The Economic Nature of the Firm: A Reader brings together the most influential essays on the economic nature of the firm. This collection demonstrates both the diversity and the vitality of research on this topic.

What economists call "the theory of the firm" is a theory of profit maximization that is now widely agreed to provide little clue as to why firms actually exist in market economies. It does not explain the sizes, scopes, internal structures, or the kinds of contractual relations that characterize business firms. However, economists from the time of Adam Smith and especially in recent years have addressed these questions and thus contributed toward a theory of the economic nature of firms.

The book begins with an original overview of the field by the editor, who sets out the major themes in the comparison of intrafirm with market coordination of economic activity. Professor Putterman goes on to draw contrasts between currently contending approaches. The readings that follow are divided into four sections. Part I presents readings on the division of labor between firms and markets. Part II focuses on the employment relationship and internal organization. Part III centers on the relationship between management and finance and on determinants of the scope of the firm. Part IV presents controversies over whether hierarchical forms of production organization are to be explained by their comparative efficiency or by the one-sided needs of employers to control labor.

The Economic Nature of the Firm will serve as a sourcebook and introduction to the literature with value to students of economics, organizational behavior, and law. It includes an integrated bibliography of all of the material referenced in the included essays and excerpts.

The economic nature of the firm

The economic nature of the firm

A reader

Edited by
Louis Putterman
BROWN UNIVERSITY

With the assistance of
Randy Kroszner

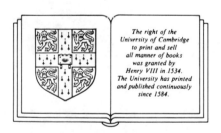

*The right of the
University of Cambridge
to print and sell
all manner of books
was granted by
Henry VIII in 1534.
The University has printed
and published continuously
since 1584.*

Cambridge University Press

Cambridge
London   New York   New Rochelle
Melbourne   Sydney

Published by the Press Syndicate of the University of Cambridge
The Pitt Building, Trumpington Street, Cambridge CB2 1RP
32 East 57th Street, New York, NY 10022, USA
10 Stamford Road, Oakleigh, Melbourne 3166, Australia

First published 1986

Printed in the United States of America

Library of Congress Cataloging-in-Publication Data
The economic nature of the firm.
Bibliography: p.
1. Managerial economics.   I. Putterman, Louis G.
II. Kroszner, Randy.
HD30.22.E25   1987   338.5   86-17111

British Library Cataloguing in Publication Data
The economic nature of the firm : a reader.
1. Microeconomics   2. Managerial economics
I. Putterman, Louis   II. Kroszner, Randy
338.5'024658   HB171
ISBN 0 521 32278 2 (hard covers)
ISBN 0 521 31140 3 (paperback)

For Vivian

Contents

CONTENTS

Editor's preface

With the exception of this Preface and the Overview, the present volume consists of selections from material previously published in books or professional journals. With each piece is included a source note that gives the full bibliographic reference of the original work and acknowledges those who granted permission to use the material. In the case of articles, the degree of completeness versus abridgement is indicated by the phrases "reprinted from," "reprinted with minor abridgements," "reprinted with abridgements," and "excerpted from," in increasing order of abridgement. Book excerpts are understood to constitute only small selections from the originals. The chapter or section from which each portion is taken has been indicated in section headings within such selections. Ellipses within both book and journal selections are used to indicate omitted portions. However, where footnotes have been deleted, no notation has been made, and the remaining notes have been renumbered consecutively.

Minor alterations in style have been made for purposes of consistency. The references have been gathered into a single listing at the end of the book, and bibliographic particulars have been added, when necessary and feasible, to make the references as complete as possible and to have them accord with the standard format of major professional journals. Reference data, except for citations of authors' names and the dates of publication, have been moved to this list from the text and notes. Authors' notes of acknowledgment, which often appear at the beginning of the original journal papers, have been removed on grounds that they are frequently dated or unimportant to the purposes of this volume, and in order to conserve space. In their place, a very brief biographical note on the authors has been added to each selection.

The inspiration for this volume can be found in Sidney Winter's graduate microeconomic theory course, in which I had the good fortune to sit several years ago at Yale, and in my subsequent reading and discussions with him around a theme he called "humans as factors." The idea that a volume like the present one should be put together, which came to me a few years later, also met with the encouragement of Lee Alston, Wesley Cohen, Gregory Dow, Victor Goldberg, Michael McPherson, Oliver Williamson, and Gordon Winston.

In the selection of the book's contents, I have benefited from the ideas of all of those mentioned. Goldberg, in particular, gave valuable advice on the structure of the book and, at an early point, suggested a number of the included items. Helpful comments on the introductory essay were provided by Alston, Dow, and Williamson, and by Colin Day, Herschel Grossman, Paul McNulty, Richard Nelson, Gilbert Skillman, Akio Yasuhara, and an anonymous reader for the Press. I confess to having been unable, for stylistic and other reasons, to incorporate some of their best suggestions into the final product. As usual, then, I take responsibility for the defects of both the book and the overview.

It would have been impossible for me to put this book together without the considerable assistance of Randy Kroszner, who was already a capable collaborator as an undergraduate at Brown when this project began. Although I must accept responsibility for all final decisions regarding editing and choice of selections, he was involved in every stage of the literature search and editing process, as well as offering detailed and incisive criticism of the introductory essay. He should share the credit for whatever is good about the result.

I would like to thank all of the authors of included contributions who gave their personal permission for the use of this material without hesitation. I thank, too, Lisa Creane and Robin Mitchell for assistance in preparing the final manuscript, and Marion Wathey for typing the reference list. The support of an Alfred P. Sloan Foundation research fellowship is also gratefully acknowledged. Finally, I would like to thank the editors and staff of Cambridge University Press whose assistance and good counsel contributed greatly to the quality of the finished product.

The economic nature of the firm: overview

LOUIS PUTTERMAN

In recent years, an increasing number of economists have shown interest in the internal nature of firms, in the firm–market relationship, and in related questions. A few papers have emerged as classics, generating new departures and appearing with regularity in citations and reading lists: Coase's 1937 paper on the nature of the firm, the impact of which Cheung recently found to be increasing;[1] Alchian and Demsetz's 1972 paper on production and information costs; and Jensen and Meckling's 1976 paper on managerial behavior, agency, and ownership structure,[2] are prime examples from the journal literature. Interest in older classics, such as writings by Knight, Schumpeter, and Adam Smith himself, can also be related to this trend. Related, too, is the challenge by radical economists to mainstream economics to show that hierarchical relations of production are not principally a tool of capitalist domination over workers, a challenge that has been accepted by some with interesting results.

How production and related activities are organized, and the relations between actors involved in these activities, is a subject interest in which crosses several disciplinary boundaries. Students of law, organizational behavior and management, finance, and other fields, should find the present compilation of economics sources on the organization problem useful. Within the economics discipline itself, to be sure, merely to raise some of these issues not long ago may have been to run the danger of appearing to take sides in a longstanding methodological debate on realism in economic models. Yet today it is increasingly being recognized that whether ordinary price theory or the developing "economics of organization" provide better characterizations of microeconomic reality depends upon the questions in which we are interested. As economists' newly honed analytical methods and newly directed lines of inquiry

---

[1] Cheung (1983) reports 17 *Social Science Citation Index* listings during 1966–70, 47 citations during 1971–5, and 105 citations during 1976–80.

[2] Incidental evidence of the popularity of the latter paper comes from a recent article on the rating of economics journals written by Laband and Sophocleus (1985). Their ranking of forty scholarly journals by number of citations per article places the *Journal of Financial Economics* in first place, ahead of the *American Economic Review,* the *Journal of Political Economy,* and other top-rated periodicals. The authors' explanation is that (p. 319) "[t]he success of the *JFE* is due, in large measure, to their publication in 1976 of Jensen and Meckling's famous piece on agency problems and the theory of the firm."

make fruitful contributions to the understanding of the organizations that inhabit our economies, controversy on the appropriate scope for inquiry gives way to the debate of views in organizational economics itself, and the discussion of why there are firms, what determines firm–market boundaries, and why firms are organized as they are becomes a topic of broad interest.[3] To celebrate, support, and promote that interest, we offer this book of readings in the economics of firms and their internal organization.

The papers and edited texts collected here fall into four overlapping groups. The first of these consists of selections from some of the older, classic writings on our topic, plus some more recent pieces, all helping to introduce the general theme of the economic nature of the firm and its place in the market system. (The term ''division of labor'' appears in the section title in its broadest meaning, that of the specialization of activities and roles, on the parts of both individuals and institutions, in complex economies.) The section begins with Adam Smith's classic discussion of the division of labor in the manufacturing establishment and in society as a whole, and its relationship to the development of markets. Next included is Karl Marx's discussion of the productivity effects of ''cooperation'' in the workshop, of the capitalist character of the factory system, and of the relations between firm and market, production and exchange. There follow excerpts from writings by Frank Knight, who emphasized the role of risk-bearing in determining economic arrangements, and Friedrich Hayek, who gave the classic discussion of the relationship between information, the level of economic decision making, and the price system.

Arguably at the core of the first section and of the volume as a whole, is Coase's now-famous paper on the firm–market boundary and the ''division of labor'' between hierarchical and simple exchange institutions. It is followed by a selection by Victor Goldberg who sets out the concept of ''relational exchange,'' an idea that both illuminates intrafirm organizational and contractual arrangements and suggests ways in which ongoing exchange affects *interfirm* relations (and thus appears also as an ''external'' market phenomenon). Finally, having begun the section with Adam Smith's ''invisible hand'' view of the market, we conclude it with a selection of Alfred Chan-

---

[3] Special circles of interest have recently been illustrated, for example, by symposia published in the *Journal of Law and Economics*, (June 1983) and the *Journal of Institutional and Theoretical Economics* (*Zeitschrift fur die gesamte Staatswissenschaft*, March 1984), in the second of which there are no fewer than 11 citations (i.e., reference listings) to the three papers singled out above (Coase, Alchian-Demsetz, and Jensen–Meckling) and 19 citations of other material included in this reader. (See also the second *J.I.T.E.* symposium issue on ''The New Institutional Economics,'' published in March 1985.) That this interest is not *isolated* in nature is suggested by a recent *nonsymposium* issue (September 1984) of the *American Economic Review,* in which five of the thirteen lead articles included between them five citations of the three mentioned papers and five citations of other selections in this volume.

dler's "visible hand" perspective on corporate resource allocation in the modern business enterprise.

Our second section contains papers treating the internal organization of firms and especially emphasizing the employment relationship and the peculiar character of human factors of production. In this category are included three now-classic and highly influential papers by Herbert Simon, by Armen Alchian and Harold Demsetz, and by Oliver Williamson, Michael Wachter, and Jeffrey Harris. Complementing these authors' concerns with the employment relation is a paper by Richard Freeman, which makes use of Albert Hirschman's concept of "voice" to understand the role of labor unions. On the human element more generally, we next sample Harvey Leibenstein's controversial argument on the importance of a nonallocative, intraorganizational form of efficiency ("X-efficiency"), and a more recent paper in which Leibenstein treats the work incentive problem as a prisoners' dilemma. The section ends with an excerpt from Richard Nelson and Sidney Winter's *An Evolutionary Theory of Economic Organization,* in which the authors highlight the organic and idiosyncratic character of the enterprise as a complex of mutually adapted behavioral routines.

The third section is composed of readings concerning the relationship between ownership structure and decision making, and expanding on the topic of which activities are integrated inside of firms and which dealt with "across markets." Like the article by Alchian and Demsetz in the previous section, most of these papers can be said to be at least partially concerned with the problem of "agency," i.e., how one actor, perhaps the owner of an asset, induces another actor, perhaps the manager of that asset, to behave in ways consistent with his or her interests. The first three papers present different approaches to the problem of "separation of ownership and control" in the modern business corporation. They begin with a brief excerpt from Henry Manne's frequently cited argument regarding the monitoring function of the market for corporate takeovers. Next comes a contribution by Eugene Fama, which develops a second view of markets as monitors of internal discretionary behavior, this one focusing on managerial compensation as an ultimate source of managerial accountability. The final piece in this group is a major portion of the article by Michael Jensen and William Meckling that has helped to spawn a significant literature in the field of finance, and that – similar to Manne but both more broadly and more subtly – answers questions about the financier–manager relationship with reference to the monitoring properties of capital markets.

The last two selections in section three leave the focus on finance and look at the determinants of contractual relations, vertical integration, and the scope of the firm. First, a contribution by Benjamin Klein, Robert Crawford, and Alchian, further develops the theory of interfirm relations and vertical integration in a manner that brings out its connections to the asset specificity, opportunism, and relational exchange considerations developed by Williamson, Goldberg, and others. The final selection, by David Teece, combines a number of approaches represented in this volume (e.g., Nelson and Winter's, and Williamson's) and others not directly represented (e.g., that of Edith Penrose) to offer a new attack on the problem raised by Coase (Part I) fifty years ago – namely, what determines which activities will come to be carried out within a given firm.

The last section of the book consists of radical interpretations of the organization of work, and of neoclassical reinterpretations and rebuttals. The radical views are represented first by an excerpt from a paper by Stephen Marglin that is often cited but obscure for "mainstream" economists due to its publication in the *Review of Radical Political Economics*. In "What Do Bosses Do?" Marglin argues that the capitalist factory arose as a response to capitalists' search for control over producers and not simply as a result of technological opportunities and changes. A second radical contribution is from Richard Edwards' recent, widely read book, *Contested Terrain*, which looks at alternative methods of control and supervision in modern business establishments.

Marglin's and Edwards' pieces are followed by a paper by Oliver Williamson that provoked considerable debate with its publication in the inaugural issue of the *Journal of Economic Behavior and Organization*. In it, Williamson sets out to evaluate the strengths and defects of six alternative organizational forms, emphasizing "transaction costs" in production processes involving more or less complex divisions of labor. Responding to several of the approaches represented in this volume, including Williamson's, the next paper, by the present writer, reviews several contributions to the literature as explanations of why it is capital that hires labor (and not the reverse) and finds them to be unconvincing. Finally, in the most recent work represented here, Samuel Bowles presents an analysis synthesizing many elements of the radical "conflict theory" of the firm, yet employing the latest developments in the mainstream literature and implicity suggesting some remarkable points of convergence in Marxist and modern information-based approaches to the nature of the firm and in particular of the labor process.

In the remainder of this introduction, I will organize my discussion of the literature on the economic nature of firms by taking two differing but complementary approaches. First, I identify seven contrasts between intraorganizational and interorganizational modes of economic coordination that feature prominently across the whole spectrum of literature surveyed. In separate sections, both a sharp view of these contrasts and a set of provisos and qualifications are presented. Second, I explicitly consider the heterogeneity of these approaches to understanding the firm and the organization of produc-

4

tion. Two broad distinctions feature prominently, here: first, that between frameworks emphasizing the *market* (or exchange, or contractual) character and those emphasizing the *hierarchical* (or planned, or authority-infused) character of firms; second, that between analysts viewing organizational form as driven by *efficiency* considerations, and those for whom, on the contrary, it is driven by considerations of *control* by subsets of agents. When combined with the further classificatory dimension of methodological orthodoxy/heterodoxy, these distinctions permit a stylized characterization of the literature in terms of a single arc ranging from the conventional neoclassical to the conventional Marxist, at its extremes, with heterodox liberal and radical camps on the adjoining flanks, and an ideologically and methodologically open ground in between them.

Firms and markets

In standard price theory, the firm is itself a primitive atom of the economy, an unindividuated, single-minded agent interacting with similarly unindividuated consumers and factor suppliers in the market economy. As Michael Jensen[4] points out, such a characterization may be appropriate to the analysis of one class of problems, inappropriate to another. With the firm as "atom," the market and the price system appear to be the exclusive mechanisms of resource allocation and economic coordination. Once the focus of attention shifts to the firm itself, however, this complex of interacting agents, resources, information, and routines presents itself as a means of organizing economic activities in its own right. Thus in his celebrated paper, Coase points out that the conceptualization of administration/plan and price system/market as alternative ways of organizing economic activity, which arises immediately in the comparison of, for example, Western and Soviet-type economic systems, can be applied internally to "market systems," which then manifest themselves as sets of administrative microeconomies interacting in largely unadministered ways. This idea is amplified in Oliver Williamson's more recent examination of microeconomic organization as an interplay of "markets and hierarchies." A strikingly similar theme is found (before Coase *or* the advent of national economic planning) in Marx's distinction between "the division of labor in society" and "the division of labor in manufacture" (or "the workshop").

Much of the literature sampled in this volume emphasizes the proposition that markets and firms are alternative forms of division of labor, methods for coordinating production, or modes of economic organization. Yet there is not complete agreement on the sharpness of this distinction. While for some the-

---

[4] See Jensen (1983), especially pp. 325–6.

5

orists the firm is a hierarchical system thoroughly distinct from the market's *price* system, for others the firm is a "nexus of contract," not readily or unambiguously distinguishable from the market environment. Thus, a good part of the substance of this literature may be seen to consist of thematic contrasts between the two modes, yet there is considerable difference in the emphasis placed upon these contrasts. With this *caveat* in mind, we proceed to survey the literature on the internal organization and economics of firms by considering themes that feature prominently and recurrently in the comparison of firms and markets. Although other breakdowns are possible, seven themes in particular will be discussed here. The distinctions involved will be drawn sharply – and perhaps overly so – in the present section; qualifications and softening of edges follow in the next section.

1. Agents interact as "free" individuals and as equals in markets but under organizational directives and in accordance with their station in a hierarchy in firms.

In an idealized market, in which there is no "market power," agents engage in exchange relations as juridical and economic equals. Decisions taken with respect to market opportunities are dictated only by agents' individual motivations; there are no directions or commands. These points apply too to an idealized labor market, and more generally, to the precontract relations between prospective participants in a business enterprise.

Once contracts are concluded, most agents are required (by their prior voluntary agreement) to act under the direction of superiors in a hierarchy.[5] According to a hierarchical conception of the firm, actions are ideally taken in response to orders and rules, rather than self-motivation and perceived opportunities. Agents interact as superior and subordinate, not as equals – although juridical equality is preserved by rights to exit the relationship, and civic equality is in theory unaffected by the particular relation entered into in the workplace.

As may be expected, the hierarchical nature of firms is emphasized by students of administration and management and by radical economists, but is downplayed, avoided, or even disputed by many economists in the neoclassical mainstream. However, the consensus in the contemporary nonradical literature on internal organization does recognize the existence of hierarchy. While hardly sharing the stridency (much less the ideological undertones) of

---

[5] As an aside here, on a point to which I return later, it is worth noting that Marx himself went to great lengths to insist that the employer and employee contract voluntarily and as equals. The crux of his theory may be seen to be an argument that exploitation occurs *inside the factory gates* and not in market exchange – an argument that might appear arcane from the standpoint of *value theory,* yet one that retains some conceptual significance in the framework of the themes of this volume. (See also McNulty, 1980, chapter 4.)

Marx's depictions of "despotism in the workshop" and indeed usually stating or implying that hierarchy is mutually beneficial to the parties involved, the concept of an "authority relation" appearing in the Coase, Simon, and Williamson pieces included here, and notions of hierarchy and supervision in the work of Cheung, Stiglitz, and others, are its obvious counterpart.[6] In the radical literature, represented here by Marglin, Edwards, and Bowles, hierarchy appears not only as a fact of work organization but also as an outgrowth of the struggle for domination of "labor" by "capital."

> *2. Intrafirm relationships are long-term and exchange is "relational," whereas pure market relationships are short-term and "anonymous." Internalization of activities to "relational" units, with their ongoing governance structures, may be motivated by the desire to minimize the incentives toward and the risks of opportunistic interactions among agents highly specialized to one another.*

A second repeating theme is the long-term nature of the relations between agents constituting the firm, as compared with agents meeting in markets. Of course, not all exchange relations commonly seen as transpiring in markets are instantaneous and one-time-only in character. These qualities may be thought of as characterizing the ideal type or pure case of market exchange, to which most neoclassical analysis refers; but relations of potentially longer-term and recurrent character, which permit the settling of accounts outside of any one transaction, and in which trust and reputation effects are important, are also common between buyers and sellers in a variety of contexts still referred to as markets. As an exchange relationship takes on some of the latter characteristics, the parties may economize on the costs of specifying and enforcing contracts, and of ascertaining quality before each transaction, and they may reduce the risks associated with having imperfect information. At the same time, the parties incur obligations to one another, protect themselves by establishing means of punishing a major breach in the relationship, and are shielded from the market at large in the sense that the immediate influence of current prices at which particular goods and services exchange, and hence shifting scarcity and demand conditions, are more weakly felt. The study of such relationships, which Goldberg has termed "relational exchange," includes the internal nature of firms and the employment relation without being limited to these areas;[7] but a stylized characterization of the firm–market di-

---

[6] In a recent treatment, for example, James Hess (1983, p. 3) argues that "The essence of an organization is presence of contracts where persons are 'united' by an authoritarian relation." And like Williamson, Wachter and Harris, Hess takes issue with Alchian and Demsetz's argument that the relationship between an employer and employee is not significantly different from that between a consumer and his grocer. "Alchian and Demsetz . . . push the argument too far when they deny the existence of voluntarily granted authority."

chotomy might take the "relational exchange" aspect of the former and the "anonymous exchange" aspect of the latter as distinguishing qualities.

Behind the removal of transactions from the domain of the open market and their internalization to a "relational" and "organizational" milieu may lie the danger of opportunistic dealing between economic agents made vulnerable by specialization. The conjunction of what Williamson calls "small numbers bargaining" and "opportunism" provides an efficiency rationale for forms of organization the existence of which would otherwise be difficult to explain in economic terms. Specifically, when resources are to become specialized to one another – as when a firm expands capacity to supply the special requirements of one major customer or when a worker acquires skills useful principally to his current employer – leaving terms of trade to future determination exposes both parties to risks so great that such specialization might be avoided, and the associated activities not be undertaken, unless a way of reducing these risks is found.[8] While specification of future terms of trade under all contingencies is ruled out by the cognitive difficulties of writing and enforcing complex contracts, establishment of rules or norms to govern the future evolution of those terms is one method of risk reduction. If only the *distribution* of returns is at issue, preference for a "relational exchange" reducing the variation of that distribution may simply imply risk aversion. However, internalization of exchange relations to organizations may also enlarge the *magnitude* of returns to be divided among the contributing parties, by reducing the costs of settling on terms and of enforcement, and by raising productivity through smoother cooperation among factors.[9]

Thus, while from one standpoint, the firm–market dichotomy presents itself as a distinction between price determination by open auction (the market) and determination by "small numbers bargaining" (the firm),[10] from another point of view the relevant quality of intraorganizational allocation is that it replaces some of the supply–demand element determining terms of exchange or distributive shares in *both* bargaining *and* the open market, with rule and norm-governed processes that reduce costs and uncertainty. An example of this is the argument by Williamson, Wachter, and Harris that the attachment

[7] See Goldberg's paper excerpted in this volume and Goldberg (1982). Goldberg himself identifies the term as a borrowing from MacNeil (1974). For an application to the economics of academic tenure, see McPherson and Winston (1983). A related discussion linking the family and friendship with firms as economically "relational" institutions is Ben-Porath (1980).

[8] For early expositions of this paradigm of interspecific investment – represented in the present volume by Klein, Crawford and Alchian's paper, among others – see Williamson (1971) and (1975). For more recent developments of this theme, see Williamson (1979), (1983a), (1984a), and (1985), and the references cited in the latter.

[9] This corresponds to an enlargement of the organizational quasi-rents in the sense of Aoki (1984) and some other recent authors.

[10] A point important enough in its own right that Gregory Dow, commenting on an earlier draft, suggests the possibility of treating it as an eighth theme in this essay.

of wage rates to jobs rather than individual workers discourages small group bargaining and replaces it with job evaluation procedures.

Routinization and subordination of bargaining to norms and structure does not, of course, imply "fair" distributive outcomes in any absolute sense. *Who determines* structure, for example by designing internal labor markets governing returns to firm-specific skills, may have a powerful effect on outcomes. Thus, the preempting of bargaining by individual employees accomplished by assigning pay to *jobs* rather than persons in the just-noted example by Williamson et al., may work to the advantage of employers more than employees when the former can control the definition of jobs, the job evaluation process, and the flow of long-term rewards extracting preferred behavior from workers. Approval of the examined institutions from a social welfare standpoint, and dismissal of concerns over distribution and balances of power, may accordingly fail to flow as directly from the analysis as is occasionally implied. Yet the "relational" perspective on economic activity, illustrated (with some differences) in the contributions in this volume by Goldberg, Klein, Crawford and Alchian, Teece, and Williamson, Wachter, and Harris, is undoubtedly one of the most fruitful insights of the body of literature in present focus, and is accordingly emphasized in our selections.

3. Whereas "history does not matter" for pure market exchange, intra-firm relations and firm structures are significantly historical in character.

Closely connected to the "relational" nature of the links between economic agents in firms is the historicity of those links and of firm structures themselves. Because "settling up" is a long-term process, the history of exchange affects the evaluation of current interactions in the trivial sense that the present status of relational accounts cannot be known without knowledge of that history, and in the more important sense that behaviors manifested in past situations – for example, a history of cooperativeness, reliability, or their opposites – affect expectations of future interactions and, hence, choices among present alternatives. Put differently, the firm is a *social* institution which has developed – and which likewise can effect changes in – its specific norms, "culture," and routines only over time. Strategies for eliciting consummate performance from managers or workers (or willingness to invest by financiers) which are open to one organization will be closed to another, at least in the short run, by virtue of history.

While it is possible to exaggerate the independence of market processes themselves from history, and too easy to forget the historicity and social specificity of market institutions, it is nonetheless true that the study of enterprises as organizations must to a far greater extent than that of markets both begin and proceed with attention to the historical dimension of institutional devel-

9

opment. Thus, whereas the firm of textbook microeconomics is a maximizing function distinguished from other firms, if at all, by its cost structure and products, firms at our own level of analysis often must be distinguished along various lines – for example, as partnerships or limited liability corporations, U-form or M-form – before useful analysis can proceed. The study of firms as organization must marry the knowledge of institutional history, such as that put forward by Chandler or discussed by Marglin, Edwards, and Williamson in the works excerpted in this volume, to the knowledge of economic and organization theory.

4. As an alternative allocative mechanism, firms take advantage of richer knowledge of inputs, and incur costs of holding inventories so as to afford secure access to an internal pool of resources.

The joining of authority to direct agents within the firm, with the long-term nature of relationships among agents, allows the firm to enjoy certain advantages as a resource-allocating mechanism. While competition for scarce resources is assumed to allocate inputs to their most productive uses in the market, since the most productive user would also (rationally) be the highest bidder, the market process assures optimal resource allocation only to the extent that the characteristics of the inputs are known to market participants. If, on the other hand, the special qualities of inputs as they work independently and in interaction with sets of complementary inputs can be known best through *use,* and/or if information about input qualities is poorly communicated across markets, for reasons of "bounded rationality" or of asymmetric information and incentive incompatability, allocation of resources by an organization controlling them over a period of time may lead to superior resource utilization. Thus Alchian and Demsetz consider firms a special kind of "market" within which resources "compete" for assignment to particular uses; and Williamson, Wachter, and Harris argue that intrafirm (as opposed to interfirm) labor allocation takes advantage of "rating" information that is difficult to communicate, or unlikely to be communicated, across markets.

The possible advantages of internal markets are illuminated by several of the perspectives represented in this volume. That the ability to utilize inputs may be specialized to particular users can be seen in notions of firm-specific human capital and learning by doing. A still more complex interaction of the skills and knowledge required to carry out effective production activities is recognized in Nelson and Winter's discussion of routines, which emphasizes the cognitive interspecialization of the team of human factors as a whole. The differences between communication within firms and across markets are addressed in Hayek's oft-cited paper on information and decentralization, where the virtue of the market in its ability to transmit a large amount of implicit information through a minimal number of signals is contrasted with the entrepreneur's command over more detailed location- or activity-specific information, especially that concerning production technology and resources.

By implying that resources are moved from one use to another within firms, the internal markets idea suggests that firms may hold on to inventories of inputs that are either not used or are put to uses of relatively low productivity until such time as specific needs arise. While short-run gaps between productivity and financial (or opportunity) outlay add to costs, secure access to such resources when needed, guarding against both the necessity of paying out high short-run scarcity rents and the possibility of total nonavailability at such times, may more than compensate. Also, it may be possible to learn about potential uses and productivity only by bringing resources into the organization, even if for low productivity uses during some periods. The implications of these practices for macroeconomic phenomena such as wage rigidity, while not highlighted in this volume, have received attention elsewhere.[11]

5. While markets are often measured against an ideal of perfect competition, the enterprise is a team within which the attenuation of competition and the promotion of cooperation may be requirements of success.

Still another perspective on the firm/market dichotomy centers upon the team nature of activities undertaken within firms. Our excerpt from Nelson and Winter emphasizes the felicitous meshing of the patterned capabilities of individual team members into a functioning, yet perhaps unreplicable, whole. "Teamness" is also emphasized by, among others, Alchian and Demsetz who argue that the relations among team members differ from simple market relations because the marginal product of the individual member is difficult to identify – and, others argue, perhaps even undefined. Interdependence of agents' *productivities*, whether they are separately and uniquely identifiable or not, creates special conditions under which output may be maximized and incentives be most effective in an organized enterprise. Because one agent's productivity enhances another's, because imperfections of monitoring contributions cause some of the results of better work to be shared by other team members, and because through timing and other details of action a team member may either assist or hinder another's work, team production is an activity having more or less cooperative, more or less jointly beneficial outcomes – a point emphasized in Leibenstein's treatment of production as a prisoner's dilemma. Among the implications of this approach are the suggestions that continuity of team membership may improve both the likelihood and the potential benefits of cooperation and that some income sharing or reward systems may be more conducive to cooperative behavior than are others.

[11] See, e.g., Okun (1981). Other examples are Goldberg (1982), and proceedings of the session entitled "The Theory of Contracts and Agency: Implications for the Behavior of Wages," in *American Economics Review* (Papers and Proceedings), May 1984.

Indeed, the essence of much of the literature that we are sampling may be summarized as follows: There are widespread gains to be had from cooperation, but the details of cooperative activity are difficult to specify in advance, contracts are difficult to enforce, and individual agents always have incentives to take advantage of cooperation by becoming free-riding members of a team. In the "open market," these difficulties can be attacked by writing better contracts, by posting bonds, and by litigating and threatening litigation. But it may prove more efficient to partially remove the relationships between co-operators from the market, leave contracts unspecified, give agents long-term incentives to cooperate and disincentives from engaging in opportunistic behavior, and institutionalize internal procedures for settling grievances, thereby economizing on costs of grievance resolution and encouraging the sense of fairness and trust.

This type of reasoning may also lead into arguments to the effect that conventional firms are *not* an efficient organizational form. Part of the radical argument that hierarchical relations add to capitalists' control without necessarily adding to the efficiency of resource utilization, is the idea that maximum cooperation cannot be achieved in conventional workplaces because internal incentive structures cannot go far enough in attenuating the *antagonistic* interests that are inherent in the structure of the capitalist employment relationship. Of course, the challenges of Alchian and Demsetz, Williamson, and others, to explain why capitalist firms are observed more frequently than co-operatives in market economies, remain. These questions are addressed in different ways by some of the pieces in Section 4 of this reader.

>*6. In firms, the incentive structures binding owner, managers, and operatives are crucial because while it is possible to hire "labor," it is effectively impossible to buy fully predetermined quantities and qualities of labor services.*

While the textbook theory of the firm depicts enterprises as hiring quantities of "labor" that translate into levels of output by way of a technologically determined production function, at our own level of analysis it is more appropriate to say that the firm contracts with laborers (including technical and managerial personnel) but that flows of labor services, which determine output, are a function not only of the type and number of workers hired but also of internal incentive structures and other variables impacting upon the motivation of effort. Neoclassical theory has been extended to treat "efficiency labor," as a magnitude determined by worker preferences and contractual incentive structures in theories of "principal–agent" interaction and of share-cropping.[12] The distinction between the worker and the "efficiency labor"

[12] See, for example, Stiglitz (1974) and (1975), Mirrlees (1976), and Shapiro and Stiglitz (1984).

that he or she provides closely parallels the distinction between "labor power" and "labor," which was emphasized by Marx and is the focus of recent conflictual theories of the firm.[13]

When the firm is pictured as an unindividuated agent, labor and managerial services are hired in standardized units and are directed to their most productive tasks with precision and certainty. Given the complexity of actual work processes, however, even a team of enterprise personnel sharing an identical objective – for example, that of maximizing the firm's profit – would face significant problems of coordination, because the exercise of judgment at the individual work station (whether in office or on shop floor) is unavoidable. The coordination problem becomes an incentive problem when the inevitably discretionary nature of work is joined to the reality of divergent individual objectives. This makes it instructive to study organizational design in terms of strategies to solve both coordination and incentive problems so as to maximize the flow of appropriate labor services per unit labor payment.

Both radical and mainstream authors assume an opposition of interest between employers and employees in the sense that it is presumed that workers will "shirk" or withdraw labor whenever the consequent income reduction is smaller than the utility of the effort reduction. The mainstream and radical depictions of this opposition differ most importantly in that whereas hierarchy and monitoring are treated by the mainstream as outcomes of mutual searches for optimal contracts beneficial to both capitalists and workers, they are seen by radicals as capitalist strategies to control the labor process and shift the terms of exchange of labor for wages *against workers*.

The principal–agent framework also plays a central role in several of the analyses of management incentives and accountability stimulated by the Berle–Means conception of "separation of ownership and control" (see below);[14] hence, the centrality of "agency" in Jensen and Meckling's paper and in other work treating the linkage of financiers' with managers' objectives. This literature is particularly rich in illustrations of the complexity, variety, and complementarity of mechanisms for solving owner–management agency problems, among which figure profit sharing, direct monitoring by boards, competition among managers, the capital market, and the "market for takeovers." Simultaneous operation of market and administrative checks[15] on agent "subgoal pursuit" in both managerial and nonmanagerial agency contexts provides an important illustration of the principle that intrafirm and market phenomena, although at one level representing alternative methods of eco-

---

[13] This parallel is drawn, too, by Goldberg (1980a). The similarity of the recent mainstream and Marxist literatures in this regard is brought out by Bowles' article reprinted in this collection.

[14] Equivalence of *this* problem with the labor–labor power approach may be controversial because of the ambivalent class position of managers.

[15] As emphasized in Fama and Jensen (1983a) and (1983b).

nomic coordination, work in concert and demand joint examination for important classes of organizational problems.

7. While there is no intentional coordinating process to impart systemic rationality to the independent decisions of agents in markets, the actions of agents within firms are subject to such a process.

Perhaps the most obvious difference between the pure market and (intra-) firm modes of economic organization has been saved for last mention. This is the distinction between unplanned and planned (Coase), market and hierarchy (Williamson), anarchic and despotic (Marx) forms of economic order alluded to earlier.

The invisibility of Adam Smith's famous "invisible hand" and Marx's "anarchy" refer to the same facet of market systems, however different the overtones: the observation that markets (at least in their conceptual ideal form) lack organs of systemwide governance, control, or conscious coordination. Although the interaction of entirely independent and uncoordinated units displays its own regularities and even a certain systemic functionality,[16] the important point is that no central plan of system operation is drawn up, and individual rules and behaviors are not dictated by a coordinating agent or agents.

Economic theory describes the price system itself as a spontaneous coordination mechanism imparting (systemic) rationality and consistency to individual agents' behaviors in the market.[17] The firm is one such agent responding to price signals in formulating its internal plans. On the other hand, the agents within the firm are no longer thought of as responding to price signals when determining their behaviors. Instead, they operate within the rubric of administrative procedures and decisions and of roles defined and allotted to them by an enterprise decision-making structure. In a simple model, the signals given to intrafirm agents and determining their behaviors can be thought of as *commands,* which serve as the analogue of price signals in markets. While richer models will replace this command conceptualization with one of internal structures motivating agents to perform enterprise-oriented tasks – that is, making such behaviors individually rational, from their own standpoints – it remains the case that the internal coordination process is one that

[16] While rejecting the welfare implication of the invisible hand theorem, even Marx concurred that the absence of conscious coordination did not imply total randomness of systemic behavior. Competition of commodity producers, limits of demand, and diffusion of techniques led to a "law of value" under which market systems could be predicted to produce definite quantities of each commodity at specific prices. Indeed, a "heterodox" reader of Marx's *Capital* may well be disappointed at the degree to which Marx makes his home among *equilibrium* economic theorists.

[17] As Hayek emphasized, such coordination can be viewed as "the result of human action but not of human design." See Hayek (1972).

is subject to attempts, at least, at intentionality and design, qualities absent from unregulated markets.

The firms–markets system

As was intimated at the outset, the above survey of firm–market distinctions, while convenient for introducing some of the themes of this volume and of the literature it represents, has definite drawbacks. Having outlined these themes, it is necessary in some measure to take back much of what has been said above – that is, to admit that some of the contrasts that have been drawn are a bit exaggerated. It is also important to point out that although firms and markets represent alternative modes of organizing individual transactions in market economies, they are also woven, together, into the cloth that is the economy as a whole. The task of analyzing the economic nature of firms ultimately must include both an understanding of the forces shaping the boundaries between firms and markets – the problem addressed, for example, by the Coase and Teece pieces in the present volume – and a sense of the way in which firm and market fit together in the larger system.

To run briefly through the disavowals: 1. The contrast between agent autonomy and equality in markets, on the one hand, and subordination and hierarchy in firms, on the other, runs the risk of obscuring actual agent discretion and the ambiguities of interagent relations within firms, leading to a view of the firm as a strictly regimented hierarchy that – as we have by now recognized – is an oversimplification for many purposes. (The characterization of agents in market as autonomous and equal may also require qualification, but the issues there are perhaps less relevant to our immediate concerns.) Agent behavior within a "hierarchy" is as often amenable to examination in a framework of constrained rational choice, with the incentive structures and resources internal to the firm generating the relevant "prices," as it is to more simplified representation as actions directly dictated by superiors.

2. The fact that transactions vary across a complete spectrum from the "relational" to the "anonymous" even within markets has already been remarked on above.[18] Here, it is also useful to point out that the long-term and

---

[18] In his application of "transaction cost" theory (see below) to governance structures, Oliver Williamson (1979) identifies both "obligational contracting" between separate entities and "internal organization" within firms as forms of "relational contracting" that arise in conditions of recurrent exchange and specific investments. In this scheme, internal organization becomes more likely the more idiosyncratic are the investments and the more uncertain is the economic environment. Victor Goldberg also cautions against overstating both theme two and theme seven when he writes: "The convenient fiction of economic theory that monolithic firms coordinate internal behavior perfectly and engage only in discrete, anonymous contracts with external parties leads us to ignore the great similarities between internal and external coordination" (1976, p.428). Goldberg approvingly cites G.B. Richardson's "The Organization of Industry" (1972), which lays emphasis on interfirm cooperative arrangements.

"relational" character of *intrafirm* relations ought not to be taken as entirely general – for example, many employment relationships will come closer to the "spot market" type than to that of the internal job ladder, the determination sometimes being associated with the degree of specialization of the labor services involved and the ease of recruitment of equivalent workers. On the whole, the material in this volume may err in the direction of treating employment relationships involving workers with relatively high degrees of skill and autonomy, and neglecting those in less skilled and more routinized jobs. The fact that some important relations are between *groups* – for example, labor unions and management – is also underplayed (except by Freeman's paper), both biases being due in part to an implicit emphasis on the professional and managerial echelon and in part to the intellectual fascination and analytical novelty of the resource specificity and relational contracting concepts.

3. The "historical–ahistorical" dichotomy must also be qualified on both sides. It may be argued that the "ahistoricity" of markets is as much a projection of neoclassical methodological propensities as of the character of markets themselves. Not only are markets as institutional structures always located on some definite historical path of development – indeed, the very word *institution,* which few would object to applying to markets, can be seen to imply a set of *norms* and, thus, a *history*. Also, insofar as prices reflect disequilibria and points on adjustment paths that fail to reach their equilibria before being shifted by further exogenous forces, even in markets *process* may matter more, and static equilibrium less, than conventional theory suggests. On the other hand, within firms as much as within markets, the degree to which current options are *determined* by history is smaller the greater the relevant horizon, so that while established structures and atmospheres influence immediate possibilities, they may be less binding for long-term changes in the internal institutions of firms.[19]

4. Our main qualification to the distinction concerning information communicated across markets and that communicated within firms is to point out that limitations on market communication will not often be as sharp as implied, and also that agents within the firm or organization and those in other units may well rely on *both* intraunit and market ratings as information sources.

---

[19] This might also be the place to mention that historical detail continues to play a relatively smaller role in the organizational economics literature than would seem to be implied by inclusion of this theme in our discussion. But perhaps the requirement of brevity in the selections for this volume has created a stronger impression of ahistoricity than is warranted. Some more historical sections of pieces excerpted here – e.g., Chandler and Marglin (and of course Smith and Marx) – do not appear in the portions selected. Nor have we included some of the more institutionally and historically specific works by other represented authors – since the primary interest of this volume is in general analytical and conceptual advances concerning the nature of the firm.

This is especially clear when considering labor markets, because an individual's career path within the organization can become a signal to prospective outside employers at the same time as his or her outside market serves as a signal within the organization. In general, the generation of information in both firms and markets can be highly complementary and more efficient than would be that by either channel operating alone, but there is also the potential for false signals and nonidentification, as when an employee's "market valuation" is taken simultaneously as an indicator of quality, labor grade, or marginal productivity, and of supply price.

5. Qualifications to treatment of the market as competitive and the firm as cooperative are obvious. On the one hand, it is somewhat inappropriate to associate active competition in the sense of "rivalry" with the "perfectly competitive" firms of textbook theory. But this is a technical point only. More important is the fact that the imperfectly competitive firms that populate actual market economies and that do display a degree of this rivalry also frequently exhibit *cooperative* behaviors, ranging from the practice of a business ethic of nonpredatorship and tacit collusion, to explicit agreements on restraint of competition. Such cooperation brings benefits to participating firms just as surely as can cooperation among the members of the internal coalitions of enterprises, although a majority of economists see society as the loser when it occurs.[20] As for cooperation within enterprises, the a priori desirability of such behavior can (as already suggested) run up against the obstructions of clashing interests, including those over the distribution of benefits. This often appears to lead to internal structures that take subordinate–superior antagonism as given and seek methods of maximizing control, not cooperation.

6. The worker, "efficiency labor" distinction has been treated rather differently by different authors. Sometimes that distinction is pointed out in what appears to be a broadside against the very concept of the production function as a relationship between inputs and outputs. However, both the neoclassical treatments by Stiglitz et al. and the radical models of Bowles (this volume), Reich and Divine (1981), Lazonick (1982), and others, draw attention to it, rather, in order to better conceptualize what the real input is. Not only is measurability not ruled out, in such frameworks, but in addition, they open the door to richer models of the firm employing much of the choice-theoretic methodology with which the production function is associated. Indeed, our thematic statement that "it is effectively impossible to buy fully predetermined quantities and qualities of labor services," might be judged to be too

---

[20] Not all interfirm cooperative relations are seen as having negative welfare implications, however. See, e.g., Richardson's (1972) discussion of the relationships between input suppliers and users, franchise operators and their parent companies, etc., and the related discussions by Goldberg (1976) and Williamson (1985).

strong if one admits models in which the supervision technology, the level at which it is employed, the state of the labor market, and other relevant variables are explicitly specified.

7. The distinction between the market as unplanned and the firm or enterprise as planned needs qualification most importantly insofar as it may tend to overstate the case for depiction of firms as hierarchies wherein subordinates strictly implement decisions made above them. As has already been remarked, it will often be more useful to view the firm as a collection of agents each of whom maintains his or her autonomy in determining certain details of rate and quality of work, volunteering of information, and so forth, responding complexly to motivational and incentive variables operating both within and perhaps also from outside of the organization. Planning by the firm's "center" may set some of the parameters and generate some of the forces to which "surbordinate" agents react, but as students of centrally planned economies know well, observed behavior may seem scarcely related to plans, as events actually unfold.[21]

Even the above disavowals will not go far enough for a significant subset of contributors to this literature who would see the entire exercise of drawing firm–market contrasts as misplaced. Writes Benjamin Klein:

> Coase mistakenly made a sharp distinction between intrafirm and interfirm transactions, claiming that while the latter represented market contracts the former represented planned direction. Economists now recognize that such a sharp distinction does not exist and that it is useful to consider also transactions occurring within the firm as representing market (contractual) relationships. *The question what is the essential characteristic of a firm now appears to be unimportant.* Thinking of all organizations as groups of explicit and implicit contracts among owners of factors of production represents a fundamental advance.[22]

To a degree, such strong statements perhaps indicate an unbridgeable difference of viewpoint with the one that has motivated the discussion above. Yet it may be pointed out that even Klein does not deny the existence of distinctions, only of *sharp* ones. Thus, the gap dividing Coase and Klein with regard to the differences between firm and market may also be seen as a matter of degree, with Klein and others placing emphasis on the market-like characteristics or "nexus-of-contracts" view of the firm, whereas Coase and others place emphasis on its planned and hierarchical character.[23] These differences will be further explored in the next section.

We end the present section with a promised word concerning firm–market

---

[21] See, for example, Nove (1983).

[22] Klein (1983, p.373), emphasis added.

[23] A related debate concerns the possibility of ascertaining precise boundaries of firms and markets. See Cheung (1983).

integration. What is to be emphasized is that while markets and firms may present themselves as alternative ways of organizing economic activity for given transactions, they are nonetheless jointly elements of a more general economic mechanism the understanding of which clearly requires a grasp of the nature of both parts, as well as of their interaction and complementarity. By focusing on the distinctiveness of the kinds of economic processes found in firms, this collection will inevitably tend to err in the direction of obscuring certain systemic factors. This seems justified in view of the present need to strengthen a broadened understanding of the nature of internal organizational economics, but the proviso should be kept in mind, so that for the future we look forward to integration of such material into a better conception of the economic system as a whole.

"All in the family"

While a difference of opinion has occasionally been alluded to, this introduction has thus far treated the literature on the internal organization and economics of firms as rather homogeneous, with the possible exception of the radical–mainstream rifts. One might indeed, at this juncture, have the impression that the (battle)field of organizational economic analysis is occupied by two internally homogeneous, mutually antagonistic, and essentially noncommunicating camps, and that insofar as one has already chosen sides in this dispute on methodological or whatever other grounds, there is little to learn from the efforts of the other group – a standpoint that raises questions about the usefulness of the grouping of materials in the present volume.

Our view of the intellectual geography being surveyed here is a rather different one. While a "mainstream–radical" distinction can be applied readily enough, in most cases this implies neither homogeneity within those groupings nor lack of fruitful interaction between them. Moreover, it is not at all clear that that particular distinction, however great its emotive and ideological import, is of greater salience with respect to the kinds of issue at hand than are other lines of classification and identification. Some comments on the range of viewpoints on the economics of the firm, beginning *within* the heterogeneous "mainstream," may illustrate this point while more generally placing the literature in perspective and further illuminating the motivation behind the selections in this volume.[24]

It may be useful to begin this discussion by noting that the greater part of the material in this collection differs from textbook microeconomic theory in ways other than the delineation of its subject matter. Methodologically or

[24] It is not intended here to present a full-fledged literature survey and critique. For that purpose, the reader may turn to a number of other sources, including Furubotn and Pejovich (1972), Leibenstein (1979), Simon (1979), and Williamson (1981).

philosophically, most of the contributions by nonradical writers, while by one definition " mainstream," are also arguably "non-neoclassical" or at least "heterodox" by virtue of their identification with such trends as "the economics of property rights,"[25] "transaction cost economics,"[26] "the new institutional economics,"[27] etc.[28] But they differ considerably in their degree and manner of unorthodoxy.

From the vantage point of a narrow definition of neoclassicism, the shared departures of nearly all of this literature are of two kinds: first, a preoccupation with institutions, categories of social reality that play almost no part in the 20th century orthodoxy of Hicks, Samuelson, Debreu and of the standard texts such as Ferguson (1969) or Henderson and Quandt (1971). Second, unlike conventional neoclassicism, this literature generally does not assume perfect and costless acquisition and transmission of information, perfect and costless calculation, or costless writing and enforcement of contracts, so that a variety of market imperfections are admitted.

Yet surely a definition of neoclassicism that permits admission to developments in economics, after, say, the mid-1960s, must find room for significant bodies of work on the economics of information and uncertainty and on choices among alternative contracts in environments characterized by uncertainty, asymmetric information, and so forth. If the literature sampled in this volume

[25] "The economics of property rights" is an analytical and descriptive trend in which the rights of persons over resources are made more explicit and receive more attention as variables in their own right than in the standard theory with its "endowments" and "trades." Both the consequences of variation in property rights, and the economic forces leading to changes in property rights, are subjects of analysis. Share-cropping, socialist firms, codetermination, nonprofits, and corporations, have all been studied by economists working within this trend. See the survey article by Furubotn and Pejovich cited in the previous note.

[26] "Transaction cost economics" is a type of analysis emphasizing the importance of the costs of carrying out economic transactions, such as those associated with the gathering of information, writing of contracts, and monitoring and enforcement of agreements. Variations in transaction costs across institutions, and the drive to economize on such costs, is made the principal basis for explaining the prevalence of specific economic institutions in given contexts. Oliver Williamson, the leading exponent of this approach who surveys it in Williamson (1984b) and provides its most comprehensive development in Williamson (1985), traces the concept back to the American institutional economist John R. Commons. See also Williamson (1975). The concept of "transaction costs" is featured in this volume in the papers by Coase and Williamson.

[27] "The new institutional economics" is a broad trend that embraces "property rights" and "transaction cost" motifs as well as other strands. Like the "old" American institutionalism and the European "historical" school, it gives explicit attention to the structure of economic institutions and (for at least some contributors) to the social, cultural, and historical forces impacting upon and delimiting those institutions. Unlike the latter schools, however, it seeks to make use of and contribute to, more than to criticize and displace, the deductive analysis of neoclassical economics. For an overview, see the special March 1984 issue of the *Journal of Institutional and Theoretical Economics*: "The New Institutional Economics: A Symposium." For another discussion, see Langlois (1981).

[28] One might add "behavioral," "modern Austrian," "evolutionary," and still other trends here. One valuable tour of heterodox trends in microeconomic theory will be found on pp. 33–45 of Nelson and Winter (1982).

differs from some of the more technical treatments of these subjects in current economics journals, the main distinction may be simply that of greater speculative license and of a corresponding inclination to conceptualize verbally rather than mathematically.[29]

If one goes beyond style and perhaps also methodology and considers the *philosophy* or, more specifically, the assumptions about economic institutions that underlie different contributions to this literature, one sees, however, that there are more fundamental distinctions between neoclassical orthodoxy and the "nonradical heterodox," which are shared in greater measure by some than by others of its contributors. One spectrum along which the varying positions can be sorted out is that of the extent to which the theorist or analyst adheres to the neoclassical presumption that the market economy is efficient, producing (in some sense) optimal outcomes for all involved, in spite of the recognition of market imperfections and of the variability and importance of institutions. The positions represented here vary from the "institutions matter but, in a free society, respond optimally to environmental requirements," to the "institutions matter, and respond *over time* to requirements" approach, to the view that "institutions matter, and there may be no reason to assume optimality." Positions along this spectrum show some correlation, although not a perfect one, with a dimension of differentiation of analysts that has already been mentioned, that of inclination to strongly delineate firm and market economic modes.

---

[29] In an interesting article, Michael Jensen (1983, cited above; see especially pp. 332–9) acknowledges a split between "mathematical-formalist" and nonmathematical literatures on "agency," noting the infrequency of citation of the one literature by the other. The "other agency literature" referred to is the formal principal–agent literature by Spence and Zeckhauser, Ross, Harris and Raviv, etc. (see references in Jensen). A laudible and important exception to this separation of literatures is recent work by James Malcomson, including Malcomson (1984). The selections for the present volume implicitly share in Jensen's preferences as between these literatures, although our preference for nonmathematical material is also based on the assumption that formalism reduces the value of contributions to a collection directed at a wider audience.

Uncertainty and asymmetric information also play important roles in the implicit contract literature that recently celebrated a decade of development in a special issue of the *Quarterly Journal of Economics.* (1983 Supplement. See especially the introductory paper by Costas Azariadis and Joseph Stiglitz.) The nonrepresentation of the latter literature in this volume results from the fact that it is primarily concerned with *macroeconomic* aspects of labor markets. Its models of employment contracts are, however, clearly related to issues discussed herein. It is of interest to note that the view of the enterprise as a seller of insurance to risk averse workers, which features prominently in the implicit contract theory, receives little mention in the papers represented here – the exception being Knight, who is explicitly criticized on this point by Alchian and Demsetz, Williamson, Wachter and Harris, and others. Rather than conclude that our authors *reject* the importance of risk aversion, however, we might recall that it is precisely avoidance of risk by parties entering into relations of specialized or idiosyncratic exchange that drives the long-term contracting/relational exchange themes of much of our material. Seen in this light, the real difference between our authors and the implicit contract theorists is the greater reluctance of the former to assume that it is workers only, as opposed to financiers, managers, and other agents, who are significantly risk averse.

On the less heretical end of the internal organization theory spectrum, we find authors such as Alchian, Demsetz, Fama, Jensen, Meckling, and Klein, who play down firm–market distinctions, play up the market-like qualities of firms and the permeation of market forces into the operation of firms, and incline to the view that unregulated competitive markets generate economically optimal institutions as allegedly indicated in the revealed preferences of market participants. For example, Alchian and Demsetz are principal dissenters from the concept of an authority relation within the firm, and they tend to minimize the duration and specificity features distinguishing the contracts defining a firm or organization from those between independent agents in the market. It is, notably, Alchian and Demsetz who refer to the firm as *a kind of market*. Rejection of a strong firm–market distinction is also exemplified in Benjamin Klein's statement, quoted in the previous section. Steven Cheung[30] argues that it is unimportant to determine exactly what constitutes a firm, and when a transaction takes place between independent agents as opposed to within firms. Fama[31] solves the problem of imperfect current period control over managerial discretion by hypothesizing that "the market will cause you to pay for today's discretions" through future evaluations of expected performance that (on average) capture past performance correctly. Jensen and Meckling[32] argue that to call the shortfalls of real market outcomes from the hypothetical outcomes that would be possible with perfect information and costless agency "inefficiencies" is to commit the "Nirvana fallacy" of comparing the possible with the imaginary. The ingenious Jensen–Meckling rejoining of corporate management and the profit motive[33] is based on an assumption that it is efficient capital markets, not intraorganizational forces, that discipline managerial behavior.

At some remove from this position are analysts such as Coase, Simon, and Williamson, who differ from Alchian et al. in drawing a sharper boundary between firm and market, giving scope to the idea of the authority relation and of control by fiat within firms, and emphasizing the difficulties of specifying economic transactions via complete and precise contracts.[34] In the cases

---

[30] See Cheung (1983).

[31] Specifically, in the 1980 paper reprinted here. Some movement on Fama's part away from this position will be referred to below.

[32] See Jensen and Meckling (1979), p. 488.

[33] (1976), reprinted in abridged form in this volume, Part III.

[34] While the authority relation concept is perhaps not always associated with Coase, one finds the following passage, strongly foreshadowing Simon's "Formal Model of the Employment Relation," in his 1937 paper:

[I]t is important to note the character of the contract into which a factor enters that is employed within a firm. The contract is one whereby the factor, for a certain remuneration (which may be fixed or fluctuating), agrees to obey the directions of an entrepreneur *within certain limits*. The

of Simon and Williamson, there is an emphasis upon human-bounded rationality that suggests departure from the neoclassical decision-making model – which identifies decision rules *normatively* (by deducing rules of optimal choice) – and *toward* behavioral models employing more realistic assumptions about human capabilities and operating strategies. Concern for organizational evolution and awareness that efficient adaptations are not necessarily automatic also separates Williamson from analysts such as Jensen. In a symposium on the 50th anniversary of Berle and Means' *The Modern Corporation and Private Property,* Williamson criticizes a paper by Fama and Jensen for suggesting that "specialized governance structures . . . have reached a high degree of refinement – on which account there is not now, if indeed there ever has been, an organization control problem with which scholars and others are legitimately concerned. On this point I have grave doubts."[35]

Yet Coase, Simon, and Williamson are as much descendants of the classical liberal tradition as are Alchian, Jensen, and colleagues. Although providing us with arguments against presuming that the results of individual choices will be systemically optimal, they too tend to suppose that competitive processes will have efficient outcomes. For example, Coase postulates that the firm–market boundary is precisely that point at which it becomes more efficient to carry out an additional transaction *between* firms than to do it *within* one firm, thus assuming an efficient sorting out of activity between markets and firms at the start of his analysis. Much the same perspective is adopted by Williamson in *Markets and Hierarchies.* Indeed, in the paper excerpted in Part IV of this collection, Williamson dons an orthodox mantle to defend capitalist production relations against radical critics, arguing (in a phrase borrowed from Frank Knight) for "decent respect for human nature as we know it." Simon's treatment of hierarchy as the efficient response to complexity[36] is arguably laden with ideological implications.

A few participants in the debate seem to go further from neoclassicism in methodology, philosophy, or both. Nelson and Winter, and Liebenstein, for

---

essence of the contract is that it should only state the limits to the powers of the entrepreneur. Within these limits, he can therefore direct the other factors of production.

Coase (1937) pp.336–7, also reprinted below.

[35] Williamson (1983b) p.351. Against the tendency to ignore real institutions on grounds of presumed competitive convergence to optimality, one could also quote *Alchian's* warnings (1950, p.220) that

[w]hat really counts is the various actions actually tried . . . not . . . some set of perfect actions. The economist may be pushing his luck too far in arguing that actions in response to changes in environment . . . will converge as a result of adaptation or adoption toward the optimum action that should have been selected, if foresight had been perfect.

[36] In Simon (1962).

example, adopt highly eclectic approaches to understanding decision-making behavior, and display little inclination to argue the a priori optimality of competitive institutions. Their work suggests that organizations and organizational cultures are complex, inarticulable, and difficult to manipulate purposively, and that in a world in which competition is imperfect because search is never exhaustive, organizational outcomes will also be imperfect and subject to indeterminacies. Sensitivity to the social and intellectual dimensions of choice, and to the myriad of factors that caution against assuming socially optimal outcomes of individually "rational" behavior, also mark the writing of such heterodox economists as Albert Hirschman, whose ideas impact upon Freeman's (and Freeman and Medoff's) view of labor unions, included in this volume. It is, arguably, a similar spirit of "nonpresumptive inquiry" that permits attempts at "bridge building" across paradigms, such as Goldberg's exploration of the radical "contested terrain" of Richard Edwards in Goldberg (1980a).

Looking over this spectrum in historical perspective, we might say, with some simplification, that contemporary economists rediscovered the firm, after it had faded to obscurity in the refinements of neoclassical theory, as something of an embarrassment. The few, such as Coase, who, though basically "mainstream" in predisposition, were willing to take the firm seriously during the heyday of the "neoclassical synthesis," were largely ignored for thirty years. Since neoclassicism was otherwise preoccupied, observations such as those of Berle and Means (1932), which presented a plausible argument that modern corporations had ceased to be vehicles of profit maximization and had become instead the private instruments of the managers *of other people's wealth,* raised questions about the real world of modern capitalism to which neoclassical theory as then constituted provided no answers. The history of the modern theory of the firm begins with those who took this challenge seriously.[37]

Looking from this perspective at the literature that has thus developed, the distinctions to which we have been pointing above come down to those between (1) analysts who answer the embarrassment of real institutions by developing new institutional analyses of highly neoclassical flavor, in that, in the absence of governmental restraints, markets are found to surface at every pass and markets *work;* (2) analysts whose methodological predispositions are somewhat less orthodox, who more sharply delineate organizations from markets, but who retain the neoclassical tendency to suppose that freely contracted arrangements incline toward social optimality unless exceptional con-

---

[37] See the special issue of the *Journal of Law and Economics* (June 1983) on the 50th anniversary of Berle and Means' book, including papers by Fama and Jensen, Williamson, and Klein. For a discussion of the disappearance and rediscovery of the firm in the history of economic thought, see McNulty (1984).

ditions argue to the contrary; and (3) analysts who not only employ heterodox methodology and take nonmarket institutions seriously, but whose inquiries also appear to be less conditioned by ideological presuppositions.

Bringing in the left

By surveying only the "mainstream," thus far, we have preserved the sense of a mainstream–radical division mentioned earlier. How absolute is that division in the theory of the firm? Emotively, ideologically, it may be all important. To be "mainstream" is almost by definition to believe in, or at least to be open to, the legitimacy of the capitalist firm and of the economic system in which it is embedded, while to be radical seems to require some display of hostility toward them. Methodologically, the distinction is also likely to be important. The radical paradigm involves a different conception of the disciplinary boundaries and scope of "political economy." And since such trends began to be identified with the new or neoclassicism in the late 19th century, radicals have taken a dim view of marginalism and of the "subjectivism" of value theories hinging, in their view, on preferences, and down-weighting the "objective" parameters of the social production process.[38]

The era in which the new literature on the firm has grown, however, is one in which scholars operating within both paradigms have recognized limitations in their inherited doctrines, and in which some have opened the doors to an eclecticism that, in the limit, sees a fading of boundaries and a meeting in discourse. Overall, it seems more reasonable to locate radical authors on a continuation of the spectrum sketched above, rather than in another plane entirely. In many respects, indeed, radical scholars find a natural place in that spectrum. An institutional and historical orientation has been part of radical economic studies at least since Marx combined value theory with studies of factory conditions and legislation in his analysis of capitalist production. The presumption of social and technical efficiency of market-selected organizational forms, which tends to characterize "mainstream" orthodoxy and our first group of "new institutional" theorists, is clearly absent.

By and large, however, radicals fit poorly into any grouping of analysts who could be labeled "nonpresumptive" in an ideological sense. This is because while they *do* consistently refrain from embracing liberal norms in their interpretations of market phenomena, the liberal worldview is replaced in their writings by an alternative normative predisposition. Since most radical economists assume a normative universe in which firms are exploitative of workers, hierarchy serves the interests of power rather than efficiency, and so

---

[38] See, for example, the editor's introduction and selections in Sweezy (1966) and Lindbeck (1977).

forth, the methodologically heterodox in their ranks might best be placed in a new group mirroring the second one discussed above. To describe Marglin, Edwards, Bowles, and similar authors as radical counterparts of Simon and Williamson seems appropriate because while the former freely borrow institutionalist and marginalist concepts, and are no more rigidly "Marxist" than Simon and Williamson are rigidly "neoclassical," the sense of a radical ideological precommitment in their writing is as evident as is the liberal precommitment of their counterparts. This leaves methodologically *orthodox* Marxists to be placed in their own group opposite the neoclassical end of the spectrum.

There is of course a "rough and ready" quality to this classificatory proposal, so that no further space need be spent on defending it. Undoubtedly, alternative schemes, emphasizing different motifs, could be at least as fruitful. For example, while it bears no obvious relationship to the arc of analytical positions that has just been sketched, it is interesting to point out that in at least one sense, namely his sharp delineation of firm and market, Marx himself[39] belongs firmly in the camp of Coase, Simon, and Williamson. In Volume I of *Capital,* Marx argues that equivalents exchange for equivalents in the market, and that consequently, profit is *not* created in the "sphere of circulation," whether by "sharp practices" or otherwise. The market is a "noisy sphere, where everything takes place on the surface and in view of all men."

This sphere . . . is in fact a very Eden of the innate rights of man. There alone rule Freedom, Equality, Property and Bentham. Freedom, because both buyer and seller of a commodity, say labour-power, are constrained only by their own free will. They contract as free agents, and the agreement they come to, is but the form in which they give legal expression to their common will. Equality, because each enters into relation with the other, as with a simple owner of commodities, and they exchange equivalent for equivalent. . . .

Whereas this sphere of circulation happily "furnishes the 'Free-trader Vulgaris' with his views and ideas, and with the standard by which he judges a society based on capital and wages," it is in the "hidden abode of production" that profit is squeezed from labor.[40]

For Marx, the secret of capitalist profit lay in the distinction, referred to earlier in this essay, between labor power as a saleable commodity and labor as a productive factor. Like other commodities, labor power exchanged for

---

[39] Does Marx not belong, by definition, in the above-proposed camp of the radical orthodox, and by his writings, too, at a methodologically intolerant left terminus of my spectrum? In spite of his vitriolic attacks on the "vulgar economists" of his day, we cannot be sure that he would be less willing to dialogue with or to make use of the tools of modern economics than, say, Bowles is in the piece included below. While some followers project a Marxist disgust for all things marginalist, Marx himself might surprise them and dissent with his quip *"Je ne suis pas marxiste."*

[40] Quotations from Marx (1967) p.176, reprinted in Part I of this collection.

its cost of production, namely the value of its subsistence requirements. However, because of its joint control over the tools, land, and other resources with which labor needed to work to be productive, the capitalist class could squeeze out of workers, upon purchase of their labor power, more labor than that needed to produce a laborer's requirements.[41] The difference between the subsistence wage and the value of commodities produced, net of nonlabor costs, constituted society's surplus production, which was captured by the owners of capital under the institutions of the capitalist order.

Given this value theory, it was natural for Marx to focus much attention upon the struggle between capitalists and workers to determine both the duration of the working day, and its intensity. But even without Marx's value theory, which is not universally insisted upon by contemporary radical economists, the struggle to wrest more work out of laborers for a given wage payment remains at the heart of the study of the labor process, which in turn remains a central focus of research. In the selections included here, Marx makes striking use of Adam Smith's reservations about the effects of division of labor upon the worker – or what is today inelegantly referred to as "deskilling." Edward's study of changes in the organization of work in selected American corporations, excerpted here, is only one notable example of this continued Marxist research tradition.[42]

Ultimately, the Marxist division of the spheres of "production" and of "circulation" – like that between division of labor in "society" (the market) and in the workshop (the firm) – must not be carried too far, for it is only by taking into account the condition of the labor market, which Marx assumes to be characterized by a pool of the unemployed created by expulsion from the land and by technological change, that the wresting of surplus labor (or, in any case, capital's ability to dictate the conditions of work) makes sense. Once market conditions are made explicit, though, the radical model (albeit *sans* value theory) not only translates sensibly into the "mainstream" terminology, as Bowles' paper in this volume shows so well; it indeed offers leads for mainstream analysis. Thus, *exempla gregia,* Shapiro and Stiglitz[43] have quite recently provided a formal demonstration of the possibility that where the labor input cannot be costlessly and perfectly monitored, firms may find a certain level of unemployment beneficial or even necessary to internal incentives, and without conspiracy or collusion, their independent hiring decisions

---

[41] Note that the idea of joint control or monopoly here is not that capitalists colluded with one another in product or even in factor markets, where in fact Marx assumed perfect competition. Rather, it is that from laborers' standpoints, the exclusive control over the complementary factors of production by another class (along with chronic unemployment) undermined bargaining power over the terms of the labor contract.

[42] For some other references, see Goldberg (1980) and Bowles (1984), reprinted in Part IV of this volume.

[43] Shapiro and Stiglitz (1984).

may lead to a labor market equilibrium characterized by just such incentive-supporting unemployment. By incorporating costly monitoring and making explicit the principal–agent problem of the workplace, the neoclassics thus appear to reinvent the "reserve army of the unemployed" and to raise again the suggestion that Marx's hierarchy, and that of Coase et al., may be quite of one piece.

The lesson of this is not that Marx or the neoclassicals or any other school or trend is after all *right* in either the totality or the detail of its analysis, but rather that just as we are likely to err by placing too much emphasis on the distinctions between market and firm, so there may also be much to lose from focusing too much attention on differences in ideology, methodological ortho-doxy, and other dimensions of characterization. While it may not be quite consolation enough, in view of the fact that understanding moves forward slowly indeed, we have, nonetheless, in this field, a clear illustration of the proposition that while "scientific" – or at least "analytic" – discourse may be hopelessly colored by ideological and methodological presumptions and motives, there is, after all, some kernel of clarified perception that emerges from debate.[44] As the modern radicals grasp the possibilities inherent in a neoclassicism awakening to the need for an economics of information, uncer-tainty, and agency, and of kindred institutional views of internal and external labor markets; as the new institutionalists build upon neoclassical methods while stressing that property rights involve relations between *individuals,* and not only personified "factors" awaiting their "returns"; and as a neoclassi-cism expanding its toolbox with asymmetric information and the like, to try to grapple with still mysterious phenomena of the macroeconomy, opens itself here and there to these other strands, some elements of a common understand-ing of *economic institutions,* and of an *economics of organizations,* begins to emerge. To grasp it all, in its present state of far from complete synthesis, may require a willingness to embrace, at least temporarily, such dialectical mysteries as relations that are at one and the same time driven by market forces, and shielded from them; at one and the same time freely entered into for mutual benefit, yet saturated with asymmetries of power and hierarchical control; and that at one and the same time manifest a coalition-like striving to

---

[44] Aside from that between Shapiro and Stiglitz and the Marxists, numerous interesting ex-amples of convergence or conciliation might be cited, for example: Alchian's apparent accep-tance (1984) of the Williamsonian critique of Alchian and Demsetz (1972, reprinted in Part II); Fama's apparent movement from the simple *"ex post* settling up" of Fama's (1980, reprinted in Part III) to a concern with internal governance mechanisms (in Fama and Jensen 1983a, 1983b); and Williamson's statements that there may be efficiency arguments favoring employee represen-tation in decision making not only (1984b) when the "need for dignity" is taken into account as a basic feature of human nature, but even (1984a) simply from the standpoint of their own exposure to specific risk, and of the governance implications (in Williamson's framework) of that exposure.

expand wealth, yet display the stamp of some members' frequently successful strategies to exploit the resources of other ''team members'' for their own advantage, and to deny options to them. It is then, to see the firm, like this body of scholarship which attempts to understand it, as a complex and evolving value-adding enterprise that is simultaneously both cooperative and competitive in character.

PART I

Within and among firms: the division of labor

From *The Wealth of Nations*

ADAM SMITH

Adam Smith (1723–90) was born in Kirkcaldy, Scotland. He received the Master of Arts degree from the University of Glasgow in 1740, and subsequently was Professor of Moral Philosophy at that University from 1752 to 1763, and Commissioner of Customs for Scotland from 1778 to 1790. *The Wealth of Nations* established Smith as the founding figure in classical political economy.

Of the division of labour

(From book I, chapter 1)

The greatest improvement in the productive powers of labour, and the greater part of the skill, dexterity, and judgment with which it is any where directed, or applied, seem to have been the effects of the division of labour.

The effects of the division of labour, in the general business of society, will be more easily understood, by considering in what manner it operates in some particular manufactures. It is commonly supposed to be carried furthest in some very trifling ones; not perhaps that it really is carried further in them than in others of more importance: but in those trifling manufactures which are destined to supply the small wants of but a small number of people, the whole number of workmen must necessarily be small; and those employed in every different branch of the work can often be collected into the same work-house, and placed at once under the view of the spectator. In those great manufactures, on the contrary, which are destined to supply the great wants of the great body of the people, every different branch of the work employs so great a number of workmen, that it is impossible to collect them all into the same workhouse. We can seldom see more, at one time, than those employed in one single branch. Though in such manufactures, therefore, the work may really be divided into a much greater number of parts, than in those of a more trifling nature, the division is not near so obvious, and has accordingly been much less observed.

From Adam Smith, *An Inquiry into the Nature and Causes of The Wealth of Nations,* originally published 1776. Excerpted from the Modern Library Edition, edited by Edwin Cannan. New York, 1937.

To take an example, therefore,[1] from a very trifling manufacture; but one in which the division of labour has been very often taken notice of, the trade of the pin-maker; a workman not educated to this business (which the division of labour has rendered a distinct trade), nor acquainted with the use of the machinery employed in it (to the invention of which the same division of labour has probably given occasion), could scarce, perhaps, with his utmost industry, make one pin in a day, and certainly could not make twenty. But in the way in which this business is now carried on, not only the whole work is a peculiar trade, but it is divided into a number of branches, of which the greater part are likewise peculiar trades. One man draws out the wire, another straights it, a third cuts it, a fourth points it, a fifth grinds it at the top for receiving the head; to make the head requires two or three distinct operations; to put it on, is a peculiar business, to whiten the pins is another; it is even a trade by itself to put them into the paper; and the important business of making a pin is, in this manner, divided into about eighteen distinct operations, which, in some manufactories, are all performed by distinct hands, though in others the same man will sometimes perform two or three of them. I have seen a small manufactory of this kind where ten men only were employed, and where some of them consequently performed two or three distinct operations. But though they were very poor, and therefore but indifferently accommodated with the necessary machinery, they could, when they exerted themselves, make among them about twelve pounds of pins in a day. There are in a pound upwards of four thousand pins of a middling size. Those ten persons, therefore, could make among them upwards of forty-eight thousand pins in a day. Each person, therefore, making a tenth part of forty-eight thousand pins, might be considered as making four thousand eight hundred pins in a day. But if they had all wrought separately and independently, and without any of them having been educated to this particular business, they certainly could not each of them have made twenty, perhaps not one pin in a day; that is, certainly, not the two hundred and fortieth, perhaps not the four thousand eight hundredth part of what they are at present capable of performing, in consequence of a proper division and combination of their different operations.

In every other art and manufacture, the effects of the division of labour are similar to what they are in this very trifling one; though, in many of them, the labour can neither be so much subdivided, nor reduced to so great a simplicity of operation. The division of labour, however, so far as it can be introduced, occasions, in every art, a proportionable increase of the productive powers of labour. The separation of different trades and employments from one another,

---

[1] Another and perhaps more important reason for taking an example like that which follows is the possibility of exhibiting the advantages of division of labour in statistical form.

seems to have taken place, in consequence of this advantage. This separation too is generally carried furthest in those countries which enjoy the highest degree of industry and improvement; what is the work of one man in a rude state of society, being generally that of several in an improved one.

. . .

This great increase of the quantity of work, which, in consequence of the division of labour, the same number of people are capable of performing, is owing to three different circumstances; first, to the increase of dexterity in every particular workman; secondly, to the saving of the time which is commonly lost in passing from one species of work to another; and lastly, to the invention of a great number of machines which facilitate and abridge labour, and enable one man to do the work of many.

First, the improvement of the dexterity of the workman necessarily increases the quantity of the work he can perform; and the division of labour, by reducing every man's business to some one simple operation, and by making this operation the sole employment of his life, necessarily increases very much the dexterity of the workman. A common smith, who, though accustomed to handle the hammer, has never been used to make nails, if upon some particular occasion he is obliged to attempt it, will scarce, I am assured, be able to make above two or three hundred nails in a day, and those too very bad ones. A smith who has been accustomed to make nails, but whose sole or principal business has not been that of a nailer, can seldom with his utmost diligence make more than eight hundred or a thousand nails in a day. I have seen several boys under twenty years of age who had never exercised any other trade but that of making nails, and who, when they exerted themselves, could make, each of them, upwards of two thousand three hundred nails in a day. The making of a nail, however, is by no means one of the simplest operations. The same person blows the bellows, stirs or mends the fire as there is occasion, heats the iron, and forges every part of the nail: In forging the head too he is obliged to change his tools. The different operations into which the making of a pin, or of a metal button, is subdivided, are all of them much more simple, and the dexterity of the person, of whose life it has been the sole business to perform them, is usually much greater. The rapidity with which some of the operations of those manufacturers are performed, exceeds what the human hand could, by those who had never seen them, be supposed capable of acquiring.

Secondly, the advantage which is gained by saving the time commonly lost in passing from one sort of work to another, is much greater than we should at first view be apt to imagine it. It is impossible to pass very quickly from one kind of work to another, that is carried on in a different place, and with quite different tools. A country weaver, who cultivates a small farm, must lose a good deal of time in passing from his loom to the field, and from the field to his loom. When the two trades can be carried on in the same workhouse, the loss of time is no doubt much less. It is even in this case, however, very considerable. A man commonly saunters a little in turning his hand from one sort of employment to another. When he first begins the new work he is seldom very keen and hearty; his mind, as they say, does not go to it, and for some time he rather trifles than applies to good purpose. The habit of sauntering and of indolent careless application, which is naturally, or rather necessarily acquired by every country workman who is obliged to change his work and his tools every half hour, and to apply his hand in twenty different ways almost every day of his life; renders him almost always slothful and lazy, and incapable of any vigorous application even on the most pressing occasions. Independent, therefore, of his deficiency in point of dexterity, this cause alone must always reduce considerable the quantity of work which he is capable of performing.

Thirdly, and lastly, every body must be sensible how much labour is facilitated and abridged by the application of proper machinery. It is unnecessary to give any example. I shall only observe, therefore, that the invention of all those machines by which labour is so much facilitated and abridged, seems to have been originally owing to the division of labour. Men are much more likely to discover easier and readier methods of attaining any object, when the whole attention of their minds is directed towards that single object, than when it is dissipated among a great variety of things. But in consequence of the division of labour, the whole of every man's attention comes naturally to be directed towards some one very simple object. It is naturally to be expected, therefore, that some one or other of those who are employed in each particular branch of labour should soon find out easier and readier methods of performing their own particular work, wherever the nature of it admits of such improvement. A great part of the machines made use of in those manufactures in which labour is most subdivided, were originally the inventions of common workmen, who, being each of them employed in some very simple operation, naturally turned their thoughts towards finding out easier and readier methods of performing it. Whoever has been much accustomed to visit such manufactures, must frequently have been shewn very pretty machines, which were the inventions of such workmen, in order to facilitate and quicken their own particular part of the work. In the first fire-engines, a boy was constantly employed to open and shut alternately the communication between the boiler and the cylinder, according as the piston either ascended or descended. One of those boys, who loved to play with his companions, observed that, by tying a string from the handle of the valve which opened this communication to another part of the machine, the valve would open and shut without his assistance, and leave him at liberty to divert himself with his play-fellows. One of the greatest improvements that has been made upon this machine, since it was first invented, was in this manner the discovery of a boy who wanted to save his own labour.

All the improvements in machinery, however, have by no means been the inventions of those who had occasion to use the machines. Many improvements have been made by the ingenuity of the makers of the machines, when to make them became the business of a peculiar trade; and some by that of those who are called philosophers or men of speculation, whose trade it is not to do any thing, but to observe every thing; and who, upon that account, are often capable of combining together the powers of the most distant and dissimilar objects. In the progress of society, philosophy or speculation becomes, like every other employment, the principal or sole trade and occupation of a particular class of citizens. Like every other employment too, it is subdivided into a great number of different branches, each of which affords occupation to a peculiar tribe or class of philosophers; and this subdivision of employment in philosophy, as well as in every other business, improves dexterity, and saves time. Each individual becomes more expert in his own peculiar branch, more work is done upon the whole, and the quantity of science is considerably increased by it.

It is the great multiplication of the productions of all the different arts, in consequence of the division of labour, which occasions, in a well-governed society, that universal opulence which extends itself to the lowest ranks of the people. Every workman has a great quantity of his own work to dispose of beyond what he himself has occasion for; and every other workman being exactly in the same situation, he is enabled to exchange a great quantity of his own goods for a great quantity, or, what comes to the same thing, for the price of a great quantity of theirs. He supplies them abundantly with what they have occasion for, and they accommodate him as amply with what he has occasion for, and a general plenty diffuses itself through all the different ranks of the society.

Observe the accommodation of the most common artificer or day labourer in a civilized and thriving country, and you will perceive that the number of people of whose industry a part, though but a small part, has been employed in procuring him this accommodation, exceeds all computation. The woollen coat, for example, which covers the day-labourer, as coarse and rough as it may appear, is the produce of the joint labour of a great multitude of workmen. The shepherd, the sorter of wool, the wool-comber or carder, the dyer, the scribbler, the spinner, the weaver, the fuller, the dresser, with many others, must all join their different arts in order to complete even this homely production. How many merchants and carriers, besides, must have been employed in transporting the materials from some of those workmen to others who often live in a very distant part of the country! how much commerce and navigation in particular, how many ship-builders, sailors, sail-makers, rope-makers, must have been employed in order to bring together the different drugs made use of by the dyer, which often come from the remotest corners of the world! What a variety of labour too is necessary in order to produce the tools of the meanest of those workmen! To say nothing of such complicated machines as the ship of the sailor, the mill of the fuller, or even the loom of the weaver, let us consider only what a variety of labour is requisite in order to form that very simple machine, the shears with which the shepherd clips the wool. The miner, the builder of the furnace for smelting the ore, the feller of the timber, the burner of the charcoal to be made use of in the smelting-house, the brick-maker, the brick-layer, the workmen who attend the furnace, the mill-wright, the forger, the smith, must all of them join their different arts in order to produce them. Were we to examine, in the same manner, all the different parts of his dress and household furniture, the coarse linen shirt which he wears next his skin, the shoes which cover his feet, the bed which he lies on, and all the different parts which compose it, the kitchengrate at which he prepares his victuals, the coals which he makes use of for that purpose, dug from the bowels of the earth, and brought him to perhaps by a long sea and a long land carriage, all the other utensils of his kitchen, all the furniture of his table, the knives and forks, the earthen or pewter plates upon which he serves up and divides his victuals, the different hands employed in preparing his bread and his beer, the glass window which lets in the heat and the light, and keeps out the wind and the rain, with all the knowledge and art requisite for preparing that beautiful and happy invention, without which these northern parts of the world could scarce have afforded a very comfortable habitation, together with the tools of all the different workmen employed in producing those different conveniences; if we examine, I say, all these things, and consider what a variety of labour is employed about each of them, we shall be sensible that without the assistance and co-operation of many thousands, the very meanest person in a civilized country could not be provided, even according to, what we very falsely imagine, the easy and simple manner in which he is commonly accommodated. Compared, indeed, with the more extravagant luxury of the great, his accommodation must no doubt appear extremely simple and easy; and yet it may be true, perhaps that the accommodation of an European prince does not always so much exceed that of an industrious and frugal peasant, as the accommodation of the latter exceeds that of many an African king, the absolute master of the lives and liberties of ten thousand naked savages.

. . .

That the division of labour is limited by the extent of
the market

(From book I, chapter 3)

As it is the power of exchanging that gives occasion to the division of labour, so the extent of this division must always be limited by the extent of that power, or in other words, by the extent of the market. When the market is very small, no person can have any encouragement to dedicate himself entirely to one employment, for want of the power to exchange all that surplus part of the produce of his own labour, which is over and above his own consumption, for such parts of the produce of other men's labour as he has occasion for.

There are some sorts of industry, even of the lowest kind, which can be carried on no where but in a great town. A porter, for example, can find employment and subsistence in no other place. A village is by much too narrow a sphere for him; even an ordinary market town is scarce large enough to afford him constant occupation. In the lone houses and very small villages which are scattered about in so desert a country as the Highlands of Scotland, every farmer must be butcher, baker and brewer for his own family. In such situations we can scarce expect to find even a smith, a carpenter, or a mason, within less than twenty miles of another of the same trade. The scattered families that live at eight or ten miles distance from the nearest of them, must learn to perform themselves a great number of little pieces of work, for which, in more populous countries, they would call in the assistance of those workmen. Country workmen are almost every where obliged to apply themselves to all the different branches of industry that have so much affinity to one another as to be employed about the same sort of materials. A country carpenter deals in every sort of work that is made of wood: a country smith in every sort of work that is made of iron. The former is not only a carpenter, but a joiner, a cabinet maker, and even a carver in wood, as well as a wheelwright, a ploughwright, a cart and wagon maker. The employments of the latter are still more various. It is impossible there should be such a trade as even that of the nailer in the remote and inland parts of the Highlands of Scotland. Such a workman at the rate of a thousand nails a day, and three hundred working days in the year, will make three hundred thousand nails in the year. But in such a situation it would be impossible to dispose of one thousand, that is, of one day's work in the year.

As by means of water-carriage a more extensive market is opened to every sort of industry than what land-carriage alone can afford it, so it is upon the sea-coast, and along the banks of navigable rivers, that industry of every kind naturally begins to subdivide and improve itself, and it is frequently not till a long time after that those improvements extend themselves to the inland parts of the country.

. . .

On joint stock companies

(From book V, chapter 1)

Joint stock companies, established either by royal charter or by act of parliament, differ in several respects, not only from regulated companies, but from private copartneries.

First, in a private copartnery, no partner, without the consent of the company, can transfer his share to another person, or introduce a new member into the company. Each member, however, may, upon proper warning, withdraw from the copartnery, and demand payment from them of his share of the common stock. In a joint stock company, on the contrary, no member can demand payment of his share from the company; but each member can, without their consent, transfer his share to another person, and thereby introduce a new member. The value of a share in a joint stock is always the price which it will bring in the market; and this may be either greater or less, in any proportion, than the sum which its owner stands credited for in the stock of the company.

Secondly, in a private copartnery, each partner is bound for the debts contracted by the company to the whole extent of his fortune. In a joint stock company, on the contrary, each partner is bound only to the extend of his share.

The trade of a joint stock company is always managed by a court of directors. This court, indeed, is frequently subject, in many respects, to the controul of a general court of proprietors. But the greater part of those proprietors seldom pretend to understand any thing of the business of the company; and when the spirit of faction happens not to prevail among them, give themselves no trouble about it, but receive contentedly such half yearly or yearly dividend, as the directors think proper to make to them. This total exemption from trouble and from risk, beyond a limited sum, encouraged many people to become adventurers in joint stock companies, who would, upon no account, hazard their fortunes in any private copartnery. Such companies, therefore, commonly draw to themselves much greater stocks than any private copartnery can boast of. The trading stock of the South Sea Company, at one time, amounted to upwards of thirty-three millions eight hundred thousand pounds. The dividend capital of the Bank of England amounts, at present, to ten millions seven hundred and eighty thousand pounds. The directors of such companies, however, being the managers rather of other people's money than of their own, it cannot well be expected, that they should watch over it with the same anxious vigilance with which the partners in a private copartnery frequently watch over their own. Like the stewards of a rich man, they are apt to consider attention to small matters as not for their master's honour, and very easily give themselves a dispensation from having it. Negligence and profusion, therefore, must always prevail, more or less, in the management of the affairs of such a company. It is upon this account that joint stock companies for foreign trade have seldom been able to maintain the competition against private adventurers. They have, accordingly, very seldom succeeded without an exclusive privilege; and frequently have not succeeded with one. Without an exclusive privilege they have commonly mismanaged the trade. With an exclusive privilege they have both mismanaged and confined it.

. . .

But a joint stock company, consisting of a small number of proprietors, with a moderate capital, approaches very nearly to the nature of the private copartnery, and may be capable of nearly the same degree of vigilance and attention.

. . .

On education

(From book V, chapter 1)

In the progress of the division of labour, the employment of the far greater part of those who live by labour, that is, of the great body of the people, comes to be confined to a few very simple operations, frequently to one or two. But the understandings of the greater part of men are necessarily formed by their ordinary employments. The man whose whole life is spent in performing a few simple operations, of which the effects too are, perhaps, always the same, or very nearly the same, has no occasion to exert his understanding, or to exercise his invention in finding out expedients for removing difficulties which never occur. He naturally loses, therefore, the habit of such exertion, and generally becomes as stupid and ignorant as it is possible for a human creature to become. The torpor of his mind renders him, not only incapable of relishing or bearing a part in any rational conversation, but of conceiving any generous, noble, or tender sentiment, and consequently of forming any just judgment concerning many even of the ordinary duties of private life. Of the great and extensive interests of his country he is altogether incapable of judging; and unless very particular pains have been taken to render him otherwise, he is equally incapable of defending his country in war. The uniformity of his stationary life naturally corrupts the courage of his mind, and makes him regard with abhorrence the irregular, uncertain, and

41

adventurous life of a soldier. It corrupts even the activity of his body, and renders him incapable of exerting his strength with vigour and perseverance, in any other employment than that to which he has been bred. His dexterity at his own particular trade seems, in this manner, to be acquired at the expense of his intellectual, social, and marital virtues. But in every improved and civilized society this is the state into which the labouring poor, that is, the great body of the people, must necessarily fall, unless government takes some pains to prevent it.

It is otherwise in the barbarous societies, as they are commonly called, of hunters, of shepherds, and even of husbandmen in that rude state of husbandry which precedes the improvement of manufactures, and the extension of foreign commerce. In such societies the varied occupations of every man oblige every man to exert his capacity, and to invent expedients for removing difficulties which are continually occurring. Invention is kept alive, and the mind is not suffered to fall into that drowsy stupidity, which, in a civilized society, seems to benumb the understanding of almost all the inferior ranks of people. In those barbarous societies, as they are called, every man, it has already been observed, is a warrior. Every man too is in some measure a statesman, and can form a tolerable judgment concerning the interest of the society, and the conduct of those who govern it. How far their chiefs are good judges in peace, or good leaders in war, is obvious to the observation of almost every single man among them. In such a society indeed, no man can well acquire that improved and refined understanding, which a few men sometimes possess in a more civilized state. Though in a rude society there is a good deal of variety in the occupations of every individual, there is not a good deal in those of the whole society. Every man does, or is capable of doing, almost every thing which any other man does, or is capable of doing. Every man has a considerable degree of knowledge, ingenuity, and invention; but scarce any man has a great degree. The degree, however, which is commonly possessed, is generally sufficient for conducting the whole simple business of the society. In a civilized state, on the contrary, though there is little variety in the occupations of the greater part of individuals, there is an almost infinite variety in those of the whole society. These varied occupations present an almost infinite variety of objects to the contemplation of those few, who, being attached to no particular occupation themselves, have leisure and inclination to examine the occupations of other people. The contemplation of so great a variety of objects necessarily exercises their minds in endless comparisons and combinations, and renders their understandings, in an extraordinary degree, both acute and comprehensive. Unless those few, however, happen to be placed in some very particular situations, their great abilities, though honourable to themselves, may contribute very little to the good government or happiness of their society. Notwithstanding the great abilities of those few, all the nobler parts of the human character may be, in a great measure, obliterated and extinguished in the great body of the people.

The education of the common people requires, perhaps, in a civilized and commercial society, the attention of the public more than that of people of some rank and fortune. People of some rank and fortune are generally eighteen or nineteen years of age before they enter upon that particular business, profession, or trade, by which they propose to distinguish themselves in the world. They have before that full time to acquire, or at least to fit themselves for afterwards acquiring, every accomplishment which can recommend them to the public esteem, or render them worthy of it.

. . .

It is otherwise with the common people. They have little time to spare for education. Their parents can scarce afford to maintain them even in infancy. As soon as they are able to work, they must apply to some trade by which they can earn their subsistence. That trade too is generally so simple uniform as to give little exercise to the understanding; while, at the same time, their labour is both so constant and so severe, that it leaves them little leisure and less inclination to apply to, or even to think of any thing else.

But though the common people cannot, in any civilized society, be so well instructed as people of some rank and fortune, the most essential parts of education, however, to read, write, and account, can be acquired at so early a period of life, that the greater part even of those who are to be bred to the lowest occupations, have time to acquire them before they can be employed in those occupations. For a very small expense the public can facilitate, can encourage, and can even impose upon almost the whole body of the people, the necessity of acquiring those most essential parts of education.

. . .

CHAPTER 2

From *Capital*

KARL MARX

Karl Marx (1818–83) was born in Trier, Germany. He earned the Ph.D. degree at the University of Jena in 1841. Beginning in 1849, he resided in London where he took up economic studies in the British Museum. His three volume work, *Capital,* is the cornerstone of what has come to be known as Marxian political economy.

The buying and selling of labor-power

(From chapters 5 and 6)

. . .

We have shown that surplus-value cannot be created by circulation, and, therefore, that in its formation, something must take place in the background, which is not apparent in the circulation itself.

. . .

The consumption of labour-power is completed, as in the case of every other commodity, outside the limits of the market or of the sphere of circulation. Accompanied by Mr. Moneybags and by the possessor of labour-power, we therefore take leave for a time of this noisy sphere, where everything takes place on the surface and in view of all men, and follow them both into the hidden abode of production, on whose threshold there stares us in the face "No admittance except on business." Here we shall see, not only how capital produces, but how capital is produced. We shall at last force the secret of profit making.

This sphere that we are deserting, within whose boundaries the sale and purchase of labor-power goes on, is in fact a very Eden of the innate rights of man. There alone rule Freedom, Equality, Property and Bentham. Freedom, because both buyer and seller of a commodity, say of labour-power, are con-

From Karl Marx, *Capital: A Critique of Political Economy, Volume I: The Process of Capitalist Production,* edited by Frederick Engels, originally published 1867. Excerpted from the translation of the Third German Edition by Samuel Moore and Edward Aveling. New York: International Publishers, 1967.

strained only by their own free will. They contract as free agents, and the agreement they come to, is but the form in which they give legal expression to their common will. Equality, because each enters into relation with the other, as with a simple owner of commodities, and they exchange equivalent for equivalent. Property, because each disposes only of what is his own. And Bentham, because each looks only to himself. The only force that brings them together and puts them in relation with each other, is the selfishness, the gain and the private interests of each. Each looks to himself only, and no one troubles himself about the rest, and just because they do so, do they all, in accordance with the preestablished harmony of things, or under the auspices of an allshrewd providence, work together to their mutual advantage, for the common weal and in the interest of all.

On leaving this sphere of simple circulation or of exchange of commodities, which furnishes the "Free-trade Vulgaris" with his views and ideas, and with the standard by which he judges a society based on capital and wages, we think we can perceive a change in the physiognomy of our dramatis personæ. He, who before was the money-owner, now strides in front as capitalist; the possessor of labour-power follows as his labourer. The one with an air of importance, smirking, intent on business; the other, timid and holding back, like one who is bringing his own hide to market and has nothing to expect but – a hiding.

Co-operation

(From chapter 13)

. . .

Capitalist production only then really begins, as we have already seen, when each individual capital employs simultaneously a comparatively large number of labourers; when consequently the labour-process is carried on on an extensive scale and yields, relatively, large quantities of products. A greater number of labourers working together, at the same time, in one place (or, if you will, in the same field of labour), in order to produce the same sort of commodity under the mastership of one capitalist, constitutes, both historically and logically, the starting-point of capitalist production. With regard to the mode of production itself, manufacture, in its strict meaning, is hardly to be distinguished, in its earliest stages, from the handicraft trades of the guilds, otherwise than by the greater number of workmen simultaneously employed by one and the same individual capital. The workshop of the mediæval master handicraftsman is simply enlarged.

. . .

Even without an alteration in the system of working, the simultaneous employment of a large number of labourers effects a revolution in the material conditions of the labour-process. The buildings in which they work, the storehouses for the raw material, the implements and utensils used simultaneously or in turns by the workmen; in short, a portion of the means of production, are now consumed in common. On the one hand, the exchange-value of these means of production is not increased; for the exchange-value of a commodity is not raised by its use-value being consumed more thoroughly and to greater advantage. On the other hand, they are used in common, and therefore on a larger scale than before. A room where twenty weavers work at twenty looms must be larger than the room of a single weaver with two assistants. But it costs less labour to build one workshop for twenty persons than to build ten to accommodate two weavers each; thus the value of the means of production that are concentrated for use in common on a large scale does not increase in direct proportion to the expansion and to the increased useful effect of those means. When consumed in common, they give up a smaller part of their value to each single product; partly because the total value they part with is spread over a greater quantity of products, and partly because their value, though absolutely greater, is, having regard to their sphere of action in the process, relatively less than the value of isolated means of production. Owing to this, the value of a part of the constant capital falls, and in proportion to the magnitude of the fall, the total value of the commodity also falls. The effect is the same as if the means of production had cost less. The economy in their application is entirely owing to their being consumed in common by a large number of workmen. Moreover, this character of being necessary conditions of social labour, a character that distinguishes them from the dispersed and relatively more costly means of production of isolated, independent labourers, or small masters, is acquired even when the numerous workmen assembled together do not assist one another, but merely work side by side. A portion of the instruments of labour acquires this social character before the labour-process itself does so.

.   .   .

When numerous labourers work together side by side, whether in one and the same process, or in different but connected processes, they are said to co-operate, or to work in co-operation.

Just as the offensive power of a squadron of cavalry, or the defensive power of a regiment of infantry, is essentially different from the sum of the offensive or defensive powers of the individual cavalry or infantry soldiers taken separately, so the sum total of the mechanical forces exerted by isolated workmen differs from the social force that is developed, when many hands take part simultaneously in one and the same undivided operation, such as raising a heavy weight, turning a winch, or removing an obstacle.[1] In such cases the effect of the combined labour could either not be produced at all by isolated individual labour, or it could only be produced by a great expenditure of time, or on a very dwarfed scale. Not only have we here an increase in the productive power of the individual, by means of co-operation, but the creation of a new power, namely, the collective power of masses.[2]

Apart from the new power that arises from the fusion of many forces into one single force, mere social contact begets in most industries an emulation and a stimulation of the animal spirits that heighten the efficiency of each individual workman. Hence it is that a dozen persons working together will, in their collective working-day of 144 hours, produce far more than twelve isolated men each working 12 hours, or than one man who works twelve days in succession. The reason of this is that man is, if not as Aristotle contends, a political, at all events a social animal.

Although a number of men may be occupied together at the same time on the same, or the same kind of work, yet the labour of each, as a part of the collective labour, may correspond to a distinct phase of the labour-process, through all whose phases, in consequence of co-operation, the subject of their labour passes with greater speed. For instance, if a dozen masons place themselves in a row, so as to pass stones from the foot of a ladder to its summit, each of them does the same thing; nevertheless, their separate acts form connected parts of one total operation; they are particular phases, which must be gone through by each stone; and the stones are thus carried up quicker by the 24 hands of the row of men than they could be if each man went separately up and down the ladder with his burden. The object is carried over this same distance in a shorter time. Again, a combination of labour occurs whenever a building, for instance, is taken in hand on different sides simultaneously; although here also the co-operating masons are doing the same, or the same kind of work. The 12 masons, in their collective working day of 144 hours, make much more progress with the building than one mason could make working for 12 days, or 144 hours. The reason is, that a body of men working in concert has hands and eyes both before and behind, and is, to a certain degree, omnipresent. The various parts of the work progress simultaneously.

In the above instances we have laid stress upon the point that the men do the same, or the same kind of work, because this, the most simple form of

[1] "There are numerous operations of so simple a kind as not to admit a division into parts, which cannot be performed without the co-operation of many pairs of hands. I would instance the lifting of a large tree on to a wain . . . everything, in short, which cannot be done unless a great many pairs of hands help each other in the same undivided employment and at the same time" (E. G. Wakefield, 1849, p. 168).

[2] "As one man cannot, and ten men must strain to lift a ton of weight, yet 100 men can do it only by the strength of a finger of each of them." (John Bellers, 1696, p. 21.)

labour in common, plays a great part in co-operation, even in its most fully developed stage. If the work be complicated, then the mere number of the men who co-operate allows of the various operations being apportioned to different hands, and, consequently, of being carried on simultaneously. The time necessary for the completion of the whole work is thereby shortened.

In many industries, there are critical periods, determined by the nature of the process, during which certain definite results must be obtained. For instance, if a flock of sheep has to be shorn, or a field of wheat to be cut and harvested, the quantity and quality of the product depends on the work being begun and ended within a certain time. In these cases, the time that ought to be taken by the process is prescribed, just as it is in herring fishing. A single person cannot carve a working-day of more than, say 12 hours, out of the natural day, but 100 men co-operating extend the working-day to 1,200 hours. The shortness of the time allowed for the work is compensated for by the large mass of labour thrown upon the field of production at the decisive moment. The completion of the task within the proper time depends on the simultaneous application of numerous combined working-days; the amount of useful effect depends on the number of labourers; this number, however, is always smaller than the number of isolated labourers required to do the same amount of work in the same period. It is owing to the absence of this kind of co-operation that, in the western part of the United States, quantities of corn, and in those parts of East India where English rule has destroyed the old communities, quantities of cotton, are yearly wasted.

On the one hand, co-operation allows of the work being carried on over an extended space; it is consequently imperatively called for in certain undertakings, such as draining, constructing dykes, irrigation works, and the making of canals, roads and railways. On the other hand, while extending the scale of production, it renders possible a relative contraction of the arena. This contraction of arena simultaneous with, and arising from, extension of scale, whereby a number of useless expenses are cut down, is owing to the conglomeration of labourers, to the aggregation of various processes, and to the concentration of the means of production.

The combined working-day produces, relatively to an equal sum of isolated working-days, a greater quantity of use-values, and, consequently, diminishes the labour-time necessary for the production of a given useful effect. Whether the combined working-day, in a given case, acquires this increased productive power, because it heightens the mechanical force of labour, or extends its sphere of action over a greater space, or contracts the field of production relatively to the scale of production, or at the critical moment sets large masses of labour to work, or excites emulation between individuals and raises their animal spirits, or impresses on the similar operations carried on by a number of men the stamp of continuity and many-sidedness, or performs simultaneously different operations, or economises the means of production by use in common, or lends to individual labour the character of average social labour – whichever of these be the cause of the increase, the special productive power of the combined working-day is, under all circumstances, the social productive power of labour, or the productive power of social labour. This power is due to co-operation itself. When the labourer co-operates systematically with others, he strips off the fetters of his individuality, and develops the capabilities of his species.

As general rule, labourers cannot co-operate without being brought together: their assemblage in one place is a necessary condition of their co-operation. Hence wage-labourers cannot co-operate, unless they are employed simultaneously by the same capital, the same capitalist, and unless therefore their labour-powers are bought simultaneously by him. The total value of these labour-powers, or the amount of the wages of these labourers for a day, or a week, as the case may be, must be ready in the pocket of the capitalist, before the workmen are assembled for the process of production. The payment of 300 workmen at once, though only for one day, requires a greater outlay of capital, than does the payment of a smaller number of men, week by week, during a whole year. Hence the number of the labourers that co-operate, or the scale of co-operation, depends, in the first instance, on the amount of capital that the individual capitalist can spare for the purchase of labour-power; in other words, on the extent to which a single capitalist has command over the means of subsistence of a number of labourers.

And as with the variable, so it is with the constant capital. For example, the outlay on raw material is 30 times as great, for the capitalist who employs 300 men, as it is for each of the 30 capitalists who employ 10 men. The value and quantity of the instruments of labour used in common do not, it is true, increase at the same rate as the number of workmen, but they do increase very considerably. Hence, concentration of large masses of the means of production in the hands of individual capitalists, is a material condition for the co-operation of wage-labourers, and the extent of the co-operation or the scale of production, depends on the extent of this concentration.

We saw in a former chapter, that a certain minimum amount of capital was necessary, in order that the number of labourers simultaneously employed, and, consequently, the amount of surplus-value produced, might suffice to liberate the employer himself from manual labour, to convert him from a small master into a capitalist, and thus formally to establish capitalist production. We now see that a certain minimum amount is a necessary condition for the conversion of numerous isolated and independent processes into one combined social process.

We also saw that at first, the subjection of labour to capital was only a formal result of the fact, that the labourer, instead of working for himself, works for and consequently under the capitalist. By the co-operation of numerous wage-labourers, the sway of capital develops into a requisite for carrying on the labour-process itself, into a real requisite of production. That a capitalist should command on the field of production, is now as indispensable as that a general should command on the field of battle.

All combined labour on a large scale requires, more or less, a directing authority, in order to secure the harmonious working of the individual activities, and to perform the general functions that have their origin in the action of the combined organism, as distinguished from the action of its separate organs. A single violin player is his own conductor; an orchestra requires a separate one. The work of directing, superintending, and adjusting, becomes one of the functions of capital, from the moment that the labour under the control of capital, becomes co-operative. Once a function of capital, it acquires special characteristics.

The directing motive, the end and aim of capitalist production, is to extract the greatest possible amount of surplus-value, and consequently to exploit labour-power to the greatest possible extent. As the number of the co-operating labourers increases, so too does their resistance to the domination of capital, and with it, the necessity for capital to overcome this resistance by counterpressure. The control exercised by the capitalist is not only a special function, due to the nature of the social labour-process, and peculiar to that process, but it is, at the same time, a function of the exploitation of a social labour-process, and is consequently rooted in the unavoidable antagonism between the exploiter and the living and labouring raw material he exploits.

Again, in proportion to the increasing mass of the means of production, now no longer the property of the labourer, but of the capitalist, the necessity increases for some effective control over the proper application of those means.[3] Moreover, the co-operation of wage-labourers is entirely brought about by the capital that employs them. Their union into one single productive body and the establishment of a connexion between their individual functions, are matters foreign and external to them, are not their own act, but the act of the capital that brings and keeps them together. Hence the connexion existing between their various labours appears to them, ideally, in the shape of a preconceived plan of the capitalist, and practically in the shape of the authority of the same capitalist, in the shape of the powerful will of another, who

[3] That Philistine paper, the *Spectator*, states that after the introduction of a sort of partnership between capitalist and workmen in the "Wirework Company of Manchester," "the first result was a sudden decrease in waste, the men not seeing why they should waste their own property any more than any other master's, and waste is, perhaps, next to bad debts, the greatest source of manufacturing loss." The same paper finds that the main defect in the Rochdale co-operative experiments is this: "They showed that associations of workmen could manage shops, mills, and almost all forms of industry with success, and they immediately improved the condition of the men but then they did not leave a clear place for masters." Quelle horreur!

subjects their activity to his aims. If, then, the control of the capitalist is in substance two-fold by reason of the two-fold nature of the process of production itself, – which, on the one hand, is a social process for producing use-values, on the other, a process for creating surplus-value – in form that control is despotic. As co-operation extends its scale, this despotism takes forms peculiar to itself. Just as at first the capitalist is relieved from actual labour so soon as his capital has reached that minimum amount with which capitalist production, as such, begins, so now, he hands over the work of direct and constant supervision of the individual workmen, and groups of workmen, to a special kind of wage-labourer. An industrial army of workmen, under the command of a capitalist, requires, like a real army, officers (managers), and sergeants (foremen, overlookers), who, while the work is being done, command in the name of the capitalist. The work of supervision becomes their established and exclusive function. When comparing the mode of production of isolated peasants and artisans with production by slave-labour, the political economist counts this labour of superintendence among the *faux frais* of production.[4] But, when considering the capitalist mode of production, he, on the contrary, treats the work of control made necessary by the cooperative character of the labour-process as identical with the different work of control, necessitated by the capitalist character of that process and the antagonism of interests between capitalist and labourer. It is not because he is a leader of industry that a man is a capitalist; on the contrary, he is a leader of industry because he is a capitalist. The leadership of industry is an attribute of capital, just as in feudal times the functions of general and judge, were attributes of landed property.

The labourer is the owner of his labour-power until he has done bargaining for its sale with the capitalist; and he can sell no more than what he has – *i.e.*, his individual, isolated labour-power. This state of things is in no way altered by the fact that the capitalist, instead of buying the labour-power of one man, buys that of 100, and enters into separate contracts with 100 unconnected men instead of with one. He is at liberty to set the 100 men to work, without letting them co-operate. He pays them the value of 100 independent labour-powers, but he does not pay for the combined labour-power of the hundred. Being independent of each other, the labourers are isolated persons, who enter into relations with the capitalist, but not with one another. This co-operation begins only with the labour-process, but they have then ceased to belong to themselves. On entering that process, they become incorporated with capital. As co-operators, as members of a working organism, they are

---

[4] Professor Cairnes, after stating that the superintendence of labour is a leading feature of production by slaves in the Southern States of North America, continues: "The peasant proprietor (of the North), appropriating the whole produce of his toil, needs no other stimulus to exertion. Superintendence is here completely dispensed with." (Cairnes, 1862, pp. 48, 49.)

but special modes of existence of capital. Hence, the productive power developed by the labourer when working in co-operation, is the productive power of capital. This power is developed gratuitously, whenever the workmen are placed under given conditions, and it is capital that places them under such conditions. Because this power costs capital nothing, and because, on the other hand, the labourer himself does not develop it before his labour belongs to capital, it appears as a power with which capital is endowed by Nature – a productive power that is immanent in capital.

.   .   .

Division of labour and manufacture

(From chapter 14)

Section 1. – Two-fold origin of manufacture

That co-operation which is based on division of labour, assumes its typical form in manufacture, and is the prevalent characteristic form of the capitalist process of production throughout the manufacturing period properly so called. That period, roughly speaking, extends from the middle of the 16th to the last third of the 18th century.

Manufacture takes its rise in two ways:

(1.) By the assemblage, in one workshop under the control of a single capitalist, of labourers belonging to various independent handicrafts, but through whose hands a given article must pass on its way to completion. A carriage, for example, was formerly the product of the labour of a great number of independent artificers, such as wheelwrights, harness-makers, tailors, locksmiths, upholsterers, turners, fringe-makers, glaziers, painters, polishers, gilders, &c. In the manufacture of carriages, however, all these different artificers are assembled in one building where they work into one another's hands. It is true that a carriage cannot be gilt before it has been made. But if a number of carriages are being made simultaneously, some may be in the hands of the gilders while others are going through an earlier process. So far, we are still in the domain of simple co-operation, which finds its materials ready to hand in the shape of men and things. But very soon an important change takes place. The tailor, the locksmith, and the other artificers, being now exclusively occupied in carriage-making, each gradually loses, through want of practice, the ability to carry on, to its full extent, his old handicraft. But, on the other hand, his activity now confined in one groove, assumes the form best adapted to the narrowed sphere of action. At first, carriage manufacture is a combination of various independent handicrafts. By degrees, it becomes the splitting up of carriage-making into its various detail processes, each of which crystallises into the exclusive function of a particular workman,

52

the manufacture, as a whole, being carried on by the men in conjunction. In the same way, cloth manufacture, as also a whole series of other manufactures, arose by combining different handicrafts together under the control of a single capitalist.

(2.) Manufacture also arises in a way exactly the reverse of this – namely, by one capitalist employing simultaneously in one workshop a number of artificers, who all do the same, or the same kind of work, such as making paper, type, or needles. This is co-operation in its most elementary form. Each of these artificers (with the help, perhaps, of one or two apprentices), makes the entire commodity, and he consequently performs in succession all the operations necessary for its production. He still works in his old handicraft-like way. But very soon external circumstances cause a different use to be made of the concentration of the workmen on one spot, and of the simultaneousness of their work. An increased quantity of the article has perhaps to be delivered within a given time. The work is therefore re-distributed. Instead of each man being allowed to perform all the various operations in succession, these operations are changed into disconnected, isolated ones, carried on side by side; each is assigned to a different artificer, and the whole of them together are performed simultaneously by the co-operating workmen. This accidental repartition gets repeated, develops advantages of its own, and gradually ossifies into a systematic division of labour. The commodity, from being the individual product of an independent artificer, becomes the social product of a union of artificers, each of whom performs one, and only one, of the constituent partial operations. The same operations which, in the case of a papermaker belonging to a German Guild, merged one into the other as the successive acts of one artificer, became in the Dutch paper manufacture so many partial operations carried on side by side by numerous co-operating labourers. The needlemaker of the Nuremberg Guild was the cornerstone on which the English needle manufacture was raised. But while in Nuremberg that single artificer performed a series of perhaps 20 operations one after another, in England it was not long before there were 20 needlemakers side by side, each performing one alone of those 20 operations, and in consequence of further experience, each of those 20 operations was again split up, isolated, and made the exclusive function of a separate workman.

The mode in which manufacture arises, its growth out of handicrafts, is therefore two-fold. On the one hand, it arises from the union of various independent handicrafts, which become stripped of their independence and specialised to such an extent as to be reduced to mere supplementary partial processes in the production of one particular commodity. On the other hand, it arises from the co-operation of artificers of one handicraft; it splits up that particular handicraft into its various detail operations, isolating, and making these operations independent of one another up to the point where each becomes the exclusive function of a particular labourer. On the one hand, therefore, manufacture either introduces division of labour into a process of production, or further develops that division; on the other hand, it unites together handicrafts that were formerly separate. But whatever may have been its particular starting-point, its final form is invariably the same – a productive mechanism whose parts are human beings.

. . .

Section 2. – The detail labourer and his implements

If we now go more into detail, it is, in the first place, clear that a labourer who all his life performs one and the same simple operation, converts his whole body into the automatic, specialised implement of that operation. Consequently, he takes less time in doing it, than the artificer who performs a whole series of operations in succession. But the collective labourer, who constitutes the living mechanism of manufacture, is made up solely of such specialised detail labourers. Hence, in comparison with the independent handicraft, more is produced in a given time, or the productive power of labour is increased. Moreover, when once this fractional work is established as the exclusive function of one person, the methods it employs become perfected. The workman's continued repetition of the same simple act, and the concentration of his attention on it, teach him by experience how to attain the desired effect with the minimum of exertion. But since there are always several generations of labourers living at one time, and working together at the manufacture of a given article, the technical skill, the tricks of the trade thus acquired, become established, and are accumulated and handed down. Manufacture, in fact, produces the skill of the detail labourer, by reproducing, and systematically driving to an extreme within the workshop, the naturally developed differentiation of trades, which it found ready to hand in society at large. . . .

. . .

An artificer, who performs one after another the various fractional operations in the production of a finished article, must at one time change his place, at another his tools. The transition from one operation to another interrupts the flow of his labour, and creates, so to say, gaps in his working-day. These gaps close up so soon as he is tied to one and the same operation all day long; they vanish in proportion as the changes in his work diminish. The resulting increased productive power is owing either to an increased expenditure of labour-power in a given time – *i.e.*, to increased intensity of labour – or to a decrease in the amount of labour-power unproductively consumed. The extra expenditure of power, demanded by every transition from rest to motion, is made up for by prolonging the duration of the normal velocity when once acquired. On the other hand, constant labour of one uniform kind disturbs the intensity and flow of a man's animal spirits, which find recreation and delight in mere change of activity.

. . .

Section 4. – Division of labour in manufacture, and division of labour in society

We first considered the origin of Manufacture, then its simple elements, then the detail labourer and his implements, and finally, the totality of the mechanism. We shall now lightly touch upon the relation between the division of labour in manufacture, and the social division of labour, which forms the foundation of all production of commodities.

. . .

Since the production and the circulation of commodities are the general prerequisites of the capitalist mode of production, division of labour in manufacture demands, that division of labour in society at large should previously have attained a certain degree of development. Inversely, the former division reacts upon and develops and multiplies the latter.

. . .

But, in spite of the numerous analogies and links connecting them, division of labour in the interior of a society, and that in the interior of a workshop, differ not only in degree, but also in kind. The analogy appears most indisputable where there is an invisible bond uniting the various branches of trade. For instance the cattle-breeder produces hides, the tanner makes the hides into leather, and the shoemaker, the leather into boots. Here the thing produced by each of them is but a step towards the final form, which is the product of all their labours combined. There are, besides, all the various industries that supply the cattle-breeder, the tanner, and the shoemaker with the means of production. Now it is quite possible to imagine, with Adam Smith, that the difference between the above social division of labour, and the division in manufacture, is merely subjective, exists merely for the observer, who, in a manufacture, can see with one glance, all the numerous operations being performed on one spot, while in the instance given above, the spreading out of the work over great areas, and the great number of people employed in each branch of labour, obscure the connexion. But what is it that forms the bond between the independent labours of the cattle-breeder, the tanner, and the shoemaker? It is the fact that their respective products are commodities. What, on the other hand, characterises division of labour in manufactures? The fact that the detail labourer produces no commodities.[5] It is only the common product of all the detail labourers that becomes a commodity. Division of labour in society is brought about by the purchase and sale of the products of different branches of industry, while the connexion between the detail operations in a workshop, is due to the sale of the labour-power of several workmen to one capitalist, who applies it as combined labour-power. The division of labour in the workshop implies concentration of the means of production in the hands of one capitalist; the division of labour in society implies their dispersion among many independent producers of commodities. While within the workshop, the iron law of proportionality subjects definite numbers of workmen to definite functions, in the society outside the workshop, chance and caprice have full play in distributing the producers and their means of production among the various branches of industry. The different spheres of production, it is true, constantly tend to an equilibrium: for, on the one hand, while each producer of a commodity is bound to produce a use-value, to satisfy a particular social want, and while the extent of these wants differs quantitatively, still there exists an inner relation which settles their proportions into a regular system, and that system one of spontaneous growth; and, on the other hand, the law of the value of commodities ultimately determines how much of its disposable working-time society can expend on each particular class of commodities. But this constant tendency to equilibrium, of the various spheres of production, is exercised, only in the shape of a reaction against the constant upsetting of this equilibrium. The *a priori* system on which the division of labour, within the workshop, is regularly carried out, becomes in the division of labour within the society, an *a posteriori*, nature-imposed necessity, controlling the lawless caprice of the producers, and perceptible in the barometrical fluctuations of the market-prices. Division of labour within the workshop implies the undisputed authority of the capitalist over men, that are but parts of a mechanism that belongs to him. The division of labour within the society brings into contact independent commodity-producers, who acknowledge no other authority but that of competition, of the coercion exerted by the pressure of their mutual interests; just as in the animal kingdom, the *bellum omnium contra omnes* more or less preserves the conditions of existence of every species. The same bourgeois mind which praises division of labour in the workshop, life-long annexation of the labourer to a partial operation, and his complete subjection to capital, as being an organisation of labour that increases its productiveness – that same bourgeois mind denounces with equal vigour every conscious attempt to socially

---

[5] "There is no longer anything which we can call the natural reward of individual labour. Each labourer produces only some part of a whole, and each part, having no value or utility in itself, there is nothing on which the labourer can seize, and say: It is my product, this I will keep to myself." (Th. Hodgeskin, 1825, p. 25.)

control and regulate the process of production, as an inroad upon such sacred things as the rights of property, freedom and unrestricted play for the bent of the individual capitalist. It is very characteristic that the enthusiastic apologists of the factory system have nothing more damning to urge against a general organisation of the labour of society, than that it would turn all society into one immense factory.

In a society with capitalist production, anarchy in the social division of labour and despotism in that of the workshop are mutual conditions the one of the other. . . .

.   .   .

While division of labour in society at large, whether such division be brought about or not by exchange of commodities, is common to economic formations of society the most diverse, division of labour in the workshop, as practised by manufacture, is a special creation of the capitalist mode of production alone.

.   .   .

In manufacture, as well as in simple co-operation, the collective working organism is a form of existence of capital. The mechanism that is made up of numerous individual detail labourers belongs to the capitalist. Hence, the productive power resulting from a combination of labours appears to be the productive power of capital. Manufacture proper not only subjects the previously independent workman to the discipline and command of capital, but, in addition, creates a hierarchic gradation of the workmen themselves. While simple co-operation leaves the mode of working by the individual for the most part unchanged, manufacture thoroughly revolutionises it, and seizes labour-power by its very roots. It converts the labourer into a crippled monstrosity, by forcing his detail dexterity at the expense of a world of productive capabilities and instincts; just as in the States of La Plata they butcher a whole beast for the sake of his hide or his tallow. Not only is the detail work distributed to the different individuals, but the individual himself is made the automatic motor of a fractional operation, and the absurd fable of Menenius Agrippa, which makes man a mere fragment of his own body, becomes realised. If, at first, the workman sells his labour-power to capital, because the material means of producing a commodity fail him, now his very labour-power refuses its services unless it has been sold to capital. Its functions can be exercised only in an environment that exists in the workshop of the capitalist after the sale. By nature unfitted to make anything independently, the manufacturing labourer develops productive activity as a mere appendage of the capitalist's workshop. As the chosen people bore in their features the sign manual of

Jehovah, so division of labour brands the manufacturing workman as the property of capital.

The knowledge, the judgment, and the will, which, though in ever so small a degree, are practised by the independent peasant or handicraftsman, in the same way as the savage makes the whole art of war consist in the exercise of his personal cunning – these faculties are now required only for the workshop as a whole. Intelligence in production expands in one direction, because it vanishes in many others. What is lost by the detail labourers, is concentrated in the capital that employs them. It is a result of the division of labour in manufactures, that the labourer is brought face to face with the intellectual potencies of the material process of production, as the property of another, and as a ruling power. This separation begins in simple co-operation, where the capitalist represents the single workman, the oneness and the will of the associated labour. It is developed in manufacture which cuts down the labourer into a detail labourer. It is completed in modern industry, which makes science a productive force distinct from labour and presses it into the service of capital.

In manufacture, in order to make the collective labourer, and through him capital, rich in social productive power, each labourer must be made poor in individual productive powers. "Ignorance is the mother of industry as well as of superstition. Reflection and fancy are subject to err; but a habit of moving the hand or the foot is independent of either. Manufactures, accordingly, prosper most where the mind is least consulted, and where the workshop may . . . be considered as an engine, the parts of which are men."[6] As a matter of fact, some few manufacturers in the middle of the 18th century preferred, for certain operations that were trade secrets, to employ half-idiotic persons.[7]

"The understandings of the greater part of men," says Adam Smith, "are necessarily formed by their ordinary employments. The man whose whole life is spent in performing a few simple operations . . . has no occasion to exert his understanding. . . . He generally becomes as stupid and ignorant as it is possible for a human creature to become." After describing the stupidity of the detail labourer he goes on: "The uniformity of his stationary life naturally corrupts the courage of his mind. . . . It corrupts even the activity of his body and renders him incapable of exerting his strength with vigour and perseverance in any other employments than that to which he has been bred. His dexterity at his own particular trade seems in this manner to be acquired at the expense of his intellectual, social, and martial virtues. But in every improved and civilised society, this is the state into which the labouring poor, that is, the great body of the people, must necessarily fall."[8] For preventing the complete deterioration of the great mass of the people by division of la-

[6] A. Ferguson, (1767) p. 280.   [7] J. D. Tuckett (1846).
[8] A. Smith (1937 [1776]) Bk. v., ch. i, art. ii.

bour, A. Smith recommends education of the people by the State, but prudently, and in homœopathic doses. G. Garnier, his French translator and commentator, who, under the first French Empire, quite naturally developed into a senator, quite as naturally opposes him on this point. Education of the masses, he urges, violates the first law of the division of labour, and with it "our whole social system would be proscribed." "Like all other divisions of labour," he says, "that between hand labour and head labour is more pronounced and decided in proportion as society (he rightly uses this word, for capital, landed property and their State) becomes richer. This division of labour, like every other, is an effect of past, and a cause of future progress . . . ought the government then to work in opposition to this division of labour, and to hinder its natural course? Ought it to expend a part of the public money in the attempt to confound and blend together two classes of labour, which are striving after division and separation?"[9]

Some crippling of body and mind is inseparable even from division of labour in society as a whole. Since, however, manufacture carries this social separation of branches of labour much further, and also, by its peculiar division, attacks the individual at the very roots of his life, it is the first to afford the materials for, and to give a start to, industrial pathology.

"To subdivide a man is to execute him, if he deserves the sentence, to assassinate him if he does not. . . . The subdivision of labour is the assassination of a people."[10]

. . .

The factory

(From chapter 15, section 4)

. . . Every kind of capitalist production, in so far as it is not only a labour-process, but also a process of creating surplus-value, has this in common, that it is not the workman that employs the instruments of labour, but the instruments of labour that employ the workman. But it is only in the factory system that this inversion for the first time acquires technical and palpable reality. By means of its conversion into an automaton, the instrument of labour confronts the labourer, during the labour-process, in the shape of capital, of dead labour, that dominates, and pumps dry, living labour-power. The separation of the intellectual powers of production from the manual labour, and the conversion of those powers into the might of capital over labour, is, as we have already shown, finally completed by modern industry erected on the foundation of machinery. The special skill of each individual insignificant factory operative vanishes as an infinitesimal quantity before the science, the gigantic

[9] G. Garnier, (1796) vol. V. of his translation of A. Smith, pp. 4–5.
[10] D. Urquhart (1855) p. 119.

physical forces, and the mass of labour that are embodied in the factory mechanism and, together with that mechanism, constitute the power of the "master." This "master," therefore, in whose brain the machinery and his monopoly of it are inseparably united, whenever he falls out with his "hands," contemptuously tells them: "The factory operatives should keep in wholesome remembrance the fact that theirs is really a low species of skilled labour; and that there is none which is more easily acquired, or of its quality more amply remunerated, or which by a short training of the least expert can be more quickly, as well as abundantly, acquired. . . . The master's machinery really plays a far more important part in the business of production than the labour and the skill of the operative, which six months' education can teach, and a common labourer can learn."[11] The technical subordination of the workman to the uniform motion of the instruments of labour, and the peculiar composition of the body of workpeople, consisting as it does of individuals of both sexes and of all ages, give rise to a barrack discipline, which is elaborated into a complete system in the factory, and which fully develops the before mentioned labour of overlooking, thereby dividing the workpeople into operatives and overlookers, into private soldiers and sergeants of an industrial army. "The main difficulty [in the automatic factory] . . . lay . . . above all in training human beings to renounce their desultory habits of work, and to identify themselves with the unvarying regularity of the complex automaton. To devise and administer a successful code of factory discipline, suited to the necessities of factory diligence, was the Herculean enterprise, the noble achievement of Arkwright! Even at the present day, when the system is perfectly organised and its labour lightened to the utmost, it is found nearly impossible to convert persons past the age of puberty, into useful factory hands."[12] The factory code in which capital formulates, like a private legislator, and at his own good will, his autocracy over his workpeople, unaccompanied by that division of responsibility, in other matters so much approved of by the bourgeoisie, and unaccompanied by the still more approved representative system, this code is but the capitalistic caricature of that social regulation of the labour-process which becomes requisite in co-operation on a great scale, and in the employment in common, of instruments of labour and especially of machinery. The place of the slave-driver's lash is taken by the overlooker's book of penalties. All punishments naturally resolve themselves into fines and deductions from wages, and the law-giving talent of the factory Lycurgus so arranges matters, that a violation of his laws is, if possible, more profitable to him than the keeping of them.

·   ·   ·

[11] "The Master Spinners' and Manufacturers' Defence Fund. Report of the Committee." (1854) p. 17.
[12] Ure (1835), p. 15.

CHAPTER 3

From *Risk, Uncertainty, and Profit*

FRANK KNIGHT

Frank Knight (1885–1972) was born in McLean County, Illinois. He received a Ph.D. degree from Cornell University in 1916. When *Risk, Uncertainty and Profit* was published in 1921, he was Associate Professor of Economics at the State University of Iowa. He later became Morton D. Hall Distinguished Service Professor of Social Science and Philosophy at the University of Chicago.

Structures and methods for meeting uncertainty

(From chapter 8)

. . .

It is therefore seen that the insurance principle can be applied even in the almost complete absence of scientific data for the computation of rates. . . .

. . . The fact which limits the application of the insurance principle to business risks generally is not therefore their inherent uniqueness alone, and the subject calls for further examination. This task will be undertaken in detail in the next chapter, which deals with entrepreneurship. At this point we may anticipate to the extent of making two observations: first, the typical uninsurable (because unmeasurable and this because unclassifiable) business risk relates to the exercise of judgment in the making of decisions by the business man; second, although such estimates do tend to fall into groups within which fluctuations cancel out and hence to approach constancy and measurability, this happens only *after the fact* and, especially in view of the brevity of a man's active life, can only to a limited extent be made the basis of prediction. Furthermore, the classification or grouping can only to a limited extent be carried out by any agency outside the person himself who makes the decisions, because of the peculiarly obstinate connection of a *moral hazard* with this sort of risks. The decisive factors in the case are so largely on the inside

Excerpted from Frank Knight, *Risk, Uncertainty and Profit*. New York: Houghton Mifflin Co., 1921; eighth impression published by Kelley and Millman, New York, 1957.

61

of the person making the decisions that the "instances" are not amenable to objective description and external control.

Manifestly these difficulties, insuperable when the "consolidation" is to be carried out by an external agency such as an insurance company or association, fall away in so far as consolidation can be effected within the scale of operations of a single individual; and the same will be true of an organization if responsibility can be adequately centralized and unity of interest secured. The possibility of thus reducing uncertainty by transforming it into a measurable risk through grouping constitutes a strong incentive to extend the scale of operations of a business establishment. This fact must constitute one of the important causes of the phenomenal growth in the average size of industrial establishments which is a familiar characteristic of modern economic life. In so far as a single business man, by borrowing capital or otherwise, can extend the scope of his exercise of judgment over a greater number of decisions or estimates, there is a greater probability that bad guesses will be offset by good ones and that a degree of constancy and dependability in the total results will be achieved. In so far uncertainty is eliminated and the desideratum of rational activity realized.

Not less important is the incentive to substitute more effective and intimate forms of association for insurance, so as to eliminate or reduce the moral hazard and make possible the application of the insurance principle of consolidation to groups of ventures too broad in scope to be "swung" by a single enterpriser. Since it is capital which is especially at risk in operations based on opinions and estimates, the form of organization centers around the provisions relating to capital. It is undoubtedly true that the reduction of risk to borrowed capital is the principal desideratum leading to the displacement of individual enterprise by the partnership and the same fact with reference to both owned and borrowed capital explains the substitution of corporate organization for the partnership. The superiority of the higher form of organization over the lower from this point of view consists both in the extension of the scope of operations to include a larger number of individual decisions, ventures, or "instances," and in the more effective unification of interest which reduces the moral hazard connected with the assumption by one person of the consequences of another person's decisions.

The close connection between these two considerations is manifest. It is the special "risk" to which large amounts of capital loaned to a single enterpriser are subject which limits the scope of operations of this form of business unit by making it impossible to secure the necessary property resources. On the other hand, it is the inefficiency of organization, the failure to secure effective unity of interest, and the consequent large risk due to moral hazard when a partnership grows to considerable size, which in turn limit its extension to still larger magnitudes and bring about the substitution of the corporate

62

form of organization. With the growth of large fortunes it becomes possible for a limited number of persons to carry on enterprises of greater and greater magnitude, and to-day we find many very large businesses organized as partnerships. Modifications of partnership law giving this form more of the flexibility of the corporation with reference to the distribution of rights of control, of participation in income, and of title to assets in case of dissolution have also contributed to this change.

With reference to the first of our two points above mentioned, the extension of the scope of operations, the corporation may be said to have solved the organization problem. There appears to be hardly any limit to the magnitude of enterprise which it is possible to organize in this form, so far as mere ability to get the public to buy the securities is concerned. On the second score, however, the effective unification of interests, though the corporation has accomplished much in comparison with other forms of organization, there is still much to be desired. Doubtless the task is impossible, in any absolute sense; nothing but a revolutionary transformation in human nature itself can apparently solve this problem finally, and such a change would, of course, obliterate all moral hazards at once, without organization. In the meanwhile the internal problems of the corporation, the protection of its various types of members and adherents against each other's predatory propensities, are quite as vital as the external problem of safeguarding the public interests against exploitation by the corporation as a unit.

Another important aspect of the relations of corporate organization to risk involves what we have called ''diffusion'' as well as consolidation. The minute divisibility of ownership and ease of transfer of shares enables an investor to distribute his holdings over a large number of enterprises in addition to increasing the size of a single enterprise. The effect of this distribution on risk is evidently twofold. In the first place, there is to the investor a further offsetting through consolidation; the losses and gains in different corporations in which he owns stock must tend to cancel out in large measure and provide a higher degree of regularity and predictability in his total returns. And again, the chance of loss of a small fraction of his total resources is of less moment even proportionally than a chance of losing a larger part.

. . .

Enterprise and profit

(From chapter 9)

. . .

When uncertainty is present and the task of deciding what to do and how to do it takes the ascendancy over that of execution, the internal organization of

63

the productive groups is no longer a matter of indifference or a mechanical detail.[1] Centralization of this deciding and controlling function is imperative, a process of "cephalization," such as has taken place in the evolution of organic life, is inevitable, and for the same reasons as in the case of biological evolution. Let us consider this process and the circumstances which condition it. The order of attack on the problem is suggested by the classification worked out in chapter VII of the elements in uncertainty in regard to which men may in large measure differ independently.

In the first place, occupations differ in respect to the kind and amount of knowledge and judgment required for their successful direction as well as in the kind of abilities and tastes adapted to the routine operation. Productive groups or establishments now compete for managerial capacity as well as skill, and a considerable rearrangement of personnel is the natural result. The final adjustment will place each producer in the place where his particular combination of the two kinds of attributes seems to be most effective.

But a more important change is the tendency of the groups themselves to specialize, finding the individuals with the greatest managerial capacity of the requisite kinds and placing them in charge of the work of the group, submitting the activities of the other members to their direction and control. It need hardly be mentioned explicitly that the organization of industry depends on the fundamental fact that the intelligence of one person can be made to direct in a general way the routine manual and mental operations of others. It will also be taken into account that men differ in their powers of effective control over other men as well as in intellectual capacity to decide what should be done. In addition, there must come into play the diversity among men in degree of confidence in their judgment and powers and in disposition to act on their opinions, to "venture." This fact is responsible for the most fundamental change of all in the form of organization, the system under which the confident and venturesome "assume the risk" or "insure" the doubtful and timid by guaranteeing to the latter a specified income in return for an assignment of the actual results.

Uncertainty thus exerts a fourfold tendency to select men and specialize functions: (1) an adaptation of men to occupations on the basis of kind of knowledge and judgment; (2) a similar selection on the basis of degree of foresight, for some lines of activity call for this endowment in a very different degree from others; (3) a specialization within productive groups, the individuals with superior managerial ability (foresight and capacity of ruling others) being placed in control of the group and the others working under their direction; and (4) those with confidence in their judgment and disposition to "back it up" in action specialize in risk-taking. The close relations obtaining among

---

[1] See above, chapter IV, p. 106, note. [ed: in the book from which this excerpt is taken]

these tendencies will be manifest. We have not separated confidence and venturesomeness at all, since they act along parallel lines and are little more than phases of the same faculty – just as courage and the tendency to minimize danger are proverbially commingled in all fields, though they are separable in thought. In addition the tendencies number (3) and (4) operate together. With human nature as we know it it would be impracticable or very unusual for one man to guarantee to another a definite result of the latter's actions without being given power to direct his work. And on the other hand the second party would not place himself under the direction of the first without such a guaranty. The result is a "double contract" of the type famous in the history of the evasion of usury laws. It seems evident also that the system would not work at all if good judgment were not in fact generally associated with confidence in one's judgment on the part both of himself and others. That is, men's judgment of their own judgment and of others' judgment as to both kind and grade must in the large be much more right than wrong.[2]

The result of this manifold specialization of function is *enterprise and the wage system of industry*. Its existence in the world is a direct result of the fact of uncertainty; our task in the remainder of this study is to examine this phenomenon in detail in its various phases and divers relations with the economic activities of man and the structure of society. It is not necessary or inevitable, not the only conceivable form or organization, but under certain conditions has certain advantages, and is capable of development in different degrees. The essence of enterprise is the specialization of the function of *responsible direction* of economic life, the neglected feature of which is the inseparability of these *two* elements, *responsibility* and *control*. Under the enterprise system, a special social class, the business men, direct economic activity; they are in the strict sense the producers, while the great mass of the population merely furnish them with productive services, placing their persons and their property at the disposal of this class; the entrepreneurs *also* guarantee to those who furnish productive services a fixed remuneration. Accurately to define these functions and trace them through the social structure will be a long task, for the specialization is never complete; but at the end of it we shall find that in a free society the two are essentially inseparable. Any degree of effective exercise of judgment, or making decisions, is in a free society coupled with a corresponding degree of uncertainty-bearing, of taking the responsibility for those decisions.

. . .

[2] The statement implies that a man's judgment has in an effective sense a true or objective value. This assumption will be justified by the further course of the argument.

CHAPTER 4

The use of knowledge in society

FRIEDRICH HAYEK

Friedrich Hayek was born in 1899 in Vienna, Austria. He earned degrees in law and politics at the University of Vienna in 1921 and 1923, and in 1940, he received the Doctor of Science degree in economics from the University of London. At the time of publication of this paper, he was Tooke Professor of Political Economy and Statistics at the London School of Economics. He is currently Professor Emeritus at the University of Chicago and the University of Freiburg. In 1974, he was awarded the Nobel Memorial Prize in Economic Science.

I

What is the problem we wish to solve when we try to construct a rational economic order?

On certain familiar assumptions the answer is simple enough. *If* we possess all the relevant information, *if* we can start out from a given system of preferences and *if* we command complete knowledge of available means, the problem which remains is purely one of logic. That is, the answer to the question of what is the best use of the available means is implicit in our assumptions. The conditions which the solution of this optimum problem must satisfy have been fully worked out and can be stated best in mathematical form: put at their briefest, they are that the marginal rates of substitution between any two commodities or factors must be the same in all their different uses.

This, however, is emphatically *not* the economic problem which society faces. And the economic calculus which we have developed to solve this logical problem, though an important step toward the solution of the economic problem of society, does not yet provide an answer to it. The reason for this is that the "data" from which the economic calculus starts are never for the whole society "given" to a single mind which could work out the implications, and can never be so given.

The peculiar character of the problem of a rational economic order is deter-

Reprinted in abridged form from Friedrich Hayek, "The Use of Knowledge in Society," *The American Economic Review*, 35 (1945): 519–30, by permission of the editors.

mined precisely by the fact that the knowledge of the circumstances of which we must make use never exists in concentrated or integrated form, but solely as the dispersed bits of incomplete and frequently contradictory knowledge which all the separate individuals possess. The economic problem of society is thus not merely a problem of how to allocate "given" resources – if "given" is taken to mean given to a single mind which deliberately solves the problem set by these "data." It is rather a problem of how to secure the best use of resources known to any of the members of society, for ends whose relative importance only these individuals know. Or, to put it briefly, it is a problem of the utilization of knowledge not given to anyone in its totality.

This character of the fundamental problem has, I am afraid, been rather obscured than illuminated by many of the recent refinements of economic theory, particularly by many of the uses made of mathematics. Though the problem with which I want primarily to deal in this paper is the problem of a rational economic organization, I shall in its course be led again and again to point to its close connections with certain methodological questions. Many of the points I wish to make are indeed conclusions toward which diverse paths of reasoning have unexpectedly converged. But as I now see these problems, this is no accident. It seems to me that many of the current disputes with regard to both economic theory and economic policy have their common origin in a misconception about the nature of the economic problem of society. This misconception in turn is due to an erroneous transfer to social phenomena of the habits of thought we have developed in dealing with the phenomena of nature.

II

In ordinary language we describe by the word "planning" the complex of interrelated decisions about the allocation of our available resources. All economic activity is in this sense planning; and in any society in which many people collaborate, this planning, whoever does it, will in some measure have to be based on knowledge which, in the first instance, is not given to the planner but to somebody else, which somehow will have to be conveyed to the planner. The various ways in which the knowledge on which people base their plans is communicated to them is the crucial problem for any theory explaining the economic process. And the problem of what is the best way of utilizing knowledge initially dispersed among all the people is at least one of the main problems of economic policy – or of designing an efficient economic system.

The answer to this question is closely connected with that other question which arises here, that of *who* is to do the planning. It is about this question that all the dispute about "economic planning" centers. This is not a dispute about whether planning is to be done or not. It is a dispute as to whether planning is to be done centrally, by one authority for the whole economic system, or is to be divided among many individuals. Planning in the specific sense in which the term is used in contemporary controversy necessarily means central planning – direction of the whole economic system according to one unified plan. Competition, on the other hand, means decentralized planning by many separate persons. The half-way house between the two, about which many people talk but which few like when they see it, is the delegation of planning to organized industries, or, in other words, monopoly.

Which of these systems is likely to be more efficient depends mainly on the question under which of them we can expect that fuller use will be made of the existing knowledge. And this, in turn, depends on whether we are more likely to succeed in putting at the disposal of a single central authority all the knowledge which ought to be used but which is initially dispersed among many different individuals, or in conveying to the individuals such additional knowledge as they need in order to enable them to fit their plans in with those of others.

.   .   .

IV

If it is fashionable today to minimize the importance of the knowledge of the particular circumstances of time and place, this is closely connected with the smaller importance which is now attached to change as such. Indeed, there are few points on which the assumptions made (usually only implicitly) by the "planners" differ from those of their opponents as much as with regard to the significance and frequency of changes which will make substantial alterations of production plans necessary. Of course, if detailed economic plans could be laid down for fairly long periods in advance and then closely adhered to, so that no further economic decisions of importance would be required, the task of drawing up a comprehensive plan governing all economic activity would appear much less formidable.

It is, perhaps, worth stressing that economic problems arise always and only in consequence of change. So long as things continue as before, or at least as they were expected to, there arise no new problems requiring a decision, no need to form a new plan. The belief that changes, or at least day-to-day adjustments, have become less important in modern times implies the contention that economic problems also have become less important. This belief in the decreasing importance of change is, for that reason, usually held by the same people who argue that the importance of economic considerations has been driven into the background by the growing importance of technological knowledge.

Is it true that, with the elaborate apparatus of modern production, economic decisions are required only at long intervals, as when a new factory is to be erected or a new process to be introduced? Is it true that, once a plant has been built, the rest is all more or less mechanical, determined by the character of the plant, and leaving little to be changed in adapting to the ever-changing circumstances of the moment?

The fairly widespread belief in the affirmative is not, so far as I can ascertain, borne out by the practical experience of the business man. In a competitive industry at any rate – and such an industry alone can serve as a test – the task of keeping cost from rising requires constant struggle, absorbing a great part of the energy of the manager. How easy it is for an inefficient manager to dissipate the differentials on which profitability rests, and that it is possible, with the same technical facilities to produce with a great variety of costs, are among the commonplaces of business experience which do not seem to be equally familiar in the study of the economist. The very strength of the desire, constantly voiced by producers and engineers, to be able to proceed untrammeled by considerations of money costs, is eloquent testimony to the extent to which these factors enter into their daily work.

. . .

V

If we can agree that the economic problem of society is mainly one of rapid adaptation to changes in the particular circumstances of time and place, it would seem to follow that the ultimate decisions must be left to the people who are familiar with these circumstances, who know directly of the relevant changes and of the resources immediately available to meet them. We cannot expect that this problem will be solved by first communicating all this knowledge to a central board which, after integrating *all* knowledge, issues its orders. We must solve it by some form of decentralization. But this answers only part of our problem. We need decentralization because only thus can we ensure that the knowledge of the particular circumstances of time and place will be promptly used. But the "man on the spot" cannot decide solely on the basis of his limited but intimate knowledge of the facts of his immediate surroundings. There still remains the problem of communicating to him such further information as he needs to fit his decisions into the whole pattern of changes of the larger economic system.

How much knowledge does he need to do so successfully? Which of the events which happen beyond the horizon of his immediate knowledge are of relevance to his immediate decision, and how much of them need he know?

There is hardly anything that happens anywhere in the world that *might* not have an effect on the decision he ought to make. But he need not know of these events as such, nor of *all* their effects. It does not matter for him *why* at the particular moment more screws of one size than of another are wanted, *why* paper bags are more readily available than canvas bags, or *why* skilled labor, or particular machine tools, have for the moment become more difficult to acquire. All that is significant for him is *how much more or less* difficult to procure they have become compared with other things with which he is also concerned, or how much more or less urgently wanted are the alternative things he produces or uses. It is always a question of the relative importance of the particular things with which he is concerned, and the causes which alter their relative importance are of no interest to him beyond the effect on those concrete things of his own environment.

It is in this connection that what I have called the economic calculus proper helps us, at least by analogy, to see how this problem can be solved, and in fact is being solved, by the price system. Even the single controlling mind, in possession of all the data for some small, self-contained economic system, would not – every time some small adjustment in the allocation of resources had to be made – go explicitly through all the relations between ends and means which might possibly be affected. It is indeed the great contribution of the pure logic of choice that it has demonstrated conclusively that even such a single mind could solve this kind of problem only by constructing and constantly using rates of equivalence (or ''values,'' or ''marginal rates of substitution''), *i.e.*, by attaching to each kind of scarce resource a numerical index which cannot be derived from any property possessed by that particular thing, but which reflects, or in which is condensed, its significance in view of the whole means-end structure. In any small change he will have to consider only these quantitative indices (or ''values'') in which all the relevant information is concentrated; and by adjusting the quantities one by one, he can appropriately rearrange his dispositions without having to solve the whole puzzle *ab initio*, or without needing at any stage to survey it at once in all its ramifications.

Fundamentally, in a system where the knowledge of the relevant facts is dispersed among many people, prices can act to coördinate the separate actions of different people in the same way as subjective values help the individual to coördinate the parts of his plan. It is worth contemplating for a moment a very simple and commonplace instance of the action of the price system to see what precisely it accomplishes. Assume that somewhere in the world a new opportunity for the use of some raw material, say tin, has arisen, or that one of the sources of supply of tin has been eliminated. It does not matter for our purpose – and it is very significant that it does not matter – which of these two causes has made tin more scarce. All that the users of tin need to know is that some of the tin they used to consume is now more profitably employed elsewhere, and that in consequence they must economize tin. There is no need for the great majority of them even to know where the more urgent need has arisen, or in favor of what other needs they ought to husband the supply. If only some of them know directly of the new demand, and switch resources over to it, and if the people who are aware of the new gap thus created in turn fill it from still other sources, the effect will rapidly spread throughout the whole economic system and influence not only all the uses of tin, but also those of its substitutes and the substitutes of these substitutes, the supply of all the things made of tin, and their substitutes, and so on; and all this without the great majority of those instrumental in bringing about these substitutions knowing anything at all about the original cause of these changes. The whole acts as one market, not because any of its members survey the whole field, but because their limited individual fields of vision sufficiently overlap so that through many intermediaries the relevant information is communicated to all. The mere fact that there is one price for any commodity – or rather that local prices are connected in a manner determined by the cost of transport, etc. – brings about the solution which (it is just conceptually possible) might have been arrived at by one single mind possessing all the information which is in fact dispersed among all the people involved in the process.

. . .

CHAPTER 5

The nature of the firm

RONALD COASE

Ronald Coase was born in Middlesex, England in 1910. He received a Bachelor's (B. Com.) degree from the University of London in 1932, and a Doctor of Science degree in economics from the same school in 1951. When this article was published, he was Assistant Lecturer at the London School of Economics. He is currently Professor Emeritus of Economics and Senior Fellow in Law and Economics at the University of Chicago Law School.

. . .

I

It is convenient if, in searching for a definition of a firm, we first consider the economic system as it is normally treated by the economist. Let us consider the description of the economic system given by Sir Arthur Salter.[1] "The normal economic system works itself. For its current operation it is under no central control, it needs no central survey. Over the whole range of human activity and human need, supply is adjusted to demand, and production to consumption, by a process that is automatic, elastic and responsive." An economist thinks of the economic system as being co-ordinated by the price mechanism and society becomes not an organization but an organism.[2] The economic system "works itself." This does not mean that there is no planning by individuals. These exercise foresight and choose between alternatives. This is necessarily so if there is to be order in the system. But this theory assumes that the direction of resources is dependent directly on the price mechanism. Indeed, it is often considered to be an objection to economic planning that it merely tries to do what is already done by the price mechanism.[3] Sir Arthur Salter's description, however, gives a very incomplete picture of our economic system. Within a firm, the description does not fit at all. For instance, in economic theory we find that the allocation of factors of production be-

Reprinted with minor abridgements from Ronald Coase, "The Nature of the Firm," *Economica*, 4 (1937): 386–405, by permission of the publisher.

[1] This description is quoted with approval by D. H. Robertson (1930), p. 85, and by Arnold Plant (1932). It appears in *Allied Shipping Control*, pp. 16–17.

[2] See F. A. Hayek (1933).   [3] See F. A. Hayek (1933).

tween different uses is determined by the price mechanism. The price of factor A becomes higher in X than in Y. As a result, A moves from Y to X until the difference between the prices in X and Y, except in so far as it compensates for other differential advantages, disappears. Yet in the real world, we find that there are many areas where this does not apply. If a workman moves from department Y to department X, he does not go because of a change in relative prices, but because he is ordered to do so. Those who object to economic planning on the grounds that the problem is solved by price movements can be answered by pointing out that there is planning within our economic system which is quite different from the individual planning mentioned above and which is akin to what is normally called economic planning. The example given above is typical of a large sphere in our modern economic system. Of course, this fact has not been ignored by economists. Marshall introduces organization as a fourth factor of production; J. B. Clark gives the co-ordinating function to the entrepreneur; Professor Knight introduces managers who co-ordinate. As D. H. Robertson points out, we find "islands of conscious power in this ocean of unconscious co-operation like lumps of butter coagulating in a pail of butter-milk."[4] But in view of the fact that it is usually argued that co-ordination will be done by the price mechanism, why is such organization necessary? Why are there these "island of conscious power"? Outside the firm, price movements direct production, which is co-ordinated through a series of exchange transactions on the market. Within a firm, these market transactions are eliminated and in place of the complicated market structure with exchange transactions is substituted the entrepreneur-co-ordinator, who directs production.[5] It is clear that these are alternative methods of co-ordinating production. Yet having regard to the fact that if production is regulated by price movements, production could be carried on without any organization at all, well might we ask, why is there any organization?

Of course, the degree to which the price mechanism is superseded varies greatly. In a department store, the allocation of the different sections to the various locations in the building may be done by the controlling authority or it may be the result of competitive price bidding for space. In the Lancashire cotton industry, a weaver can rent power and shop-room and can obtain looms and yarn on credit.[6] This co-ordination of the various factors of production is, however, normally carried out without the intervention of the price mechanism. As is evident, the amount of "vertical" integration, involving as it does the supersession of the price mechanism, varies greatly from industry to industry and from firm to firm.

[4] D. H. Robertson (1930) p. 85.

[5] In the rest of this paper I shall use the term entrepreneur to refer to the person or persons who, in a competitive system, take the place of the price mechanism in the direction of resources.

[6] *Survey of Textile Industries*, p. 26.

It can, I think, be assumed that the distinguishing mark of the firm is the supersession of the price mechanism. It is, of course, as Professor Robbins points out, "related to an outside network of relative prices and costs,"[7] but it is important to discover the exact nature of this relationship. This distinction between the allocation of resources in a firm and the allocation in the economic system has been very vividly described by Mr. Maurice Dobb when discussing Adam Smith's conception of the capitalist:

. . . It began to be seen that there was something more important than the relations inside each factory or unit captained by an undertaker; there were the relations of the undertaker with the rest of the economic world outside his immediate sphere . . . the undertaker busies himself with the division of labour inside each firm and he plans and organises consciously,

but

. . . he is related to the much larger economic specialisation of which he himself is merely one specialised unit. Here, he plays his part as a single cell in a larger organism, mainly unconscious of the wider role he fills.[8]

In view of the fact that while economists treat the price mechanism as a co-ordinating instrument, they also admit the co-ordinating function of the "entrepreneur," it is surely important to inquire why co-ordination is the work of the price mechanism in one case and of the entrepreneur in another. The purpose of this paper is to bridge what appears to be a gap in economic theory between the assumption (made for some purposes) that resources are allocated by means of the price mechanism and the assumption (made for other purposes) that this allocation is dependent on the entrepreneur-coodinator. We have to explain the basis on which, in practice, this choice between alternatives is effected.[9]

II

Our task is to attempt to discover why a firm emerges at all in a specialized exchange economy. The price mechanism (considered purely from the side of

[7] L. Robbins (1932) p. 71.

[8] Maurice Dobb (1925), p. 20 Cf., also, Henderson, (1922) pp. 3–5.

[9] It is easy to see when the State takes over the direction of an industry that, in planning it, it is doing something which was previously done by the price mechanism. What is usually not realized is that any business man in organizing the relations between his departments is also doing something which could be organized through the price mechanism. There is therefore point in Mr. Durbin's answer to those who emphasize the problems involved in economic planning that the same problems have to be solved by business men in the competitive system. (See Durbin, 1936). The important difference between these two cases is that economic planning is imposed on industry while firms arise voluntarily because they represent a more efficient method of organizing production. In a competitive system, there is an "optimum" amount of planning!

the direction of resources) might be superseded if the relationship which replaced it was desired for its own sake. This would be the case, for example, if some people preferred to work under the direction of some other person. Such individuals would accept less in order to work under someone, and firms would arise naturally from this. But it would appear that this cannot be a very important reason, for it would rather seem that the opposite tendency is operating if one judges from the stress normally laid on the advantage of "being one's own master."[10] Of course, if the desire was not to be controlled but to control, to exercise power over others, then people might be willing to give up something in order to direct others; that is, they would be willing to pay others more than they could get under the price mechanism in order to be able to direct them. But this implies that those who direct pay in order to be able to do this and are not paid to direct, which is clearly not true in the majority of cases.[11] Firms might also exist if purchasers preferred commodities which are produced by firms to those not so produced; but even in spheres where one would expect such preferences (if they exist) to be of negligible importance, firms are to be found in the real world.[12] Therefore there must be other elements involved.

The main reason why it is profitable to establish a firm would seem to be that there is a cost of using the price mechanism. The most obvious cost of "organizing" production through the price mechanism is that of discovering what the relevant prices are.[13] This cost may be reduced but it will not be eliminated by the emergence of specialists who will sell this information. The costs of negotiating and concluding a separate contract for each exchange transaction which takes place on a market must also be taken into account.[14] Again, in certain markets, e.g., produce exchanges, a technique is devised for minimizing these contract costs; but they are not eliminated. It is true that contracts are not eliminated when there is a firm but they are greatly reduced. A factor of production (or the owner thereof) does not have to make a series of contracts with the factors with whom he is co-operating within the firm, as would be necessary, of course, if this co-operation were as a direct result of

---

[10] See Harry Dawes (1934), who instances "the trek to retail shopkeeping and insurance work by the better paid of skilled men due to the desire (often the main aim in life of a worker) to be independent" (p. 86).

[11] None the less, this is not altogether fanciful. Some small shopkeepers are said to earn less than their assistants.

[12] G. F. Shove (1933) p. 116, note I, points out that such preferences may exist, although the example he gives is almost the reverse of the instance given in the text.

[13] According to N. Kaldor (1934) it is one of the assumptions of static theory that "All the relevant prices are known to all individuals." But this is clearly not true of the real world.

[14] This influence was noted by Professor Usher when discussing the development of capitalism. He says: "The successive buying and selling of partly finished products were sheer waste of energy" (1921, p. 13). But he does not develop the idea nor consider why it is that buying and selling operations still exist.

the working of the price mechanism. For this series of contracts is substituted one. At this stage, it is important to note the character of the contract into which a factor enters that is employed within a firm. The contract is one whereby the factor, for a certain remuneration (which may be fixed or fluctuating), agrees to obey the directions of an entrepreneur *within certain limits*.[15] The essence of the contract is that it should only state the limits to the powers of the entrepreneur. Within these limits, he can therefore direct the other factors of production.

There are, however, other disadvantages – or costs – of using the price mechanism. It may be desired to make a long-term contract for the supply of some article or service. This may be due to the fact that if one contract is made for a longer period, instead of several shorter ones, then certain costs of making each contract will be avoided. Or, owing to the risk attitude of the people concerned, they may prefer to make a long rather than a short-term contract. Now, owing to the difficulty of forecasting, the longer the period of the contract is for the supply of the commodity or service, the less possible, and indeed, the less desirable it is for the person purchasing to specify what the other contracting party is expected to do. It may well be a matter of indifference to the person supplying the service or commodity which of several courses of action is taken, but not to the purchaser of that service or commodity. But the purchaser will not know which of these several courses he will want the supplier to take. Therefore, the service which is being provided is expressed in general terms, the exact details being left until a later date. All that is stated in the contract is the limits to what the persons supplying the commodity or service are expected to do. The details of what the supplier is expected to do are not stated in the contract but are decided later by the purchaser. When the direction of resources (within the limits of the contract) becomes dependent on the buyer in this way, that relationship which I term a "firm" may be obtained.[16] A firm is likely therefore to emerge in those cases where a very short term contract would be unsatisfactory. It is obviously of more importance in the case of services – labor – than it is in the case of the buying of commodities. In the case of commodities, the main items can be stated in advance and the details which will be decided later will be of minor significance.

We may sum up this section of the argument by saying that the operation of a market costs something and by forming an organization and allowing

[15] It would be possible for no limits to the powers of the entrepreneur to be fixed. This would be voluntary slavery. According to Professor Batt (1929) p. 18, such a contract would be void and unenforceable.

[16] Of course, it is not possible to draw a hard and fast line which determines whether there is a firm or not. There may be more or less direction. It is similar to the legal question of whether there is the relationship of master and servant or principal and agent. See the discussion of this problem presented later.

some authority (an "entrepreneur") to direct the resources, certain marketing costs are saved. The entrepreneur has to carry out his function at less cost, taking into account the fact that he may get factors of production at a lower price than the market transactions which he supersedes, because it is always possible to revert to the open market if he fails to do this.

The question of uncertainty is one which is often considered to be very relevant to the study of the equilibrium of the firm. It seems improbable that a firm would emerge without the existence of uncertainty. But those, for instance, Professor Knight, who make the *mode of payment* the distinguishing mark of the firm – fixed incomes being guaranteed to some of those engaged in production by a person who takes the residual, and fluctuating, income – would appear to be introducing a point which is irrelevant to the problem we are considering. One entrepreneur may sell his services to another for a certain sum of money, while the payment to his employees may be mainly or wholly a share in profits.[17] The significant question would appear to be why the allocation of resources is not done directly by the price mechanism.

Another factor that should be noted is that exchange transactions on a market and the same transactions organized within a firm are often treated differently by Governments or other bodies with regulatory powers. If we consider the operation of a sales tax, it is clear that it is a tax on market transactions and not on the same transactions organized within the firm. Now since these are alternative methods of "organization" – by the price mechanism or by the entrepreneur – such a regulation would bring into existence firms which otherwise would have no *raison d'être*. It would furnish a reason for the emergence of a firm in a specialized exchange economy. Of course, to the extent that firms already exist, such a measure as a sales tax would merely tend to make them larger than they would otherwise be. Similarly, quota schemes, and methods of price control which imply that there is rationing, and which do not apply to firms producing such products for themselves, by allowing advantages to those who organize within the firm and not through the market, necessarily encourage the growth of firms. But it is difficult to believe that it is measures such as have been mentioned in this paragraph which have brought firms into existence. Such measures would, however, tend to have this result if they did not exist for other reasons.

These, then, are the reasons why organizations such as firms exist in a specialized exchange economy in which it is generally assumed that the distribution of resources is "organized" by the price mechanism. A firm, therefore, consists of the system of relationships which comes into existence when the direction of resources is dependent on an entrepreneur.

The approach which has just been sketched would appear to offer an ad-

---

[17] The views of Professor Knight are examined later in more detail.

vantage in that it is possible to give a scientific meaning to what is meant by saying that a firm gets larger or smaller. A firm becomes larger as additional transactions (which could be exchange transactions co-ordinated through the price mechanism) are organized by the entrepreneur and becomes smaller as he abandons the organization of such transactions. The question which arises is whether it is possible to study the forces which determine the size of the firm. Why does the entrepreneur not organize one less transaction or one more? It is interesting to note that Professor Knight considers that:

> . . . the relation between efficiency and size is one of the most serious problems of theory, being, in contrast with the relation for a plant, largely a matter of personality and historical accident rather than of intelligible general principles. But the question is peculiarly vital because the possibility of monopoly gain offers a powerful incentive to *continuous and unlimited* expansion of the firm, which force must be offset by some equally powerful one making for decreased efficiency (in the production of money income) with growth in size, if even boundary competition is to exist.[18]

Professor Knight would appear to consider that it is impossible to treat scientifically the determinants of the size of the firm. On the basis of the concept of the firm developed above, this task will now be attempted.

It was suggested that the introduction of the firm was due primarily to the existence of marketing costs. A pertinent question to ask would appear to be (quite apart from the monopoly considerations raised by Professor Knight), why, if by organizing one can eliminate certain costs and in fact reduce the cost of production, are there any market transactions at all?[19] Why is not all production carried on by one big firm? There would appear to be certain possible explanations.

First, as a firm gets larger, there may be decreasing returns to the entrepreneur function, that is, the costs of organizing additional transactions within the firm may rise.[20] Naturally a point must be reached where the costs of organizing an extra transaction within the firm are equal to the costs involved in carrying out the transaction in the open market, or, to the costs of organizing by another entrepreneur. Secondly, it may be that as the transactions which are organized increase, the entrepreneur fails to place the factors of production in the uses where their value is greatest, that is, fails to make the best use of the factors of production. Again, a point must be reached where the loss through the waste of resources is equal to the marketing costs of the exchange

---

[18] Frank Knight (1933).

[19] There are certain marketing costs which could only be eliminated by the abolition of "consumers' choice" and these are the costs of retailing. It is conceivable that these costs might be so high that people would be willing to accept rations because the extra product obtained was worth the loss of their choice.

[20] This argument assumes that exchange transactions on a market can be considered as homogeneous; which is clearly untrue in fact. This complication is taken into account later.

transaction in the open market or to the loss if the transaction was organized by another entrepreneur. Finally, the supply price of one or more of the factors of production may rise, because the "other advantages" of a small firm are greater than those of a large firm.[21] Of course, the actual point where the expansion of the firm ceases might be determined by a combination of the factors mentioned above. The first two reasons given most probably correspond to the economists' phrase of "diminishing returns to management."[22]

The point has been made in the previous paragraph that a firm will tend to expand until the costs of organizing an extra transaction within the firm become equal to the costs of carrying out the same transaction by means of an exchange on the open market or the costs of organizing in another firm. But if the firm stops its expansion at a point below the costs of marketing in the open market and at a point equal to the costs of organizing in another firm, in most cases (excluding the case of "combination"[23]), this will imply that there is a market transaction between these two producers, each of whom could organize it at less than the actual marketing costs. How is the paradox to be resolved? If we consider an example the reason for this will become clear. Suppose A is buying a product from B and that both A and B could organize this marketing transaction at less than its present cost. B, we can assume, is not organizing one process or stage of production, but several. If A therefore wishes to avoid a market transaction, he will have to take over all the processes of production controlled by B. Unless A takes over all the processes of production, a market transaction will still remain, although it is a different product that is bought. But we have previously assumed that as each producer expands he becomes less efficient; the additional costs of organizing extra transactions increase. It is probable that A's cost of organizing the transactions previously organized by B will be greater than B's cost of doing the same thing. A therefore will take over the whole of B's organization only if his cost of organizing B's work is not greater than B's cost by an amount equal to the costs of carrying out an exchange transaction on the open market. But once it becomes economical to have a market transaction, it also pays to divide production in such a way that the cost of organizing an extra transaction in each firm is the same.

[21] For a discussion of the variation of the supply price of factors of production to firms of varying size, see E. A. G. Robinson (1931). It is sometimes said that the supply price of organizing ability increases as the size of the firm increases because men prefer to be the heads of small independent businesses rather than the heads of departments in a large business. See Jones (1927) p. 531, and Macgregor (1906) p. 63. This is a common argument of those who advocate Rationalization. It is said that larger units would be more efficient, but owing to the individualistic spirit of the smaller entrepreneurs, they prefer to remain independent, apparently in spite of the higher income which their increased efficiency under Rationalization makes possible.

[22] This discussion is, of course, brief and incomplete. For a more thorough discussion of this particular problem, see N. Kaldor (1934) and E. A. G. Robinson (1934).

[23] A definition of this term is given later.

Up to now it has been assumed that the exchange transactions which take place through the price mechanism are homogeneous. In fact, nothing could be more diverse than the actual transactions which take place in our modern world. This would seem to imply that the costs of carrying out exchange transactions through the price mechanism will vary considerably as will also the costs of organizing these transactions within the firm. It seems therefore possible that quite apart from the question of diminishing returns the costs of organizing these transactions within the firm may be greater than the costs of carrying out the exchange transactions in the open market. This would necessarily imply that there were exchange transactions carried out through the price mechanism, but would it mean that there would have to be more than one firm? Clearly not, for all those areas in the economic system where the direction of resources was not dependent directly on the price mechanism could be organized within one firm. The factors which were discussed earlier would seem to be the important ones, though it is difficult to say whether "diminishing returns to management" or the rising supply price of factors is likely to be the more important.

Other things being equal, therefore, a firm will tend to be larger:

(a)   the less the costs of organizing and the slower these costs rise with an increase in the transactions organized;

(b)   the less likely the entrepreneur is to make mistakes and the smaller the increase in mistakes with an increase in the transactions organized;

(c)   the greater the lowering (or the less the rise) in the supply price of factors of production to firms of larger size.

Apart from variations in the supply price of factors of production to firms of different sizes, it would appear that the costs of organizing and the losses through mistakes will increase with an increase in the spatial distribution of the transactions organized, in the dissimilarity of the transactions, and in the probability of changes in the relevant prices.[24] As more transactions are organized by an entrepreneur, it would appear that the transactions would tend to be either different in kind or in different places. This furnishes an additional reason why efficiency will tend to decrease as the firm gets larger. Inventions which tend to bring factors of production nearer together, by lessening spatial distribution, tend to increase the size of the firm.[25] Changes like the telephone

[24] This aspect of the problem is emphasized by N. Kaldor (1934). Its importance in this connection had been previously noted by E. A. G. Robinson (1931) pp. 83–106. This assumes that an increase in the probability of price movements increases the costs of organizing within a firm more than it increases the cost of carrying out an exchange transaction on the market – which is probable.

[25] This would appear to be the importance of the treatment of the technical unit by E. A. G. Robinson (1931) pp. 27–33. The larger the technical unit, the greater the concentration of factors and therefore the firm is likely to be larger.

and the telegraph which tend to reduce the cost of organizing spatially will tend to increase the size of the firm. All changes which improve managerial technique will tend to increase the size of the firm.[26,27]

It should be noted that the definition of a firm which was given above can be used to give more precise meanings to the terms "combination" and "integration."[28] There is a combination when transactions which were previously organized by two or more entrepreneurs become organized by one. This becomes integration when it involves the organization of transactions which were previously carried out between the entrepreneurs on a market. A firm can expand in either or both of these two ways. The whole of the "structure of competitive industry" becomes tractable by the ordinary technique of economic analysis.

III

The problem which has been investigated in the previous section has not been entirely neglected by economists and it is now necessary to consider why the reasons given above for the emergence of a firm in a specialized exchange economy are to be preferred to the other explanations which have been offered.

It is sometimes said that the reason for the existence of a firm is to be found in the division of labor. This is the view of Professor Usher, a view which has been adopted and expanded by Mr. Maurice Dobb. The firm becomes

. . . the result of an increasing complexity of the division of labour. . . . The growth of this economic differentiation creates the need for some integrating force without which differentiation would collapse into chaos; and it is as the integrating force in a differentiated economy that industrial forms are chiefly significant.[29]

[26] It should be noted that most inventions will change both the costs of organizing and the costs of using the price mechanism. In such cases, whether the invention tends to make firms larger or smaller will depend on the relative effect on these two sets of costs. For instance, if the telephone reduces the costs of using the price mechanism more than it reduces the costs of organizing, then it will have the effect of reducing the size of the firm.

[27] An illustration of these dynamic forces is furnished by Maurice Dobb (1928) p. 68. "With the passing of bonded labour the factory, as an establishment where work was organised under the whip of he overseer, lost its *raison d'être* until this was restored to it with the introduction of power machinery after 1846." It seems important to realize that the passage from the domestic system to the factory system is not a mere historical accident, but is conditioned by economic forces. This is shown by the fact that it is possible to move from the factory system to the domestic system, as in the Russian example, as well as vice versa. It is the essence of serfdom that the price mechanism is not allowed to operate. Therefore, there has to be direction from some organizer. When, however, serfdom passed, the price mechanism was allowed to operate. It was not until machinery drew workers into one locality that it paid to supersede the price mechanism and the firm again emerged.

[28] This is often called "vertical integration," combination being termed "lateral integration."

[29] Maurice Dobb (1928) p. 10. Professor Usher's views are to be found in Usher (1921) pp. 1–18.

The answer to this argument is an obvious one. The "integrating force in a differentiated economy" already exists in the form of the price mechanism. It is perhaps the main achievement of economic science that it has shown that there is no reason to suppose that specialization must lead to chaos.[30] The reason given by Mr. Maurice Dobb is therefore inadmissible. What has to be explained is why one integrating force (the entrepreneur) should be substituted for another integrating force (the price mechanism).

The most interesting reasons (and probably the most widely accepted) which have been given to explain this fact are those to be found in Professor Knight's *Risk, Uncertainty and Profit*. His views will be examined in some detail.

Professor Knight starts with a system in which there is no uncertainty:

. . . acting as individuals under absolute freedom but without collusion men are supposed to have organised economic life with the primary and secondary division of labour, the use of capital, etc., developed to the point familiar in present-day America. The principal fact which calls for the exercise of the imagination is the internal organisation of the productive groups or establishments. With uncertainty entirely absent, every individual being in possession of perfect knowledge of the situation, there would be no occasion for anything of the nature of responsible management or control of productive activity. Even marketing transactions in any realistic sense would not be found. The flow of raw materials and productive services to the consumer would be entirely automatic.[31]

Professor Knight says that we can imagine this adjustment as being "the result of a long process of experimentation worked out by trial-and-error methods alone," while it is not necessary "to imagine every worker doing exactly the right thing at the right time in a sort of 'pre-established harmony' with the work of others. There might be managers, superintendents, etc., for the purpose of co-ordinating the activities of individuals," though these managers would be performing a purely routine function, "without responsibility of any sort."[32]

Professor Knight then continues:

With the introduction of uncertainty – the fact of ignorance and the necessity of acting upon opinion rather than knowledge – into this Eden-like situation, its character is entirely changed. . . . With uncertainty present doing things, the actual execution of activity, becomes in a real sense a secondary part of life; the primary problem or function is deciding what to do and how to do it.[33]

This fact of uncertainty brings about the two most important characteristics of social organization.

---

[30] Cf. J. B. Clark (1900) p. 19, who speaks of the theory of exchange as being the "theory of the organisation of industrial society."
[31] Frank Knight (1921) p. 267.   [32] Knight (1921) pp. 267–8.   [33] Knight (1921) p. 268.

In the first place, goods are produced for a market, on the basis of entirely impersonal prediction of wants, not for the satisfaction of the wants of the producers themselves. The producer takes the responsibility of forecasting the consumers' wants. In the second place, the work of forecasting and at the same time a large part of the technological direction and control of production are still further concentrated upon a very narrow class of producers, and we meet with a new economic functionary, the entrepreneur. . . . When uncertainty is present and the task of deciding what to do and how to do it takes the ascendancy over that of execution the internal organisation of the productive groups is no longer a matter of indifference or a mechanical detail. Centralisation of this deciding and controlling function is imperative, a process of "cephalisation" is inevitable.[34]

The most fundamental change is:

. . . the system under which the confident and venturesome assume the risk or insure the doubtful and timid by guaranteeing to the latter a specified income in return for an assignment of the actual results. . . . With human nature as we know it it would be impracticable or very unusual for one man to guarantee to another a definite result of the latter's actions without being given power to direct his work. And on the other hand the second party would not place himself under the direction of the first without such a guarantee. . . . The result of this manifold specialisation of function is the enterprise and wage system of industry. Its existence in the world is the direct result of the fact of uncertainty.[35]

These quotations give the essence of Professor Knight's theory. The fact of uncertainty means that people have to forecast future wants. Therefore, you get a special class springing up who direct the activities of others to whom they give guaranteed wages. It acts because good judgment is generally associated with confidence in one's judgment.[36]

Professor Knight would appear to leave himself open to criticism on several grounds. First of all, as he himself points out, the fact that certain people have better judgment or better knowledge does not mean that they can only get an income from it by themselves actively taking part in production. They can sell advice or knowledge. Every business buys the services of a host of advisers. We can imagine a system where all advice or knowledge was bought as required. Again, it is possible to get a reward from better knowledge or judgment not by actively taking part in production but by making contracts with people who are producing. A merchant buying for future delivery represents an example of this. But this merely illustrates the point that it is quite possible to give a guaranteed reward providing that certain acts are performed without directing the performance of those acts. Professor Knight says that "with human nature as we know it it would be impracticable or very unusual for one man to guarantee to another a definite result of the latter's actions without

---

[34] Knight (1921) pp. 268–95.   [35] Knight (1921) pp. 269–70.   [36] Knight (1921) p. 270.

being given power to direct his work.'' This is surely incorrect. A large proportion of jobs are done to contract, that is, the contractor is guaranteed a
certain sum providing he performs certain acts. But this does not involve any
direction. It does mean, however, that the system of relative prices has been
changed and that there will be a new arrangement of the factors of production.[37] The fact that Professor Knight mentions that the ''second party would
not place himself under the direction of the first without such a guarantee'' is
irrelevant to the problem we are considering. Finally, it seems important to
notice that even in the case of an economic system where there is no uncertainty Professor Knight considers that there would be co-ordinators, though
they would perform only a routine function. He immediately adds that they
would be ''without responsibility of any sort,'' which raises the question by
whom are they paid and why? It seems that nowhere does Professor Knight
give a reason why the price mechanism should be superseded.

· · ·

V

Only one task now remains; and that is, to see whether the concept of a firm
which has been developed fits in with that existing in the real world. We can
best approach the question of what constitutes a firm in practice by considering the legal relationship normally called that of ''master and servant'' or
''employer and employee.''[38] The essentials of this relationship have been
given as follows:

(1) The servant must be under the duty of rendering personal services to the master
or to others on behalf of the master, otherwise the contract is a contract for sale of
goods or the like.

(2) The master must have the right to control the servant's work, either personally
or by another servant or agent. It is this right of control or interference, of being
entitled to tell the servant when to work (within the hours of service) and when not to
work, and what work to do and how to do it (within the terms of such service) which
is the dominant characteristic in this relation and marks off the servant from an independent contractor, or from one employed merely to give to his employer the fruits of
his labour. In the latter case, the contractor or performer is not under the employer's

[37] This shows that it is possible to have a private enterprise system without the existence of
firms. Though, in practice, the two functions of enterprise, which actually influences the system
of relative prices by forecasting wants and acting in accordance with such forecasts, and management, which accepts the system of relative prices as being given, are normally carried out by
the same persons, yet it seems important to keep them separate in theory. This point is further
discussed later.

[38] The legal concept of ''employer and employee'' and the economic concept of a firm are not
identical, in that the firm may imply control over another person's property as well as over their
labor. But the identity of these two concepts is sufficiently close for an examination of the legal
concept to be of value in appraising the worth of the economic concept.

control in doing the work or effecting the service; he has to shape and manage his work so as to give the result he has contracted to effect.[39]

We thus see that it is the fact of direction which is the essence of the legal concept of "employer and employee," just as it was in the economic concept which was developed above. It is interesting to note that Professor Batt says further:

> That which distinguishes an agent from a servant is not the absence or presence of a fixed wage or the payment only of commission on business done, but rather the freedom with which an agent may carry out his employment.[40]

We can, therefore, conclude that the definition we have given is one which approximates closely to the firm as it is considered in the real world.

Our definition is, therefore, realistic. Is it manageable? This ought to be clear. When we are considering how large a firm will be the principle of marginalism works smoothly. The question always is, will it pay to bring an extra exchange transaction under the organizing authority? At the margin, the costs of organizing within the firm will be equal either to the costs of organizing in another firm or to the costs involved in leaving the transaction to be "organized" by the price mechanism. Business men will be constantly experimenting, controlling more or less, and in this way, equilibrium will be maintained. This gives the position of equilibrium for static analysis. But it is clear that the dynamic factors are also of considerable importance, and an investigation of the effect changes have on the cost of organizing within the firm and on marketing costs generally will enable one to explain why firms get larger and smaller. We thus have a theory of moving equilibrium. The above analysis would also appear to have clarified the relationship between initiative or enterprise and management. Initiative means forecasting and operates through the price mechanism by the making of new contracts. Management proper merely reacts to price changes, rearranging the factors of production under its control. That the business man normally combines both functions is an obvious result of the marketing costs which were discussed above. Finally, this analysis enables us to state more exactly what is meant by the "marginal product" of the entrepreneur. But an elaboration of this point would take us far from our comparatively simple task of definition and clarification.

[39] Batt (1929), p. 6.   [40] Batt (1929) p. 7.

CHAPTER 6

Relational exchange: economics and complex contracts

VICTOR GOLDBERG

Victor Goldberg was born in 1941 in Washington, D.C. He received the Ph.D. in economics at Yale University in 1970. At the time of publication of this paper, he was Professor of Economics at the University of California, Davis. He is currently Professor of Law at Northwestern University.

For the past few decades the primary thrust of microeconomic theory has been to abstract from real-world complexity and to focus on the workings of impersonal markets. While that line of analysis has been highly productive, the great emphasis on impersonal markets has not been without cost. The standard paradigm influences the direction of research, suggesting certain questions and ignoring others. It does not, for example, help us discover why certain activities are carried on within firms rather than in the impersonal markets. Moreover, it provides wrong or misleading answers to other questions. Why do we observe sharing contracts, cost-plus pricing, or sticky wages? In recent years a countermovement has developed emphasizing the costs of the current focus and the virtues of explicitly confronting those issues that have been abstracted from. This new literature has not, in general, entailed a rejection of standard microeconomics. Rather it has complemented it.

This new literature is still in its infancy and its jargon, not surprisingly, is in disarray. The contributors have labeled their work the new institutionalism, markets and hierarchies, the transactions cost-, property rights-, obligational markets-, administered contracts-, or relational exchange-, approach. I will try to sweep aside terminological quibbles and force on the various approaches a common language. Taking an author's prerogative, I will use my own – relational exchange.[1]

In the following section I will present the essential elements of the rela-

Reprinted in abridged form from Victor Goldberg, "Relational Exchange: Economics and Complex Contracts," *American Behavioral Scientist*, vol. 23. no. 3, January/February 1980, 337–52. Copyright © 1980 by Sage Publications. Reprinted by permission of Sage Publications, Inc.

[1] In fact, it is borrowed from Ian Macneil (1974). In earlier papers I used the administered contracts nomenclature (see Goldberg, 1976, 1977, 1979). See also Williamson (1975), Wachter and Williamson (1978); Klein, Crawford, and Alchian (1978); Alchian and Demsetz (1972); Cheung (1969) and Jensen and Meckling (1976a).

tional exchange framework. The following sections will consider some of the implications of this approach for regulation, macroeconomics, and antitrust. Concluding remarks follow.

Relational exchange

We begin with an obvious empirical fact. Much economic activity takes place within long-term, complex, perhaps multiparty contractual (or contract-like) relationships; behavior is, in varying degrees, sheltered from market forces. The implicit contract of utility regulation, the contractual network that constitutes a firm, franchise agreements, pensions, and collective bargaining agreements are examples. Granted this, we can then proceed along two different lines. First, we can attempt to explain why relationships take the form that they do; why does a particular firm own its retail outlets rather than selling through franchised outlets or discount stores? Second, what impact does the relationship's structure have beyond the relationship? Do the price adjustment rules used in employment contracts or in regulated industries give the wrong short-run signals thereby exacerbating unemployment? Since economists attempt both to explain and prescribe, these questions can also be recast in normative terms: How should parties structure their relationships (from the point of view of the parties or other groups – perhaps society as a whole)?

To make headway in understanding the essential features of relational exchange it is convenient to set up a stylized problem. Consider two parties contemplating entering into a contract who must establish rules to structure their future relationship. The parties can have competing alternatives both at the formation stage and within the relationship. The choice of rules will depend upon the anticipated outcomes. The choice will also reflect three significant facts about the world that are so obvious that only an economist would feel compelled to recognize them explicitly. First, people are not omniscient; their information is imperfect and improvable only at a cost. Second, not all people are saints all of the time; as the relationship unfolds there will be opportunities for one party to take advantage of the other's vulnerability, to engage in strategic behavior, or to follow his own interests at the expense of the other party. The actors will, on occasion, behave opportunistically. Third, the parties cannot necessarily rely on outsiders to enforce the agreement cheaply and accurately.

If we assume that the agreement reflects the balancing of the parties' interests given the tools available, the efficacy of those tools in different contexts, and the constraints facing the decision makers, then we have the framework for a predictive model. Under conditions M we should expect to observe structure N; or if we observe structure N, then we should expect to find conditions M. This is, of course, an overly mechanical representation. A more modest formulation is that the agreements reflect the purposive behavior of the parties.

The relational exchange framework directs attention to a number of concerns often overlooked in standard microeconomics. It also suggests that in many contexts the significance of the static optimality sort of questions, with which economists typically deal, has been overrated. The parties will be willing to absorb a lot of apparent static inefficiency in pursuit of their relational goals.

Within the contract each party makes expenditures, receives benefits, and confers benefits on the other party at various times. The timing of the streams of benefits and costs need not coincide. For example, X might have planted crops and contracted with Y for harvesting them. Or X might agree to paint Y's house with Y paying upon completion. If X had cheap, effective legal remedies available (or if he could rely on Y's need to maintain his reputation)[2] then the noncoincidence of the streams of costs and benefits to the parties would be immaterial. But if external enforcement is imperfect, X is vulnerable to being held up by Y.

If as the relationship unfolds the costs incurred by X are much greater than the benefits he has received (as in the harvesting example), Y can convincingly threaten to breach the contract even though at this point Y has incurred no costs and received no benefits. Y could conceivably force X to revise the contract price down (or wage up) to the point at which X is indifferent between completing the agreement or terminating it. In the other case, X's vulnerability is even greater. Not only does he incur a cost before receiving payment, but Y also receives benefits before paying.

The vulnerability can, of course, be reduced by deliberately structuring the relationship to make the stream of benefits and costs for each party more nearly coincident. Progress payments (for custom-made capital goods or defense contracts) and instalment sales contracts are examples of such phased performance in which one party's performance consists of making payment. The parties' options are not restricted to adjusting the payment stream to a fixed production schedule. The timing of production as well as the techniques used in production (e.g., less fixed, specialized capital), and the characteristics of the output (e.g., greater standardization) can all be altered to enhance the contract's enforceability.

Suppose that one party has to make a considerable initial investment and that the value of the investment depends on continuation of the relationship.

---

[2] The discipline of future dealings, either with a particular party or with the market, is in many instances a more effective constraint on a party's behavior than is the formal law.

An employee investing in firm-specific capital is one example[3]; a second would be an electric utility building a plant to serve a particular area. Both will be reluctant to incur the high initial costs without some assurance of subsequent rewards. Other things equal, the firmer that assurance the more attractive the investment. So, for example, if the utility customers agree to give it the exclusive right to serve them for twenty years, then the utility would find construction of a long-lived plant more attractive than if it did not have such assurance. Of course, if a new, superior technology were likely to appear within three years, the customers would not want the long lived plant built. Nevertheless, there will be lots of instances in which the parties will find it efficacious to protect one party's reliance on the continuation of the relationship.

Since circumstances will change in ways not anticipated at the formation stage, the parties will desire some means for adjusting the relationship to take those new circumstances into account. As an example, consider a contract in which X agrees to build a custom-made machine for Y who will use it to produce a new product. Before the machine's construction is completed, Y decides that marketing the new product will be unprofitable and wants to cancel its order. Ideally, X would want some mechanism in the contract which would require that Y take his reliance into account when weighing the merits of continuation versus breach. (Likewise, Y would want X to take into account his costs of continuing if X had the legal right to enforce the initial agreement.) If the parties acted totally in good faith – if we assume no opportunistic behavior – then this does not present a problem. They can simply inform each other of the costs of continuation versus breach (accurately, by assumption), choose the optimal strategy, and divide in some manner the benefits or costs arising from this optimal solution. But, of course, both X and Y will have incentives to be less than completely honest. The spectre of opportunistic behavior hangs over the relationship. If the parties cannot draw upon a reservoir of trust or rely on the discipline of future dealings, they will require some mechanisms for balancing the reliance and flexibility interests.

The parties must establish some sort of governance mechanism for the relationship. The initial agreement will, in general, be neither self-enforcing nor self-adjusting. Prices (deductibles and co-payments in insurance contracts for example) and simple adjustment rules (like indexing) can, of course, be used to influence the parties' behavior. These passive devices can be supplemented by – or supplanted by – more activist forms of governance. These

---

[3] Learning how to use an information-processing system that is unique to a single firm would be an example. The skill is valuable so long as the worker remains with the firm; if he were fired that skill would be worthless and the time spent acquiring it goes for nought.

activist forms include extensive monitoring or policing of behavior to detect and punish violations of the agreement. In addition, it will often be advantageous to postpone decisions until more facts are known and to assign to someone the task of making that future decision. If that someone is one of the parties, this arrangement can be characterized as establishing an authority relationship – the decider has authority over the future behavior of the other party (see Simon, 1951). X agrees that Y can tell him what to do. The question of the scope of Y's authority can be a source of great friction as those familiar with labor history can attest.

Because standard microeconomics emphasizes market exchange and suppresses consideration of behavior that occurs within relationships sheltered from market forces, economists have tended to view elements that facilitate such sheltering with hostility and suspicion. The spirit of the relational exchange approach is quite different. It recognizes that the sheltering is inevitable and, moreover, that it can be functional. Contracting parties will often find it in their mutual interest to increase the isolation of at least one of them from alternatives – to make it more difficult (costly) to leave this particular relationship. To protect X's reliance, for example, the parties would want to make exit expensive for Y. Or, as a second example, A's ability to exercise authority over B can be enhanced if he can threaten to impose costs on a recalcitrant B; that threat can be made credible by making termination costly for B. The relational exchange approach focuses our attention on the reasons why parties might want to erect exit barriers and on the rich array of institutional devices which might be utilized for that purpose.

The organizing theme of much of the new literature is "efficiency." People will adopt certain arrangements because these are more efficient than alternatives, given the opportunities and difficulties confronting them. The analysis need not, however, be an apology for existing institutions: Whatever is, is right. Efficiency is contextual. Given the social context, the parties will attempt to arrange their affairs as best they can. If the context were different, then the efficient structure would also differ. So, to take an extreme example, one might argue that in the best of all possible worlds collective bargaining agreements would be inefficient; but they might be an intelligent (efficient) response in a world characterized by the threat of labor violence.[4] At a different level of analysis, we can take the existence of collective bargaining as given – it is part of the social context. We need not worry about whether it is good, bad, efficient, stupid, or immoral. It simply is. Granted that, we can then ask such questions as: Will increased job security for union members result in predictable changes in the organization of work? For example, will

---

[4] I develop this point at some length in Goldberg (1980b). This approach runs the risk of becoming an empty tautology. It should be viewed as a plausible research strategy rather than as a more grandiose statement about social institutions.

employers now invest more heavily in giving workers firm-specific skills and redesign the production process to take advantage of these skilled workers? Or we might investigate the techniques employed to govern the relationship (less authority, more "due process" or "voice"). Likewise, on the prescriptive level, we will be led to search for mechanisms for adjusting ongoing relationships to changing conditions, and other problems foreign to the world of conventional economic theory.

.   .   .

CHAPTER 7

From *The Visible Hand*

ALFRED CHANDLER

Alfred Chandler was born in 1918 in Guyencourt, Delaware. He received the Ph.D. degree from Harvard University in 1952. He is Straus Professor of Business History at Harvard Business School. *The Visible Hand* was awarded the Bancroft and Pulitzer prizes.

Introduction: the visible hand

The title of this book indicates its theme but not its focus or purpose. Its purpose is to examine the changing processes of production and distribution in the United States and the ways in which they have been managed. To achieve this end it focuses on the business enterprise that carried out these processes. Because the large enterprise administered by salaried managers replaced the small traditional family firm as the primary instrument for managing production and distribution, the book concentrates specifically on the rise of modern business enterprise and its managers. It is a history of a business institution and a business class.

The theme propounded here is that modern business enterprise took the place of market mechanisms in coordinating the activities of the economy and allocating its resources. In many sectors of the economy the visible hand of management replaced what Adam Smith referred to as the invisible hand of market forces. The market remained the generator of demand for goods and services, but modern business enterprise took over the functions of coordinating flows of goods through existing processes of production and distribution, and of allocating funds and personnel for future production and distribution. As modern business enterprise acquired functions hitherto carried out by the market, it became the most powerful institution in the American economy and its managers the most influential group of economic decision makers. The rise of modern business enterprise in the United States, therefore, brought with it managerial capitalism.

From The Visible Hand

Modern business enterprise defined

Modern business enterprise is easily defined. . . . It has two specific characteristics: it contains many distinct operating units and it is managed by a hierarchy of salaried executives.

Each unit within the modern multiunit enterprise has its own administrative office. Each is administered by a full-time salaried manager. Each has its own set of books and accounts which can be audited separately from those of the large enterprise. Each could theoretically operate as an independent business enterprise.

In contrast, the traditional American business firm was a single-unit business enterprise. In such an enterprise an individual or a small number of owners operated a shop, factory, bank, or transportation line out of a single office. Normally this type of firm handled only a single economic function, dealt in a single product line, and operated in one geographic area. Before the rise of the modern firm, the activities of one of these small, personally owned and managed enterprises were coordinated and monitored by market and price mechanisms.

Modern enterprise, by bringing many units under its control, began to operate in different locations, often carrying on different types of economic activities and handling different lines of goods and services. The activities of these units and the transactions between them thus became internalized. They became monitored and coordinated by salaried employees rather than market mechanisms.

Modern business enterprise, therefore, employs a hierarchy of middle and top salaried managers to monitor and coordinate the work of the units under its control. Such middle and top managers form an entirely new class of businessmen. Some traditional single-unit enterprises employed managers whose activities were similar to those of the lowest level managers in a modern business enterprise. Owners of plantations, mills, shops, and banks hired salaried employees to administer or assist them in administering the unit. As the work within single operating units increased, these managers employed subordinates – foremen, drivers, and mates – to supervise the work force. But as late as 1840 there were no middle managers in the United States – that is, there were no managers who supervised the work of other managers. At that time nearly all top managers were owners; they were either partners or major stockholders in the enterprise they managed.

The multiunit enterprise administered by a set of salaried middle and top managers can then properly be termed modern. Such enterprises did not exist in the United States in 1840. By World War I this type of firm had become the dominant business institution in many sectors of the American economy. By the middle of the twentieth century, these enterprises employed hundreds and even thousands of middle and top managers who supervised the work of dozens and often hundreds of operating units employing tens and often hundreds of thousands of workers. These enterprises were owned by tens or hundreds of thousands of shareholders and carried out billions of dollars of business annually. Even a relatively small business enterprise operating in local or regional markets had its top and middle managers. Rarely in the history of the world has an institution grown to be so important and so pervasive in so short a period of time.

. . .

Before I enter the complexities of the historical experience, it seems wise to outline a list of general propositions to make more precise the primary concerns of the study. They give some indication at the outset of the nature of modern business enterprise and suggest why the visible hand of management replaced the invisible hand of market mechanisms. I set these forth as a guide through the intricate history of interrelated institutional changes that follows.

The first proposition is that modern multiunit business enterprise replaced small traditional enterprise when administrative coordination permitted greater productivity, lower costs, and higher profits than coordination by market mechanisms.

This proposition is derived directly from the definition of a modern business enterprise. Such an enterprise came into being and continued to grow by setting up or purchasing business units that were theoretically able to operate as independent enterprises – in other words, by internalizing the activities that had been or could be carried on by several business units and the transactions that had been or could be carried on between them.

Such an internalization gave the enlarged enterprise many advantages.[1] By routinizing the transactions between units, the costs of these transactions were lowered. By linking the administration of producing units with buying and distributing units, costs for information on markets and sources of supply were reduced. Of much greater significance, the internalization of many units permitted the flow of goods from one unit to another to be administratively coordinated. More effective scheduling of flows achieved a more intensive use of facilities and personnel employed in the processes of production and distribution and so increased productivity and reduced costs. In addition, administrative coordination provided a more certain cash flow and more rapid

[1] Ronald Coase (1937) provides a pioneering analysis of the reasons for internalizing of operating units. His work is expanded upon by Oliver Williamson, particularly in Williamson (1970), p. 7. Useful articles on coordination and allocation within the enterprise are Kenneth J. Arrow, (1964); H. Leibenstein, (1966); A. A. Alchian and H. Demsetz, (1972); and G. B. Richardson (1972).

payment for services rendered. The savings resulting from such coordination were much greater than those resulting from lower information and transactions costs.

The second proposition is simply that the advantages of internalizing the activities of many business units within a single enterprise could not be realized until a managerial hierarchy had been created.

Such advantages could be achieved only when a group of managers had been assembled to carry out the functions formerly handled by price and market mechanisms. Whereas the activities of single-unit traditional enterprises were monitored and coordinated by market mechanisms, the producing and distributing units within a modern business enterprise are monitored and coordinated by middle managers. Top managers, in addition to evaluating and coordinating the work of middle managers, took the place of the market in allocating resources for future production and distribution. In order to carry out these functions, the managers had to invent new practices and procedures which in time became standard operating methods in managing American production and distribution.

Thus the existence of a managerial hierarchy is a defining characteristic of the modern business enterprise. A multiunit enterprise without such managers remains little more than a federation of autonomous offices. Such federations were formed to control competition between units or to assure enterprises of sources of raw materials or outlets for finished goods and services. The owners and managers of the autonomous units agreed on common buying, pricing, production, and marketing policies. If there were no managers, these policies were determined and enforced by legislative and judicial rather than administrative means. Such federations were often able to bring small reductions in information and transactions costs, but they could not lower costs through increased productivity. They could not provide the administrative coordination that became the central function of modern business enterprise.

The third proposition is that modern business enterprise appeared for the first time in history when the volume of economic activities reached a level that made administrative coordination more efficient and more profitable than market coordination.

Such an increase in volume of activity came with new technology and expanding markets. New technology made possible an unprecedented output and movement of goods. Enlarged markets were essential to absorb such output. Therefore modern business enterprise first appeared, grew, and continued to flourish in those sectors and industries characterized by new and advancing technology and by expanding markets. Conversely in those sectors and industries where technology did not bring a sharp increase in output and where markets remained small and specialized, administrative coordination was rarely more profitable than market coordination. In those areas modern business enterprise was late in appearing and slow in spreading.

The fourth proposition is that once a managerial hierarchy had been formed and had successfully carried out its function of administrative coordination, the hierarchy itself became a source of permanence, power, and continued growth.

In Werner Sombart's phrase, the modern business enterprise took on "a life of its own."[2] Traditional enterprises were normally short-lived. They were almost always partnerships which were reconstituted or disbanded at the death or retirement of a partner. If a son carried on the father's business, he found new partners. Often the partnership was disbanded when one partner decided he wanted to work with another businessman. On the other hand, the hierarchies that came to manage the new multiunit enterprises had a permanence beyond that of any individual or group of individuals who worked in them. When a manager died, retired, was promoted, or left an office, another was ready and trained to take his place. Men came and went. The institution and its offices remained.

The fifth proposition is that the careers of the salaried managers who directed these hierarchies became increasingly technical and professional.

In these new business bureaucracies, as in other administrative hierarchies requiring specialized skills, selection and promotion became increasingly based on training, experience, and performance rather than on family relationship or money. With the coming of modern business enterprise, the businessman, for the first time, could conceive of a lifetime career involving a climb up the hierarchical ladder. In such enterprises, managerial training became increasingly longer and more formalized. Managers carrying out similar activities in different enterprises often had the same type of training and attended the same types of schools. They read the same journals and joined the same associations. They had an approach to their work that was closer to that of lawyers, doctors, and ministers than that of the owners and managers of small traditional business enterprises.

The sixth proposition is that as the multiunit business enterprise grew in size and diversity and as its managers became more professional, the management of the enterprise became separated from its ownership.

[2] Werner Sombart (1930), vol. III, p. 200. Though there is very little written on the nature of coordination and allocation of resources and activities within the firm, there is a vast literature on the bureaucratic nature of modern business enterprise and on the goals and motives of business managers. Almost none of this literature, however, looks at the historical development of managerial hierarchies or the role and functions of managers over a period of time.

From The Visible Hand

The rise of modern business enterprise brought a new definition of the relationship between ownership and management and therefore a new type of capitalism to the American economy. Before the appearance of the multiunit firm, owners managed and managers owned. Even when partnerships began to incorporate, their capital stock stayed in the hands of a few individuals or families. These corporations remained single-unit enterprises which rarely hired more than two or three managers. The traditional capitalist firm can, therefore, be properly termed a personal enterprise.

From its very beginning, however, modern business enterprise required more managers than a family or its associates could provide. In some firms the entrepreneur and his close associates (and their families) who built the enterprise continued to hold the majority of stock. They maintained a close personal relationship with their managers, and they retained a major say in top management decisions, particularly those concerning financial policies, allocation of resources, and the selection of senior managers. Such a modern business enterprise may be termed an entrepreneurial or family one, and an economy or sectors of an economy dominated by such firms may be considered a system of entrepreneurial or family capitalism.

Where the creation and growth of an enterprise required large sums of outside capital, the relationship between ownership and management differed. The financial institutions providing the funds normally placed part-time representatives on the firm's board. In such enterprises, salaried managers had to share top management decisions, particularly those involving the raising and spending of large sums of capital, with representatives of banks and other financial institutions. An economy or sector controlled by such firms has often been termed one of financial capitalism.

In many modern business enterprises neither bankers nor families were in control. Ownership became widely scattered. The stockholders did not have the influence, knowledge, experience, or commitment to take part in the high command. Salaried managers determined long-term policy as well as managing short-term operating activities. They dominated top as well as lower and middle management. Such an enterprise controlled by its managers can properly be identified as managerial, and a system dominated by such firms is called managerial capitalism.

As family- and financier-controlled enterprises grew in size and age they became managerial. Unless the owners or representatives of financial houses became full-time career managers within the enterprise itself, they did not have the information, the time, or the experience to play a dominant role in top-level decisions. As members of the boards of directors they did hold veto power. They could say no, and they could replace the senior managers with other career managers; but they were rarely in a position to propose positive alternative solutions. In time, the part-time owners and financiers on the board

97

normally looked on the enterprise in the same way as did ordinary stockholders. It became a source of income and not a business to be managed. Of necessity, they left current operations and future plans to the career administrators. In many industries and sectors of the American economy, managerial capitalism soon replaced family or financial capitalism.

The seventh proposition is that in making administrative decisions, career managers preferred policies that favored the long-term stability and growth of their enterprises to those that maximized current profits.

For salaried managers the continuing existence of their enterprises was essential to their lifetime careers. Their primary goal was to assure continuing use of and therefore continuing flow of material to their facilities. They were far more willing than were the owners (the stockholders) to reduce or even forego current dividends in order to maintain the long-term viability of their organizations. They sought to protect their sources of supplies and their outlets. They took on new products and services in order to make more complete use of existing facilities and personnel. Such expansion, in turn, led to the addition of still more workers and equipment. If profits were high, they preferred to reinvest them in the enterprise rather than pay them out in dividends. In this way the desire of the managers to keep the organization fully employed became a continuing force for its further growth.

The eighth and final proposition is that as the large enterprises grew and dominated major sectors of the economy, they altered the basic structure of these sectors and of the economy as a whole.

The new bureaucratic enterprises did not, it must be emphasized, replace the market as the primary force in generating goods and services. The current decisions as to flows and the long-term ones as to allocating resources were based on estimates of current and long-term market demand. What the new enterprises did do was to take over from the market the coordination and integration of the flow of goods and services from the production of raw materials through the several processes of production to the sale to the ultimate consumer. Where they did so, production and distribution came to be concentrated in the hands of a few large enterprises. At first this occurred in only a few sectors or industries where technological innovation and market growth created high-speed and high-volume throughput. As technology became more sophisticated and as markets expanded, administrative coordination replaced market coordination in an increasingly larger portion of the economy. By the middle of the twentieth century the salaried managers of a relatively small number of large mass producing, large mass retailing, and large mass transporting enterprises coordinated current flows of goods through the processes of production and distribution and allocated the resources to be used for future production and distribution in major sectors of the American economy. By then, the managerial revolution in American business had been carried out.[3]

These basic propositions fall into two parts. The first three help to explain the initial appearance of modern business enterprise: why it began when it did, where it did, and in the way it did. The remaining five concern its continuing growth: where, how, and why an enterprise once started continued to grow and to maintain its position of dominance. This institution appeared when managerial hierarchies were able to monitor and coordinate the activities of a number of business units more efficiently than did market mechanisms. It continued to grow so that these hierarchies of increasingly professional managers might remain fully employed. It emerged and spread, however, only in those industries and sectors whose technology and markets permitted administrative coordination to be more profitable than market coordination. Because these areas were at the center of the American economy and because professional managers replaced families, financiers, or their representatives as decision makers in these areas, modern American capitalism became managerial capitalism.

Historical realities are, of course, far more complicated than these general propositions suggest. Modern business enterprise and the new business class that managed it appeared, grew, and flourished in different ways even in the different sectors and in the different industries they came to dominate. Varying needs and opportunities meant that the specific substance of managerial tasks differed from one sector to another and from one industry to another. So too did the specific relationships between managers and owners. And once a managerial hierarchy was fully established, the sequence of its development varied from industry to industry and from sector to sector.

Nevertheless, these differences can be viewed as variations on a single theme. The visible hand of management replaced the invisible hand of market forces where and when new technology and expanded markets permitted a historically unprecedented high volume and speed of materials through the processes of production and distribution. Modern business enterprise was thus the institutional response to the rapid pace of technological innovation and increasing consumer demand in the United States during the second half of the nineteenth century.

[3] James Burnham (1941) who was the first to describe and analyze that phenomenon, gives in chap. 7 a definition of the managerial class in American business but makes no attempt to describe the history of that class or the institution that brought it to power.

PART II

The employment relation, the human factor, and internal organization

CHAPTER 8

A formal theory of the employment
relationship

HERBERT SIMON

Herbert Simon was born in Milwaukee, Wisconsin in 1916. He received
a Ph.D. degree from the University of Chicago in 1943. When this paper
was published, he was Professor at the Carnegie Institute of Technology
and consultant to the Cowles Commission for Research in Economics.
He is currently Mellon Professor of Computer Science and Psychology,
Carnegie-Mellon University. In 1978, he was awarded the Nobel Memorial Prize in Economic Science.

In traditional economic theory employees (persons who contract to exchange
their services for a wage) enter into the system in two sharply distinct roles.
Initially, they are owners of a factor of production (their own labor) which
they sell for a definite price. Having done so, they become completely passive
factors of production employed by the entrepreneur in such a way as to maximize his profit.

This way of viewing the employment contract and management of labor
involves a very high order of abstraction – such a high order, in fact, as to
leave out of account the most striking empirical facts of the situation as we
observe it in the real world. In particular, it abstracts away the most obvious
peculiarities of the employment contract, those which distinguish it from other
kinds of contracts; and it ignores the most significant features of the administrative process, i.e., the process of actually managing the factors of production, including labor. It is the aim of this paper to set forth a theory of the
employment relationship that reintroduces some of the more important of these
empirical realities into the economic model. Perhaps in this way a bridge can
be constructed between the economist, with his theories of the firm and of
factor allocation, and the administrator, with his theories of organization – a
bridge wide enough to permit some free trade in ideas between two intellectual domains that have hitherto been quite effectively isolated from each other.

Reprinted in abridged form from Herbert Simon, "A Formal Theory of the Employment Relationship," *Econometrica*, 19 (1951): 293–305, by permission of the publisher. The full paper
is reprinted in Herbert Simon, *Models of Bounded Rationality, Vol. II*, Cambridge, Massachusetts: M.I.T. Press, 1982, Chapter 5.2 (pp. 11–23).

1. The concept of authority

The authority relationship that exists between an employer and an employee, a relationship created by the employment contract, will play a central role in our theory. What is the nature of this relationship?

We will call our employer B (for "boss"), and our employee W (for "worker"). The collection of specific actions that W performs on the job (typing and filing certain letters, laying bricks, or what not) we will call his *behavior*. We will consider the set of all possible behavior patterns of W and we will let x designate an element of this set. A particular x might then represent a given set of tasks, performed at a particular rate of working, a particular level of accuracy, and so forth.[1]

We will say that B exercises *authority* over W if W permits B to select x. That is, W accepts authority when his behavior is determined by B's decision. In general, W will accept authority only if x_0, the x chosen by B, is restricted to some given subset (W's "area of acceptance") of all the possible values. This is the definition of authority that is most generally employed in modern administrative theory.[2]

2. The employment contract

We will say that W enters into an employment contract with B when the former agrees to accept the authority of the latter and the latter agrees to pay the former a stated wage (w). This contract differs fundamentally from a sales contract – the kind of contract that is assumed in ordinary formulations of price theory. In the sales contract each party promises a specific consideration in return for the consideration promised by the other. The buyer (like B) promises to pay a stated sum of money; but the seller (unlike W) promises in return a specified quantity of a completely specified commodity. Moreover, the seller is not interested in the way in which his commodity is used once it is sold, while the worker *is* interested by what the entrepreneur will want him to do (what x will be chosen by B).[3]

We notice that certain services are obtained by buyers in our society sometimes by a sales contract, sometimes by an employment contract. For example, if I want a new concrete sidewalk, I may contract for the sidewalk or I may employ a worker to construct it for me. However, there are certain classes

---

[1] Our theory is closely related to the theory of a two-person nonzero-sum game, in the sense of von Neumann and Morgenstern (1944). The various x's (the elements of the set of possible behavior patterns) correspond to the several strategies available to W.

[2] See Simon (1947), p. 125 and Barnard (1938), p. 163.

[3] A contract to rent durable property is intermediate between the sales contract and the employment contract insofar as the lessor is interested in the effect that the use of the property will have upon its condition when it is returned to him.

of services that are typically secured by purchase and others that are typically secured by employing someone to perform them. Most labor today is performed by persons who are in an employment relation with their immediate contractors.

We may now attempt to answer two related questions about the employment contract. Why is W willing to sign a blank check, so to speak, by giving B authority over his behavior? If both parties are behaving rationally – in some sense – under what circumstances will they enter into a sales contract and under what circumstances an employment contract?

The following two conjectures, which, if correct, provide a possible answer to these questions, will be examined in the framework of a formal model:

1. W will be willing to enter an employment contract with B only if it does not matter to him "very much" which x (within the agreed-upon area of acceptance) B will choose or if W is compensated in some way for the possibility that B will choose an x that is not desired by W (i.e., that B will ask W to perform an unpleasant task).

2.   It will be advantageous to B to offer W added compensation for entering into an employment contract if B is unable to predict with certainty, at the time the contract is made, which x will be the optimum one, from his standpoint. That is, B will pay for the privilege of postponing, until some time after the contract is made, the selection of x.

3. The satisfaction functions

Let us suppose that W and B are each trying to maximize their respective *satisfaction functions*. Let the satisfaction of each depend on:

(a)   the particular x that is chosen. (For W this affects, for example, the pleasantness of his work; for B this determines the product that will be produced by W's labor.)

(b)   the particular wage (w) that is received or paid.

We assume further that these two components of the satisfaction function enter additively into it as follows:

$$S_1 = F_1(x) - a_1 w, \tag{3.1}$$

$$S_2 = F_2(x) + a_2 w, \tag{3.2}$$

where S_1 and S_2 are the satisfactions of B and W, respectively, and $w > 0$ is the wage paid by B to W. The opportunity cost to each participant of entering into the contract may be used to define the zero point of his satisfaction function. That is, if W does not contract with B, then $S_1 = 0$, $S_2 = 0$. Further, for the situations with which we wish to deal it seems reasonable to assume that $F_1(x) \geqslant 0$, $F_2(x) \leqslant 0$, $a_1 > 0, a_2 > 0$ for the relevant range of x.

Since $S_1 = 0$, $S_2 = 0$ if B and W fail to reach an agreement, we may assume that, for any agreement they do reach, $S_1 \geqslant 0$, $S_2 \geqslant 0$. When an x and a w exist satisfying these conditions, we say the system is *viable*. The condition may be stated thus:

$$F_1(x) \geqslant a_1w, \tag{3.3}$$

$$-F_2(x) \leqslant a_2w. \tag{3.4}$$

Equations (3.3) and (3.4) imply

$$a_2F_1 \geqslant a_2a_1w \geqslant -a_1F_2. \tag{3.5}$$

Conversely, if for some x, $a_2F_1(x) \geqslant -a_1F_2(x)$, we can always find a $w \geqslant 0$ such that (3.5) holds. Hence (3.5) is a necessary and sufficient condition that the system be viable.

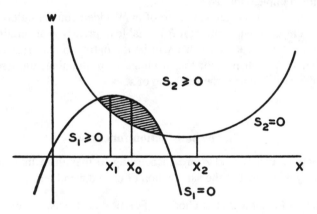

Figure 1

· · ·

5. Effect of uncertainty

The argument thus far suggests that the rational procedure for B and W would be first to determine a preferred x, and then to proceed to bargain about w so as to fix S_1 and S_2.[4] If they follow this procedure they will arrive at a sales contract of the ordinary kind in which W agrees to perform a specific, determinate act (x_0) in return for an agreed-upon price (w_0).

---

[4] Of course, $T(x)$ may assume its greatest value for several elements, x, but this complication is inessential.

Let us suppose now that $F_1(x)$ and $F_2(x)$, the satisfactions associated with x for B and W, respectively, are not known with certainty at the time B and W must reach agreement. W is to perform some future acts for B, but it is not known at the time they make their agreement what future acts would be most advantageous. Under these circumstances there are two basically different ways in which the parties could proceed.

1. From a knowledge of the probability distribution functions of $F_1(x)$ and $F_2(x)$, for each x, they could estimate what x would be optimal in the sense of maximizing the expected value of, say, $T(x)$. They could then contract for W to perform this specified x for a specified wage, w. This is essentially the sales contract procedure with mathematical expectations substituted for certain outcomes.[5]

2. B and W could agree upon a specified wage, w, to be paid by the former to the latter, and upon a specified procedure that will be followed, *at a later time when the actual values for all x of $F_1(x)$ and $F_2(x)$ are known*, for selecting a specific x. There are any number of conceivable procedures that B and W could employ for the subsequent selection of x. One of the simplest is for W to permit B to select x from some specified set, X (i.e., for W to accept B's authority). Then B would presumably select that x in X which would be optimal for him (i.e., the x that maximizes $F_1(x)$, since w is already fixed). But this arrangement is precisely what we have previously defined as an employment contract.

At the time of contract negotiations F_1 and F_2 have a known joint probability density function for each element x: $p(F_1, F_2; x) \, dF_1 dF_2$. Defining the expectation operator, $\mathcal{E}$, in the usual way, we have, for fixed x,

$$\mathcal{E}[T(x)] = \mathcal{E}[a_2 F_1(x) + a_1 F_2(x)] = a_2 \mathcal{E}[F_1(x)] + a_1 \mathcal{E}[F_2(x)]. \tag{5.1}$$

Alternative 1: sales contract. We suppose that at the time of contract negotiations B and W agree upon a particular x that will maximize $\mathcal{E}[T(x)]$ and agree on a w that divides the total satisfaction between them. We can measure the advantage of this procedure by the quantity $\max_x \mathcal{E}[T(x)]$.

Alternative 2: employment contract. We suppose that at the time of contract negotiations B and W agree upon a set X from which x will subsequently be chosen by B and agree on a w that divides the total satisfaction between them. Subsequently [when $F_1(x)$ and $F_2(x)$ become known with certainty], B chooses

---

[5] Von Neumann and Morgenstern (1944) have shown that introduction of mathematical expectations is equivalent to the definition of a cardinal utility function. We have already cardinalized our satisfaction functions by the simplifying assumptions leading to equations(3.1) and (3.2).

x so as to maximize $F_1(x)$, i.e., he chooses $\max_{x \text{ in } X} F_1(x)$. We can measure the advantage of this procedure by the quantity

$$T_x = \mathcal{E}[a_2 F_1(x_m) + a_1 F_2(x_m)], \tag{5.2}$$

where x_m is the x in X which maximizes $F_1(x)$.

. . . We can define a *preferred* set, X, as a set for which T_x assumes its maximum value. Our previous theorem can also be extended to show that, if B and W agree upon an X which is not preferred, the expected satisfactions of both could be increased by substituting a preferred X and adjusting w appropriately.

Our notion of a preferred set provides us with a rational theory for determining the range of authority of B over W (W's area of acceptance). Moreover, the sales contract is subsumed as a special case in which X contains a single element. Hence, the difference between max T_x for all sets and max T_x for single-element sets provides us with a measure of the advantage of an employment contract over a sales contract for specified distribution functions of $F_1(x)$, $F_2(x)$.

. . .

In another important respect the model can be brought into closer conformity with reality without serious difficulty. Any actual employment contract, unlike the hypothetical arrangements we have thus far discussed, specifies much more than the wage to be paid and the authority relationship. The kinds of matters over which the employer will not exercise his authority are often spelled out in considerable detail; e.g., hours of work, nature of duties (in general or specifically), and so forth. If the employment relationship endures for an extended period, all sorts of informal understandings grow up in addition to formal agreements that are made when the contract is periodically renewed. Under modern conditions when a labor union is involved, many of these contract terms are spelled out specifically and in detail in the union agreement. Our model has taken care of this fact in recognizing that authority is accepted within limits, but such limits can be introduced in another way.

In order to extend the model in this direction, let us suppose that the behavior of the worker (or a whole group of workers) is specified, not by a single element x, but by a sequence of such elements $(x, y, z, \cdots)$, where the elements in the sequence can be varied independently. Let us suppose that each of these determines a separate component in the satisfaction functions and that these components enter additively:

$$S_1 = f_{1x}(x) + f_{1y}(y) + \cdots - aw, \tag{7.2}$$

and similarly for S_2.

Then the parties may enter into a contract in which certain of the elements, say, x, $\cdots$, are specified as terms in the contract (as in the sales contract); a second set of elements, say, y, $\cdots$, is to be subject to the authority of the employer; and a third set of elements, say, z, $\cdots$ is to be left to the discretion of the worker or workers. Analogously to our previous assumptions, we may assume that if the element y is subject to the authority of B, he will fix it so as to maximize $f_{1y}(y)$ while, if z is left to the discretion of W, he will fix it so as to maximize $f_{2z}(z)$. We can now derive inequalities analogous to (6.8) that will indicate which elements should, on rational grounds, fall in each of these three categories.

Reviewing the results we have already obtained, we can see that the conditions making it advantageous (1) to stipulate the value of a particular variable in the contract are

(a) sharp conflict of interest with respect to the optimum value of the element (f_1 high when f_2 low and vice versa);

(b) little uncertainty as to the optimum values of the element (σ_{f1} and σ_{f2} small).

The conditions making it advantageous (2) to give B authority over an element or (3) to leave it to the discretion of W are, of course, just the opposite of those listed above. Moreover, (2) will be preferable to (3) if B's sensitivity to departures from optimality is greater than W's.

8. Application to planning under uncertainty

The model proposed here deals with a particular problem of planning under uncertainty. It analyzes a situation in which it may be advantageous to postpone decision (selection of x) in order to gain from information obtained subsequently. The postponement of choice may be regarded as a kind of "liquidity preference" where the liquid resource is the employee's time instead of money.

The same general approach can be applied to the problem of choosing among more or less liquid forms for holding assets. The function $F_1(x)$ would then represent the gain derived from using assets in the pursuit of strategy x. The function $F_2(x)$ would need to be replaced by some measure of the cost of holding assets in liquid form (e.g., interest costs). Then, the advantage of postponement, given by an expression like (6.8), with $\beta = \alpha$, would have to be compared with the cost of holding assets.

Indeed, comparison of the methods of this paper with Marschak's theory of liquidity under the assumption of complete information but uncertainty (particularly 1949, pp. 182–195) reveals a close similarity of approach. In both problems the central question is to determine the optimum degree of postponement of commitment. In Marschak's case this is measured by the

109

amount of assets not invested in the first period; in our case, by the range of elements included in the set X (area of acceptance).

9. Conclusion

We have constructed a model that incorporates rational grounds for the choice by two individuals between an employment contract and a contract of the ordinary kind (which we have called a sales contract). By a generalization of this model we are able to account for the fact that in an employment contract certain aspects of the worker's behavior are stipulated in the contract terms, certain other aspects are placed within the authority of the employer, and still other aspects are left to the worker's choice. Since administrative theory has been interested in explaining behavior within the framework of employment relations, and economic theory in explaining behavior within the area of market relations, the model suggests one possible way of relating these two bodies of theory. The most serious limitations of the model lie in the assumptions of rational utility-maximizing behavior incorporated in it.

CHAPTER 9

Production, information costs, and economic organization

ARMEN ALCHIAN and HAROLD DEMSETZ

Armen Alchian was born in 1914 in Fresno, California. He received a
Ph.D. in economics at Stanford University in 1943. When this article
was published, he was Professor of Economics at the University of California, Los Angeles, where he is currently Professor Emeritus and John
M. Olin Distinguished Scholar in the Graduate School of Management.

Harold Demsetz was born in Chicago, Illinois in 1930. He received a
Ph.D. in economics at Northwestern University in 1959. This article
was written during his last months at the University of Chicago and his
first months at the University of California, Los Angeles, where he has
been Professor of Economics since 1971.

The mark of a capitalistic society is that resources are owned and allocated by
such nongovernmental organizations as firms, households, and markets. Resource owners increase productivity through cooperative specialization and
this leads to the demand for economic organizations which facilitate cooperation. When a lumber mill employs a cabinetmaker, cooperation between
specialists is achieved within a firm, and when a cabinetmaker purchases wood
from a lumberman, the cooperation takes place across markets (or between
firms). Two important problems face a theory of economic organization – to
explain the conditions that determine whether the gains from specialization
and cooperative production can better be obtained within an organization like
the firm, or across markets, and to explain the structure of the organization.

It is common to see the firm characterized by the power to settle issues by
fiat, by authority, or by disciplinary action superior to that available in the
conventional market. This is delusion. The firm does not own all its inputs.
It has no power of fiat, no authority, no disciplinary action any different in
the slightest degree from ordinary market contracting between any two people. I can "punish" you only by withholding future business or by seeking
redress in the courts for any failure to honor our exchange agreement. That is
exactly all that any employer can do. He can fire or sue, just as I can fire my

Reprinted with minor abridgements from Armen Alchian and Harold Demsetz, "Production,
Information Costs, and Economic Organization," *The American Economic Review*, 62 (1972):
777–95, by permission of the editors.

111

grocer by stopping purchases from him or sue him for delivering faulty products. What then is the content of the presumed power to manage and assign workers to various tasks? Exactly the same as one little consumer's power to manage and assign his grocer to various tasks. The single consumer can assign his grocer to the task of obtaining whatever the customer can induce the grocer to provide at a price acceptable to both parties. That is precisely all that an employer can do to an employee. To speak of managing, directing, or assigning workers to various tasks is a deceptive way of noting that the employer continually is involved in renegotiation of contracts on terms that must be acceptable to both parties. Telling an employee to type this letter rather than to file that document is like my telling a grocer to sell me this brand of tuna rather than that brand of bread. I have no contract to continue to purchase from the grocer and neither the employer nor the employee is bound by any contractual obligations to continue their relationship. Long-term contracts between employer and employee are not the essence of the organization we call a firm. My grocer can count on my returning day after day and purchasing his services and goods even with the prices not always marked on the goods – because I know what they are – and he adapts his activity to conform to my directions to him as to what I want each day . . . he is not my employee.

Wherein then is the relationship between a grocer and his employee different from that between a grocer and his customers? It is in a *team* use of inputs and a centralized position of some party in the contractual arrangements of *all* other inputs. It is the *centralized contractual agent in a team productive process* – not some superior authoritarian directive or disciplinary power. Exactly what is a team process and why does it induce the contractual form, called the firm? These problems motivate the inquiry of this paper.

I. The metering problem

The economic organization through which input owners cooperate will make better use of their comparative advantages to the extent that it facilitates the payment of rewards in accord with productivity. If rewards were random, and without regard to productive effort, no incentive to productive effort would be provided by the organization; and if rewards were negatively correlated with productivity the organization would be subject to sabotage. Two key demands are placed on an economic organization – metering input productivity and metering rewards.[1]

Metering problems sometimes can be resolved well through the exchange

[1] Meter means to measure and also to apportion. One can meter (measure) output and one can also meter (control) the output. We use the word to denote both; the context should indicate which.

of products across competitive markets, because in many situations markets yield a high correlation between rewards and productivity. If a farmer increases his output of wheat by 10 percent at the prevailing market price, his receipts also increase by 10 percent. This method of organizing economic activity meters the *output directly,* reveals the marginal product and apportions the *rewards* to resource owners in accord with that direct measurement of their outputs. The success of this decentralized, market exchange in promoting productive specialization requires that changes in market rewards fall on those responsible for changes in *output.*[2]

The classic relationship in economics that runs from marginal productivity to the distribution of income implicitly *assumes* the existence of an organization, be it the market or the firm, that allocates rewards to resources in accord with their productivity. The problem of economic organization, the economical means of metering productivity and rewards, is not confronted directly in the classical analysis of production and distribution. Instead, that analysis tends to assume sufficiently economic – or zero cost – means, as if productivity automatically created its reward. We conjecture the direction of causation is the reverse – the specific system of rewarding which is relied upon stimulates a particular productivity response. If the economic organization meters poorly, with rewards and productivity only loosely correlated, then productivity will be smaller; but if the economic organization meters well productivity will be greater. What makes metering difficult and hence induces means of economizing on metering costs?

---

[2] A producer's wealth would be reduced by the present capitalized value of the future income lost by loss of reputation. Reputation, i.e., credibility, is an asset, which is another way of saying that reliable information about expected performance is both a costly and a valuable good. For acts of God that interfere with contract performance, both parties have incentives to reach a settlement akin to that which would have been reached if such events had been covered by specific contingency clauses. The reason, again, is that a reputation for "honest" dealings – i.e., for actions similar to those that would probably have been reached had the contract provided this contingency – is wealth.

Almost every contract is open-ended in that many contingencies are uncovered. For example, if a fire delays production of a promised product by *A* to *B,* and if *B* contends that *A* has not fulfilled the contract, how is the dispute settled and what recompense, if any, does *A* grant to *B?* A person uninitiated in such questions may be surprised by the extent to which contracts permit either party to escape performance or to nullify the contract. In fact, it is hard to imagine any contract, which, when taken solely in terms of its stipulations, could not be evaded by one of the parties. Yet that is the ruling, viable type of contract. Why? Undoubtedly the best discussion that we have seen on this question is by Stewart Macaulay (1963).

There are means not only of detecting or preventing cheating, but also for deciding how to allocate the losses or gains of unpredictable events or quality of items exchanged. Sales contracts contain warranties, guarantees, collateral, return privileges and penalty clauses for specific non-performance. These are means of assignment of *risks* of losses of cheating. A lower price without warranty – an "as is" purchase – places more of the risk on the buyer while the seller buys insurance against losses of his "cheating." On the other hand, a warranty or return privilege or service contract places more risk on the seller with insurance being bought by the buyer.

II. Team production

Two men jointly lift heavy cargo into trucks. Solely by observing the total weight loaded per day, it is impossible to determine each person's marginal productivity. With team production it is difficult, solely by observing total output, to either define or determine *each* individual's contribution to this output of the cooperating inputs. The output is yielded by a team, by definition, and it is not a *sum* of separable outputs of each of its members. Team production of Z involves at least two inputs, X_i and X_j, with $\partial^2 Z/\partial X_i \partial X_j \neq 0$.[3] The production function is *not* separable into two functions each involving only inputs X_i or only inputs X_j. Consequently there is no *sum* of Z of two separable functions to treat as the Z of the team production function. (An example of a *separable* case is $Z = aX_i^2$ and $Z_j = bX_j^2$, and $Z = Z_i + Z_j$. This is not team production.) There exist production techniques in which the Z obtained is greater than if X_i and X_j had produced separable Z. Team production will be used if it yields an output enough larger than the sum of separable production of Z to cover the costs of organizing and disciplining team members – the topics of this paper.[4]

Usual explanations of the gains from cooperative behavior rely on exchange and production in accord with the comparative advantage specialization principle with separable additive production. However, as suggested above there is a source of gain from cooperative activity involving working as a *team,* wherein individual cooperating inputs do not yield identifiable, separate products which can be *summed* to measure the total output. For this cooperative productive activity, here called "team" production, measuring *marginal* productivity and making payments in accord therewith is more expensive by an order of magnitude than for separable production functions.

Team production, to repeat, is production in which (1) several types of resources are used and (2) the product is not a sum of separable outputs of each cooperating resource. An additional factor creates a team organization problem – (3) not all resources used in team production belong to one person.

We do not inquire into why all the jointly used resources are not owned by one person, but instead into the types of organization, contracts, and informational and payment procedures used among owners of teamed inputs. With respect to the one-owner case, perhaps it is sufficient merely to note that (a) slavery is prohibited, (b) one might assume risk aversion as a reason for one person's not borrowing enough to purchase all the assets or sources of ser-

---

[3] The function is separable into additive functions if the cross partial derivative is zero, i.e., if $\partial^2 Z/\partial X_i \partial X_j = 0$.

[4] With sufficient generality of notation and conception this team production function could be formulated as a case of the generalized production function interpretation given by our colleague, E. A. Thompson (1970).

vices rather than renting them, and (c) the purchase-resale spread may be so large that costs of short-term ownership exceed rental costs. Our problem is viewed basically as one of organization among different people, not of the physical goods or services, however much there must be selection and choice of combination of the latter.

How can the members of a team be rewarded and induced to work efficiently? In team production, marginal products of cooperative team members are not so directly and separably (i.e., cheaply) observable. What a team offers to the market can be taken as the marginal product of the team but not of the team members. The costs of metering or ascertaining the marginal products of the team's members is what calls forth new organizations and procedures. Clues to each input's productivity can be secured by observing *behavior* of individual inputs. When lifting cargo into the truck, how rapidly does a man move to the next piece to be loaded, how many cigarette breaks does he take, does the item being lifted tilt downward toward his side?

If detecting such behavior were costless, neither party would have an incentive to shirk, because neither could impose the cost of his shirking on the other (if their cooperation was agreed to voluntarily). But since costs must be incurred to monitor each other, each input owner will have more incentive to shirk when he works as part of a team, than if his performance could be monitored easily or if he did not work as a team. If there is a net increase in productivity available by team production, net of the metering cost associated with disciplining the team, then team production will be relied upon rather than a multitude of bilateral exchanges of separable individual outputs.

Both leisure and higher income enter a person's utility function.[5] Hence, each person should adjust his work and realized reward so as to equate the marginal rate of substitution between leisure and production of real output to his marginal rate of substitution in consumption. That is, he would adjust his rate of work to bring his demand prices of leisure and output to equality with their true costs. However, with detection, policing, monitoring, measuring or metering costs, each person will be induced to take more leisure, because the effect of relaxing on *his realized* (reward) rate of substitution between output and leisure will be less than the effect on the *true* rate of substitution. His realized cost of leisure will fall more than the true cost of leisure, so he "buys" more leisure (i.e., more nonpecuniary reward).

If his relaxation cannot be detected perfectly at zero cost, part of its effects will be borne by others in the team, thus making *his* realized cost of relaxation less than the true total cost to the team. The difficulty of detecting such actions permits the private costs of his actions to be less than their full costs. Since each person responds to his private realizable rate of substitution (in produc-

---

[5] More precisely: "if anything other than pecuniary income enters his utility function." Leisure stands for all nonpecuniary income for simplicity of exposition.

tion) rather than the true total (i.e. social) rate, and so long as there are costs for other people to detect his shift toward relaxation, it will not pay (them) to force him to readjust completely by making him realize the true cost. Only enough efforts will be made to equate the marginal gains of detection activity with the marginal costs of detection; and that implies a lower rate of productive effort and more shirking than in a costless monitoring, or measuring, world.

In a university, the faculty use office telephones, paper, and mail for personal uses beyond strict university productivity. The university administrators could stop such practices by identifying *the* responsible person in each case, but they can do so only at higher costs than administrators are willing to incur. The extra costs of identifying each party (rather than merely identifying the presence of such activity) would exceed the savings from diminished faculty "turpitudinal peccadilloes." So the faculty is allowed some degree of "privileges, perquisites, or fringe benefits." And the total of the pecuniary wages paid is lower because of this irreducible (at acceptable costs) degree of amenity-seizing activity. Pay is lower in pecuniary terms and higher in leisure, conveniences, and ease of work. But still every person would prefer to see detection made more effective (if it were somehow possible to monitor costlessly) so that he, as part of the now more effectively producing team, could thereby realize a higher pecuniary pay and less leisure. If everyone could, at zero cost, have his reward-realized rate brought to the true production possibility real rate, all could achieve a more preferred position. But detection of the responsible parties is costly; that cost acts like a tax on work rewards.[6] Viable shirking is the result.

What forms of organizing team production will lower the cost of detecting "performance" (i.e., marginal productivity) and bring personally realized rates of substitution closer to true rates of substitution? Market competition, in principle, could monitor some team production. (It already *organizes* teams.) Input owners who are not team members can offer, in return for a smaller share of the team's rewards, to replace excessively (i.e., overpaid) shirking members. Market competition among potential team members would determine team membership and individual rewards. There would be no team leader, manager, organizer, owner, or employer. For such decentralized organizational control to work, outsiders, possibly after observing each team's total output, can speculate about their capabilities as team members and, by a mar-

---

[6] Do not assume that the sole result of the cost of detecting shirking is one form of payment (more leisure and less take home money). With several members of the team, each has an incentive to cheat against each other by engaging in more than the average amount of such leisure if the employer can not tell at zero cost which employee is taking more than average. As a result the total productivity of the team is lowered. Shirking detection costs thus change the form of payment and also result in lower total rewards. Because the cross partial derivatives are positive, shirking reduces other people's marginal products.

ket competitive process, revised teams with greater production ability will be formed and sustained. Incumbent members will be constrained by threats of replacement by outsiders offering services for lower reward shares or offering greater rewards to the other members of the team. Any team member who shirked in the expectation that the reduced output effect would not be attributed to him will be displaced if his activity is detected. Teams of productive inputs, like business units, would evolve in apparent spontaneity in the market – without any central organizing agent, team manager, or boss.

But completely effective control cannot be expected from individualized market competition for two reasons. First, for this competition to be completely effective, new challengers for team membership must know where, and to what extent, shirking is a serious problem, i.e., know they can increase net output as compared with the inputs they replace. To the extent that this is true it is probably possible for existing fellow team members to recognize the shirking. But, by definition, the detection of shirking by observing team output is costly for team production. Secondly, assume the presence of detection costs, and assume that in order to secure a place on the team a new input owner must accept a smaller share of rewards (or a promise to produce more). Then his incentive to shirk would still be at least as great as the incentives of the inputs replaced, because he still bears less than the entire reduction in team output for which he is responsible.

III. The classical firm

One method of reducing shirking is for someone to specialize as a monitor to check the input performance of team members.[7] But who will monitor the monitor? One constraint on the monitor is the aforesaid market competition offered by other monitors, but for reasons already given, that is not perfectly effective. Another constraint can be imposed on the monitor: give him title to the net earnings of the team, net of payments to other inputs. If owners of cooperating inputs agree with the monitor that he is to receive any residual product above prescribed amounts (hopefully, the marginal value products of the other inputs), the monitor will have an added incentive not to shirk as a monitor. Specialization in monitoring plus reliance on a residual claimant

---

[7] What is meant by performance? Input energy, initiative, work attitude, perspiration, rate of exhaustion? Or output? It is the latter that is sought – the *effect* or output. But performance is nicely ambiguous because it suggests both input and output. It is *nicely* ambiguous because as we shall see, sometimes by inspecting a team member's input activity we can better judge his output effect, perhaps not with complete accuracy but better than by watching the output of the *team*. It is not always the case that watching input activity is the only or best means of detecting, measuring or monitoring output effects of each team member, but in some cases it is a useful way. For the moment the word performance glosses over these aspects and facilitates concentration on other issues.

117

status will reduce shirking; but additional links are needed to forge the firm of classical economic theory. How will the residual claimant monitor the other inputs?

We use the term monitor to connote several activities in addition to its disciplinary connotation. It connotes measuring output performance, apportioning rewards, observing the input behavior of inputs as a means of detecting or estimating their marginal productivity and giving assignments or instructions in what to do and how to do it. (It also includes, as we shall show later, authority to terminate or revise contracts.) Perhaps the contrast between a football coach and team captain is helpful. The coach selects strategies and tactics and sends in instructions about what plays to utilize. The captain is essentially an observer and reporter of the performance at close hand of the members. The latter is an inspector-steward and the former a supervisor manager. For the present all these activities are included in the rubric "monitoring." All these tasks are, in principle, negotiable across markets, but we are presuming that such market measurement of marginal productivities and job reassignments are not so cheaply performed for team production. And in particular our analysis suggests that it is not so much the costs of spontaneously negotiating contracts in the markets among groups for team production as it is the detection of the performance of individual members of the team that calls for the organization noted here.

The specialist *who receives the residual rewards* will be the monitor of the members of the team (i.e., will manage the use of cooperative inputs). The monitor earns his residual through the reduction in shirking that he brings about, not only by the prices that he agrees to pay the owners of the inputs, but also by observing and directing the actions or uses of these inputs. *Managing or examining the ways to which inputs are used in team production is a method of metering the marginal productivity of individual inputs to the team's output.*

To discipline team members and reduce shirking, the residual claimant must have power to revise the contract terms and incentives of *individual* members without having to terminate or alter every other input's contract. Hence, team members who seek to increase their productivity will assign to the monitor not only the residual claimant right but also the right to alter individual membership and performance on the team. Each team member, of course, can terminate his own membership (i.e., quit the team), but only the monitor may unilaterally terminate the membership of any of the other members without necessarily terminating the team itself or his association with the team; and he alone can expand or reduce membership, alter the mix of membership, or sell the right to be the residual claimant-monitor of the team. It is this entire bundle of rights: (1) to be a residual claimant; (2) to observe input behavior; (3) to be the central party common to all contracts with inputs; (4) to alter the membership of the team; and (5) to sell these rights, that defines the *owner-ship* (or the employer) of the *classical* (capitalist, free-enterprise) firm. The coalescing of these rights has arisen, our analysis asserts, because it resolves the shirking-information problem of team production better than does the non-centralized contractual arrangement.

The relationship of each team member to the *owner* of the firm (i.e., the party common to all input contracts *and* the residual claimant) is simply a "quid pro quo" contract. Each makes a purchase and sale. The employee "orders" the owner of the team to pay him money in the same sense that the employer directs the team member to perform certain acts. The employee can terminate the contract as readily as can the employer, and long-term contracts, therefore, are not an essential attribute of the firm. Nor are "authoritarian," "dictational," or "fiat" attributes relevant to the conception of the firm or its efficiency.

In summary, two necessary conditions exist for the emergence of the firm on the prior assumption that more than pecuniary wealth enter utility functions: (1) It is possible to increase productivity through team-oriented production, a production technique for which it is costly to directly measure the marginal outputs of the cooperating inputs. This makes it more difficult to restrict shirking through simple market exchange between cooperating inputs. (2) It is economical to estimate marginal productivity by observing or specifying input behavior. The simultaneous occurrence of both these preconditions leads to the contractual organization of inputs, known as the *classical capitalist firms* with (a) joint input production, (b) several input owners, (c) one party who is common to all the contracts of the joint inputs, (d) who has rights to renegotiate any input's contract independently of contracts with other input owners, (e) who holds the residual claim, and (f) who has the right to sell his central contractual residual status.[8]

Other theories of the firm

At this juncture, as an aside, we briefly place this theory of the firm in the contexts of those offered by Ronald Coase and Frank Knight.[9] Our view of the firm is not necessarily inconsistent with Coase's; we attempt to go further and identify refutable implications. Coase's penetrating insight is to make more of the fact that markets do not operate costlessly, and he relies on the cost of using markets to *form* contracts as his basic explanation for the existence of firms. We do not disagree with the proposition that, *ceteris paribus*, the higher is the cost of transacting across markets the greater will be the

[8] Removal of (b) converts a capitalist proprietary firm to a socialist firm.
[9] Recognition must also be made to the seminal inquiries by Morris Silver and Richard Auster (1969) and by H. B. Malmgren (1961).

comparative advantage of organizing resources within the firm; it is a difficult proposition to disagree with or to refute. We could with equal ease subscribe to a theory of the firm based on the cost of managing for surely it is true that, *ceteris paribus,* the lower is the cost of managing the greater will be the comparative advantage of organizing resources within the firm. To move the theory forward, it is necessary to know what is meant by a firm and to explain the circumstances under which the cost of "managing" resources is low relative to the cost of allocating resources through market transaction. The conception of and rationale for the classical firm that we propose takes a step down the path pointed out by Coase toward that goal. Consideration of team production, team organization, difficulty in metering outputs, and the problem of shirking are important to our explanation but, so far as we can ascertain, not in Coase's. Coase's analysis insofar as it had heretofore been developed would suggest open-ended contracts but does not appear to imply anything more − neither the residual claimant status nor the distinction between employee and subcontractor status (nor any of the implications indicated below). And it is not true that employees are generally employed on the basis of long-term contractual arrangements any more than on a series of short-term or indefinite length contracts.

The importance of our proposed additional elements is revealed, for example, by the explanation of why the person to whom the control monitor is responsible receives the residual, and also by our later discussion of the implications about the corporation, partnerships, and profit sharing. These alternative forms for organization of the firm are difficult to resolve on the basis of market transaction costs only. Our exposition also suggests a definition of the classical firm − something crucial that was heretofore absent.

In addition, sometimes a technological development will lower the cost of market transactions while, at the same time, it expands the role of the firm. When the "putting out" system was used for weaving, inputs were organized largely through market negotiations. With the development of efficient central sources of power, it became economical to perform weaving in proximity to the power source and to engage in team production. The bringing in of weavers surely must have resulted in a reduction in the cost of negotiating (forming) contracts. Yet, what we observe is the beginning of the factory system, in which inputs are organized within a firm. Why? The weavers did not simply move to a common source of power that they could tap like an electric line, purchasing power while they used their own equipment. Now team production in the joint use of equipment became more important. The measurement of marginal productivity, which now involved interactions between workers, especially through their joint use of machines, became more difficult though contract negotiating cost was reduced, while managing the *behavior* of inputs became easier because of the increased centralization of activity.

120

The firm as an organization expanded even though the cost of transactions was reduced by the advent of centralized power. The same could be said for modern assembly lines. Hence the emergence of central power sources expanded the scope of productive activity in which the firm enjoyed a comparative advantage as an organizational form.

Some economists, following Knight, have identified the bearing of risks of wealth changes with the director or central employer without explaining why that is a viable arrangement. Presumably, the more risk-averse inputs become employees rather than owners of the classical firm. Risk averseness and uncertainty *with regard to the firm's fortunes* have little, if anything, to do with our explanation although it helps to explain why all resources in a team are not owned by one person. That is, the role of risk taken in the sense of absorbing the windfalls that buffet the firm because of unforeseen competition, technological change, or fluctuations in demand are not central to our theory, although it is true that imperfect knowledge and, therefore, risk, in *this* sense of risk, underlie the problem of monitoring team behavior. We deduce the system of paying the manager with a residual claim (the equity) from the desire to have efficient means to reduce shirking so as to make team production economical and not from the smaller aversion to the risks of enterprise in a dynamic economy. We conjecture that "distribution-of-risk" is not a valid rationale for the *existence* and organization of the *classical* firm.

Although we have emphasized team production as creating a costly metering task and have treated team production as an essential (necessary?) condition for the firm, would not other obstacles to cheap metering also call forth the same kind of contractual arrangement here denoted as a firm? For example, suppose a farmer produces wheat in an easily ascertained quantity but with subtle and difficult to detect quality variations determined by how the farmer grew the wheat. A vertical integration could allow a purchaser to control the farmer's behavior in order to more economically estimate productivity. But this is not a case of joint or team production, unless "information" can be considered part of the product. (While a good case could be made for that broader conception of production, we shall ignore it here.) Instead of forming a firm, a buyer can contract to have his inspector on the site of production, just as home builders contract with architects to supervise building contracts; that arrangement is not a firm. Still, a firm might be organized in the production of many products wherein no team production or jointness is involved.

This possibility rather clearly indicates a broader, or complementary, approach to that which we have chosen. (1) As we do in this paper, it can be argued that the firm is the particular policing device utilized when joint team production is present. If other sources of high policing costs arise, as in the wheat case just indicated, some other form of contractual arrangement will be

121

used. Thus to each source of informational cost there may be a different type of policing and contractual arrangement. (2) On the other hand, one can say that where policing is difficult across markets, various forms of contractual arrangements are devised, but there is no reason for that known as the firm to be uniquely related or even highly correlated with team production, as defined here. It might be used equally probably and viably for other sources of high policing cost. We have not intensively analyzed other sources, and we can only note that our current and readily revisable conjecture is that (1) is valid, and has motivated us in our current endeavor. In any event, the test of the theory advanced here is to see whether the conditions we have identified are necessary for firms to have long-run viability rather than merely births with high infant mortality. Conglomerate firms or collections of separate production agencies into one owning organization can be interpreted as an investment trust or investment diversification device – probably Knight's interpretation. A holding company can be called a firm, because of the common association of the word firm with any ownership unit that owns income sources. The term firm as commonly used is so turgid of meaning that we can not hope to explain every entity to which the name is attached in common or even technical literature. Instead, we seek to identify and explain a particular contractual arrangement induced by the cost of information factors analyzed in this paper.

IV. Types of firms

A. Profit-sharing firms

Explicit in our explanation of the capitalist firm is the assumption that the cost of *managing* the team's inputs by a central monitor, who disciplines himself because he is a residual claimant, is low relative to the cost of metering the marginal outputs of team members.

If we look within a firm to see who monitors – hires, fires, changes, promotes, and renegotiates – we should find him being a residual claimant or, at least, one whose pay or reward is more than any others correlated with fluctuations in the residual value of the firm. They more likely will have options or rights or bonuses than will inputs with other tasks.

An implicit "auxiliary" assumption of our explanation of the firm is that the cost of team production is increased if the residual claim is not held entirely by the central monitor. That is, we assume that if profit sharing had to be relied upon for *all* team members, losses from the resulting increase in central monitor shirking would exceed the output gains from the increased incentives of other team members not to shirk. If the optimal team size is only two owners of inputs, then an equal division of profits and losses between them will leave each with stronger incentives to reduce shirking than if the optimal team size is large, for in the latter case only a smaller percentage of the losses occasioned by the shirker will be borne by him. Incentives to shirk are positively related to the optimal size of the team under an equal profit-sharing scheme.[10]

The preceding does not imply that profit sharing is never viable. Profit sharing to encourage self-policing is more appropriate for small teams. And, indeed, where input owners are free to make whatever contractual arrangements suit them, as generally is true in capitalist economies, profit sharing seems largely limited to partnerships with a relatively small number of *active*[11] partners. Another advantage of such arrangements for smaller teams is that it permits more effective reciprocal monitoring among inputs. Monitoring need not be entirely specialized.

Profit sharing is more viable if small team size is associated with situations where the cost of specialized management of inputs is large relative to the increased productivity potential in team effort. We conjecture that the cost of managing team inputs increases if the productivity of a team member is difficult to correlate with his behavior. In "artistic" or "professional" work, watching a man's activities is not a good clue to what he is actually thinking or doing with his mind. While it is relatively easy to manage or direct the loading of trucks by a team of dock workers where input activity is so highly related in an obvious way to output, it is more difficult to manage and direct a lawyer in the preparation and presentation of a case. Dock workers can be directed in detail without the monitor himself loading the truck, and assembly line workers can be monitored by varying the speed of the assembly line, but detailed direction in the preparation of a law case would require in much greater degree that the monitor prepare the case himself. As a result, artistic or professional inputs, such as lawyers, advertising specialists, and doctors, will be given relatively freer reign with regard to individual behavior. If the management of inputs is relatively costly, or ineffective, as it would seem to be in these cases, but, nonetheless if team effort is more productive than separable production with exchange across markets, then there will develop a tendency to use profit-sharing schemes to provide incentives to avoid shirking.[12]

---

[10] While the degree to which residual claims are centralized will affect the size of the team, this will be only one of many factors that determine team size, so as an approximation, we can treat team size as exogenously determined. Under certain assumptions about the shape of the "typical" utility function, the incentive to avoid shirking with unequal profit-sharing can be measured by the Herfindahl index.

[11] The use of the word active will be clarified in our discussion of the corporation, which follows below.

[12] Some sharing contracts, like crop sharing, or rental payments based on gross sales in retail stores, come close to profit sharing . However, it is gross output sharing rather than profit shar-

B. Socialist firms

We have analyzed the classical proprietorship and the profit-sharing firms in the context of free association and choice of economic organization. Such organizations need not be the most viable when political constraints limit the forms of organization that can be chosen. It is one thing to have profit sharing when professional or artistic talents are used by small teams. But if political or tax or subsidy considerations induce profit-sharing techniques when these are not otherwise economically justified, then additional management techniques will be developed to help reduce the degree of shirking.

For example, most, if not all, firms in Jugoslavia are owned by the employees in the restricted sense that all share in the residual. This is true for large firms and for firms which employ nonartistic, or nonprofessional, workers as well. With a decay of political constraints, most of these firms could be expected to rely on paid wages rather than shares in the residual. This rests on our auxiliary assumption that general sharing in the residual results in losses from enhanced shirking by the monitor that exceed the gains from reduced shirking by residual-sharing employees. If this were not so, profit sharing with employees should have occurred more frequently in Western societies where such organizations are neither banned nor preferred politically. Where residual sharing by employees is politically imposed, as in Jugoslavia, we are led to expect that some management technique will arise to reduce the shirking by the central monitor, a technique that will not be found frequently in Western societies since the monitor retains all (or much) of the residual in the West and profit sharing is largely confined to small, professional-artistic team production situations. We do find in the larger scale residual-sharing firms in Jugoslavia that there are employee committees that can recommend (to the state) the termination of a manager's contract (veto his continuance) with the enterprise. We conjecture that the workers' committee is given the right to recommend the termination of the manager's contract precisely because the general sharing of the residual increases "excessively" the manager's incentive to shirk.[13]

---

ing. We are unable to specify the implications of the difference. We refer the reader to S. N. Cheung (1969).

[13] Incidentally, investment activity will be changed. The inability to capitalize the investment value as "take-home" private property *wealth* of the members of the firm means that the benefits of the investment must be taken as annual income by those who are employed at the time of the income. Investment will be confined more to those with shorter life and with higher rates or pay-offs if the alternative of investing is paying out the firm's income to employees to take home and use as private property. For a development of this proposition, see the papers by Eirik Furubotn and Svetozar Pejovich (1974) and by Pejovich (1969).

C. The corporation

All firms must initially acquire command over some resources. The corporation does so primarily by selling promises of future returns to those who (as creditors or owners) provide financial capital. In some situations resources can be acquired in advance from consumers by promises of future delivery (for example, advance sale of a proposed book). Or where the firm is a few artistic or professional persons, each can "chip in" with time and talent until the sale of services brings in revenues. For the most part, capital can be acquired more cheaply if many (risk-averse) investors contribute small portions to a large investment. The economies of raising large sums of equity capital in this way suggest that modifications in the relationship among corporate inputs are required to cope with the shirking problem that arises with profit sharing among large numbers of corporate stockholders. One modification is limited liability, especially for firms that are large relative to a stockholder's wealth. It serves to protect stockholders from large losses no matter how they are caused.

If every stock owner participated in each decision in a corporation, not only would large bureaucratic costs be incurred, but many would shirk the task of becoming well informed on the issue to be decided, since the losses associated with unexpectedly bad decisions will be borne in large part by the many other corporate shareholders. More effective control of corporate activity is achieved for most purposes by transferring decision authority to a smaller group, whose main function is to negotiate with and manage (renegotiate with) the other inputs of the team. The corporate stockholders retain the authority to revise the membership of the management group and over major decisions that affect the structure of the corporation or its dissolution.

As a result a new modification of partnerships is induced – the right to sale of corporate shares without approval of any other stockholders. Any share holder can remove his wealth from control by those with whom he has differences of opinion. Rather than try to control the decisions of the management, which is harder to do with many stockholders than with only a few, unrestricted salability provides a more acceptable escape to each stockholder from continued policies with which he disagrees.

Indeed, the policing of managerial shirking relies on across-market competition from new groups of would-be managers as well as competition from members within the firm who seek to displace existing management. In addition to competition from outside and inside managers, control is facilitated by the temporary congealing of share votes into voting blocs owned by one or a few contenders. Proxy battles of stock-purchases concentrate the votes required to displace the existing management or modify managerial policies.

But it is more than a change in policy that is sought by the newly formed financial interests, whether of new stockholders or not. It is the capitalization of expected future benefits into stock prices that concentrates on the innovators the wealth gains of their actions if they own large numbers of shares. Without capitalization of future benefits, there would be less incentive to incur the costs required to exert informed decisive influence on the corporation's policies and managing personnel. Temporarily, the structure of ownership is reformed, moving away from diffused ownership into decisive power blocs, and this is a transient resurgence of the classical firm with power again concentrated in those who have title to the residual.

In assessing the significance of stockholders' power it is not the usual diffusion of voting power that is significant but instead the frequency with which voting congeals into decisive changes. Even a one-man owned company may have a long term with just one manager – continuously being approved by the owner. Similarly a dispersed voting power corporation may be also characterized by a long-lived management. The question is the probability of replacement of the management if it behaves in ways not acceptable to a majority of the stockholders. The unrestricted stability of stock and the transfer of proxies enhances the probability of decisive action in the event current stockholders or any outsider believes that management is not doing a good job with the corporation. We are not comparing the corporate responsiveness to that of a single proprietorship; instead, we are indicating features of the corporate structure that are induced by the problem of delegated authority to manager-monitors.[14]

[14] Instead of thinking of shareholders as joint *owners,* we can think of them as investors, like bondholders, except that the stockholders are more optimistic than bondholders about the enterprise prospects. Instead of buying bonds in the corporation, thus enjoying smaller risks, shareholders prefer to invest funds with a greater realizable return if the firm prospers as expected, but with smaller (possibly negative) returns if the firm performs in a manner closer to that expected by the more pessimistic investors. The pessimistic investors, in turn, regard only the bonds as likely to pay off.

If the entrepreneur-organizer is to raise capital on the best terms to him, it is to his advantage, as well as that of prospective investors, to recognize these differences in expectations. The residual claim on earnings enjoyed by shareholders does not serve the function of enhancing their efficiency as monitors in the general situation. The stockholders are "merely" the less risk-averse or the more optimistic member of the group that finances the firm. Being more optimistic than the average and seeing a higher mean value future return, they are willing to pay more for a certificate that allows them to realize gain on their expectations. One method of doing so is to buy claims to the distribution of returns that "they see" while bondholders, who are more pessimistic, purchase a claim to the distribution that they see as more likely to emerge. Stockholders are then comparable to warrant holders. They care not about the voting rights (usually not attached to warrants); they are in the same position in so far as voting rights are concerned as are bondholders. The only difference is in the probability distribution of rewards and the terms on which they can place their bets.

If we treat bondholders, preferred and convertible preferred stockholders, and common stockholders and warrant holders as simply different classes of investors – differing not only in their risk averseness but in their beliefs about the probability distribution of the firm's future earnings,

D. Mutual and nonprofit firms

The benefits obtained by the new management are greater if the stock can be purchased and sold, because this enables *capitalization* of anticipated future improvements into present *wealth* of new managers who bought stock and created a larger capital by their management changes. But in nonprofit corporations, colleges, churches, country clubs, mutual savings banks, mutual insurance companies, and "coops," the future consequences of improved management are not capitalized into present wealth of stockholders. (As if to make more difficult that competition by new would-be monitors, multiple shares of ownership in those enterprises cannot be bought by one person.) One should, therefore, find greater shirking in nonprofit, mutually owned enterprises. (This suggests that nonprofit enterprises arc especially appropriate in realms of en-

why should stockholders be regarded as "owners" in any sense distinct from the other financial investors? The entrepreneur-organizer, who let us assume is the chief operating officer and sole repository of control of the corporation, does not find his authority residing in common stockholders (except in the case of a take over). Does this type of control make any difference in the way the firm is conducted? Would it make any difference in the kinds of behavior that would be tolerated by competing managers and investors (and we here deliberately refrain from thinking of them as owner-stockholders in the traditional sense)?

Investment old timers recall a significant incidence of nonvoting common stock, now prohibited in corporations whose stock is traded on listed exchanges. (Why prohibited?) The entrepreneur in those days could hold voting shares while investors held nonvoting shares, which in every other respect were identical. Nonvoting share holders were simply investors devoid of ownership connotations. The control and behavior of inside owners in such corporations has never, so far as we have ascertained, been carefully studied. For example, at the simplest level of interest, does the evidence indicate that nonvoting shareholders fared any worse because of not having voting rights? Did owners permit the nonvoting holders the normal return available to voting shareholders? Though evidence is prohibitively expensive to obtain, it is remarkable that voting and nonvoting shares sold for essentially identical prices, even during some proxy battles. However, our casual evidence deserves no more than interest-initiating weight.

One more point. The facade is deceptive. Instead of nonvoting shares, today we have warrants, convertible preferred stocks all of which are solely or partly "equity" claims without voting rights, though they could be converted into voting shares.

In sum, is it the case that the stockholder-investor relationship is one emanating from the *division* of *ownership* among several people, or is it that the collection of investment funds from people of varying anticipations is the underlying factor? If the latter, why should any of them be thought of as the owners in whom voting rights, whatever they may signify or however exercisable, should reside in order to enhance efficiency? Why voting rights in any of the outside, participating investors?

Our initial perception of this possibly significant difference in interpretation was precipitated by Henry Manne (1967). A reading of his paper makes it clear that it is hard to understand why an investor who wishes to back and "share" in the consequences of some new business should necessarily have to acquire voting power (i.e., power to change the manager-operator) in order to invest in the venture. In fact, we invest in some ventures in the hope that no other stockholders will be so "foolish" as to try to toss out the incumbent management. We want him to have the power to stay in office, and for the prospect of sharing in his fortunes we buy nonvoting common stock. Our willingness to invest is enhanced by the knowledge that we can act legally via fraud, embezzlement and other laws to help assure that we outside investors will not be "milked" beyond our initial discounted anticipations.

deavor where more shirking is desired and where redirected use of the enterprise in response to market-revealed values is less desired.)

E. Partnerships

Team production in artistic or professional intellectual skills will more likely be by partnerships than other types of team production. This amounts to market-organized team activity and to a non-employer status. Self-monitoring partnerships, therefore, will be used rather than employer-employee contracts, and these organizations will be small to prevent an excessive dilution of efforts through shirking. Also, partnerships are more likely to occur among relatives or long-standing acquaintances, not necessarily because they share a common utility function, but also because each knows better the other's work characteristics and tendencies to shirk.

F. Employee unions

Employee unions, whatever else they do, perform as monitors for employees. Employers monitor employees and similarly employees monitor an employer's performance. Are correct wages paid on time and in good currency? Usually, this is extremely easy to check. But some forms of employer performance are less easy to meter and are more subject to employer shirking. Fringe benefits often are in non-pecuniary, contingent form; medical, hospital, and accident insurance, and retirement pensions are contingent payments or performances partly in *kind* by employers to employees. Each employee cannot judge the character of such payments as easily as money wages. Insurance is a contingent payment – what the employee will get upon the contingent event may come as a disappointment. If he could easily determine what other employees had gotten upon such contingent events he could judge more accurately the performance by the employer. He could "trust" the employer not to shirk in such fringe contingent payments, but he would prefer an effective and economic monitor of those payments. We see a specialist monitor – the union employees' agent – hired by them and monitoring those aspects of employer payment most difficult for the employees to monitor. Employees should be willing to employ a specialist monitor to administer such hard-to-detect employer performance, even though their monitor has incentives to use pension and retirement funds not entirely for the benefit of employees.

V. Team spirit and loyalty

Every team member would prefer a team in which no one, not even himself, shirked. Then the true marginal costs and values could be equated to achieve more preferred positions. If one could enhance a common interest in non-shirking in the guise of a team loyalty or team spirit, the team would be more efficient. In those sports where team activity is most clearly exemplified, the sense of loyalty and team spirit is most strongly urged. Obviously the team is better, with team spirit and loyalty, because of the reduced shirking – not because of some other feature inherent in loyalty or spirit as such.[15]

Corporations and business firms try to instill a spirit of loyalty. This should not be viewed simply as a device to increase profits by *over*-working or misleading the employees, nor as an adolescent urge for belonging. It promotes a closer approximation to the employees' potentially available true rates of substitution between production and leisure and enables each team member to achieve a more preferred situation. The difficulty, of course, is to create economically that team spirit and loyalty. It can be preached with an aura of moral code of conduct – a morality with literally the same basis as the ten commandments – to restrict our conduct toward what we would choose if we bore our full costs.

---

[15] *Sports Leagues:* Professional sports contests among teams are typically conducted by a *league* of teams. We assume that sports consumers are interested not only in absolute sporting skill but also in skills *relative* to other teams. Being slightly better than opposing teams enables one to claim a major portion of the receipts; the inferior team does not release resources and reduce costs, since they were expected in the play of contest. Hence, absolute skill is developed beyond the equality of marginal investment in sporting skill with its true social marginal value product. It follows there will be a tendency to overinvest in training athletes and developing teams. "Reverse shirking" arises, as budding players are induced to overpractice hyperactively relative to the social marginal value of their enhanced skills. To prevent overinvestment, the teams seek an agreement with each other to restrict practice, size of teams, and even pay of the team members (which reduces incentives of young people to overinvest in developing skills). Ideally, if all the contestant teams were owned by one owner, overinvestment in sports would be avoided, much as ownership of common fisheries or underground oil or water reserves would prevent overinvestment. This hyperactivity (to suggest the opposite of shirking) is controlled by the league of teams, wherein the league adopts a common set of constraints on each team's behavior. In effect, the teams are no longer really owned by the team owners but are supervised by them, much as the franchisers of some product. They are not full-fledged owners of their business, including the brand name, and can not "do what they wish" as franchises. Comparable to the franchiser, is the league commissioner or conference president, who seeks to restrain hyperactivity, as individual team supervisors compete with each other and cause external diseconomies. Such restraints are usually regarded as anticompetitive, antisocial, collusive-cartel devices to restrain free open competition, and reduce players' salaries. However, the interpretation presented here is premised on an attempt to avoid hyperinvestment in team sports production. Of course, the team operators have an incentive, once the league is formed and restraints are placed on hyperinvestment activity, to go further and obtain the private benefits of monopoly restriction. To what extent overinvestment is replaced by monopoly restriction is not yet determinable; nor have we seen an empirical test of these two competing, but mutually consistent interpretations. (This interpretation of league-sports activity was proposed by Earl Thompson (1970) and formulated by Michael Canes (1970)). Again, athletic teams clearly exemplify the specialization of monitoring with captains and coaches; a captain detects shirkers while the coach trains and selects strategies and tactics. Both functions may be centralized in one person.

129

VI. Kinds of inputs owned by the firm

To this point the discussion has examined why firms, as we have defined them, exist? That is, why is there an owner-employer who is the common party to contracts with other owners of inputs in team activity? The answer to that question should also indicate the kind of the jointly used resources likely to be owned by the central-owner-monitor and the kind likely to be hired from people who are not team-owners. Can we identify characteristics or features of various inputs that lead to their being hired or to their being owned by the firm?

How can residual-claimant, central-employer-owner demonstrate ability to pay the other hired inputs the promised amount in the event of a loss? He can pay in advance or he can commit wealth sufficient to cover negative residuals. The latter will take the form of machines, land, buildings, or raw materials committed to the firm. Commitments of labor-wealth (i.e., human wealth) given the property rights in people, is less feasible. These considerations suggest that residual claimants – owners of the firm – will be investors of resalable capital equipment in the firm. The goods or inputs more likely to be invested, than rented, by the owners of the enterprise, will have higher resale values relative to the initial cost and will have longer expected use in a firm relative to the economic life of the good.

But beyond these factors are those developed above to explain the existence of the institution known as the firm – the costs of detecting output performance. When a durable resource is used it will have a marginal product and a depreciation. Its use requires payment to cover at least use-induced depreciation; unless that user cost is specifically detectable, payment for it will be demanded in accord with *expected* depreciation. And we can ascertain circumstances for each. An indestructible hammer with a readily detectable marginal product has zero user cost. But suppose the hammer were destructible and that careless (which is easier than careful) use is more abusive and causes greater depreciation of the hammer. Suppose in addition the abuse is easier to detect by observing the way it is used than by observing only the hammer after its use, or by measuring the output scored from a hammer by a laborer. If the hammer were rented and used in the absence of the owner, the depreciation would be greater than if the use were observed by the owner and the user charged in accord with the imposed depreciation. (Careless use is more likely than careful use – if one does not pay for the greater depreciation.) An absentee owner would therefore ask for a higher rental price because of the higher *expected* user cost than if the item were used by the owner. The expectation is higher because of the greater difficulty of observing specific user cost, by inspection of the hammer after use. Renting is therefore in this case more costly than owner use. This is the valid content of the misleading expressions about ownership being more economical than renting – ignoring all other factors that may work in the opposite direction, like tax provision, short-term occupancy and capital risk avoidance.

Better examples are tools of the trade. Watch repairers, engineers, and carpenters tend to own their own tools especially if they are portable. Trucks are more likely to be employee owned rather than other equally expensive team inputs because it is relatively cheap for the driver to police the care taken in using a truck. Policing the use of trucks by a nondriver owner is more likely to occur for trucks that are not specialized to one driver, like public transit busses.

The factor with which we are concerned here is one related to the costs of monitoring not only the gross product performance of an input but also the abuse or depreciation inflicted on the input in the course of its use. If depreciation or user cost is more cheaply detected when the owner can see its use than by only seeing the input before and after, there is a force toward owner use rather than renting. Resources whose user cost is harder to detect when used by someone else, tend on this count to be owner-used. Absentee ownership, in the lay language, will be less likely. Assume momentarily that labor service cannot be performed in the absence of its owner. The labor owner can more cheaply monitor any abuse of himself than if somehow labor-services could be provided without the labor owner observing its mode of use or knowing what was happening. Also his incentive to abuse himself is increased if he does not own himself.[16]

The similarity between the preceding analysis and the question of absentee landlordism and of sharecropping arrangements is no accident. The same fac-

[16] Professional athletes in baseball, football, and basketball, where athletes have sold their source of service to the team owners upon entering into sports activity, are owned by team owners. Here the team owners must monitor the athletes' physical condition and behavior to protect the team owners' wealth. The athlete has *less* (not, *no*) incentive to protect or enhance his athletic prowess since capital value changes have less impact on his own wealth and more on the team owners. Thus, some athletes sign up for big initial bonuses (representing present capital value of future services). Future salaries are lower by the annuity value of the prepaid "bonus" and hence the athlete has *less* to lose by subsequent abuse of his athletic prowess. Any decline in his subsequent service value would in part be borne by the team owner who owns the players' future service. This does not say these losses of future salaries have no effect on preservation of athletic talent (we are not making a "sunk cost" error). Instead, we assert that the preservation is reduced, not eliminated, because the amount of loss of wealth suffered is smaller. The athlete will spend less to maintain or enhance his prowess thereafter. The effect of this revised incentive system is evidenced in comparisons of the kinds of attention and care imposed on the athletes at the "expense of the team owner" in the case where athletes' future services are owned by the team owner with that where future labor service values are owned by the athlete himself. Why athletes' future athletic services are owned by the team owners rather than being hired is a question we should be able to answer. One presumption is cartelization and monopsony gains to team owners. Another is exactly the theory being expounded in this paper – costs of monitoring production of athletes; we know not on which to rely.

tors which explain the contractual arrangements known as a firm help to explain the incidence of tenancy, labor hiring or sharecropping.[17]

VII. Firms as a specialized market institution for collecting, collating, and selling input information

The firm serves as a highly specialized surrogate market. Any person contemplating a joint-input activity must search and detect the qualities of available joint inputs. He could contact an employment agency, but that agency in a small town would have little advantage over a large firm with many inputs. The employer, by virtue of monitoring many inputs, acquires special superior information about their productive talents. This aids his *directive* (i.e., market hiring) efficiency. He "sells" his information to employee-inputs as he aids them in ascertaining good input combinations for team activity. Those who work as employees or who rent services to him are using him to discern superior combinations of inputs. Not only does the director-employer "decide" what each input will produce, he also estimates which heterogeneous inputs will work together jointly more efficiently, and he does this in the context of a privately owned market for forming teams. The department store is a firm and is a superior private market. People who shop and work in one town can as well shop and work in a privately owned firm.

This marketing function is obscured in the theoretical literature by the assumption of homogeneous factors. Or it is tacitly left for individuals to do themselves via personal market search, much as if a person had to search without benefit of specialist retailers. Whether or not the firm arose because of this efficient information service, it gives the director-employer more knowledge about the productive talents of the team's inputs, and a basis for superior decisions about efficient or profitable combinations of those heterogeneous resources.

In other words, opportunities for profitable team production by inputs already within the firm may be ascertained more economically and accurately than for resources outside the firm. Superior combinations of inputs can be more economically identified and formed from resources already used in the organization than by obtaining new resources (and knowledge of them) from the outside. Promotion and revision of employee assignments (contracts) will be preferred by a firm to the hiring of new inputs. To the extent that this occurs there is reason to expect the firm to be able to operate as a conglomerate rather than persist in producing a single product. Efficient production

---

[17] The analysis used by Cheung (1969) in explaining the prevalence of sharecropping and land tenancy arrangements is built squarely on the same factors – the costs of detecting output performance of jointly used inputs in team production and the costs of detecting user costs imposed on the various inputs if owner used or if rented.

with heterogeneous resources is a result not of having *better* resources but in *knowing more accurately* the relative productive performances of those resources. Poorer resources can be paid less in accord with their inferiority; greater accuracy of knowledge of the potential and actual productive actions of inputs rather than having high productivity resources makes a firm (or an assignment of inputs) profitable.[18]

VIII. Summary

While ordinary contracts facilitate efficient specialization according to comparative advantage, a special class of contracts among a group of joint inputs to a team production process is commonly used for team production. Instead of multilateral contracts among all the joint inputs owners, a central common party to a set of bilateral contracts facilitates efficient organization of the joint inputs in team production. The terms of the contracts form the basis of the entity called the firm – especially appropriate for organizing team production processes.

Team productive activity is that in which a union, or joint use, of inputs yields a larger output than the sum of the products of the separately used inputs. This team production requires – like all other production processes – an assessment of marginal productivities if efficient production is to be achieved. Nonseparability of the products of several differently owned joint inputs raises the cost of assessing the marginal productivities of those resources or services of each input owner. Monitoring or metering the productivities to match marginal productivities to costs of inputs and thereby to reduce shirking can be achieved more economically (than by across market bilateral negotiations among inputs) in a firm.

The essence of the classical firm is identified here as a contractual structure with: (1) joint input production; (2) several input owners; (3) one party who

[18] According to our interpretation, the firm is a specialized surrogate for a market for team use of inputs; it provides superior (i.e., cheaper) collection and collation of knowledge about heterogeneous resources. The greater the set of inputs about which knowledge of performance is being collated within a firm the greater are the present costs of the collation activity. Then, the larger the firm (market) the greater the attenuation of monitor control. To counter this force, the firm will be divisionalized in ways that economize on those costs – just as will the market be specialized. So far as we can ascertain, other theories of the reasons for firms have no such implications.

In Japan, employees by custom work nearly their entire lives with one firm, and the firm agrees to that expectation. Firms will tend to be large and conglomerate to enable a broader scope of input revision. Each firm is, in effect, a small economy engaging in "intranational and international" trade. Analogously, Americans expect to spend their whole lives in the United States, and the bigger the country, in terms of variety of resources, the easier it is to adjust to changing tastes and circumstances. Japan, with its lifetime employees, should be characterized more by large, conglomerate firms. Presumably, at some size of the firm, specialized knowledge about inputs becomes as expensive to transmit across divisions of the firms as it does across markets to other firms.

is common to all the contracts of the joint inputs; (4) who has rights to renegotiate any input's contract independently of contracts with other input owners; (5) who holds the residual claim; and (6) who has the right to sell his central contractual residual status. The central agent is called the firm's owner and the employer. No authoritarian control is involved; the arrangement is simply a contractual structure subject to continuous renegotiation with the central agent. The contractual structure arises as a means of enhancing efficient organization of team production. In particular, the ability to detect shirking among owners of jointly used inputs in team production is enhanced (detection costs are reduced) by this arrangement and the discipline (by revision of contracts) of input owners is made more economic.

Testable implications are suggested by the analysis of different types of organizations – nonprofit, proprietary for profit, unions, cooperatives, partnerships, and by the kinds of inputs that tend to be owned by the firm in contrast to those employed by the firm.

We conclude with a highly conjectural but possibly significant interpretation. As a consequence of the flow of information to the central party (employer), the firm takes on the characteristic of an efficient market in that information about the productive characteristics of a large set of specific inputs is now more cheaply available. Better recombinations or new uses of resources can be more efficiently ascertained than by the conventional search through the general market. In this sense inputs compete with each other within and via a firm rather than solely across markets as conventionally conceived. Emphasis on interfirm competition obscures intrafirm competition among inputs. Conceiving competition as the *revelation and exchange* of knowledge or information about qualities, potential uses of different inputs in different potential applications indicates that the firm is a device for enhancing competition among sets of input resources as well as a device for more efficiently rewarding the inputs. In contrast to markets and cities which can be viewed as publicly or nonowned market places, the firm can be considered a privately owned market; if so, we could consider the firm and the ordinary market as competing types of markets, competition between private proprietary markets and public or communal markets. Could it be that the market suffers from the defects of communal property rights in organizing and influencing uses of valuable resources?

CHAPTER 10

Understanding the employment relation: the analysis of idiosyncratic exchange

OLIVER WILLIAMSON, MICHAEL WACHTER, and
JEFFREY HARRIS

Oliver Williamson was born in Superior, Wisconsin in 1932. He received the Ph.D. in economics at Carnegie-Mellon University in 1963. When this paper was published, he was Professor of Economics, Law, and Public Policy at the University of Pennsylvania. He is currently Gordon Tweedy Professor of Economics of Law and Organization at Yale University.

Michael Wachter was born in 1943 in New York City. He received the Ph.D. from Harvard University in 1970. When this paper was published, he was Associate Professor of Economics at the University of Pennsylvania, where he is currently Professor of Economics, Law and Management and Director of the Institute for Law and Economics.

Jeffrey Harris was born in 1948. He earned an M.D. and a Ph.D. in economics from the University of Pennsylvania in 1974 and 1975, respectively. At the time of publication of this paper, he was Resident in Medicine at Massachusetts General Hospital. He is currently Associate Professor of Economics at the Massachusetts Institute of Technology.

. . .

2. Background

A brief review of the literature. The internal labor market literature has its roots in the industrial relations – labor economics literature of the 1950s and early 1960s. The important contributions in this area include the work of Dunlop, Kerr, Livernash, Meij, Raimon, and Ross.[1] This work, which is descriptively oriented, has since been developed and extended by Doeringer and Piore.[2]

Reprinted with abridgements from Oliver Williamson, Michael Wachter, and Jeffrey Harris, "Understanding the Employment Relation: The Analysis of Idiosyncratic Exchange," *The Bell Journal of Economics,* 6 (1975): 250–78. Copyright 1975. Reprinted with permission of the Rand Corporation. (A variant of this paper also appears as Chapter 4 of Williamson's *Markets and Hierarchies: Analysis and Antitrust Implications.* New York: The Free Press, 1975.)

[1] See Dunlop (1957, 1958), Kerr (1954), Livernash (1957), Meij (1963), Raimon (1953), and Ross (1958).

[2] Although acknowledging some of the efficiency aspects of the internal labor market, Doeringer and Piore also stress nonneoclassical attributes. Subsequent work in this tradition moves even further away from an efficiency orientation. Harrison (1972), Piore (1973), Thurow (1971),

The distinction between structured and structureless labor markets is especially notable. Whereas spot market contracting characterizes the latter (as Kerr puts it, the "only nexus is cash"),[3] structured markets are ones for which a large number of institutional restraints have developed. Outside access to jobs in structured markets is limited to specific "ports of entry" into the firm, these generally being lower level appointments. Higher level jobs within the firm are filled by the promotion or transfer of employees who have previously secured entry. Training for these jobs involves the acquisition of task-specific and firm-specific skills, occurs in an on-the-job context, and often involves a team element. The internal due process rules which develop in these internal markets "are thought to effectuate standards of equity that a competitive market cannot or does not respect."[4]

Though coming from a somewhat more theoretical tradition, the study of human capital represents a second and related approach to labor market analysis. It likewise makes the distinction between specific and general training. Incumbent employees who have received specific training become valuable resources to the firm. Turnover is costly, since a similarly qualified but inexperienced employee would have to acquire the requisite task-specific skills before he would reach a level of productivity equivalent to that of an incumbent. A premium is accordingly offered to specifically trained employees to discourage turnover, although in principle a long-term contract would suffice.[5]

The present analysis is both similar to and different from both of these traditions. It relies extensively on the institutional literature for the purpose of identifying the structural elements associated with internal labor markets. Also, our interpretation of the institutional restraints that have developed in such markets is consonant with much of this literature. What distinguishes our treatment from prior institutional discussions is that it is more microanalytic, in that it expressly identifies and evaluates alternative contracting modes, and it employs the proposed organizational failures framework apparatus throughout.

Like Becker, we are much concerned with the organizational implications of task-specific training. But whereas he finds that long-term contracts are vitiated because the courts regard them as a form of involuntary servitude[6]; we emphasize that the transaction costs of writing, negotiating, and enforcing such contracts are prohibitive.[7]

---

and Wachtel and Betsy (1972) have pushed this nonneoclassical interpretation to the point that efficiency considerations become, at most, a minor theme and at times disappear altogether in the study of collective organization.

[3] Kerr (1959) p. 95. [4] Doeringer and Piore (1971) p. 29. [5] See Becker (1962) pp. 10–25.
[6] See Becker (1962) p. 23.
[7] Becker hints at this in his remark that "any enforceable contract could at best specify the hours required on a job, not the quality of performance" (1962) p. 24. But rather than develop

Technology. It is widely felt that technology has an important, if not fully determinative, influence on the employment relationship. We agree, but take exception with the usual view in several respects. First, we argue that indivisibilities (of the usual kinds) are neither necessary nor sufficient for market contracting to be supplanted by internal organization. Second, we contend that nonseparabilities at most explain small group organization. Third, and most important, we find that the leading reason why an internal labor market supplants spot contracting is because of small numbers exchange relations.

Conventional treatments – indivisibilities

Indivisibilities of both physical capital and informational types are said to lead to the substitution of internal for market organization. The former involves scale economies associated with physical assets and is reasonably familiar. Larger scale units, provided they are utilized at design capacity, permit lower average costs to be realized. The group may thus be formed so as to assure that utilization demands will be sufficient.

Somewhat less familiar are the indivisibilities associated with information. Radner observes in this connection that "the acquisition of information often involves a 'set up cost'; i.e., the resources needed to obtain the information may be independent of the scale of the production process in which the information is used."[8] Consequently, groups may also be formed so as to economize on information costs.

That there are economies of either of these types to be realized, however, does not clearly imply, as a technological imperative, collective organization. Thus, technologically speaking, there is nothing that prevents one individual from procuring the physical asset in requisite size to realize the economies in question and contracting to supply the services of this asset to all of the members of the group. Similarly, there is no technological bar that prevents one individual from assuming the information gathering and dissemination function. All parties, suppliers of the specialized services and users alike, could be independent, yet scale economies of both types could be fully realized. If, therefore, such specialization fails to materialize, it is not because monopoly ownership of the physical assets and information services in question is impeded in technological respects. Rather, the problems are to be traced to transactional difficulties that predictably attend market exchange in these circumstances. Accordingly, the incentive to collectivize activities for which indi-

---

this line of analysis, and address the underlying transactional factors that explain such a condition, he merely notes that workers could always secure a release from long term contracts by "sabotaging" operations (p. 24). The implications for collective organization are nowhere addressed.

[8] Radner (1970) p. 457.

visibilities are large in relation to the market is ultimately of a transactional kind.

Conventional treatments – nonseparabilities

Alchian and Demsetz[9] contend that normal sales relationships are supplanted by an employment relation on account of nonseparabilities. The standard example is the manual loading of freight into a truck by two men, both of whom must work coordinately to lift the cargo in question. The inability to impute marginal products to each man on the basis of observed output is what, in Alchian and Demsetz' scheme of things, warrants hierarchical organization. A "boss" is introduced who monitors the work of both, thereby checking malingering and yielding a larger team output.

We agree, but make two further points. First, it is not the nonseparability by itself that occasions the problem. Rather it is this in conjunction with what we shall refer to below as "opportunism" and a condition of "information impactedness" that poses the difficulties. Absent these transactional considerations, the purported metering problems associated with nonseparability vanish. Second, and more important, we contend that most tasks are separable in the sense that – provided that successive stages of production are in balance – it is possible to sever the connection between stages by introducing buffer inventories.

Consider Adam Smith's pin-making example.[10] Pin manufacture involved a series of technologically distant operations (wire straightening, cutting, pointing, grinding, etc.). In principle, each of these activities could be performed by an independent specialist and work passed from station to station by contract. Autonomous contracting would be facilitated, moreover, by introducing buffer inventories at each station, since coordination requirements and hence contractual complexity would thereby be reduced. Each worker could then proceed at his own pace, subject only to the condition that he maintain his buffer inventory at some minimum level. A series of independent entrepreneurs rather than a group of employees, each subject to an authority relation, could thus perform the tasks in question.

Transaction costs militate against such an organization of tasks, however. For one thing, it may be possible to economize on buffer inventories by designating someone to act as a coordinator,[11] which entails, albeit in limited degree, a shift toward hierarchy. But more germane to our purposes here are the economies attributable to the structure of internal labor markets – provided that the jobs in question are idiosyncratic in nontrivial degree. The ways

---

[9] Alchian and Demsetz (1972).   [10] Smith (1937) p. 457.

[11] For a discussion of some of the ways in which buffer inventory savings can be realized, see Williamson (1964a) pp. 1454–5.

138

in which the structured bargaining features of internal labor markets permit such economies to be realized are developed below. We nevertheless take this opportunity to emphasize that small numbers exchange relations *evolve* much more frequently than is usually acknowledged, and that the prospect of costly haggling among autonomous agents is a consequence. The interesting institutional design question that is thereby posed is how can such haggling be attenuated? Examining the structural bargaining attributes of alternative contracting modes is plainly relevant in this connection.

Small numbers – general

Arrow illustrates the problem of small numbers exchange with the lighthouse example. Indivisibility is no problem, since the light can be either on or off. He furthermore abstracts from uncertainty, by assuming that the lighthouse keeper knows exactly when each ship will need its services, and assumes that exclusion is possible since only one ship will be within lighthouse range at any one time. A trading problem nevertheless arises, because "there would be only one buyer and one seller and no competitive forces to drive the two of them into competitive equilibrium."[12] As will be evident, this condition, together with the stipulation that the firm is confronted with changing internal and market circumstances, is what we mainly rely on to explain the employment relation.

Small numbers – task idiosyncracies

Doeringer and Piore describe idiosyncratic tasks in the following way[13]:

Almost every job involves some specific skills. Even the simplest custodial tasks are facilitated by familiarity with the physical environment specific to the workplace in which they being performed. The apparently routine operation of standard machines can be importantly aided by familiarity with the particular piece of operating equipment. . . . In some cases workers are able to anticipate trouble and diagnose its source by subtle changes in the sound or smell of the equipment. Moreover, performance in some production or managerial jobs involves a team element, and a critical skill is the ability to operate effectively with the given members of the team. This ability is dependent upon the interaction skills of the personalities of the members, and the individual's work "skills" are specific in the sense that skills necessary to work on one team are never quite the same as those required on another.

Hayek describes the consequences of idiosyncracy as follows[14]:

[12] Arrow (1969) p. 58.   [13] Doeringer & Piore (1971) pp. 15–16.
[14] Hayek (1945) pp. 521–2.

. . . practically every individual has some advantage over all others in that he possesses unique information of which beneficial use might be made, but of which use can be made only if the decisions depending on it are left to him or are made with his active cooperation. We need to remember only how much we have to learn in any occupation after we have completed our theoretical training, how big a part of our working life we spend learning particular jobs, and how valuable an asset in all walks of life is knowledge of people, of local conditions, and special circumstances.

More generally, task idiosyncrasies can arise in at least four ways: (1) equipment idiosyncrasies, due to incompletely standardized, albeit common, equipment, the unique characteristics of which become known through experience; (2) process idiosyncrasies, which are fashioned or "adopted" by the worker and his associates in specific operating contexts; (3) informal team accommodations, attributable to mutual adaptation among parties engaged in recurrent contact but which are upset, to the possible detriment of group performance, when the membership is altered; and (4) communication idiosyncrasies with respect to information channels and codes that are of value only within the firm. Given that "technology is [partly] unwritten and that part of the specificity derives from improvements which the work force itself introduces, workers are in a position to perfect their monopoly over the knowledge of the technology should there be an incentive to do so."[15]

Training for idiosyncratic jobs ordinarily takes place in an on-the-job context. Classroom training is unsuitable both because the *uniqueness* attributes associated with particular operations, machines, the work group, and, more generally, the atmosphere of the workplace may be impossible to replicate in the classroom, and because job incumbents, who are in possession of the requisite skills and knowledge with which the new recruit or candidate must become familiar, may be unable to describe, demonstrate, or otherwise impart this information except in an operational context.[16] Teaching by doing thus facilitates the learning by doing process. Where such uniqueness and teaching attributes are at all important, specific exposure in the workplace at some stage becomes essential. Outsiders who lack specific experience can thus achieve parity with insiders only by being hired and incurring the necessary start up costs.

The success of on-the-job training is plainly conditional on the information disclosure attitudes of incumbent employees. Both individually and as a group, incumbents are in possession of a valuable resource (knowledge) and can be expected to reveal it fully and candidly only in exchange for value. The way the employment relation is structured turns out to be important in this connection. The danger is that incumbent employees will hoard information to their personal advantage and engage in a series of bilateral monopolistic exchanges

---

[15] Doeringer and Piore (1971) p. 84.   [16] See Doeringer and Piore (1971) p. 20.

with the management – to the detriment of both the firm and other employees as well.

An additional feature of these tasks not described above but nevertheless important to an understanding of the contractual problems associated with the employment relation is that the activity in question is subject to periodic disturbance by environmental changes.[17] Shifts in demand due to changes in the prices of complements or substitutes or to changes in consumer incomes or tastes occur; relative factor price changes appear; and technological changes of both product design and production technique types take place. Successive adaptations to changes of each of these kinds are typically needed if efficient production performance is to be realized. In addition, life cycle changes in the work force occur which occasion turnover, upgrading, and continuous training. The tasks in question are thus to be regarded in moving equilibrium terms. Put differently, they are not tasks for which a once-for-all adaptation by workers is sufficient, thereafter to remain unchanged.

4. Individualistic bargaining models

Four types of individualistic contracting modes can be distinguished.[18] (1) contract now for the specific performance of x in the future; (2) contract now for the delivery of x_i contingent on event e_i obtaining in the future; (3) wait until the future materializes and contract for the appropriate (specific) x at the time; and (4) contract now for the right to select a specific x from within an admissible set X, the determination of the particular x to be deferred until the future. Simon's study of the employment relation[19] treats contracts of the first type, which he characterizes as sales contracts, as the main alternative to the

[17] Omitted from the discussion of the framework in this paper is a systems related condition referred to as "atmosphere." Failure to include atmosphere does not imply that we think it unimportant. But the concept is somewhat difficult to explicate in what is already a rather long paper.

[18] Lest the ensuing discussion of autonomous bargaining modes be thought to be contrived and/or unnecessary, since "everyone knows" such bargaining modes are inapposite, we make the following observations. First, though it is widely recognized that complex contingent claims contracting is infeasible (e.g., Radner notes that the Arrow–Debreu contracting model "requires that the economic agents possess capabilities of imagination and calculation that exceed reality by many orders of magnitude" (1970), p. 457), the reasons for this are rarely fully spelled out – either in general or, even less, with respect to labor market contracting. We attempt to rectify this condition in Section 4 below. Second, as our discussion of Alchian and Demsetz below reveals, it is plainly not the case that everyone appreciates that idiosyncratic tasks need to be distinguished from tasks in general and that sequential spot contracting is singularly unsuited for jobs of the idiosyncratic kind. Third, so as to correct the widely held belief that the authority relation represents a well defined alternative to "normal" market contracting (as recently illustrated by Arrow's (1974, pp. 25, 63–64) reliance on Simon's treatment of the authority relation), we think it important that the ambiguities of the authority relation be exposed.

[19] Simon (1957) pp. 183–195.

so-called authority relation (type 4). This, however, is unfortunate because type 1 contracts, being rigid, are singularly unsuited to permit adaptation in response to changing internal and market circumstances. By contrast, contingent claims contracts (type 2) and sequential spot sales contract (type 3) both permit adaptation. If complexity/uncertainty is held to be a central feature of the environment with which we are concerned, which it is, the deck is plainly stacked against contracts of type 1 from the outset. Accordingly, type 1 contracts will hereafter be disregarded.

Contingent claims contracts. Suppose that the efficient choice of x on each date depends on how the future unfolds. Suppose furthermore that the parties are instructed to negotiate a once-for-all labor contract in which the obligations of both employer and employee are fully stipulated at the outset. A complex contingent claims contract would then presumably result. The employer would agree to pay a particular wage now in return for which the employee agrees to deliver stipulated future services of a contingent kind, the particular services being dependent upon the circumstances which eventuate.

Contracting problems of several kinds can be anticipated. First, can the complex contract be written? Second, even if it can, is a meaningful agreement between the parties feasible? Third, can such agreements be implemented in a low cost fashion? The issues posed can all usefully be considered in the context of the framework sketched out above.

The feasibility of writing complex contingent claims contracts reduces fundamentally to a bounded rationality issue. The discussion by Feldman and Kanter of complex decision trees is instructive in this connection[20]:

For even moderately complex problems . . . the entire decision trees cannot be generated. There are several reasons why this is so: one is the size of the tree. The number of alternative paths in complex decision problems if very large. . . . A second reason is that in most decision situations, unlike chess, neither the alternative paths nor a rule for generating them is available. . . . A third reason is the problem of estimating consequences. . . . For many problems, consequences of alternatives are difficult, if not impossible to estimate. The comprehensive decision model is not feasible for most interesting decision problems.

Plainly, the complex labor agreements needed to describe the idiosyncratic tasks in question are of this kind. Not only are changing market circumstances (product demand, rivalry, factor prices, technological conditions, and the like) impossibly complex to enumerate, but the appropriate adaptations thereto cannot be established with any degree of confidence *ex ante*. Changing life cycle conditions with respect to the internal labor force compound the complexities.

The enumeration problems referred to are acknowledged by Meade in his

---

[20] Feldman and Kanter (1965) p. 615.

discussion of contingent claims contracts: "When environmental uncertainties are so numerous that they cannot all be considered . . . or, what comes perhaps to much the same thing, when any particular environmental risks are so hard to define and to distinguish from each other that it is impossible to base a firm betting or insurance contract upon the occurrence or nonoccurrence of any of them, then for this reason alone it is impossible to have a system of contingency . . . markets."[21] But for bounded rationality, Meade's concerns with excessive numbers, undefinable risks, and indistinguishable events would vanish.

But suppose, *arguendo,* that exhaustive complex contracts could be written at reasonable expense. Would such contracts be acceptable to the parties? We submit that a problem of incomprehensibility will frequently arise and impede reaching agreement. At least one of the parties, probably the worker, will be unable meaningfully to assess the implications of the complex agreement to which he is being asked to accede. Sequential contracting, in which experience permits the implications of various contingent commitments to be better understood, is thus apt to be favored instead.

Assume, however, that *ex ante* understanding poses no bar to contracting. *Ex post* enforcement issues then need to be addressed. First, there is the problem of declaring what state of the world has obtained. Meade's remarks that contingent claims contracts are infeasible in circumstances where it is impossible, on the contract execution date, "to decide precisely enough for the purposes of a firm legal contract" what state of the world has eventuated bear on this.[22] While it is easy to agree with Meade's contentions, we think it noteworthy to observe that, were it not for opportunism and information impactedness, the impediments to contracting to which he refers vanish. Absent these conditions, the responsibility for declaring what state of the world had obtained could simply be assigned to the "best informed" party. Once he has made the determination, the appropriate choice of x is found by consulting the contract. Execution then follows directly.

It is hazardous, however, to permit the best informed party unilaterally to make state of the world declarations where opportunism can be anticipated. If the worker is not indifferent between supplying services of type x_j rather than x_k, and if the declaration of the state of the world were to be left to him, he will be inclined, when circumstances permit, to represent the state of the world in terms most favorable to him. Similar problems are to be expected for those events for which the employer is thought to be the best informed party and unilaterally declares, from among a plausible set, which e_i has eventuated.[23] Moreover, mediation by a third party is no answer since, by as-

---

[21] Meade (1971) p. 183.   [22] Meade (1971) p. 183.

[23] The issue here is somewhat more subtle, however. The employer, when he assumes the role of the best informed party, will not wish to declare a false state of the world *unless*, at the time

sumption, an information impactedness condition prevails with respect to the observations in question.

Finally, even were it that state of the world issues could be settled conclusively at low cost, there is still the problem of execution. Did the worker really supply x_i in response to condition e_i, as he should, or did he (opportunistically) supply x_j instead? If the latter, how does the employer show this in a way that entitles him to a remedy? These are likewise information impactedness issues. Problems akin to moral hazard are posed.

Ordinarily, bounded rationality renders the description of once-for-all contingent claims employment contracts strictly infeasible. Occasions to examine the negotiability and enforcement properties of such contracts thus rarely develop. It is sufficient for our purposes here, however, merely to establish that problems of any of these kinds impair contingent claims contracting. In consideration of these difficulties, alternatives to the once-for-all supply relation ought presumably to be examined.

Sequential spot contracts. Alchian and Demsetz take the position that it is delusion to characterize the relation between employer and employee by reference to fiat, authority, or the like. Rather, it is their contention that the relation between an employer and his employee is identical to that which exists between a shopper and his grocer in fiat and authority respects[24]:

> The single consumer can assign his grocer to the task of obtaining whatever the customer can induce the grocer to provide at a price acceptable to both parties. That is precisely all that an employer can do to an employee. To speak of managing, directing, or assigning workers to various tasks is a deceptive way of noting that the employer continually is involved in renegotiation of contracts on terms that must be acceptable to both parties. . . . Long term contracts between employer and employee are not the essence of the organization we call a firm.

Implicit in their argument, we take it, is an assumption that the transition costs associated with employee turnover are negligible. Employers, therefore, are able easily to adapt to changing market circumstances by filling jobs on a spot market basis. Although job incumbents may continue to hold jobs for a considerable period of time, and may claim to be subject to an authority relationship, all that they are essentially doing is continuously meeting bids for

he got the worker to agree to a wage w, he represented to the worker that services of type x_i would be called for when event e_i obtained when in fact x_i' services, which the worker dislikes, yield a greater e_i gain. The worker, being assured that he would be called on to perform x_i' services only when the unlikely event e_i' occurred, agreed to a lower wage than he would have if he realized that an x_i' response would be called for in both e_i and e_i' situations – because the employer will falsely declare e_i to be e_i' so as to get x_i' performed.

[24] Alchian & Demsetz (1972) p. 777.

their jobs in the spot market. This is option number three, among the contracting alternatives described at the beginning of this section, done repeatedly.

That adaptive, sequential decisionmaking can be effectively implemented in sequential spot labor markets which satisfy the low transition cost assumption (as some apparently do, e.g., migrant farm labor),[25] without posing issues that differ in kind from the usual grocer-customer relationship, seems uncontestable. We submit, however, that many jobs do not satisfy this assumption. In particular, the tasks of interest here are not of this primitive variety. Where tasks are idiosyncratic, in nontrivial degree, the worker–employer relationship is no longer contractually equivalent to the usual grocer-customer relationship and the feasibility of sequential spot market contracting breaks down.

Whereas the problems of contingent claims contracts were attributed to bounded rationality and opportunism conditions, sequential spot contracts are principally impaired only by the latter. (Bounded rationality poses a less severe problem because no effort is made to describe the complex decision tree from the outset. Instead, adaptations to uncertainty are devised as events unfold.) Wherein does opportunism arise and how is sequential spot contracting impaired?

Recall from the discussion of opportunism in Section 3 that opportunism poses a contractual problem only to the extent that it appears in a small numbers bargaining context. Otherwise, large numbers bidding effectively checks opportunistic inclinations and competitive outcomes result. The problem with the tasks in question is that while large numbers bidding conditions obtain at the outset, before jobs are first assigned and the work begun, the idiosyncratic nature of the work experience effectively destroys parity at the contract renewal interval. Incumbents who enjoy nontrivial advantages over similarly qualified but inexperienced bidders are well situated to demand some fraction of the cost savings which their idiosyncratic experience has generated.

One possible adaptation is for employers to avoid idiosyncratic technologies and techniques in favor of more well-standardized operations. Although least-cost production technologies are sacrificed in the process, pecuniary gains may nevertheless result since incumbents realize little strategic advantage over otherwise qualified but inexperienced outsiders. Structuring the initial bidding in such a way as to permit the least-cost technology and techniques to be employed without risking untoward contract renewal outcomes is, however, plainly to be preferred. Two possibilities warrant consideration: (1) extract a promise from each willing bidder at the outset that he will not use his idiosyncratic knowledge and experience in a monopolistic way at the contract renewal interval; or (2) require incumbents to capitalize the prospective monop-

---

[25] See Doeringer and Piore (171) pp. 4–5; also Kerr (1954) p. 95.

oly gains that each will accrue and extract corresponding lump-sum payments from winning bidders at the outset.

The first of these can be dismissed as utopian. It assumes that promises not to behave opportunistically are either self-enforcing or can be enforced in the courts. Self-enforcement is tantamount to denying that human agents are prone to be opportunists, and fails for want of reality testing. Enforcement of such promises by the courts is likewise unrealistic. Neither case by case litigation nor simple rule-making disposition of the issues is feasible. Litigation on the merits of each case is prohibitively costly, while rules to the effect that "all workers shall receive only competitive wages" fail because courts cannot, for information impactedness reasons, determine whether workers put their energies and inventiveness into the job in a way which permits task-specific cost savings to be fully realized – in which case disaffected workers can counter such rules by withholding effort.

The distinction between consummate and perfunctory cooperation is important in this connection. Consummate cooperation is an affirmative job attitude – to include the use of judgment, filling gaps, and taking initiative in an instrumental way.[26] Perfunctory cooperation, by contrast, involves job performance of a minimally acceptable sort. Incumbents, who through experience have acquired task-specific skills, need merely to maintain a slight margin over the best available inexperienced candidate (whose job attitude, of necessity, is an unknown quantity). The upshot is that workers, by shifting to a perfunctory performance mode, are in a position to "destroy" idiosyncratic efficiency gains. Reliance on preemployment promises as a means by which to deny workers from participating in such gains is accordingly self-defeating.

Consider therefore the second alternative in which, though worker participation in realized cost savings is assumed to be normal, workers are required to submit lump-sum bids for jobs at the outset. Assuming that large numbers of applicants are qualified to bid for these jobs at the outset, will such a scheme permit employers fully to appropriate the expected, discounted value of future cost savings by awarding the job to whichever worker offers to make the highest lump-sum payment?

---

[26] Consummate cooperation involves working in a fully functional, undistorted mode. Efforts are not purposefully withheld; neither is behavior of a knowingly inapt kind undertaken. Blau and Scott are plainly concerned with the difference between perfunctory and consummate cooperation in the following passage (1962, p. 140):

the contract obligates employees to perform only a set of duties in accordance with minimum standards and does not assure their striving to achieve optimum performance. . . . [L]egal authority does not and cannot command the employee's willingness to devote his ingenuity and energy to performing his tasks to the best of his ability. . . . It promotes compliance with directives and discipline, but does not encourage employees to exert effort, to accept responsibilities, or to exercise initiative.

Such a contracting scheme amounts to long-term contracting in which many of the details of the agreement are left unspecified. As might be anticipated, numerous problems are posed. For one thing, it assumes that workers are capable of assessing complex future circumstances in a sophisticated way and of making a determination of what the prospective gains are. Plainly, a serious bounded rationality issue is raised. Second, even if workers had the competence to complete such an exercise, it is seriously to be doubted that they could raise the funds, if their personal assets were deficient, to make the implied full valuation bids. As Malmgren has observed, in a somewhat different but nevertheless related context, "some [individuals] will see opportunities, but be unable to communicate their own information and expectations favorably to bankers, and thus be unable to acquire finance, or need to pay a higher charge for the capital borrowed."[27] The communication difficulties referred to are due to language limitations (attributable to bounded rationality) that the parties experience. That bankers are unwilling to accept the representations of loan-seekers at face value is because of the risks of opportunism.

Third, and crucially, the magnitude of the estimated future gains to be realized by workers often depends not merely on exogenous events and/or activities that each worker fully controls but also on the posture of coworkers and the posture of the employer. Problems with coworkers arise if, despite steady state task separability, the consent or active cooperation of workers who interface with the task in question must be secured each time an adaptation is proposed. This effectively means that related sets of workers must enter bids as teams, which complicates the bidding scheme greatly and offers opportunities for free riding. Problems also arise if gains cannot be realized independently of the decisions taken by management with respect, for example, to the organization of production, complementary new asset acquisitions, equipment repair policy, etc. Lump sum bidding is plainly hazardous where workers are entering bids on life cycle earnings streams that are repeatedly exposed to rebargaining.[28]

Finally, but surely of negligible importance in relation to the issues already raised, there is the question of efficient risk bearing: which party is best situated to bear the risks of future uncertainties, individual workers or the firm? That individual workers may be poorly suited to bear such risks and, as a

---

[27] Malmgren (1961) p. 46.

[28] There is the related problem of comparing the bids of workers who have different age, health, and other characteristics. Possibly this could be handled by stipulating that winners have claims to jobs in perpetuity, so that a job can be put up for rebidding by the estate of a worker who dies or retires. Such rebidding, however, is hazardous if the new worker must secure anew the cooperation of his colleagues. Established workers are then in a position strategically to appropriate some of the gains. (This assumes that coalition asymmetries exist which favor old workers in relation to the new.)

group, can pool risks only with difficulty, seems evident and further argues against the bidding scheme proposed.

Transactional difficulties thus beset both contingent claims and sequential spot market contracting for the idiosyncratic tasks of interest in this chapter. Consider therefore the so-called authority relation as the solution to the contracting problems in question.

The authority relation. Simon has made one of the few attempts to assess the employment relation formally. Letting B designate the employer (or boss), W be the employee (or worker), and x be an element in the set of possible behavior patterns of W, he defines an authority relation as follows[29]:

We will say that B exercises *authority* over W if W permits B to select x. That is, W accepts authority when his behavior is determined by B's decision. In general, W will accept authority only if x_o, the x chosen by B, is restricted to some subset (W's "area of acceptance") of all the possible values.

An employment contract is then said to exist whenever W agrees to accept the authority of B in return for which B agrees to pay W a stated wage.[30]

Simon then asks when will such an employment relationship be preferred to a sales contract, and offers the following two conjectures[31]:

(1) W will be willing to enter into an employment contract with B only if it does not matter to him "very much" which x (within the agreed upon area of acceptance) B will choose, or if W is compensated in some way for the possibility that B will choose x that is not desired by W (i.e., that B will ask W to perform an unpleasant task).

(2) It will be advantageous to B to offer W added compensation for entering into an employment contract if B is unable to predict with certainty, at the time the contract is made, which x will be the optimum one, from his standpoint. That is, B will pay for the privilege of postponing, until some time after the contract is made, the selection of x.

He then goes on to develop a formal model in which he demonstrates that the employment contract commonly has attractive properties, under conditions of uncertainty, *provided that the alternatives are* (1) the promise of a particular x in exchange for a given wage w (what he considers to be the sales contract option), or (2) a set of X from which a particular x will subsequently be chosen in exchange for a given wage w' (the employment contract option).

Put differently, the deterministic sales contract is shown to be inferior to an incompletely specified employment relation in which W and B do not agree on all terms *ex ante,* but "agree to agree later" – or better, "agree to tell and be told." But plainly the terms are rigged from the outset. As noted previ-

---

[29] Simon (1957) p. 184.   [30] See Simon (1957) p. 184.   [31] Simon (1957) p. 185.

ously, the particular type of sales contract to which Simon refers in attempting to establish the rationale for an authority relation is the only one of the three types of sales contracts described at the beginning of this section that lacks for adaptability in response to changing market circumstances. Since employment contracts of both the contingent claim and sequential spot marketing kinds are not similarly flawed, a better test of the authority relation would be to compare it with either of these instead.

Simon's modeling apparatus, unfortunately, does not lend itself to such purposes. It is simply silent with respect to the efficiency properties of alternative contracts in which adaptability is featured. Not only is it unable to discriminate between the authority relation, contingent claims contract, and spot market contracting in adaptability respects, but Simon's model fails to raise transaction cost issues of the types described here.

This is not, however, to suggest that the authority relation had nothing to commend it. To the contrary, such a relation does not require that the complex decision tree be generated in advance, and thus does not pose the severe bounded rationality problems to which the contingent claims contracting model is subject. The authority relation also, presumably, reduces the frequency with which contracts must be negotiated in comparison with the sequential spot contracting mode. Adaptations in the small can be costlessly accomplished under an authority relation because such changes, to the worker, do not matter ''very much.''

Assuming, however, that the parties are prospectively joined in a long-term association and the jobs in question are of the idiosyncratic kind, most of the problems of sequential spot contracting still need to be faced. Thus how are wage and related terms of employment to be adjusted through time in response to either small, but cumulative, or large, discrete changes in the data? What happens when hitherto unforeseen and unforeseeable contingencies eventuate? How are differences between the parties regarding state of the world determinations, the definition of the task, and job performance to be reconciled? Substantially all of the problems that are posed by idiosyncratic tasks in the sequential spot contracting mode appear, we submit, under the authority relation as well.

5. The efficiency implications of internal labor market structures

The upshot is that none of the above contracting schemes has acceptable properties for tasks of the idiosyncratic variety. Contingent claims contracting[32] fails principally on account of bounded rationality. Spot marketing contracting[33]

---

[32] See Meade (1971) Chapter 10.   [33] See Alchian and Demsetz (1972) p. 777.

is impaired by first mover advantages and problems of opportunism. The authority relation[34] is excessively vague and, ultimately, is confronted with the same types of problems as is spot market contracting. Faced with this result, the question of alternative contracting schemes naturally arises. Can more effective schemes be designed? Do more efficient contracting modes exist?

Our analysis here is restricted to the latter of these questions, which we answer in the affirmative. Although we do not contend that the internal labor market structures which we describe are optimally efficient with respect to idiosyncratic tasks, we think it significant that their efficiency properties have been little noted or understated by predominantly nonneoclassical interpretations of these markets in the past.

Our assessment of the efficiency implications of internal labor market structures is in three parts. The occasion for and purposes of collective organization are sketched first. The salient structural attributes of internal labor markets are then described and the efficiency implications of each, expressed in terms of the language of the organizational failures framework, are indicated. Several caveats follow.

Collective organization. To observe that the pursuit of perceived individual interests can sometimes lead to defective collective outcomes is scarcely novel. Schelling has treated the issue extensively in the context of the "ecology of micromotives."[35] The individual in each of his examples is both small in relation to the system – and thus his behavior, by itself, has no decisive influence on the system – and is unable to appropriate the collective gains that would obtain were he voluntarily to forego individual self-interest seeking. Schelling then observes that the remedy involves collective action. An enforceable social contract which imposes a cooperative solution on the system is needed.[36]

Although it is common to think of collective action as state action, this is plainly too narrow. As Arrow and Schelling[37] emphasize, both private collective action (of which the firm, with its hierarchical controls, is an example) and norms of socialization are also devices for realizing cooperative solutions. The internal labor market, we contend, is usefully interpreted in this same spirit.

Thus, although it is in the interest of each worker, bargaining individually or as a part of a small team, to acquire and exploit monopoly positions, it is plainly not in the interest of the *system* that employees should behave in this way. Opportunistic bargaining not only itself absorbs real resources, but efficient adaptations will be delayed and possibly foregone altogether. What

[34] See Simon (1957) pp. 183–95.   [35] Schelling (1971).   [36] See Schelling (1971) p. 69.
[37] See Arrow (1969) p. 62 and Schelling (1971) p. 69.

this suggests, accordingly, is that the employment relation be transformed in such a way that systems concerns are made more fully to prevail and the following objectives are realized: (1) bargaining costs are made lower, (2) the internal wage structure is rationalized in terms of objective task characteristics, (3) consummate rather than perfunctory cooperation is encouraged, and (4) investments of idiosyncratic types, which constitute a potential source of monopoly, are undertaken without risk of exploitation. For the reasons and in the ways developed below, internal labor markets can have, and some do have, the requisite properties to satisfy this prescription.[38]

Structural attributes and their efficiency consequences

Wage bargaining. A leading difficulty with individual contracting schemes where jobs are idiosyncratic is that workers are strategically situated to bargain opportunistically. The internal labor market achieves a fundamental transformation by shifting to a system where wage rates attach mainly to jobs rather than to workers. Not only is individual wage bargaining thereby discouraged, but it may even be legally foreclosed.[39] Once wages are expressly removed from individual bargaining, there is really no occasion for the worker to haggle over the incremental gains that are realized when adaptations of degree are proposed by the management. The incentives to behave opportunistically, which infect individual bargaining schemes, are correspondingly attenuated.

Moreover, not only are affirmative incentives lacking, but there are disincentives, of group disciplinary and promotion ladder types, which augur against resistance to authority on matters that come within the range customarily covered by the authority relation.[40] Promotion ladder issues are taken up in conjunction with the discussion of ports of entry below; consider, therefore, group disciplinary effects.

Barnard observes in this connection[41]:

---

[38] Commons' discussion with Sidney Hillman concerning the transformation of membership attitudes among the Amalgamated Clothing Workers illustrates some of the systems attributes of collective agreements (1970, p. 130):

Ten years after World War I, I asked Sidney Hillman . . . why his members were less revolutionary than they had been when I knew them twenty-five years before in the sweatshop. . . . Hillman replied, "They know now that they are citizens of the industry. They know that they must make the corporation a success on account of their own jobs." They were citizens because they had an arbitration system which gave them security against arbitrary foremen. They had an unemployment system by agreement with the firm which gave them security of earnings. This is an illustration of the meaning of part-whole relations.

[39] See Summers (1969) pp. 538, 573.

[40] Authority relation is used here in the *qualified* short-run sense suggested in our discussion of Simon in Section 4 above.

[41] Barnard (1962) p. 169.

151

Since the efficiency of organization is affected by the degree to which individuals assent to orders, denying the authority of an organization communication is a threat to the interests of all individuals who derive a net advantage from their connection with the organization, unless the orders are unacceptable to them also. Accordingly, at any given time there is among most of the contributors an active personal interest in the maintenance of the authority of all orders which to them are within the zone of indifference. The maintenance of this interest is largely a function of informal organization.

The application of group pressures thus combines with promotional incentives to facilitate adaptations in the small.[42] Even individuals who have exhausted their promotional prospects can thereby be induced to comply. System interests are made more fully to prevail. This concern with viability possibly explains the position taken in labor law that those orders which are ambiguous with respect to, and perhaps even exceed, the scope of authority, are to be fulfilled first and disputed later.[43]

Contractual incompleteness/arbitration. Internal labor market agreements are commonly reached through collective bargaining. Cox observes in this connection that the collective bargaining agreement should be understood as an instrument of government as well as an instrument of exchange: "the collective agreement governs complex, many-sided relations between large numbers of people in a going concern for very substantial periods of time."[44] Provision for unforeseeable contingencies is made by writing the contract in general and flexible terms and supplying the parties with a special arbitration machinery: "One simply cannot spell out every detail of life in an industrial establishment, or even of that portion which both management and labor agree is a matter of mutual concern."[45] Such contractual incompleteness is an implicit concession to bounded rationality. Rather than attempt to anticipate all bridges that might conceivably be faced, which is impossibly ambitious and excessively costly, bridges are crossed as they appear.

But however attractive adaptive, sequential decision making is in bounded rationality respects, admitting gaps into the contract also poses hazards: where parties are not indifferent with respect to the manner in which gaps are to be filled, fractious bargaining or litigation commonly results. It is for the purpose of forestalling worst outcomes of this kind that the special arbitration apparatus is devised.

[42] Of course informal organization does not operate exclusively in the context of a collectivized wage bargain. Autonomous bargainers, however, are ordinarily expected to behave in autonomous ways. The extent to which group powers serve as a check on challenges to authority is accordingly much weaker where the individual bargaining mode prevails (see March and Simon, 1958, pp. 59, 66). By contrast, the individual in the collectivized system who refuses to accede to orders on matters that fall within the customarily defined zone of acceptance is apt to be regarded as cantankerous or malevolent, since there is no private pecuniary gain to be appropriated, and will be ostracized by his peers.

[43] See Summers (1969) pp. 538, 573.   [44] Cox (1958) p. 22.   [45] Cox (1958) p. 23.

Important differences between commercial and labor arbitration are to be noted in this connection. For one thing, "the commercial arbitrator finds facts – did the cloth meet the sample – while the labor arbitrator necessarily pours meaning into the general phrases and interstices of a document."[46] In addition, the idiosyncratic practices of the firm and its employees also constitute "shop law" and, to the labor arbitrator, are essential background for purposes of understanding a collective agreement and interpreting its intent.[47]

In the language of Section 3, the creation of such a special arbitration apparatus serves to overcome information impactedness, in that the arbitrator is able to explore the facts in greater depth and with greater sensitivity to idiosyncratic attributes of the enterprise than could judicial proceedings. Furthermore, once it becomes recognized that the arbitrator is able to apprise himself of the facts in a discerning and low cost way, opportunistic misrepresentations of the data are discouraged as well.

Grievances. Also of interest in relation to the above is the matter of who is entitled to activate the arbitration machinery when an individual dispute arises. Cox takes the position that[48]

> . . . giving the union control over all claims arising under the collective agreement comports so much better with the functional nature of a collective bargaining agreement. . . . Allowing an individual to carry a claim to arbitration whenever he is dissatisfied with the adjustment worked out by the company and the union . . . discourages the kind of day-to-day cooperation between company and union which is normally the mark of sound industrial relations – a relationship in which grievances are treated as problems to be solved and contracts are only guideposts in a dynamic human relationship. When . . . the individual's claim endangers group interests, the union's function is to resolve the competition by reaching an accommodation or striking a balance.

The practice described by Cox of giving the union control over arbitration claims plainly permits group interests, whence concern for system viability, to supersede individual interests, thereby curbing small numbers opportunism.

---

[46] Cox (1958) p.. 23.   [47] Cox (1958) p. 24.

[48] Cox (1958) p. 24. We are informed that this practice is changing and offer three comments in this regard. First, institutional change does not always promote efficiency outcomes; backward steps will sometimes occur – possibly because the efficiency implications are not understood. Second, relegating control to the union as to whether a grievance is to be submitted to arbitration can sometimes lead to capricious results. Disfavored workers can be unfairly disadvantaged by those who control the union decision-making machinery. Some form of appeal may therefore be a necessary corrective. Third, that workers are given rights to bring grievances on their own motion does not imply that this will happen frequently. Grievances that fail to secure the support of peers are unlikely to be brought unless they represent egregious conditions on which the grievant feels confidently he will prevail. The bringing of trivial grievances not only elicits the resentment of peers but impairs the grievant's standing when more serious matters are posed.

Internal promotion/ports of entry. Acceding to authority on matters that fall within the zone of acceptance[49] merely requires that the employee respond in a minimally acceptable, even perfunctory way. This may be sufficient for tasks that are reasonably well structured. In such circumstances, the zeal with which an instruction to "do this" or "do that" is discharged may have little effect on the outcome. As indicated, however, consummate cooperation is valued for the tasks of interest here. But how is cooperation of this more extensive sort to be realized?

A simple answer is to reward cooperative behavior by awarding incentive payments on a transaction-specific basis. The employment relation would then revert to a series of haggling encounters over the nature of the *quid pro quo*, however, and would hardly be distinguishable from a sequential spot contract. Moreover, such payments would plainly violate the nonindividualistic wage bargaining attributes of internal labor markets described above.

The internal promotion practices in internal labor markets are of special interest in this connection. Access to higher level positions on internal promotion ladders is not open to all comers on an unrestricted basis. Rather, as part of the internal incentive system, higher level positions (of the prescribed kinds)[50] are filled by promotion from within whenever this is feasible. This practice, particularly if it is followed by other enterprises to which the worker might otherwise turn for upgrading opportunities, ties the interests of the worker to the firm in a continuing way.[51] Given these ties, the worker looks to internal promotion as the principal means of improving his position.[52]

The practice of restricting entry to lower level jobs and promoting from within has interesting experience-rating implications. It permits firms to protect themselves against low productivity types, who might otherwise successfully represent themselves to be high productivity applicants, by bringing employees in at low level positions and then upgrading them as experience warrants.[53] Furthermore, employees who may have been incorrectly upgraded

[49] The zone of acceptance is discussed in the quotation from Barnard in Section 5 above.

[50] For a discussion, see Doeringer and Piore (1971) pp. 42–47.

[51] Since access to idiosyncratic types of jobs is limited by requiring new employees to accept a lower job at the bottom of promotion ladders, individuals can usually not shift laterally between firms without cost: "employees in nonentry jobs in one enterprise often have access only to entry-level jobs in other enterprises. The latter will often pay less than those which the employees currently hold" (Doeringer and Piore (1971) p. 78).

[52] Assuming that unit costs are equalized across rival enterprises (as a condition of competitive viability), the internal wage structure will be everywhere lower, including port of entry wages, if straight seniority is adopted.

[53] For a more general discussion of the special powers of internal organization in auditing and experience rating respects, see Williamson (1975). The treatment in the text is keyed to an efficiency interpretation of the Doeringer and Piore (1971) discussion of ports of entry limitation.

but later have been "found out," and hence barred from additional internal promotions, are unable to move to a new organization without penalty.[54] Were unpenalized lateral moves possible, workers might, considering the problems of accurately transmitting productivity valuations between firms, be able to disguise their true productivity attributes from new employers sufficiently long to achieve additional promotions. Restricting access to low level positions serves to protect the firm against exploitation by opportunistic types who would, if they could, change jobs strategically for the purpose of compounding errors between successive independent organizations.

Were it, however, that markets could equally well perform these experience-rating functions, the port of entry restrictions described would be unnecessary. The (comparative) limitations of markets in experience-rating respects accordingly warrant attention. The principal impediment to effective interfirm experience-rating is one of communication.[55] By comparison with the firm, markets lack a rich and common rating language. The language problem is particularly severe where the judgments to be made are highly subjective. The advantages of hierarchy in these circumstances are especially great if those who are the most familiar with an agent's characteristics, usually his immediate supervisor, also do the experience rating. The need to rationalize subjective assessments that are confidently held but, by reason of bounded rationality, difficult to articulate is reduced. Put differently, interfirm experience-rating is impeded in information impactedness respects.

Reliance on internal promotion has affirmative incentive properties in that workers can anticipate that differential talent and degrees of cooperativeness will be rewarded. Consequently, although the attachment of wages to jobs rather than to individuals may result in an imperfect correspondence between wages and marginal productivity at ports of entry, productivity differentials will be recognized over time and a more perfect correspondence can be expected for higher level assignments in the internal labor market job hierarchy.

. . .

[54] Agents seeking transfer may have gotten ahead in an organization by error. Experiencing rating, after all, is a statistical inference process and is vulnerable to "Type II" error. When a mistake has been discovered and additional promotions are not forthcoming, the agent might seek transfer in the hope that he can successfully disguise his true characteristics in the new organization and thereby secure further promotions. Alternatively, the agent may have been promoted correctly, but changed his work attitudes subsequently – in which case further promotion is denied. Again, he might seek transfer in the hope of securing additional promotion in an organization that, because of the difficulty of interfirm communication about agent characteristics, is less able to ascertain his true characteristics initially.

[55] Interfirm experience rating may also suffer in veracity respects, since firms may choose deliberately to mislead rivals. The major impediment, however, is one of communication.

CHAPTER 11

Individual mobility and union voice in the labor market

RICHARD FREEMAN

Richard Freeman was born in 1945 in Newburgh, New York. He received the Ph.D. in economics at Harvard University in 1969. When this paper was published, he was a member of the Department of Economics at Harvard University, where he is currently Professor.

Standard economic analysis of the impact of trade unions on the labor market is straightforward: unions are monopolistic organizations that raise wages and create inefficiency in resource allocation. Industrial relations experts tell a more complex story, stressing the diverse effect of unions on work rules, managerial decision making, and "virtually every aspect" of the activity of enterprises. To what extent do the non-wage effects of collective bargaining make the monopoly model incomplete or misleading? Do unions perform economically significant functions beyond altering wage rates?

This paper examines the non-wage effects of trade unions in the context of the "exit-voice" model of the social system developed by Albert O. Hirschman (1970). Unions are treated as the institution of collective voice in the job market; voluntary quits as the expression of exit. Comparisons are made between the free market quit and union voice mechanisms for transmitting worker desires for conditions of employment, compensation packages, and rules of the work place to employers; some empirical implications of the analysis are drawn and preliminary empirical findings described.

I. Employment relations and conditions of work

What makes the exit-voice framework a potentially fruitful way of looking at trade unions are "the peculiarities of the employment contract . . . which distinguish it from other kinds of contracts." (Herbert Simon, 1957) In a world of uncertainty, imperfect information, and transactions costs, employment involves an authority relation in which workers sell "labor power" to enterprises for extended periods of time. As Ronald Coase puts it, "the contract is one whereby the factor (labor) for a certain remuneration . . . agrees

Reprinted from "Individual Mobility and Union Voice in the Labor Market," *The American Economic Review (Papers and Proceedings)*, 66 (1976): 361–8, by permission of the editors.

to obey the directions of an entrepreneur *with certain limits"* (Coase, 1952). Because of on-the-job skills specific to enterprises (a learning curve phenomenon) and the cost of mobility and turnover, there are gains to be had from regular employment, a continuing relation between firms and much of their work force, in which allocative and remunerative decisions are not directly determined by the price mechanism.[1] Because workers care about nonpecuniary conditions of employment and rules of the work place, and because different conditions, rules, and methods of organization have different costs, the labor contract tends to be complex and multidimensional, involving numerous issues beyond wages, including the "social relations of production." (John R. Hicks, 1973, p. 317) Because workers have some control over their own activities and can affect the productivity of others, particularly in "team" settings where monitoring of individuals is expensive, their attitudes or morale are potentially important inputs into the production process.

The complex, multidimensional and continuing nature of the employment relation creates a substantial information problem in the job market (Oliver Williamson, Michael Wachter, and J. Harris, 1975). Within firms, prices convey only crude information about preferences and costs. In the external market, workers and employers must appraise diverse conditions, rules, and compensation packages across enterprises. Over time technological changes continually alter the structure of the work place and jobs while changes in real income lead workers to demand new conditions of employment and methods of compensation. Firms or organizations have continual need for information from workers not only as Hirschman stresses because of decline or decay but because of changes in opportunities and efficient modes of behavior.

From the perspective of the exit-voice framework information about conditions and preferences can be provided by: free market "exit," consisting of quits and related behavior and/or by "voice" consisting of the collective bargaining system by which workers elect union leaders to represent them in bargaining. Each mechanism has certain strengths and weaknesses, which must enter any welfare economics calculation. Each is, from the perspective of positive economics, likely to produce different market outcomes in the various aspects of the labor contract.

II. Quits as an information system

Worker control of their own effort in work places creates several forms of "exit-behavior": quitting, rejecting a job offer; absenteeism, the partial withdrawal of labor time; reduction of work effort in the form of malingering and slack or in extreme cases "quiet sabotage." Strikes, which involve temporary

---

[1] Because I focus on the situation with regular work relations, the analysis is not directly applicable to the case of craftsmen who change jobs regularly.

collective exit, are best viewed as a tool of voice since they involve expression of demands by union or union-like group organizations.

Employers can learn about worker preferences and the causes of discontent from individual quits either inferentially by linking different levels of exit to different or changing characteristics of the employment relation in what amounts to hedonic price type calculations or through direct questioning, "exit interviews," of those who quit or make related decisions.

The amount of information provided by either channel is, unfortunately, likely to be small relative to the costs of processing the data. Inferring reasons for discontent from "abnormally" high quits requires specification of underlying multidimensional characteristics of work places; a reasonably large sample; and sufficient variation in conditions or in changes in conditions to permit the assignment of causality. Inferences about the preferences of workers who quit may, because of "selectivity bias," yield incorrect information about average evaluations or the evaluations of future potential quitters. The wider the variation in tastes among workers due to differences in preferences and position in the work place (especially seniority) and the greater the different modes of expressing exit (the young quit, while older employees choose less drastic actions), the more difficult will the inferential process be. If all persons had the same tastes, introspection by managers or foremen would yield answers at no cost.

Exit interviews run into a different difficulty – that of motivating the worker who leaves to detail work place problems. There is no gain to quitters from providing management with desired information about dissatisfaction, and there are possible losses via bad references – retaliation for conveying bad news. As a result, the leading personnel management text reports that "it is extremely difficult to get reliable information by means of exit interviews" (C. Meyers and P. Pigors, 1973, p. 222). The information content in other forms of exit behavior will be even smaller. A worker guilty of absenteeism for reasons of discontent with work relations will hide the reasons for fear of being fired, while malingering or quiet sabotage are by their nature covert activities.

Finally, whatever information the quit mechanism provides about current conditions of work, it provides much less about changes in conditions and, more importantly, about the trade-offs workers are willing to make in wages or other conditions for desired improvements; especially when the changes involve more than marginal adjustments in the work place. Innovations in the labor contract can be appraised only by potentially costly trial and error experimentation: changing conditions or compensation and observing outcomes.

Despite the high noise to signal ratio in labor market quits, the mechanism has desirable properties. Quit behavior depends solely on individual free market "marginal decisions" and does not require collective organizations like unions. Such behavior has well-known efficiency properties. Over time, some employers will extract the signal from the noise in quits or by trial and error find the "optimal" labor contract and come to dominate production or be imitated by competitors.

Certain features of the quit mechanism suggest, however, that there may be some divergence from optimum for extended periods of time. Since workers who leave an enterprise do not benefit from the improvement in conditions that may result, the extent of quitting to convey information may be suboptimal. That is when quits are effective in altering work conditions, the irreversibility of the decision provides too little incentive for workers to leave. Even if the level of *quitting* were optimal, however, the possibility that quitters differ in their evaluation of conditions from other workers (notably older or specifically trained persons who are unlikely to quit and whose position in the firm gives them a different set of interests) makes reliance on quits potentially misleading. Other forms of exit behavior must also be evaluated. In recessions or declining markets, moreover, quits will be ineffective as a mode of workers expressing preferences and obtaining desired changes.

Hirschman's analysis suggests other malfunctioning. Consider the situation in which all employers offer the same work conditions and where workers quit particular enterprises in the hope of attaining better conditions but in fact cannot do so. Each firm has a constant pool of applicants for jobs and a constant quit rate; no information is conveyed about what to change and there are no advantages in profitability. More generally, the same result would occur if the firms had different but similarly undesirable work conditions. Workers disliking bad condition A in firm A would move to firm B where they would find bad condition B and so forth. In this musical chairs equilibrium, quits are ineffective and excessive, at least until "random mutations" by enterprises produce a better wage-benefits-conditions package, so that quits differ substantially among employers. As a result there will be a long period of adjustment to equilibrium.

From the perspective of workers, the information flow is especially likely to be faulty with respect to aspects of jobs, ranging from treatment by supervisors and coworkers to actual (as opposed to nominal) work responsibilities to evaluations of hazard (W. Kip Viscusi, 1979) which cannot be calculated without actually accepting employment. Under the quit system, each worker, would, say, learn about the bad qualities of a job only after a trial period of work and quit. If all workers knew about the job, no one would apply (without larger compensating differentials), but the information each gains is lost.

The question is not, however, whether individual mobility *ultimately* provides enough information to attain something akin to the optimal labor contract in the long run but rather how it does relative to the alternative institutional mechanism of voice, to whose operation I turn next.

III. Collective voice by trade unionism

The institution of voice in the labor market is trade unionism and collective bargaining. There are several reasons why collective rather than individual activity is necessary for voice to be effective within firms. First, the authority relation makes it difficult for individuals to express discontent due to the danger of being fired – it is clearly easier to retaliate against a single worker than the entire work force. Even with unionization, however, some protection of voice is needed, particularly for activists, as is recognized in the Wagner Act, which makes it an unfair labor practice to fire or otherwise discriminate against persons for trade union activity. Second, the communal nature of work conditions and rules which apply to all workers in the establishment creates a public good problem of preference relation. Individuals cannot bargain over plant-wide conditions nor trade wages for fringes when there are sizeable set up costs. They will not have the incentive to reveal their preferences when the activity of others may produce the public goods at no cost to them. Elicitation of preferences and determination of acceptable bargaining packages are one of the major tasks of trade unions and critical components in the operation of successful collective bargaining systems. Third, because of the regularity of employment, there is a need to "police" or monitor contracts and thus for a collective agency specializing in information about the contract and in representation of workers. The úbiquity of grievance systems (found in 96 percent of contracts) or grievance and arbitration (93 percent) reflects the importance of contract interpretation in the operation of collective voice (U.S. Department of Labor, 1972).

The major advantages of unionization are that it provides: a direct channel of communication between workers and management; an alternative mode of expressing discontent than quitting, with consequent reductions in turnover costs and increases in specific training and work conditions; and social relations of production which can mitigate the problems associated with the authority relation in firms.

Union voice proffers very different information about workers' preferences than individual mobility – specific facts about areas of discontent and actual tradeoff possibilities (albeit masked by negotiating strategies). It creates an institutional mechanism for innovation in labor contracts and what may be termed a "new market" for labor contracts.[2] It focuses managerial attention and effort on labor issues on a regular basis, alerting firms to problems fairly continually rather than by sudden sharp outbursts of discontent. In large enterprises, union voice provides central management with information about

---

[2] Recent theoretical work on the existence of contingent claims markets and constrained transactions is thus relevant, surprising as this may be to the theorists, to analysis of the trade union institution. See Jerry Green and Eytan Sheshinski (1975).

local conditions and operations that is likely to differ greatly from that obtained from the organizational hierarchy.

By providing a mode of expressing discontent beyond exiting, direct information about worker desires and certain preferred work conditions that cannot be readily offered by nonunion establishments, union voice can be expected to reduce quit rates, absenteeism and related exit behavior. In the exit-voice model, there is *ceteris paribus,* a reasonably well-defined and economically significant trade-off between the two mechanisms. The reduction in quits will reduce labor turnover and training costs and increase firm-specific investments in human capital and possibly have efficiency gains.[3]

One desirable nonpecuniary condition of work, an industrial jurisprudence system with formal grievance, arbitration and related protection against managerial authority in establishments, may be "produced" only by unionization or some related mechanism. The essence of industrial jurisprudence is the dilution of the power of the foremen and other supervisors, which would presumably be difficult to attain in nonunion establishments where management has the "last word." Desire for such rules and procedures implies that union voice enters as a direct argument in utility functions (suggesting that in the absence of monopoly wage gains, workers would take lower pay for collective bargaining) and by affecting morale and the social relations in the firm, possibly in the production function as well.

On the negative side, the major disadvantage of union voice is that, as the standard monopoly model stresses, it creates monopoly power in the job market and wages above and employment below competitive levels. There are other costs to unionization as well: government, management, and workers invest considerable resources in bargaining which might have been spent on direct production; the productivity of the work force may be reduced by "featherbedding" (one possible exercise of monopoly power which would not show up in wages per se). Some work rules, like closed shops, may be "inequitable" to some workers; and more generally as a "political organization" unions may not reflect the desires of all members in a reasonable or "fair" manner.

Accepting the costs of collective bargaining the normative question is whether these costs exceed the benefits due to reduction in exit behavior, improved flow of information, and provision of protection against managerial authority. There is, in our analysis, a trade-off: by providing information and a mechanism for potentially complex bargaining among workers and between workers and management that is more efficient than quits, collective bargaining is likely to yield a better "mix" among wages, work conditions, rules of the

---

[3] Of course the reduction in quits could be too great with bad consequences for overall labor mobility.

work place and a reduction in turnover costs and increased firm specific human capital, at the expense of higher price of labor.

IV. Union voice and market outcomes

The fact that unions are ''political'' organizations whose activities depend on the preferences of workers as a group has important implications regarding the impact of collective bargaining.[4] Whereas quits reflect the desires of marginal workers, voice reflects the demands of some average of workers. If as a first approximation the median voter model is applied to union behavior, policy will be set by the median member (who is the marginal voter) with the consequence that greater weight will be placed on the preferences of relatively immobile workers (such as older workers and the specifically trained) than under the quit mechanism.[5] Trade unionism transforms the supply side of the job market by *making median (or some other average) rather than marginal preferences the ''determinant'' of the labor contract*. In the job market, individuals for whom there is a great gap between (pecuniary and nonpecuniary) wages in an establishment and opportunity wages are especially likely to exercise voice when work conditions change in an undesirable way. This contrasts with Hirschman's product market case in which those with higher consumer surplus are most likely to exit when quality of goods deteriorates.

The switch from a marginal to median (or other average) supply calculus might be expected to create inefficiencies since optimality criteria invariably require marginal first order conditions. Because of the union's role in facilitating information flows and coordinating worker preferences in bargaining, however, the situation is more complex. Bargaining among workers (which would not exist in the absence of unions) and potential worker demands for public or lumpy goods at the work place *could* offset inefficiency losses. Consider, for example, a situation in which management can choose one of two modes of organizing work, which, exclusive of their impact on workers, have equal profitability. Method A greatly reduces the well-being of immobile senior workers, while method B has no effect on them but displeases the mobile young slightly. In a market where information is conveyed by quits, the behavior of the young would lead management to choose method A, despite the loss of consumer ''surplus'' to older personnel. In a market with collective bargaining, the union might arbitrage the differences in prefer-

---

[4]While recognizing the political and organizational nature of unions, in this essay I neglect the effect of these factors on behavior, treating unions solely as an institution that conveys the desires of members. This omission will be rectified in future work.

[5]The median voter model is used as the simplest voting model. With many dimensions to contracts and groups within unions, it is obvious that a more complex game-theoretic model is needed to explain actual events.

ences, so that the firm will pick B, with a negotiated redistribution giving the young some compensatory benefit and the old a less onerous loss than under A. This scenario can be expanded, to take account of different frequencies of quitting under A and B with similar results. The greater the difference between the losses under the two modes, the greater is the possibility that a superior bargain could be struck through the voice mechanism. I do not claim that the union will, in fact, arbitrage worker preferences correctly for the behavior of the union will depend on its internal organization, organizational goals, and political power of the various groups which are neglected here. The possibility is, however, there.

A second situation in which average preferences may yield better outcomes occurs when desirable work conditions or fringe benefits involve substantial fixed costs. Marginal evaluation could, as is well-known, lead enterprises to reject provision of employment conditions which would pass a benefit–cost test.

Advantages or disadvantages of union voice aside, by providing a distinct market mechanism for imparting information, aggregating preferences, altering authority relations, and changing marginal to average evaluations, collective bargaining will yield outcomes that differ from those in competitive markets. I conclude by sketching briefly some of the empirical implications of the model and the evidence regarding them.

As noted earlier, unionization is expected to reduce quits and raise investments in firm specific training. Studies of interindustrial variation in quits have generally found a negative relation (John Pencavel (1970), John M. Burton and J. Parker (1969), Vladimir Stoikov and Robert Raimon (1968)), as does my preliminary analysis of the relation between unionization and quits using disaggregate data files, which provide a superior test, through the route of the linkage remains to be determined. At least one potential proxy for "specific training," years of tenure with an employer, is also positively affected by unionization (Freeman, forthcoming).

Reversing lines of causality, the exit-voice model suggests that when quitting is nonviable, workers may be more prone to unionization. This is roughly consistent with Alan Blinder's evidence that older workers and those with family responsibility are more likely to be union members; with *U.S.* trade union history, in which unionism has grown rapidly following major recessions or depressions; and with union activities in coal, lumber, and similar locales from which exit is costly. Other factors are obviously also important, however.

Trade unionism can be expected to increase the fringe benefits share of total compensation, both for information considerations (Richard Lester, 1967) and preference aggregation reasons. Analysis of data from individual establishments finds a significant positive relation (Freeman, forthcoming).

163

As a relatively permanent market institution, preserving information about work conditions that might otherwise be lost through individual quits, trade unions can also be expected to *increase* differentials for bad working conditions relative to the competitive market outcome, a result supported by Viscusi's analysis of compensating differentials for dangerous work.

Through the various nonwage effects outlined here, unions might be expected to alter the overall production process and worker productivity. James Medoff and C. Brown (1975) find, in fact, positive trade union productivity effects in cross-industry, cross state regressions, holding capital-labor and worker quality fixed.

Finally the model suggests that by directing attention to work place problems and encouraging expressions of discontent and by keeping dissatisfied workers from quitting, unions may *increase* job dissatisfaction, other factors (wages, conditions) held fixed. My preliminary investigation of job satisfaction in large data tapes finds such a relation.

If the unionization-satisfaction result stands up to more detailed analysis, it has significant implications for understanding the entire voice mechanism. It suggests that voice, of necessity, produces "dissatisfaction" by making individuals especially sensitive to and willing to criticize conditions. To be effective, voice cannot be silent, even when it may produce "the goods."

CHAPTER 12

Allocative efficiency and X-efficiency

HARVEY LEIBENSTEIN

Harvey Leibenstein was born in 1922. He received the Ph.D. in economics at Princeton University in 1951. When this paper was published, he was Professor of Economics at the University of California, Berkeley. Since 1967, he has been Andelot Professor of Economics and Population at Harvard University.

At the core of economics is the concept of efficiency. Microeconomic theory is concerned with allocative efficiency. Empirical evidence has been accumulating that suggests that the problem of allocative efficiency is trivial. Yet it is hard to escape the notion that efficiency in some broad sense is significant. In this paper I want to review the empirical evidence briefly and to consider some of the possible implications of the findings, especially as they relate to the theory of the firm and to the explanation of economic growth. The essence of the argument is that microeconomic theory focuses on allocative efficiency to the exclusion of other types of efficiencies that, in fact, are much more significant in many instances. Furthermore, improvement in "nonallocative efficiency" is an important aspect of the process of growth.

. . .

II. X-Efficiency: the empirical evidence

We have seen that the welfare loss due to allocational inefficiency is frequently no more than 1/10 of 1 per cent. Is it conceivable that the value of X-inefficiency would be larger than that? One way of looking at it is to return to the problem of the welfare loss due to monopoly. Suppose that one-third of the industries are in the monopolized sector. Is it possible that the lack of competitive pressure of operating in monopolized industries would lead to cost 3/10 of a per cent higher than would be the case under competition? This magnitude seems to be very small, and hence it certainly seems to be a possibility. The question essentially, is whether we can visualize managers bestirring themselves sufficiently, if the environment forced them to do so, in

Excerpted from Harvey Leibenstein, "Allocative Efficiency and X-Efficiency," *The American Economic Review*, 56 (1966): 392–415, by permission of the editors.

order to reduce costs by more than 3/10 of 1 per cent. Some of the empirical evidence available suggests that not only is this a possibility, but that the magnitudes involved are very much larger. As we shall see, the spotty evidence on this subject does not prove the case but it does seem to be sufficiently persuasive to suggest the possibility that X-efficiency exists, and that it frequently is much more significant than allocational efficiency.

Professor Eric Lundberg in his studies of Swedish industries points to the case of the steel plant at Horndal that was left to operate without any new capital investment of *technological change,* and furthermore maintenance and replacement were kept at a minimum, and yet output per man hour rose by 2 per cent per annum. Professor Lundberg asserts that according to his interviews with industrialists and technicians "sub-optimal disequilibrium in regard to technology and utilization of existing capital stock is a profoundly important aspect of the situation at any time." (This according to Gorin Ohlin's summary of Lundberg's findings, 1962). If a suboptimal disequilibrium exists at any time, then it would seem reasonable that under the proper motivations managers and workers could bestir themselves to produce closer to optimality, and that under other conditions they may be motivated to move farther away from optimality.

Frederick Harbison reports visiting two petroleum refineries in Egypt less than one-half mile apart. "The labor productivity of one had been nearly double that in the other for many years. But recently, under completely new management, the inefficient refinery was beginning to make quite spectacular improvements in efficiency with the same labor force" (1956, p. 373). We may inquire why the management was changed only recently whereas the difference in labor productivity existed for many years. It is quite possible that had the motivation existed in sufficient strength, this change could have taken place earlier.

In a recent book on the firm, Neil Chamberlain (1962, p. 341) visualizes his firms reacting to variances between forecasted revenues and expenditures and actual. He quotes from the president of a corporation: "Actual sales revenue for the fiscal year varied one per cent from the original forecast. Expenditures varied 30 per cent. The reasons were practically entirely due to manufacturing problems of inefficiency and quality. . . . The only actions specifically taken were in attempted changes in methods of production . . . [and] the use of an engineering consulting firm. . . ." One would have thought that the cost-reducing activities mentioned could be carried out irrespective of the variance. Nevertheless, the quotation clearly implies that, in fact, they would not have been motivated to attempt changes were it not that they were stimulated by the variance.

.   .   .

166

That changes in incentives will change productivity per man (and cost per unit of output) is demonstrated clearly by a wide variety of studies on the effects of introducing payments by results schemes. Davison, Florence, Gray, and Ross (1958, p. 203) review the literature in this area for British industry, survey the results for a number of manufacturing operations, and present illustrative examples of their findings from a number of firms. The summary of their findings follows: "The change in output per worker was found to vary among the different operations all the way from an increase of 7.5 per cent to one of 291 per cent, about half the cases falling between 43 per cent and 76 per cent. Such increases in output, most of them large, from our 'first-line' case histories, and from additional evidence, were found not to be just a 'flash in the pan' but were sustained over the whole period of study."

Roughly similar findings were obtained for the consequences of introducing payments by results in Australia, Belgium, India, the Netherlands, and the United States (ILO, 1956). In Victoria it was found that "soundly designed and properly operated incentive plans have in practice increased production rate in the reporting firms from 20 to 50 per cent." In the Netherlands labor efficiency increases of 36.5 per cent were reported. It seems clear that with the same type of equipment the working tempo varies considerably both between different workers and different departments. Appropriate incentives can obviously change such tempos considerably and reduce costs, without any changes in purchasable inputs per unit.

The now-famous Hawthorne Studies (Roethlisberger & Dickson, 1939) suggest that the mere fact that management shows a special interest in a certain group of workers can increase output. That is, management's greater interest in the group on whom the experiments were tried, both when working conditions were improved and when they were worsened, created a positive motivation among the workers. (The magnitudes were from 13 to 30 per cent, Landsberger, 1958). In one of the ILO missions to Pakistan an improvement in labor relations in a textile mill in Lyallpur resulted in a productivity increase of 30 per cent. Nothing else was changed except that labor turnover was reduced by one-fifth (ILO, July & August, 1958).

Individual variations in worker proficiency are probably larger than plant differences. Frequently the variation between the best to poorest worker is as much as four to one. Certainly improved worker selection could improve productivity at the plant level. To the extent that people are not working at what they are most proficient at, productivity should rise as a consequence of superior selection methods (Ghiselli & Brown, 1948).

Although there is a large literature on the importance of psychological factors on productivity, it is usually quite difficult to assess this literature because many psychologists work on the basis of high- and low-productivity groups

H. LEIBENSTEIN

but do not report the actual numerical differences. In general, it seems that some of the psychological factors studied in terms of small-group theory can account for differences in productivity of from 7 to 18 per cent. The discoveries include such findings as (1) up to a point smaller working units are more productive than larger ones; (2) working units made up of friends are more productive than those made up of nonfriends; (3) units that are generally supervised are more efficient than those that are closely supervised (Argyle, Gardner & Cioffi, 1958); and (4) units that are given more information about the importance of their work are more proficient than those given less information (Tomekovic, 1962). A partial reason for these observed differences is probably the likelihood that individual motivation towards work is differently affected under the different circumstances mentioned.

III. The residual and X-efficiency: an interpretation

The main burden of these findings is that X-inefficiency exists, and that improvement in X-efficiency is a significant source of increased output. In general, we may specify three elements as significant in determining what we have called X-efficiency: (1) intra-plant motivational efficiency, (2) external motivational efficiency, and (3) nonmarket input efficiency.

The simple fact is that neither individuals nor firms work as hard, nor do they search for information as effectively, as they could. The importance of motivation and its association with degree of effort and search arises because the relation between inputs and outputs is *not* a determinate one. There are four reasons why given inputs cannot be transformed into predetermined outputs: (a) contracts for labor are incomplete, (b) not all factors of production are marketed, (c) the production function is not completely specified or known, and (d) interdependence and uncertainty lead competing firms to cooperate tacitly with each other in some respects, and to imitate each other with respect to technique, to some degree.

The conventional theoretical assumption, although it is rarely stated, is that inputs have a fixed specification and yield a fixed performance. This ignores other likely possibilities. Inputs may have a fixed specification that yields a variable performance, or they may be of a variable specification and yield a variable performance. Some types of complex machinery may have fixed specifications, but their performance may be variable depending on the exact nature of their employment. The most common case is that of labor services of various kinds that have variable specifications and variable performance – although markets sometimes operate as if much of the labor of a given class has a fixed specification. Moreover, it is exceedingly rare for all elements of performance in a labor contract to be spelled out. A good deal is left to custom, authority, and whatever motivational techniques are available to management as well as to individual discretion and judgment.

Similarly, the production function is neither completely specified nor known. There is always an experimental element involved so that something may be known about the current state; say the existing relation between inputs and outputs, but not what will happen given changes in the input ratios. In addition, important inputs are frequently not marketed or, if they are traded, they are not equally accessible (or accessible on equal terms) to all potential buyers. This is especially true of management knowledge. In many areas of the world managers may not be available in well-organized markets. But even when they are available, their capacities may not be known. One of the important capacities of management may be the degree to which managers can obtain factors of production that in fact are not marketed in well-organized markets or on a universalistic basis. In underdeveloped countries the capacity to obtain finance may depend on family connections. Trustworthiness may be similarly determined. Some types of market information may be available to some individuals but not purchasable in the market. For these and other reasons it seems clear that it is one thing to purchase or hire inputs in a given combination; it is something else to get a predetermined output of them.

169

The prisoners' dilemma in the invisible hand: an analysis of intrafirm productivity

HARVEY LEIBENSTEIN

Harvey Leibenstein is Andelot Professor of Economics and Population at Harvard University. See also the previous paper by Leibenstein.

This paper attempts to show that it is useful to view productivity as a prisoners' dilemma problem, that conventions are alternative solutions to the prisoners' dilemma, that effort conventions are usually nonoptimal, and that a "shock" is necessary in order to shift from one nonoptimal solution to another. Within this framework the invisible hand does *not* produce a Pareto optimal result. It is consistent with any number of nonoptimal effort conventions.

1. Effort discretion and the game theory view of production

Under neoclassical assumptions decision units follow parametric maximization; they control all the variables, and they view other influences as parameters. Game theory takes a different view: no single decision unit controls all the variables; the outcome depends on decisions made by two or many parties. I argue that once we look at productivity from the viewpoint of X-efficiency theory postulates, effort discretion is implied, and productivity becomes a game theoretic problem. Two X-efficiency theory postulates concern us: incomplete firm membership contracts; and frequent nonoptimal "conventional" behavior. Employment contracts are incomplete since remuneration is usually well specified but effort is not. Agents (employees), in principal-agent relations, need not behave exactly as the principals wish. As a consequence some effort discretion exists. Hence, firm members can choose, within bounds, the amount of effort they put forth. The productivity outcome depends in part on effort choices made by firm members, and in part on the wage and work condition choices made by the firm. Note: I distinguish "firm decisions" from the decisions of firm members whether or not the latter are managers or other employees.

Reprinted from Harvey Leibenstein, "The Prisoners' Dilemma in the Invisible Hand: An Analysis of Intrafirm Productivity," *The American Economic Review (Papers and Proceedings)*, 72 (1982): 92–7, by permission of the editors.

I now turn to the basic behavioral postulate which relaxes the usual max-imization assumption. It can be seen in terms of a three-stage process. First, people behave in terms of habits or conventions. A convention is a routine that has an interpersonal component. Second, when pressure is increased, the individual shifts to a more calculating mode of behavior. Third, under a high degree of pressure, individuals are complete calculators, that is, maximizers. Related to conventional behavior is the assumption of inert areas; that is, the existence of upper and lower bounds within which behavior does not change. Thus, routine behavior continues unaltered unless some variable changes so that the value of this variable goes beyond the upper or lower bounds of the inert area. Essentially, we visualize a process whereby external variables change the amount of pressure on the individual so that the pressure goes beyond the inert area bounds, which in turn results in a new type of behavior – say a new convention or a shift to partial calculation. We will see that conventions play an essential role in determining the outcome of the prisoners' dilemma prob-lem.

Now consider an illustration which looks at productivity from a game the-ory viewpoint. Suppose all employees make the same effort choice, but they have two options: a "Golden Rule" effort option; and a maximizing private satisfaction option. Under the Golden Rule every employee acts in the best interest of the firm. He treats the firm as he would like the firm to treat him, and puts forth effort as if the enterprise was his own. The alternative option is at the other extreme: the individual works as little as possible in the firm's interest and does other things (on the job) to pursue his own private interests.

The firm has two similar symmetrical options. It could behave in a Golden Rule fashion in which it provides employees with the maximal conditions, salaries, and security, consistent with "sustainable profits"; it is as if the firm operates *almost* entirely in the interest of the employees. The other alternative is parametric maximization, which implies cost minimization. That is, the firm *attempts* to minimize working conditions and wages cost while trying to get the most effort from employees. In the payoff table (Table 1) the payoffs to each side are shown in the four corners of the table in terms of utilities of the two types of options. As illustrated the symmetrical choices give higher values for the mutual Golden Rule choice than to the individual maximizing choice.

Given the numbers in Table 1 we can readily see that it involves a pris-oners' dilemma situation. First, consider the choice problem from the firm's viewpoint. If employees operate according to the Golden Rule, then it cer-tainly pays for the firm to choose maximization. Similarly, if the firm assumes that employees are private maximizers, it also makes sense for the firm to choose maximization. A very similar argument can be made for employees. They also choose maximization under both cases of the choices by the firm.

TABLE 1

Employee Options	Firm Options		
	W_1 Golden Rule	W_2 Peer Group Standard	W_3 Indiv Maxi
π_1 Golden Rule	15 \ 15	17 \ 6	20 \ 3
π_2 Peer Group Standard	6 \ 17	10 \ 10	12 \ 4
π_3 Indiv Max.	3 \ 20	4 \ 12	5 \ 5

As a consequence, the joint choice is maximization. But this joint choice is clearly inferior to the cooperative choice of the dual Golden Rule. Thus, if each side attempts to behave "rationally" and maximize given the other's behavior, then the result is the prisoners' dilemma outcome.

Now consider the 3×3 payoff table reflecting a slightly more complicated productivity game. Two of the options are the same as before: the Golden Rule, and maximization. In between we indicate a "peer group standard" effort option. Under this option employees consider the average effort level in terms of pace, quality, and choice of activities, and perform (as a group) according to the established average. Individual effort levels are distributed more or less symmetrically around the average level. This average is a *convention* determined and supported by peer group pressures. I consider later how such conventions are formed. From the point of view of the firm, the same choices exist. In between the Golden Rule and maximization there is a third option under which the employer recognizes the existing peer group effort standard, and provides wages and working conditions in accordance with the average peer group effort.

In Table 1 the utilities associated with the various joint choices are shown. As the utilities are listed, we can readily see that what we have is a prisoners' dilemma situation. As in the 2×2 case, the choices made by the two parties will be those under parametric maximization, and, as a result, the prisoners' dilemma outcome occurs. However, by introducing the peer group standard, we add a new possibility. "Rational" choice still leads to the prisoners' dilemma outcome. In practice, however, the prisoners' dilemma outcome frequently does not occur; and a peer group standard frequently is chosen. Most of what follows is to explain why this should be the case.

We may view the three diagonal outcomes as the symmetrical cooperative choices. If these were the *only* alternatives, then obviously the choice made would be the joint Golden Rule. However, if we add the adversarial options, and since both sides can do better through adversarial behavior when the other does not choose an adversary position, then the joint adversarial choices dominate. Is productivity, in general, really a prisoners' dilemma problem? A basic criterion is that a prisoners' dilemma occurs wherever there are possibilities for adversarial behavior between the parties, and by all parties, which reduces the joint cooperative outcome. Now, it seems reasonable to presume that adversarial behavior between employees and the firm will usually decrease productivity, while cooperative behavior will increase it. This is certainly not the case in all types of games. But this is the case for the particular "game" set where productivity is the outcome.

II. Effort conventions as solutions

An alternative way of finding a solution to prisoners' dilemma problems is for an individual to behave in a not necessarily maximizing fashion: that is, to use conventions or convention-like elements such as ethics. It is important to distinguish (a) the rationale behind a convention, and (b) behavior given a convention. The rationale behind conventions has been developed by D. Lewis (1969), Edna Ullman-Margalit (1978), and reviewed by Andrew Schotter (1981). The basic idea is that conventions represent solutions to game theory coordination problems. Special interest is attached to those cases that involve multiple equilibria, and hence a multiplicity of possible conventions, any one of which, *including nonoptimal ones,* are better than none.

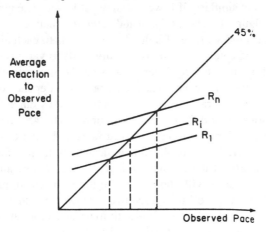

Figure 1

173

Let me give a few examples. Consider the choice on which side of the road to drive. Individuals should be indifferent whether everyone drives on the left, or on the right; but the payoffs for all individuals driving on the left, or the right, are the same. The payoffs are negative if one drives on the left and others drive on the right, or vice versa. Thus we have multiple solutions (everyone driving on the left or on the right). The choice of either convention is superior to none. Similarly, languages and writing systems are conventions. There is a multiplicity of possible connections between sounds and meanings. Hence many possible languages. Thus, the reason for a convention (say a specific language) lies in the fact that once the convention exists, dropping the convention may have a very high cost. Recall the biblical Tower of Babel story. Thus a writing or spelling system which is clearly nonoptimal may persist. Hence conventions are solutions to multiple equilibria problems. However, such latent equilibria need not all be equally good. It is only required that not having the convention (any equilibrium point) makes people worse off.

Once a convention exists people do not normally reappraise it; rather behavior becomes part of a *stimulus–response* mechanism. When the context (i.e., the stimulus) for the use of a convention arises, people employ the convention. Thus, people who know many languages will normally speak in the language of the community once they determine that it is appropriate for the context.

In the same spirit we can think of an effort convention as determined by a peer group standard. Entrants to the firm observe the average effort level, and set their own effort approximately at or fairly close to the observed average. If the observed level were higher, many would simply shift their own level to a higher level, and similarly if it were somewhat lower. The general notion is illustrated in Figure 1. The abscissa indicates alternative pace levels. The ordinate indicates the average of individual reactions to each alternative. The reaction curves indicate the reactions of individuals to various observed rates and is denoted by the letter R_i. There is a large set of possible reactions to a given observed rate; and, hence, each reaction curve depends on some initial (or historical) observed rate, so that the reaction curves range from R_1 to R_n. Different histories yield different reaction curves. The 45° line indicates the set of possible equilibria between observed rates and reactions to them. The distance between R_1, R_n on the 45° line indicates all the possible equilibrium effort levels. Clearly, if the convention is R_1, it need not be an optimal solution, but once chosen it will continue to be the solution in question. In the illustration I choose "pace" to signify effort. However, other components of effort, such as the quality levels of the activities carried out are implicit in the example. The main point is that individual reactions to the observed *components* of effort determine the equilibrium effort *convention*.

174

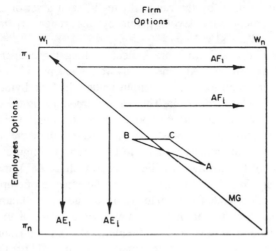

Figure 2

An effort convention need not depend only on the peer group standard. It is also possible that some type of work ethic, or the Japanese consensus system, creates conventions which are superior to some or all possible peer group standards. Thus there may exist a wide range of alternative latent solutions along the cooperative diagonal. (See Figure 2.)

Note especially that an effort convention solves (i.e., avoids) the prisoners' dilemma.[1] The convention is clearly superior to permitting the latent prisoners' dilemma solution to assert itself. Thus, what may appear as an inferior convention to other alternatives will turn out to be stable. If that convention were not supported, the result (the latent prisoners' dilemma outcome) could be worse.[2]

III. The continuous model

Let us now consider a model which generalizes the 3×3 options case to continuous option sets. Certainly effort is a continuous variable. Wages and working conditions offered by the firm are also continuous. This is illustrated in Figure 2. From the top (the NW corner), we have a set of wage-working

[1]This general notion is spelled out in a paper I wrote in 1978 (published 1980). Ullman-Margalit's book (1978), which I was not aware of when I wrote my paper, explores these matters very carefully.
[2]Despite the repeated game aspect of the problem a nonoptimal convention can be stable since (1) convention followers can agree implicitly to police deviants, (2) to police those who might be tempted by free-rider low-effort incentives, and (3) to continually reinforce veneration for the convention. These elements can be sufficiently strong so that it takes a large perturbation (shock) to generate a movement out of a nonoptimal cooperative position.

condition options given by the range W_1 to W_n, and a set of effort options which imply productivity levels given by the range π_1 to π_n. Note: $W_1 > W_2 > \cdots > W_n$, and $\pi_1 > \pi_2 > \cdots > \pi_n$.

The cooperative possibilities are indicated along the cooperative mutual gain diagonal marked MG. Assume that as we move from a lower to a higher effort level, there is an increase in output value which is divided between a higher W and a higher firm profit. Thus, a movement along the diagonal MG leads to successively Pareto-superior points since both employees and the firm gain by such movements. We must keep in mind that there are many cooperative diagonals approximately parallel to the one in the figure. However, a shift along any of the horizontal option sets (say along AF_1) involves adversarial movements for which the firm gains at the expense of employees. Similarly, vertical movements from top to bottom are adversarial movements (say along AE_1) for which the employees gain at the expense of the firm. What makes this general case a prisoners' dilemma case is the postulate that joint choices which are adversarial lead to smaller joint payoffs than would otherwise be the case.

If we consider horizontal movements away from the cooperative diagonal or vertical movements (towards the bottom), then we obtain adversarial behavior under which one party gains and the other loses. But it is the possibility of such shifts in options which creates the lower values along the cooperative diagonal as we move from west to east and from north to south simultaneously.

There is the possibility of shifts which combine both a change in distribution and a change in the cooperative valuation. For example, in the figure the shift from A to B is a shift under which the distribution shifts towards employees. At the same time it represents a move towards a higher cooperative level and, hence, a higher joint output. We can decompose this movement into two segments shown by the sides of the triangle AC and CB. The net effect can still be beneficial to both parties even if some redistribution also takes place.

IV. Example and implications

The view of a convention as a solution to a prisoners' dilemma problem requires that we focus on the stability of the convention. This is related to a concept of inert areas. Each convention is embedded in an inert area. Only if the values of certain variables get beyond the inert area bounds is the convention destabilized. Thus, to obtain a desirable change requires two elements: a necessary "shock" in order to destabilize the operating effort convention; and a movement towards a new convention. A purely static theory does not allow us to determine whether the movement is to a superior convention, an inferior one, or to the prisoners' dilemma solution.

A recent article in the New York Times (October 13, 1981) compared two identically designed plants, with identically designed labor requirements, producing the same Ford automobiles; but the plant in Germany produced 50 percent more cars per day with 22 percent *less* labor. Obviously, despite the design, the effort conventions in the two countries are extremely different.

Now consider (without proof) a few of the implications of nonoptimal effort conventions in our model. Firms operate within, and not on, their production frontier. For a given output, costs are generally not minimized. Innovations are not introduced when it optimally pays to do so. Firm equilibrium is not Pareto optimal. Less output is not necessarily associated with more desired leisure. Firms do not necessarily maximize profits.

V. The prisoners' dilemma and the invisible hand – interrelations

This paper suggests that the invisible hand theory has to be reconsidered. Even if we assume decreasing returns to scale, and no externalities, we can still end up with nontraditional conclusions. The invisible hand theorem which leads to an optimal exchange situation no longer represents an unalloyed optimum in the sense that the *produced* commodities exchanged could have been produced under an infinity of different conventions some of which are very much inferior to others. Thus, two countries with identical inputs, identical knowledge, identical capital accumulation, and the same level of employment, may yet produce significantly different outputs because production takes place on the basis of very different effort conventions.

In addition to visualizing the prisoners' dilemma *in* the invisible hand, as it were, we must also take note that the invisible hand is embedded in a wider *latent* prisoners' dilemma framework. At any specific time the latent prisoners' dilemma possibilities are held in abeyance by conventions, institutions, and laws, involving trust, enforcement of contracts, etc. In other words, we can view a set of cooperative diagonals as exchange options available under a market mechanism. If the adversarial portions are absent, then the mutual choice is the optimal position on the cooperative diagonal. Adversarial portions of the payoff table may be made essentially nonaccessible through nonmarket conventions, such as trust, honesty, fairness, legal recourse for misunderstanding or fraud, emphasis on reputation for fair dealings, etc. Thus, a convention of honesty in contractual relations eliminates adversarial behavior in which both sides attempt to cheat the other. Similarly, an effective low-cost system of laws which enforces contracts may minimize the inducement to use other types of adversarial behavior. To the extent that such conventions are absent, the invisible hand is weakened, the exchange mechanism flawed, and the outcome is no longer optimal.

CHAPTER 14

From *An Evolutionary Theory of Economic Change*

RICHARD NELSON and SIDNEY WINTER

Richard Nelson was born in 1930 in New York City. He received the Ph.D. in economics at Yale University in 1956. He has been Professor of Economics at Yale since 1969.

Sidney Winter was born in Iowa City, Iowa, in 1935. He received the Ph.D. in economics at Yale University in 1964. He has been Professor of Economics and of Organization and Management at Yale since 1976.

From chapter 5, Organizational capabilities and behavior

. . .

1. Routine as organizational memory

It is easy enough to suggest that a plausible answer to the question "Where does the knowledge reside?" is "In the organization's memory." But where and what is the memory of an organization? We propose that the routinization of activity in an organization constitutes the most important form of storage of the organization's specific operational knowledge. Basically, we claim that organizations *remember* by *doing* – although there are some important qualifications and elaborations.

The idea that organizations "remember" a routine largely by exercising it is much like the idea that an individual remembers skills by exercising them. The point that remembering is achieved largely through exercise, and could not be assured totally through written records or other formal filing devices, does not deny that firms keep formal memories and that these formal memories play an important role. But there must be much more to organizational memory than formal records. Further, cost considerations make "doing" the dominant mode of information storage even in many cases where formal records could in principle be kept.

To see how exercise of a routine serves as parsimonious organizational memory, consider an organization in fully routine operation and ask what really needs to be remembered, given that such a state has been achieved. Under such a regime, the situations of individual members and of the organization as a whole contain no significant novelties: the situations confronted replicate ones that were confronted the previous day (or week, month, or year) and are handled in the same way. The scope of the activity that actually takes place in such a static condition and the operational knowledge involved are extremely restricted. Members perform only a minute fraction of the routines they have in repertoire. The lathe operator and the lathe turn out a few specific parts; there is an indeterminately larger number that they could (after appropriate setup and learning) produce. The operator's skills as truck driver and short-order cook are never drawn upon, and perhaps are unknown to other organization members. Routine operation of the organization as a whole certainly does not require that the lathe operator maintain his skill in cooking bacon and eggs, or in the machining of parts for products that were discontinued three years previously; neither does it require that other members remember that the lathe operator possesses or once possessed these skills. If the same state of routine operation is expected to continue indefinitely, there is no economic benefit to be anticipated from holding this sort of information in the organization's memory. (As an obvious corollary, if there is a positive cost to storing information, this sort of ''irrelevant'' information will tend *not* to be held in memory under the ''equilibrium'' condition of continuing routine operation.)

What is required for the organization to continue in routine operation is simply that all members continue to ''know their jobs'' as those jobs are defined by the routine. This means, first of all, that they retain in their repertoires all routines actually invoked in the given state of routine operation of the organization.

There is, however, much more to ''knowing one's job'' in an organization than merely having the appropriate routines in repertoire. There is also the matter of knowing what routines to perform and when to perform them. For the individual member, this entails the ability to receive and interpret a stream of incoming messages from other members and from the environment. Having received and interpreted a message, the member uses the information contained therein in the selection and performance of an appropriate routine from his own repertoire. (This may, of course, be merely a ''relay message'' routine, or even a ''file and forget'' routine.)

The class of things that count as ''messages'' in this characterization is large and diverse. There are, first of all, the obvious examples of written and oral communications that take overtly the form of directives to do this or that. Such directives involve the exercise of formal authority, a phenomenon that has been the focus of a great deal of organizational literature. Then there are the written and oral communications that do not take this form but that are responded to in much the same way. For example, descriptions of what is "needed," when directed to the member whose job it is to meet that need, often function as directives. Even a simple description of the situation, without explicit reference to a need, may function this way. Then there are all the hand signals, gestures, glances, whistles, bell ringing, and so on that can serve in lieu of oral and written communication for these same purposes. Another broad subclass of examples follows a pattern wherein the performance of a routine by one member produces an alteration in the local working environment of another, and the alteration simultaneously makes the performance of a particular routine feasible and carries the message that it should be performed. An assembly line is one example: the arrival of the partly assembled product at a particular station (as a consequence of the performances of other members) both makes possible the performance of the operation done at that station and indicates that the performance is now called for. The arrival of a draft of a letter or document on a secretary's desk makes possible its typing, and may also indicate that its typing is now called for. In still another large subclass, there are messages to which an individual member responds that do not, in any immediate sense, come from other human members. They may come from clocks and calendars – the start of the working day is an obvious example. They may come from meters, gauges, and display boards that convey information on the current state of machines or of other aspects of the working environment and the progress of activity. Or they may come from outside the organization, as when an order or invoice or application form arrives in the mail.[1]

The ability to receive these various sorts of messages involves the possession of certain sensory capacities, plus, let us say, an ordinary ability to understand the natural language of written and oral communication in the wider society of which the organization is a part. These are abilities that usually characterize an organization member quite apart from his role in the organization – that is, they are the sorts of things a new member typically brings to the organization.

What about the ability to interpret the messages – to make the link between a message and the performance that it calls for? It is just as necessary as knowing the job, but much more specific to the organization and the job. It is

---

[1] The fact that there are such diverse sources and media for the messages to which organization members respond in carrying out their duties is suggestive of the problems of defining "authority" in a useful way. To confine attention to directives from superior to subordinate, or even to communications of all sorts from superior to subordinate, is to ignore most of the details of the coordinating information flow. On the other hand, it is hard to deny that the relations of superior and subordinate often have a lot to do with how the subordinate responds to, for example, messages from the clock.

one thing to know how to tell time; it is another to know when to arrive at work, and what it is that you do at about 10 A.M. on the last working day of the month. It is one thing to see a partly assembled automobile in front of you on the line and another to see it as a call for the particular steps that are yours to perform. Even directives that appear to be in "plain Engligh" often require interpretation in a manner that is quite specific to the organizational context. For example, they often omit reference to the typical locations of objects or individuals named in the directives; only someone who has been around the place long enough can easily supply the interpretation. But, in addition, the internal language of communication in an organization is never plain English: it is a dialect full of locally understood nouns standing for particular products, parts, customers, plant locations, and individuals and involving very localized meanings for "promptly," "slower," "too hot," and so on.[2]

The activity of formulating and sending appropriate messages we regard as the performance of a routine by the organization member concerned. This view seems convenient because, as we have noted, there is an important range of cases in which message origination occurs incidentally in the performance of a routine that nominally is directed to other ends. For example, no distinct problem of message formulation arises if the message is conveyed by the partly finished product, passed along to the member who should deal with it next. The burden of the communication process in this case and many similar ones falls upon the receiver who (to know his job) must be able to discern the implications for his own action that are implicit in the changes in his immediate environment – changes that others, by merely doing *their* jobs, have produced. But there are, of course, many organizational roles whose performance does involve message formulation in a conventional sense. For organization members in such roles, there are additional requisites of knowing the job that parallel the ones involved in receiving and interpreting such messages. These include, again, the abilities to speak and write the natural language of the society to which the organization belongs, but also the important additional requirement of command of the organizational dialect. Such command is certainly not to be taken for granted in a new organization member, but is imputed by assumption to members in an organization in a state of routine operation.

The overall picture of an organization in routine operation can now be drawn. A flow of messages comes into the organization from the external environment and from clocks and calendars. The organization members receiving these messages interpret them as calling for the performance of routines from their repertoires. These performances include ones that would be

---

[2] Kenneth Arrow, among others, has given particular emphasis to the internal dialect or "code" of an organization as a key source of the economies that formal organization provides and as an important cause of persistent differences among organizations. See Arrow (1974) pp. 53–9.

thought of as directly productive – such as unloading the truck that has arrived at the loading dock – and others of a clerical or information-processing nature – such as routing a customer's inquiry or order to the appropriate point in the organization. Either as an incidental consequence of other sorts of action or as deliberate acts of communication, the performance of routines by each organization member generates a stream of messages to others. These messages in turn are interpreted as calling for particular performances by their recipients, which generate other performances, messages, interpretations, and so on. At any given time, organization members are responding to messages originating from other members as well as from the environment; the above description of the process as starting with information input from external sources or timekeeping devices is merely an expositional convenience. There is, indeed, an internal equilibrium "circular flow" of information in an organization in routine operation, but it is a flow that is continuously primed by external message sources and timekeeping devices.

For such a system to accomplish something productive, such as building computers or carrying passengers between airports or teaching children to read and write, some highly specific conditions must be satisfied, different in each particular case. The specific features that account for the ability of a particular organization to accomplish particular things are reflected, first of all, in the character of the collection of individual members' repertoires. Airlines are the sorts of organizations that have pilots as members, while schools have teachers. The capabilities of a particular sort of organization are similarly associated with the possession of particular collections of specialized plant and equipment, and the repertoires of organization members include the ability to operate that plant and equipment. Finally, of course, the actual exercise of productive capability requires that there be something upon which to exercise it – some computer components to assemble, or passengers to carry, or children to teach. These are the considerations recognized in the "list of ingredients" level of discussion of productive capability, which is standard in economic analysis. There is also a "recipe" level of discussion, at which "technologies" are described in terms of the principles that underlie them and the character and sequencing of the subtasks that must be performed to get the desired result. This is the province of engineers and other technologists, and to some extent of designers and production managers.

But just as an individual member does not come to know his job merely by mastering the required routines in the repertoire, so an organization does not become capable of an actual productive performance merely by acquiring all the "ingredients," even if it also has the "recipe." What is central to a productive organizational performance is coordination; what is central to coordination is that individual members, knowing their jobs, correctly interpret and respond to the messages they receive. The interpretations that members

183

give to messages are the mechanism that picks out, from a vast array of possibilities consistent with the roster of member repertoires, a collection of individual member performances that actually constitute a productive performance for the organization as a whole.[3] To the extent that the description above is valid, skills, organization, and "technology" are intimately intertwined in a functioning routine, and it is difficult to say exactly where one aspect ends and another begins. This is another way of arguing that "blueprints" are only a small part of what needs to be in an organizational memory in order that production proceed effectively. Furthermore, once the set of routines is in memory by virtue of use, blueprints may not be necessary save, perhaps, as a checkpoint to assess what might be wrong when the routine breaks down.

Given this picture, it is easy to see the relationship between routine operation and organizational memory – or, alternatively, to identify the routinization of activity as the "locus" of operational knowledge in an organization. Information is actually stored primarily in the memories of the members of the organization, in which reside all the knowledge, articulable and tacit, that constitutes their individual skills and routines, the generalized language competence and the specific command of the organizational dialect, and, above all, the associations that link the incoming messages to the specific performances that they call for. In the sense that the memories of individual members do store so much of the information required for the performance of organizational routines, there is substantial truth in the proposition that the knowledge an organization possesses is reducible to the knowledge of its individual members. This is the perspective that one is led to emphasize if one is committed to the view that "knowing" is something that only humans can do.

But the knowledge stored in human memories is meaningful and effective only in some context, and for knowledge exercised in an organizational role that context is an organizational context. It typically includes, first, a variety of forms of external memory – files, message boards, manuals, computer memories, magnetic tapes – that complement and support individual memories but that are maintained in large part as a routine organizational function. One might, therefore, want to say that they are part of organizational memory rather than an information storage activity of individual members. Second, the context includes the physical state of equipment and of the work environment generally. Performance of an organizational memory function is in part implicit in the simple fact that equipment and structures are relatively durable: they and the general state of the work environment do not undergo radical and

184

discontinuous change. A fire or severe storm may break the continuity. The destruction caused by such an event is informational as well as physical, for there is a disruption of the accustomed interpretive context for the information possessed by human members. One might therefore be tempted to say that an organization "remembers" in part by keeping – and to the extent that it succeeds in keeping – its equipment, structures, and work environment in some degree of order and repair. Finally, and most important, the context of the information possessed by an individual member is established by the information possessed by all other members. Without the crane operator's ability to interpret the hand signal for "down a little more" and to lower the hook accordingly, the abilities to perceive the need for the signal and to generate it are meaningless. To view organizational memory as reducible to individual member memories is to overlook, or undervalue, the linking of those individual memories by shared experiences in the past, experiences that have established the extremely detailed and specific communication system that underlies routine performance.

What requires emphasis in the foregoing account is the power of the supposition that "the organization is in a state of routine operation" to limit the scope of the organizational memory function that needs to be performed. While each organization member must know his job, there is no need for anyone to know anyone *else*'s job. Neither is there any need for anyone to be able to articulate or conceptualize the procedures employed by the organization as a whole. Some fraction of the necessary coordinating information may be communicated among members in explicit, articulated form, but there is heavy reliance on the communication implicit in performances that nominally serve other, directly productive purposes. There is no need for an exhaustive symbolic account of the organization's methods; in any case, because much of the knowledge involved is tacit knowledge held by individual members, such an account cannot exist. Yet the amount of information storage implicit in the successful continuation of the routinized performance of the organization as a whole may dwarf the capacity of an individual human memory. The complexity and scale of the productive process may far surpass what any "chief engineer," however skilled, could conceivably guide.[4]

It is by no means the case, however, that routinization entirely frees organizational memory and organizational performance from constraints imposed by human memory limitations. It is important here to distinguish between the memory requirements of a complex coordinated performance taking place at a given time and the requirements of a flexible performance in which the organization as a whole does quite different things at different times. The

---

[4]We have already noted in Chapter 3 [ed.: of the book from which this excerpt is taken] the limitations of the "chief engineer" and "book of blueprints" parables that occur in orthodox accounts of productive knowledge.

complexity of performance at a given time can be greater in a larger organization. With a larger number of members and thus a larger number of human memories among which the organizational memory function can be divided, greater complexity can be consistent with constant or declining demands on the memories of individual members. All members can, simultaneously, remember their jobs by doing them. The situation is quite different with respect to flexibility of organizational performance over time. Flexibility involves variation of the organizational performance in response to variation in the environment.[5] For the organization to respond routinely with a wide variety of specialized routine performances, each "customized" for a particular configuration of the environment, members must be able to retain in repertoire the specialized individual routines involved, and to recall the meaning of a set of messages sufficiently rich to differentiate all the required performances from one another. They must do so in spite of the long time intervals elapsing between the performances of at least some specialized routines and the receipts of some particular messages. (That there are such intervals is of course implied by the supposition that the list of performances or messages to be distinguished is long.) Especially in the case of the tacit components of high skill, the phenomenon of memory loss or increasing rustiness over time is important. A skill that is only exercised briefly every year or two cannot be expressed with the smoothness and reliability of one consistently exercised five days a week. And unexpected lapses by individual members tend to have amplified disruptive effects on organizational performance, since by themselves they create further novelties in the organization's state – novelties with which existing routines and communication systems may be unprepared to deal.

These are the considerations that link routine operation with remembering by doing. It is not just that routinization reflects the achievement of coordination and the establishment of an organizational memory that sustains such coordination. It is that coordination is preserved, and organizational memory refreshed, by exercise – just as, and partly because, individual skills are maintained by being exercised. It may be possible to achieve flexibility by scheduling drills for the specific purpose of maintaining infrequently exercised capabilities, or even by having standby units that do nothing but drill for particular contingencies. But these are obviously costly ways of maintaining organizational memory, at least as compared with genuine "doing" that is directly productive. And, as is well known, the quality of the practice afforded by a drill is inevitably degraded by the fact that it is merely a drill.

[5] It might also involve response to variations in directives from top management, but presumably those variations reflect changes in the environment. In any case, the story would be much the same for arbitrary changes in directives.

From An Evolutionary Theory of Economic Change

2. Routine as truce

Our discussion to this point has been concerned with the cognitive aspects of the performances of organization members – with the question of whether they know what to do and how to do it. We have ignored the motivational aspect – the question of whether they would actually choose to do what is "required" of them in the routine operation of the organization as a whole. Relatedly, the image of coordination that we have presented involves no mention of authority figures, backed by a system of incentives and sanctions, who cajole or coerce the required performances from other members. It is not, however, part of our intention to ignore the divergence of interests among organization members, or to assume implicitly that members are somehow fully committed to the smooth functioning of the organization. Here we fill in the part of the picture of routine operation that involves motivational considerations and intraorganizational conflict.[6]

First of all, our concept of routine operation should not be confused with performance according to the nominal standards of the organization. Neither should the proposition that members correctly interpret and appropriately respond to messages they receive be taken to imply that members do what they are told. Nominally, the workday in a particular organization may run from 9:00 to 5:00, but it may be the case (routinely) that very little activity that is productive from the organization's point of view gets done before 9:30 or after 4:45. Similarly, days or weeks may pass between the nominal deadlines for the completion of particular tasks and the typical dates at which they are actually completed. Repeated follow-up requests or orders may, quite routinely, be part of the system of messages that ultimately results in "timely" performance by other organization members. The priority system used by a particular member in allocating effort among tasks may make use, routinely, of the information contained in the overtones of panic or fury in the incoming messages. In short, routine operation is consistent with routinely occurring laxity, slippage, rule-breaking, defiance, and even sabotage. Such behaviors typically violate nominal standards and expectations in an organization, but they do not necessarily violate empirically based expectations or have consequences for output that are inconsistent with results being statistically stable and within the expected range. They may be expected, adapted to, and allowed for – even to the point where a sudden reversion to nominal standards by some organization members would be disruptive of the achieved state of coordination.

[6]In regard to the context of this section, we acknowledge a diffuse intellectual indebtedness to a large number of authors: Coase (1937), Simon (1951), March and Simon (1958), Doeringer and Piore (1971), Ross (1973), Williamson (1975, ch. 4), and Leibenstein (1976).

Although nominal standards of performance are not necessarily relevant, it is nevertheless true that some sort of stable accommodation between the requirements of organizational functioning and the motivations of all organization members is a necessary concomitant of routine operation. What signals the existence of an accommodation is not the conformity of behavior to standards of performance laid down by supervisors or codified in job descriptions, but that members are rarely surprised at each other's behavior and also that involuntary separations of members from the organization do not occur.

The usual mechanisms of internal control are, of course, a part of the context that helps define the *de facto* contracts that individual members make with the organization. Some of the clerks in the retail store might simply ignore the customers if the manager did not check up occasionally – but the manager does, routinely, check up occasionally, and this keeps the problem within limits. Some fraction of workers may in fact take every opportunity to shirk. This means that the "contracts" of these workers call for them to deliver an amount of work that is defined by the level of managerial supervision; a change in that level would mean a change in the *de facto* contract, but no such change occurs in the context of routine operation. Again, if banks did not have elaborate routinized systems of financial control, it is likely that more bank employees would exploit their positions to their own financial advantage, whether by dipping directly into the till or by approving doubtful loans to undertakings in which they have an interest. As it is, the operation of the control system is a major component of the routine tasks of many bank employees: every job is partially defined by the system's existence and illicit appropriation of bank funds is not (routinely) an important form of compensation.

The examples just given illustrate the way in which control of organization members is effected through mechanisms operating routinely as part of the jobs of other organization members, and serving primarily to threaten sanctions, including dismissal, for behavior that deviates from organizational requirements in specified prohibited directions and in excessive degree. Such rule-enforcement mechanisms play a crucial but limited role in making routine operation possible. On the one hand, they largely prevent or deter individual members from pursuing their own interests along lines that are so strongly antithetical to organizational requirements as to threaten the feasibility of any coordinated performance at all. In this sense, they are crucial in keeping the underlying conflicts among organization members from being expressed in highly disruptive forms.

Ordinarily, however, control systems of this type leave individual members with substantial areas of behavioral discretion, areas that embrace performances of widely differing appropriateness or value from the organizational perspective. Except for tasks involving very low levels of skill, performed under conditions favorable to close observation of several workers by a single supervisor, it is not practical to monitor and control behavior so closely that only organizationally appropriate behaviors are permitted. Within the substantial zone of discretion that exists in most cases, the conformity of individual member behavior to organizational requirements is motivated by considerations other than the routinized organizational mechanisms that "enforce the rules." A variety of other motivating considerations exist. In some cases it is possible to measure individual member "output" reasonably well; reward (or freedom from sanction) can then be conditioned on achievement of a satisfactory output level. In others, organizationally appropriate behavior may be as attractive to the individual member as any other behavior in the zone of discretion left by the rule-enforcement system. Or members may regard themselves as being in a long-term exchange relationship with the organization and may expect future rewards for effective behavior in the present. The importance and efficacy of these motivators and of others not mentioned may be expected to vary among tasks, among rule enforcement, output monitoring and promotion systems, and also, importantly, across member cultures and subcultures that inculcate differing attitudes toward the responsibilities and rewards of organizational membership.[7]

In routine operation, the combined effect of the rule-enforcement mechanism and other motivators is such as to leave members content to play their roles in the organizational routine – but "content" only in the sense that they are willing to continue to perform up to their usual standard, to the accompaniment of the usual amount of griping and squabbling. Conflict, both manifest and latent, persists, but manifest conflict follows largely predictable paths and stays within predictable bounds that are consistent with the ongoing routine. In short, routine operation involves a comprehensive truce in intraorganizational conflict. There is a truce between the supervisor and those supervised at every level in the organizational hierarchy: the usual amount of work gets done, reprimands and compliments are delivered with the usual frequency, and no demands are presented for major modifications in the terms of the relationship. There is similarly a truce in the struggle for advancement, power, and perquisites among high-level executives. Nobody is trying to steer the organizational ship into a sharp turn in the hope of throwing a rival overboard – or if someone is trying, he correctly expects to be thwarted.

When one considers routine operation as the basis of organizational memory, one is led to expect to find routines patterned in ways that reflect characteristics of the information storage problem that they solve. When one considers routine operation as involving a truce in intraorganizational conflict,

---

[7] The considerations just mentioned are among those involved in discussion of "internal" labor markets and the "dual labor market" theory. See Doeringer and Piore (1971) and Williamson (1975, ch. 4).

189

one is led to expect routines to be patterned in ways that reflect features of the underlying problem of diverging individual member interests. The obvious example of such patterning is the existence of rule-enforcement mechanisms as an ongoing feature of organizational routine, even when serious breaches of the rules are infrequent and most of the sanctions that are nominally available are not applied.

But more subtle manifestations, specific to a particular organizational context, frequently exist. Like a truce among nations, the truce among organization members tends to give rise to a peculiar symbolic culture shared by the parties. A renewal of overt hostilities would be costly and would also involve a sharp rise in uncertainty about the future positions of the parties. Accordingly, the state of truce is ordinarily considered valuable, and a breach of its terms is not to be undertaken lightly. But the terms of a truce can never be fully explicit, and in the case of the intraorganizational truce are often not explicit at all. The terms become increasingly defined by a shared tradition arising out of the specific contingencies confronted and the responses of the parties to those contingencies. In the interpretive context of such a tradition, actions by individual members have connotations related to the terms of the truce. In particular, a contemplated action otherwise sensible both for the organization and for the member taking it may have to be rejected if it is likely to be interpreted as "provocative" – that is, as signaling a lessened commitment to the preservation of the truce and a corresponding willingness to risk overt conflict for the sake of modifying the routine in a manner favored by the member who initiates the change. On the defensive side, each member strives to protect his interests by standing prepared to deliver a firm rebuff not only to actions by others that clearly threaten those interests, but also to actions that might be quite innocuous were it not for their possible interpretation as probes of his alertness or determination to defend his rights under the truce.

The apparent fragility of the prevailing truce and the implied need for caution in undertaking anything that looks like a new initiative is thus reinforced by the defensive alertness (or alert defensiveness) of organization members seeking to assure that their interests continue to be recognized and preserved. The result may be that the routines of the organization as a whole are confined to extremely narrow channels by the dikes of vested interest. Adaptations that appear "obvious" and "easy" to an external observer may be foreclosed because they involve a perceived threat to internal political equilibrium.

Of course, organizations vary in the extent to which these mechanisms operate, as they do in other respects. But it seems safe to say that fear of breaking the truce is, in general, a powerful force tending to hold organizations on the path of relatively inflexible routine.

. . .

PART III

Management, finance, and the scope of the firm

CHAPTER 15

Mergers and the market for corporate control

HENRY MANNE

Henry Manne was born in 1928. He received the J.D. at the University of Chicago in 1952 and the J.S.D. at Yale University in 1966. He was Professor at George Washington University Law School when this paper was published. In 1986, he became Dean of the School of Law and University Professor at George Mason University.

The corporate-control market

The conventional approach to a merger problem takes corporations merely as decision-making units or firms within the classical market framework. This approach dictates a ban on many horizontal mergers almost by definition. The basic proposition advanced in this paper is that the control of corporations may constitute a valuable asset; that this asset exists independent of any interest in either economies of scale or monopoly profits; that an active market for corporate control exists; and that a great many mergers are probably the result of the successful workings of this special market.

Basically this paper will constitute an introduction to a study of the market for corporation control. The emphasis will be placed on the antitrust implications of this market, but the analysis to follow has important implications for a variety of economic questions. Perhaps the most important implications are those for the alleged separation of ownership and control in large corporations. So long as we are unable to discern any control relationship between small shareholders and corporate management, the thrust of Berle and Means's famous phrase remains strong. But, as will be explained below, the market for corporate control gives to these shareholders both power and protection commensurate with their interest in corporate affairs.

A fundamental premise underlying the market for corporate control is the existence of a high positive correlation between corporate managerial efficiency and the market price of shares of that company.[1] As an existing com-

Excerpted from Henry Manne, "Mergers and the Market for Corporate Control," *Journal of Political Economy*, 73 (1965):110–20. Copyright 1965. Reprinted with the permission of the University of Chicago Press.

[1] The claim of a positive correlation between managerial efficiency and the market price of shares would seem at first blush to raise an empirical question. In fact, however, the concept of

pany is poorly managed – in the sense of not making as great a return for the shareholders as could be accomplished under other feasible managements – the market price of the shares declines relative to the shares of other companies in the same industry or relative to the market as a whole. This phenomenon has a dual importance for the market for corporate control.

In the first place, a lower share price facilitates any effort to take over high-paying managerial positions. The compensation from these positions may take the usual forms of salary, bonuses, pensions, expense accounts, and stock options. Perhaps more important, it may take the form of information useful in trading in the company's shares; or, if that is illegal, information may be exchanged and the trading done in other companies' shares. But it is extremely doubtful that the full compensation recoverable by executives for managing their corporations explains more than a small fraction of outsider[2] attempts to take over control. Take-overs of corporations are too expensive generally to make the "purchase" of management compensation an attractive proposition.[3]

It is far more likely that a second kind of reward provides the primary motivation for most take-over attempts. The market price of shares does more than measure the price at which the normal compensation of executives can be "sold" to new individuals. Share price, or that part reflecting managerial efficiency, also measures the potential capital gain inherent in the corporate stock. The lower the stock price, relative to what it could be with more efficient management, the more attractive the take-over becomes to those who believe that they can manage the company more efficiently. And the potential

corporate managerial efficiency, with its overtones of an entrepreneurial function, is one for which there are no objective standards. But there are compelling reasons, apart from empirical data, for believing that this correlation exists. Insiders, those who have the most reliable information about corporate affairs, are strongly motivated financially to perform a kind of arbitrage function for their company's stock. That is, given their sense of what constitutes efficient management, they will cause share prices to rise or decline in accordance with that standard.

The contention is often made that stock-market prices are not accurate gauges, since far more trades take place without reliable information than with it. But there is reason to believe that intelligence rather than ignorance ultimately determines the course of individual share prices. Stock-market decisions tend to be of the one-out-of-two-alternatives variety, such as buy or not buy, hold or sell, or put or call. To the extent that decisions on these questions are made by shareholders or potential shareholders operating without reliable information, over a period of time the decisions will tend to be randomly distributed and the effect will therefore be neutral. Decisions made by those with a higher degree of certainty will to that extent not meet a canceling effect since they will not be made on a random basis. Over some period of time it would seem that the average market price of a company's shares must be the "correct" one.

[2] "Outsider" here refers to anyone not presently controlling the affairs of the corporation, even though it may include one or more individuals on the corporation's board of directors.

[3] To the extent that executive compensation increases with higher share prices, the take-over is most attractive at the time when it is also most expensive. Indeed, the danger of a take-over may account for managers' voluntarily decreasing their compensation when the company's share price is down.

return from the successful takeover and revitalization of a poorly run company can be enormous.

Additional leverage in this operation can be obtained by borrowing the funds with which the shares are purchased, although American commercial banks are generally forbidden to lend money for this purpose. A comparable advantage can be had from using other shares rather than cash as the exchange medium. Given the fact of special tax treatment for capital gains, we can see how this mechanism for taking over control of badly run corporations is one of the most important "get-rich-quick" opportunities in our economy today.

But the greatest benefits of the take-over scheme probably inure to those least conscious of it. Apart from the stock market, we have no objective standard of managerial efficiency. Courts, as indicated by the so-called business-judgment rule, are loath to second-guess business decisions or remove directors from office. Only the take-over scheme provides some assurance of competitive efficiency among corporate managers and thereby affords strong protection to the interests of vast numbers of small, non-controlling shareholders. Compared to this mechanism, the efforts of the SEC and the courts to protect shareholders through the development of a fiduciary duty concept and the shareholder's derivative suit seem small indeed. It is true that sales by dissatisfied shareholders are necessary to trigger the mechanism and that these shareholders may suffer considerable losses. On the other hand, even greater capital losses are prevented by the existence of a competitive market for control.[4]

. . .

[4] Unfortunately the suppression of this market would be the consequence of proposals made by several writers in the field. For a review and a criticism of this literature see Henry G. Manne, (1962) 399–432. For another defense of this market see Harry G. Johnson (1963), pp. xvii–xviii.

CHAPTER 16

Agency problems and the theory of the firm

EUGENE FAMA

Eugene Fama was born in 1939 in Somerville, Massachusetts. He received the Ph.D. at the University of Chicago in 1964. He has been Theodore Yntema Professor of Finance at the Graduate School of Business, the University of Chicago, since 1963.

Economists have long been concerned with the incentive problems that arise when decision making in a firm is the province of managers who are not the firm's security holders.[1] One outcome has been the development of "behavioral" and "managerial" theories of the firm which reject the classical model of an entrepreneur, or owner-manager, who single-mindedly operates the firm to maximize profits, in favor of theories that focus more on the motivations of a manager who controls but does not own and who has little resemblance to the classical "economic man." Examples of this approach are Baumol (1959), Simon (1959), Cyert and March (1963), and Williamson (1964b).

More recently the literature has moved toward theories that reject the classical model of the firm but assume classical forms of economic behavior on the part of agents within the firm. The firm is viewed as a set of contracts among factors of production, with each factor motivated by its self-interest. Because of its emphasis on the importance of rights in the organization established by contracts, this literature is characterized under the rubric "property rights." Alchian and Demsetz (1972) and Jensen and Meckling (1976a) are the best examples. The antecedents of their work are in Coase (1937, 1960).

The striking insight of Alchian and Demsetz (1972) and Jensen and Meckling (1976a) is in viewing the firm as a set of contracts among factors of production. In effect, the firm is viewed as a team whose members act from self-interest but realize that their destinies depend to some extent on the survival of the team in its competition with other teams. This insight, however, is not carried far enough. In the classical theory, the agent who personifies the firm is the entrepreneur who is taken to be both manager and residual risk

[1] Jensen and Meckling (1976a) quote from Adam Smith (1776). The modern literature on the problem dates back at least to Berle and Means (1932).

bearer. Although his title sometimes changes – for example, Alchian and Demsetz call him "the employer" – the entrepreneur continues to play a central role in the firm of the property rights literature. As a consequence, this literature fails to explain the large modern corporation in which control of the firm is in the hands of managers who are more or less separate from the firm's security holders.

The main thesis of this paper is that separation of security ownership and control can be explained as an efficient form of economic organization within the "set of contracts" perspective. We first set aside the typical presumption that a corporation has owners in any meaningful sense. The attractive concept of the entrepreneur is also laid to rest, at least for the purposes of the large modern corporation. Instead, the two functions usually attributed to the entrepreneur, management and risk bearing, are treated as naturally separate factors within the set of contracts called a firm. The firm is disciplined by competition from other firms, which forces the evolution of devices for efficiently monitoring the performance of the entire team and of its individual members. In addition, individual participants in the firm, and in particular its managers, face both the discipline and opportunities provided by the markets for their services, both within and outside of the firm.

The irrelevance of the concept of ownership of the firm

To set a framework for the analysis, let us first describe roles for management and risk bearing in the set of contracts called a firm. Management is a type of labor but with a special role – coordinating the activities of inputs and carrying out the contracts agreed among inputs, all of which can be characterized as "decision making." To explain the role of the risk bearers, assume for the moment that the firm rents all other factors of production and that rental contracts are negotiated at the beginning of each production period with payoffs at the end of the period. The risk bearers then contract to accept the uncertain and possibly negative difference between total revenues and costs at the end of each production period.

When other factors of production are paid at the end of each period, it is not necessary for the risk bearers to invest anything in the firm at the beginning of the period. Most commonly, however, the risk bearers guarantee performance of their contracts by putting up wealth ex ante, with this front money used to purchase capital and perhaps also the technology that the firm uses in its production activities. In this way the risk bearing function is combined with ownership of capital and technology. We also commonly observe that the joint functions of risk bearing and ownership of capital are repackaged and sold in different proportions to different groups of investors. For example, when front money is raised by issuing both bonds and common stock, the bonds involve a combination of risk bearing and ownership of capital with a low amount of risk bearing relative to the combination of risk bearing and ownership of capital inherent in the common stock. Unless the bonds are risk free, the risk bearing function is in part borne by the bondholders, and ownership of capital is shared by bondholders and stockholders.

However, ownership of capital should not be confused with ownership of the firm. Each factor in a firm is owned by somebody. The firm is just the set of contracts covering the way inputs are joined to create outputs and the way receipts from outputs are shared among inputs. In this "nexus of contracts" perspective, ownership of the firm is an irrelevant concept. Dispelling the tenacious notion that a firm is owned by its security holders is important because it is a first step toward understanding that control over a firm's decisions is not necessarily the province of security holders. The second step is setting aside the equally tenacious role in the firm usually attributed to the entrepreneur.

Management and risk bearing: a closer look

The entrepreneur (manager–risk bearer) is central in both the Jensen–Meckling and Alchian–Demsetz analyses of the firm. For example, Alchian–Demsetz state: "The essence of the classical firm is identified here as a contractual structure with: (1) joint input production; (2) several input owners; (3) one party who is common to all the contracts of the joint inputs; (4) who has the right to renegotiate any input's contract independently of contracts with other input owners; (5) who holds the residual claim; and (6) who has the right to sell his central contractual residual status. The central agent is called the firm's owner and the employer" (1972, p. 794).

To understand the modern corporation, it is better to separate the manager, the agents of points 3 and 4 of the Alchian–Demsetz definition of the firm, from the risk bearer described in points 5 and 6. The rationale for separating these functions is not just that the end result is more descriptive of the corporation, a point recognized in both the Alchian–Demsetz and Jensen–Meckling papers. The major loss in retaining the concept of the entrepreneur is that one is prevented from developing a perspective on management and risk bearing as separate factors of production, each faced with a market for its services that provides alternative opportunities and, in the case of management, motivation toward performance.

Thus, any given set of contracts, a particular firm, is in competition with other firms, which are likewise teams of cooperating factors of production. If there is a part of the team that has a special interest in its viability, it is not obviously the risk bearers. It is true that if the team does not prove viable

198

factors like labor and management are protected by markets in which rights to their future services can be sold or rented to other teams. The risk bearers, as residual claimants, also seem to suffer the most direct consequences from the failings of the team. However, the risk bearers in the modern corporation also have markets for their services – capital markets – which allow them to shift among teams with relatively low transaction costs and to hedge against the failings of any given team by diversifying their holdings across teams.

Indeed, portfolio theory tells us that the optimal portfolio for any investor is likely to be diversified across the securities of many firms.[2] Since he holds the securities of many firms precisely to avoid having his wealth depend too much on any one firm, an individual security holder generally has no special interest in personally overseeing the detailed activities of any firm. In short, efficient allocation of risk bearing seems to imply a large degree of separation of security ownership from control of a firm.

On the other hand, the managers of a firm rent a substantial lump of wealth – their human capital – to the firm, and the rental rates for their human capital signaled by the managerial labor market are likely to depend on the success or failure of the firm. The function of management is to oversee the contracts among factors and to ensure the viability of the firm. For the purposes of the managerial labor market, the previous associations of a manager with success and failure are information about his talents. The manager of a firm, like the coach of any team, may not suffer any immediate gain or loss in current wages from the current performance of his team, but the success or failure of the team impacts his future wages, and this gives the manager a stake in the success of the team.

The firm's security holders provide important but indirect assistance to the managerial labor market in its task of valuing the firm's management. A security holder wants to purchase securities with confidence that the prices paid reflect the risks he is taking and that the securities will be priced in the future to allow him to reap the rewards (or punishments) of his risk bearing. Thus, although an individual security holder may not have a strong interest in directly overseeing the management of a particular firm, he has a strong interest in the existence of a capital market which efficiently prices the firm's securities. The signals provided by an efficient capital market about the values of a firm's securities are likely to be important for the managerial labor market's revaluations of the firm's management.

We come now to the central question. To what extent can the signals provided by the managerial labor market and the capital market, perhaps along with other market-induced mechanisms, discipline managers? We first dis-

---

[2] Detailed discussions of portfolio models can be found in Fama and Miller (1972, chaps. 6 and 7), Jensen (1972), and Fama (1976, chaps. 7 and 8).

199

cuss, still in general terms, the types of discipline imposed by managerial labor markets, both within and outside of the firm. We then analyze specific conditions under which this discipline is sufficient to resolve potential incentive problems that might be associated with the separation of security ownership and control.

The viability of separation of security ownership and control of the firm: general comments

The outside managerial labor market exerts many direct pressures on the firm to sort and compensate managers according to performance. One form of pressure comes from the fact that an ongoing firm is always in the market for new managers. Potential new managers are concerned with the mechanics by which their performance will be judged, and they seek information about the responsiveness of the system in rewarding performance. Moreover, given a competitive managerial labor market, when the firm's reward system is not responsive to performance the firm loses managers, and the best are the first to leave.

There is also much internal monitoring of managers by managers themselves. Part of the talent of a manager is his ability to elicit and measure the productivity of lower managers, so there is a natural process of monitoring from higher to lower levels of management. Less well appreciated, however, is the monitoring that takes place from bottom to top. Lower managers perceive that they can gain by stepping over shirking or less competent managers above them. Moreover, in the team or nexus of contracts view of the firm, each manager is concerned with the performance of managers above and below him since his marginal product is likely to be a positive function of theirs. Finally, although higher managers are affected more than lower managers, all managers realize that the managerial labor market uses the performance of the firm to determine each manager's outside opportunity wage. In short, each manager has a stake in the performance of the managers above and below him and, as a consequence, undertakes some amount of monitoring in both directions.

All managers below the very top level have an interest in seeing that the top managers choose policies for the firm which provide the most positive signals to the managerial labor market. But by what mechanism can top management be disciplined? Since the body designated for this function is the board of directors, we can ask how it might be constructed to do its job. A board dominated by security holders does not seem optimal or endowed with good survival properties. Diffuse ownership of securities is beneficial in terms of an optimal allocation of risk bearing, but its consequence is that the firm's security holders are generally too diversified across the securities of many firms to take much direct interest in a particular firm.

If there is competition among the top managers themselves (all want to be the boss of bosses), then perhaps they are the best ones to control the board of directors. They are most directly in the line of fire from lower managers when the markets for securities and managerial labor give poor signals about the performance of the firm. Because of their power over the firm's decisions, their market-determined opportunity wages are also likely to be most affected by market signals about the performance of the firm. If they are also in competition for the top places in the firm, they may be the most informed and responsive critics of the firm's performance.

Having gained control of the board, top management may decide that collusion and expropriation of security holder wealth are better than competition among themselves. The probability of such collusive arrangements might be lowered, and the viability of the board as a market-induced mechanism for low-cost internal transfer of control might be enhanced, by the inclusion of outside directors. The latter might best be regarded as professional referees whose task is to stimulate and oversee the competition among the firm's top managers. In a state of advanced evolution of the external markets that buttress the corporate firm, the outside directors are in their turn disciplined by the market for their services which prices them according to their performance as referees. Since such a system of separation of security ownership from control is consistent with the pressures applied by the managerial labor market, and since it likewise operates in the interests of the firm's security holders, it probably has good survival properties.[3]

This analysis does not imply that boards of directors are likely to be composed entirely of managers and outside directors. The board is viewed as a market-induced institution, the ultimate internal monitor of the set of contracts called a firm, whose most important role is to scrutinize the highest decision makers within the firm. In the team or nexus of contracts view of the firm, one cannot rule out the evolution of boards of directors that contain many different factors of production (or their hired representatives), whose common trait is that their marginal products are affected by those of the top decision makers. On the other hand, one also cannot conclude that all such factors will naturally show up on boards since there may be other market-

---

[3] Watts and Zimmerman (1978) provide a similar description of the market-induced evolution of "independent" outside auditors whose function is to certify and, as a consequence, stimulate the viability of the set of contracts called the firm. Like the outside directors, the outside auditors are policed by the market for their services which prices them in large part on the basis of how well they resist perverting the interests of one set of factors (e.g., security holders) to the benefit of other factors (e.g., management). Like the professional outside director, the welfare of the outside auditor depends largely on "reputation."

induced institutions, for example, unions, that more efficiently monitor managers on behalf of specific factors. All one can say is that in a competitive environment lower-cost sets of monitoring mechanisms are likely to survive. The role of the board in this framework is to provide a relatively low-cost mechanism for replacing or reordering top managers; lower cost, for example, than the mechanism provided by an outside takeover, although, of course, the existence of an outside market for control is another force which helps to sensitize the internal managerial labor market.

The perspective suggested here owes much to, but is nevertheless different from, existing treatments of the firm in the property rights literature. Thus, Alchian (1969) and Alchian and Demsetz (1972) comment insightfully on the disciplining of management that takes place through the inside and outside markets for managers. However, they attribute the task of disciplining management primarily to the risk bearers, the firm's security holders, who are assisted to some extent by managerial labor markets and by the possibility of outside takeover. Jensen and Meckling (1976a) likewise make control of management the province of the firm's risk bearers, but they do not allow for any assistance from the managerial labor market. Of all the authors in the property-rights literature, Manne (1965, 1967) is most concerned with the market for corporate control. He recognizes that with diffuse security ownership management and risk bearing are naturally separate functions. But for him, disciplining management is an "entrepreneurial job" which in the first instance falls on a firm's organizers and later on specialists in the process of outside takeover.

When management and risk bearing are viewed as naturally separate factors of production, looking at the market for risk bearing from the viewpoint of portfolio theory tells us that risk bearers are likely to spread their wealth across many firms and so not be interested in directly controlling the management of any individual firm. Thus, models of the firm, like those of Alchian-Demsetz and Jensen-Meckling, in which the control of management falls primarily on the risk bearers, are not likely to allay the fears of those concerned with the apparent incentive problems created by the separation of security ownership and control. Likewise, Manne's approach, in which the control of management relies primarily on the expensive mechanism of an outside takeover, offers little comfort. The viability of the large corporation with diffuse security ownership is better explained in terms of a model where the primary disciplining of managers comes through managerial labor markets, both within and outside of the firm, with assistance from the panoply of internal and external monitoring devices that evolve to stimulate the ongoing efficiency of the corporate form, and with the market for outside takeovers providing discipline of last resort.

202

The viability of separation of security ownership and control: details

The preceding is a general discussion of how pressure from managerial labor markets helps to discipline managers. We now examine somewhat more specifically conditions under which the discipline imposed by managerial labor markets can resolve potential incentive problems associated with the separation of security ownership and control of the firm.

To focus on the problem we are trying to solve, let us first examine the situation where the manager is also the firm's sole security holder, so that there is clearly no incentive problem. When he is sole security holder, a manager consumes on the job, through shirking, perquisites, or incompetence, to the point where these yield marginal expected utility equal to that provided by an additional dollar of wealth usable for consumption or investment outside of the firm. The manager is induced to make this specific decision because he pays directly for consumption on the job; that is, as manager he cannot avoid a full ex post settling up with himself as security holder.

In contrast, when the manager is no longer sole security holder, and in the absence of some form of full ex post settling up for deviations from contract, a manager has an incentive to consume more on the job than is agreed in his contract. The manager perceives that, on an ex post basis, he can beat the game by shirking or consuming more perquisites than previously agreed. This does not necessarily mean that the manager profits at the expense of other factors. Rational managerial labor markets understand any shortcomings of available mechanisms for enforcing ex post settling up. Assessments of ex post deviations from contract will be incorporated into contracts on an ex ante basis; for example, through an adjustment of the manager's wage.

Nevertheless, a game which is fair on an ex ante basis does not induce the same behavior as a game in which there is also ex post settling up. Herein lie the potential losses from separation of security ownership and control of a firm. There are situations where, with less than complete ex post settling up, the manager is induced to consume more on the job than he would like, given that on average he pays for his consumption ex ante.

Three general conditions suffice to make the wage revaluation imposed by the managerial labor market a form of full ex post settling up which resolves the managerial incentive problem described above. The first condition is that a manager's talents and his tastes for consumption on the job are not known with certainty, are likely to change through time, and must be imputed by managerial labor markets at least in part from information about the manager's current and past performance. Since it seems to capture the essence of

203

the task of managerial labor markets in a world of uncertainty, this assumption is no real restriction.

The second assumption is that managerial labor markets appropriately use current and past information to revise future wages and understand any enforcement power inherent in the wage revision process. In short, contrary to much of the literature on separation of security ownership and control, we impute efficiency or rationality in information processing to managerial labor markets. In defense of this assumption, we note that the problem faced by managerial labor markets in revaluing the managers of a firm is much entwined with the problem faced by the capital market in revaluing the firm itself. Although we do not understand all the details of the process, available empirical evidence (e.g., Fama 1976, chaps. 5 and 6) suggests that the capital market generally makes rational assessments of the value of the firm in the face of imprecise and uncertain information. This does not necessarily mean that information processing in managerial labor markets is equally efficient or rational, but it is a warning against strong presumptions to the contrary.

The final and key condition for full control of managerial behavior through wage changes is that the weight of the wage revision process is sufficient to resolve any potential problems with managerial incentives. In this general form, the condition amounts to assuming the desired result. More substance is provided by specific examples.

·   ·   ·

Example: stochastic processes for marginal products

The next example of ex post settling up through the wage revision process is somewhat more formal than that described above. We make specific assumptions about the stochastic evolution of a manager's measured marginal product and about how the managerial labor market uses information from the process to adjust the manager's future wages – in a manner which amounts to precise, full ex post settling up for the results of past performance.

Suppose the manager's measured marginal product for any period t is composed of two terms: (i) an expected value, given his talents, effort exerted during t, consumption of perquisites, etc.; and (ii) random noise. The random noise may in part result from measurement error, that is, the sheer difficulty of accurately measuring marginal products when there is team production, but it may also arise in part from the fact that effort exerted and talent do not yield perfectly certain consequences. Moreover, because of the uncertain evolution of the manager's talents and tastes, the expected value of his marginal product is itself a stochastic process. Specifically, we assume that the expected value, $\bar{z}_t$, follows a random walk with steps that are independent of the random noise, ϵ_t, in the manager's measured marginal product, z_t. Thus, the measured marginal product,

$$z_t = \bar{z}_t + \epsilon_t, \tag{1}$$

is a random walk plus white noise. For simplicity, we also assume that this process describes the manager's marginal product both in his current employment and in the best alternative employment.

The characteristics (parameters) of the evolution of the manager's marginal product depend to some extent on endogenous variables like effort and perquisites consumed, which are not completely observable. Our purpose is to set up the managerial labor market so that the wage revision process resolves any potential incentive problems that may arise from the endogeneity of z_t in a situation where there is separation of security ownership and control of the firm.

Suppose next that risk bearers are all risk neutral and that 1-period market interest rates are always equal to zero. Suppose also that managerial wage contracts are written so that the manager's wage in any period t is the expected value of his marginal product, $\bar{z}_t$, conditional on past measured values of his marginal product, with the risk bearers accepting the noise ϵ_t, in the ex post measurement of the marginal product. We shall see below that this is an optimal arrangement for our risk-neutral risk bearers. However, it is not necessarily optimal for the manager if he is risk averse. A risk-averse manager may want to sell part of the risk inherent in the uncertain evolution of his expected marginal product to the risk bearers, for example, through a long-term wage contract.

We avoid this issue by assuming that, perhaps because of the more extreme moral hazard problems in long-term contracts (remember that $\bar{z}_t$ is in part under the control of the manager) and the contracting costs to which these moral hazard problems give rise, simple contracts in which the manager's wage is reset at the beginning of each period are dominant, at least for some nontrivial subset of firms and managers.[4] If we could also assume away any remaining moral hazard (managerial incentive) problems, then with risk-averse managers, risk-neutral risk bearers, and the presumed fixed recontracting period, the contract which specifies ex ante that the manager will be paid the

---

[4] Institutions like corporations, that are subject to rapid technological change with a large degree of uncertainty about future managerial needs, may find that long-term managerial contracts can only be negotiated at high cost. On the other hand, institutions like governments, schools, and universities may be able to forecast more reliably their future needs for managers (and other professionals) and so may be able to offer long-term contracts at relatively low cost. These institutions can then be expected to attract the relatively risk-averse members of the professional labor force, while the riskier employment offered by corporations attracts those who are willing to accept shorter-term contracts.

current expected value of his marginal product dominates any contract where the manager also shares the ex post deviation of his measured marginal product from its ex ante expected value (see, e.g., Spence and Zeckhauser 1971).

However, contracts which specify ex ante that the manager will be paid the current expected value of his marginal product seem to leave the typical moral hazard problem that arises when there is less than complete ex post enforcement of contracts. The noise ϵ_t in the manager's marginal product is borne by the risk bearers. Once the manager's expected marginal product $\bar{z}_t$ ($=$ his current wage) has been assessed, he seems to have an incentive to consume more perquisites and provide less effort than are implied in $\bar{z}_t$.

A mechanism for ex post enforcement is, however, built into the model. With the expected value of the manager's marginal product wandering randomly through time, future assessments of expected marginal products (and thus of wages) will be determined in part by ϵ_t, the deviation of the current measured marginal product from its ex ante expected value. In the present scenario, where $\bar{z}_t$ is assumed to follow a random walk, Muth (1960) has shown that the expected value of the marginal product evolves according to

$$\bar{z}_t = \bar{z}_{t-1} + (1 - \phi)\epsilon_{t-1}, \tag{2}$$

where the parameter ϕ ($0 < \phi < 1$) is closer to zero the smaller the variance of the noise term in the marginal product equation (1) relative to the variance of the steps in the random walk followed by the expected marginal product.

In fact, the process by which future expected marginal products are adjusted on the basis of past deviations of marginal products from their expected values leads to a precise form of full ex post settling up. This is best seen by writing the marginal product z_t in its inverted form, that is, in terms of past marginal products and the current noise. The inverted form for our model, a random walk embedded in random noise, is

$$z_t = (1 - \phi)z_{t-1} + \phi(1 - \phi)z_{t-2} + \phi^2(1 - \phi)z_{t-3} + \cdots + \epsilon_t, \tag{3}$$

so that

$$\bar{z}_t = (1 - \phi)z_{t-1} + \phi(1 - \phi)z_{t-2} + \phi^2(1 - \phi)z_{t-3} + \cdots \tag{4}$$

(see, e.g., Nelson 1973, chap. 4, or Muth 1960).

For our purposes, the interesting fact is that, although he is paid his ex ante expected marginal product, the manager does not get to avoid his ex post marginal product. For example, we can infer from (4) that z_{t-1} has weight $1 - \phi$ in $\bar{z}_t$; then it has weight $\phi(1 - \phi)$ in $\bar{z}_{t+1}$, $\phi^2(1 - \phi)$ in $\bar{z}_{t+2}$, and so on. In the end, the sum of the contributions of z_{t-1} to future expected marginal products, and thus to future wages, is exactly z_{t-1}. With zero interest rates, this means that the risk bearers simply allow the manager to smooth his marginal product across future periods at the going opportunity cost of all such

206

temporal wealth transfers. As a consequence, the manager has no incentive to try to bury shirking or consumption of perquisites in his ex post measured marginal product.

Since the managerial labor market is presumed to understand the weight of the wage revision process, which in this case amounts to precise full ex post settling up, any potential managerial incentive problems in the separation of risk bearing, or security ownership, from control are resolved. The manager can contract for and take an optimal amount of consumption on the job. The wage set ex ante need not include any allowance for ex post incentives to deviate from the contract since the wage revision process neutralizes any such incentives. Note, moreover, that the value of ϕ in the wage revision process described by (4) determines how the observed marginal product of any given period is subdivided and spread across future periods, but whatever the value of ϕ, the given marginal product is fully accounted for in the stream of future wages. Thus, it is now clear what was meant by the earlier claim that although the parameter ϕ in the process generating the manager's marginal product is to some extent under his control, this is not a matter of particular concern to the managerial labor market.

A somewhat evident qualification is in order. The smoothing process described by (4) contains an infinite number of terms, whereas any manager has a finite working life. For practical purposes, full ex post settling up is achieved as long as the manager's current marginal product is "very nearly" fully absorbed by the stream of wages over his future working life. This requires a value of ϕ in (4) which is sufficiently far from 1.0, given the number of periods remaining in the manager's working life. Recall that ϕ is closer to 1.0 the larger the variance of the noise in the manager's measured marginal product relative to the variance of the steps of the random walk taken by the expected value of his marginal product. Intuitively, when the variance of the noise term is large relative to that of the changes in the expected value, the current measured marginal product has a weak signal about any change in the expected value of the marginal product, and the current marginal product is only allocated slowly to expected future marginal products.

Some extensions

Having qualified the analysis, let us now indicate some ways in which it is robust to changes in details of the model.

1. More complicated models for the manager's marginal product.

The critical ingredient in enforcing precise full ex post settling up through wage revisions on the basis of reassessments of expected marginal products is that when the marginal product and its expected value are expressed in inverted form, as in (3) and (4), the sum of the weights on past marginal products is exactly 1.0. This will be the case (see, e.g., Nelson 1973, chap. 4) whenever the manager's marginal product conforms to a nonstationary stochastic process, but the changes from period to period in the marginal product conform to some stationary ARMA (mixed autoregressive moving average) process. The example summarized in equations (1)–(4) is the interesting but special case where the expected marginal product follows a random walk so that the differences of the marginal product are a stationary, first-order moving average process. The general case allows the expected value of the marginal product to follow any more complicated nonstationary process which has the property that the differences of the marginal product are stationary, so that the marginal product and its expected value can be expressed in inverted form as

$$z_t = \pi_1 z_{t-1} + \pi_2 z_{t-2} + \cdots + \epsilon_t \tag{5}$$

$$\bar{z}_t = \pi_1 z_{t-1} + \pi_2 z_{t-2} + \cdots \tag{6}$$

with

$$\sum_{i=1}^{\infty} \pi_i = 1. \tag{7}$$

These can be viewed as the general conditions for enforcing precise full ex post settling through the wage revision process when the manager's wage is equal to the current expected value of his marginal product.[5]

· · ·

[5] When $\bar{z}_t$ follows a stationary process, the long-run average value toward which the process always tends will eventually be known with near perfect certainty. Thus, the case of a stationary expected marginal product is of little interest, at least for the purposes of ex post settling up enforced by the wage revision process.

CHAPTER 17

Theory of the firm: managerial behavior, agency costs, and ownership structure

MICHAEL JENSEN and WILLIAM MECKLING

Michael Jensen was born in Rochester, Minnesota, in 1939. He received the Ph.D. in economics at the University of Chicago in 1968. When this paper was published, he was Associate Professor at the University of Rochester. He is currently LaClare Professor of Finance and Director of the Managerial Economics Research Center at the Graduate School of Management, the University of Rochester, and Professor of Business Administration, Harvard Business School.

William Meckling was born in 1921 in McKeesport, Pennsylvania. He received the M.B.A. degree at the University of Denver in 1947 and did postgraduate work at the University of Chicago from 1949 to 1952. When this paper was published, he was Dean of the Graduate School of Management, University of Rochester.

The directors of such [joint-stock] companies, however, being the managers rather of other people's money than of their own, it cannot well be expected, that they should watch over it with the same anxious vigilance with which the partners in a private copartnery frequently watch over their own. Like the stewards of a rich man, they are easily apt to consider attention to small matters as not for their master's honour, and very easily give themselves a dispensation from having it. Negligence and profusion, therefore, must always prevail, more or less, in the management of the affairs of such a company.

Adam Smith, *The Wealth of Nations,* 1776, Cannan Edition
(Modern Library, New York, 1937) p. 700.

1. Introduction and summary

1.1. Motivation of the paper

In this paper we draw on recent progress in the theory of (1) property rights, (2) agency, and (3) finance to develop a theory of ownership structure[1] for the firm. In addition to tying together elements of the theory of each of these

Reprinted in abridged form from Michael Jensen and William Meckling, "Theory of the Firm: Managerial Behavior, Agency Costs, and Ownership Structure," *The Journal of Financial Economics,* 3 (1976): 305–60.
[1] We do not use the term "capital structure" because that term usually denotes the relative quantities of bonds, equity, warrants, trade credit, etc., which represent the liabilities of a

three areas, our analysis casts new light on and has implications for a variety of issues in the professional and popular literature such as the definition of the firm, the ''separation of ownership and control'', the ''social responsibility'' of business, the definition of a ''corporate objective function'', the determination of an optimal capital structure, the specification of the content of credit agreements, the theory of organizations, and the supply side of the completeness of markets problem.

Our theory helps explain:

(1) why an entrepreneur or manager in a firm which has a mixed financial structure (containing both debt and outside equity claims) will choose a set of activities for the firm such that the total value of the firm is *less* than it would be if he were the sole owner and why this result is independent of whether the firm operates in monopolistic or competitive produce or factor markets;

(2) why his failure to maximize the value of the firm is perfectly consistent with efficiency;

(3) why the sale of common stock is a viable source of capital even though managers do not literally maximize the value of the firm;

(4) why debt was relied upon as a source of capital before debt financing offered any tax advantage relative to equity;

(5) why preferred stock would be issued;

(6) why accounting reports would be provided voluntarily to creditors and stockholders, and why independent auditors would be engaged by management to testify to the accuracy and correctness of such reports;

(7) why lenders often place restrictions on the activities of firms to whom they lend, and why firms would themselves be led to suggest the imposition of such restrictions;

(8) why some industries are characterized by owner-operated firms whose sole outside source of capital is borrowing;

(9) why highly regulated industries such as public utilities or banks will have higher debt equity ratios for equivalent levels of risk than the average non-regulated firm;

(10) why security analysis can be socially productive even if it does not increase portfolio returns to investors.

firm. Our theory implies there is another important dimension to this problem – namely the relative amounts of ownership claims held by insiders (management) and outsiders (investors with no direct role in the management of the firm).

1.2. Theory of the firm: an empty box?

While the literature of economics is replete with references to the "theory of the firm", the material generally subsumed under that heading is not a theory of the firm but actually a theory of markets in which firms are important actors. The firm is a "black box" operated so as to meet the relevant marginal conditions with respect to inputs and outputs, thereby maximizing profits, or more accurately, present value. Except for a few recent and tentative steps, however, we have no theory which explains how the conflicting objectives of the individual participants are brought into equilibrium so as to yield this result. The limitations of this black box view of the firm have been cited by Adam Smith and Alfred Marshall, among others. More recently, popular and professional debates over the "social responsibility" of corporations, the separation of ownership and control, and the rash of reviews of the literature on the "theory of the firm" have evidenced continuing concern with these issues.[2]

A number of major attempts have been made during recent years to construct a theory of the firm by substituting other models for profit or value maximization; each attempt motivated by a conviction that the latter is inadequate to explain managerial behavior in large corporations.[3] Some of these reformulation attempts have rejected the fundamental principle of maximizing behavior as well as rejecting the more specific profit maximizing model. We retain the notion of maximizing behavior on the part of all individuals in the analysis to follow.[4]

1.3. Property rights

An independent stream of research with important implications for the theory of the firm has been stimulated by the pioneering work of Coase, and ex-

[2]Reviews of this literature are given by Peterson (1965), Alchian (1965, 1968), Machlup (1967), Shubik (1970), Cyert and Hedrick (1972), Branch (1973), Preston (1975).

[3]See Williamson (1964b, 1970, 1975), Marris (1964), Baumol (1959), Penrose (1958), and Cyert and March (1963). Thorough reviews of these and other contributions are given by Machlup (1961) and Alchian (1965). •

Simon (1955) developed a model of human choice incorporating information (search) and computational costs which also has important implications for the behavior of managers. Unfortunately, Simon's work has often been misinterpreted as a denial of maximizing behavior, and misused, especially in the marketing and behavioral science literature. His later use of the term "satisficing" (Simon, 1959) has undoubtedly contributed to this confusion because it suggests rejection of maximizing behavior rather than maximization subject to costs of information and of decision making.

[4]See Meckling (1976) for a discussion of the fundamental importance of the assumption of resourceful, evaluative, maximizing behavior on the part of individuals in the development of theory. Klein (1976) takes an approach similar to the one we embark on in this paper in his review of the theory of the firm and the law.

tended by Alchian, Demsetz and others.[5] A comprehensive survey of this literature is given by Furubotn and Pejovich (1972). While the focus of this research has been "property rights",[6] the subject matter encompassed is far broader than that term suggests. What is important for the problems addressed here is that specification of individual rights determines how costs and rewards will be allocated among the participants in any organization. Since the specification of rights is generally effected through contracting (implicit as well as explicit), individual behavior in organizations, including the behavior of managers, will depend upon the nature of these contracts. We focus in this paper on the behavioral implications of the property rights specified in the contracts between the owners and managers of the firm.

1.4. Agency costs

Many problems associated with the inadequacy of the current theory of the firm can also be viewed as special cases of the theory of agency relationships in which there is a growing literature.[7] This literature has developed independently of the property rights literature even though the problems with which it is concerned are similar; the approaches are in fact highly complementary to each other.

We define an agency relationship as a contract under which one or more persons (the principal(s)) engage another person (the agent) to perform some service on their behalf which involves delegating some decision making authority to the agent. If both parties to the relationship are utility maximizers there is good reason to believe that the agent will not always act in the best interests of the principal. The *principal* can limit divergences from his interest by establishing appropriate incentives for the agent and by incurring monitoring costs designed to limit the aberrant activities of the agent. In addition in some situations it will pay the *agent* to expend resources (bonding costs) to guarantee that he will not take certain actions which would harm the principal or to ensure that the principal will be compensated if he does take such actions. However, it is generally impossible for the principal or the agent at zero cost to ensure that the agent will make optimal decisions from the principal's viewpoint. In most agency relationships the principal and the agent will incur positive monitoring and bonding costs (non-pecuniary as well as pecuniary),

---

[5] See Coase (1937, 1959, 1960), Alchian (1965, 1968), Alchian and Kessel (1962), Demsetz (1967), Alchian and Demsetz (1972), Monsen and Downs (1965), Silver and Auster (1969), and McManus (1975).

[6] Property rights are of course human rights, i.e., rights which are possessed by human beings. The introduction of the wholly false distinction between property rights and human rights in many policy discussions is surely one of the all time great semantic flimflams.

[7] Cf. Berhold (1972), Ross (1973, 1974), Wilson (1968, 1969), and Heckerman (1975).

and in all there will be some divergence between the agent's decisions[8] and those decisions which would maximize the welfare of the principal. The dollar equivalent of the reduction in welfare experienced by the principal due to this divergence is also a cost of the agency relationship, and we refer to this latter cost as the "residual loss". We define *agency costs* as the sum of:

(1) the monitoring expenditures by the principal,[9]
(2) the bonding expenditures by the agent,
(3) the residual loss.

Note also that agency costs arise in any situation involving cooperative effort (such as the co-authoring of this paper) by two or more people even though there is no clear cut principal–agent relationship. Viewed in this light it is clear that our definition of agency costs and their importance to the theory of the firm bears a close relationship to the problem of shirking and monitoring of team production which Alchian and Demsetz (1972) raise in their paper on the theory of the firm.

Since the relationship between the stockholders and manager of a corporation fit the definition of a pure agency relationship it should be no surprise to discover that the issues associated with the "separation of ownership and control" in the modern diffuse ownership corporation are intimately associated with the general problem of agency. We show below that an explanation of why and how the agency costs generated by the corporate form are born leads to a theory of the ownership (or capital) structure of the firm.

Before moving on, however, it is worthwhile to point out the generality of the agency problem. The problem of inducing an "agent" to behave as if he were maximizing the "principal's" welfare is quite general. It exists in all organizations and in all cooperative efforts – at every level of management in firms,[10] in universities, in mutual companies, in cooperatives, in governmen-

---

[8] Given the optimal monitoring and bonding activities by the principal and agent.

[9] As it is used in this paper the term monitoring includes more than just measuring or observing the behavior of the agent. It includes efforts on the part of the principal to "control" the behavior of the agent through budget restrictions, compensation policies, operating rules etc.

[10] As we show below the existence of positive monitoring and bonding costs will result in the manager of a corporation possessing control over some resources which he can allocate (within certain constraints) to satisfy his own preferences. However, to the extent that he must obtain the cooperation of others in order to carry out his tasks (such as divisional vice presidents) and to the extent that he cannot control their behavior perfectly and costlessly they will be able to appropriate some of these resources for their own ends. In short, there are agency costs generated at every level of the organization. Unfortunately, the analysis of these more general organizational issues is even more difficult than that of the "ownership and control" issue because the nature of the contractual obligations and rights of the parties are much more varied and generally not as well specified in explicit contractual arrangements. Nevertheless, they exist and we believe that extensions of our analysis in these directions show promise of producing insights into a viable theory of organization.

tal authorities and bureaus, in unions, and in relationships normally classified as agency relationships such as are common in the performing arts and the market for real estate. The development of theories to explain the form which agency costs take in each of these situations (where the contractual relations differ significantly), and how and why they are born will lead to a rich theory of organizations which is now lacking in economics and the social sciences generally. We confine our attention in this paper to only a small part of this general problem – the analysis of agency costs generated by the contractual arrangements between the owners and top management of the corporation.

Our approach to the agency problem here differs fundamentally from most of the existing literature. That literature focuses almost exclusively on the normative aspects of the agency relationship; that is how to structure the contractual relation (including compensation incentives) between the principal and agent to provide appropriate incentives for the agent to make choices which will maximize the principal's welfare given that uncertainty and imperfect monitoring exist. We focus almost entirely on the positive aspects of the theory. That is, we assume individuals solve these normative problems and given that only stocks and bonds can be issued as claims we investigate the incentives faced by each of the parties and the elements entering into the determination of the equilibrium contractual form characterizing the relationship between the manager (i.e., agent) of the firm and the outside equity and debt holders (i.e., principals).

1.5. Some general comments on the definition of the firm

Ronald Coase (1937) in his seminal paper on "The Nature of the Firm" pointed out that economics had no positive theory to determine the bounds of the firm. He characterized the bounds of the firm as that range of exchanges over which the market system was suppressed and resource allocation was accomplished instead by authority and direction. He focused on the cost of using markets to effect contracts and exchanges and argued that activities would be included within the firm whenever the costs of using markets were greater than the costs of using direct authority. Alchian and Demsetz (1972) object to the notion that activities within the firm are governed by authority, and correctly emphasize the role of contracts as a vehicle for voluntary exchange. They emphasize the role of monitoring in situations in which there is joint input or team production.[11] We sympathize with the importance they

---

[11] They define the classical capitalist firm as a contractual organization of inputs in which there is "(a) joint input production, (b) several inputs owners, (c) one party who is common to all the contracts of the joint inputs, (d) who has rights to renegotiate any input's contract independently of contracts with other input owners, (e) who holds the residual claim, and (f) who has the right to sell his contractual residual status."

attach to monitoring, but we believe the emphasis which Alchian–Demsetz place on joint input production is too narrow and therefore misleading. Contractual relations are the essence of the firm, not only with employees but with suppliers, customers, creditors, etc. The problem of agency costs and monitoring exists for all of these contracts, independent of whether there is joint production in their sense; i.e., joint production can explain only a small fraction of the behavior of individuals associated with a firm. A detailed examination of these issues is left to another paper.

It is important to recognize that most organizations are simply *legal fictions*[12] *which serve as a nexus for a set of contracting relationships among individuals.* This includes firms, non-profit institutions such as universities, hospitals and foundations, mutual organizations such as mutual savings banks and insurance companies, and co-operatives, some private clubs, and even governmental bodies such as cities, states and the Federal government, government enterprises such as TVA, the Post Office, transit systems, etc.

The private corporation or firm is simply one form of *legal fiction which serves as a nexus for contracting relationships and which is also characterized by the existence of divisible residual claims on the assets and cash flows of the organization which can generally be sold without permission of the other contracting individuals.* While this definition of the firm has little substantive content, emphasizing the essential contractual nature of firms and other organizations focuses attention on a crucial set of questions – why particular sets of contractual relations arise for various types of organizations, what the consequences of these contractual relations are, and how they are affected by changes exogenous to the organization. Viewed this way, it makes little or no sense to try to distinguish those things which are ''inside'' the firm (or any other organization) from those things that are ''outside'' of it. There is in a very real sense only a multitude of complex relationships (i.e., contracts between the legal fiction (the firm) and the owners of labor, material and capital inputs and the consumers of output.[13]

Viewing the firm as the nexus of a set of contracting relationships among individuals also serves to make it clear that the personalization of the firm implied by asking questions such as ''what should be the objective function of the firm'', or ''does the firm have a social responsibility'' is seriously misleading. *The firm is not an individual.* It is a legal fiction which serves as a focus for a complex process in which the conflicting objectives of individ-

[12] By legal fiction we mean the artificial construct under the law which allows certain organizations to be treated as individuals.

[13] For example, we ordinarily think of a product as leaving the firm at the time it is sold, but implicitly or explicitly such sales generally carry with them continuing contracts between the firm and the buyer. If the product does not perform as expected the buyer often can and does have a right to satisfaction. Explicit evidence that such implicit contracts do exist is the practice we occasionally observe of specific provision that ''all sales are final.''

uals (some of whom may "represent" other organizations) are brought into equilibrium within a framework of contractual relations. In this sense the "behavior" of the firm is like the behavior of a market; i.e., the outcome of a complex equilibrium process. We seldom fall into the trap of characterizing the wheat or stock market as an individual, but we often make this error by thinking about organizations as if they were persons with motivations and intentions.[14]

1.6. An overview of the paper

We develop the theory in stages. Sections 2 and 4 provide analyses of the agency costs of equity and debt respectively. These form the major foundation of the theory. Section 3 poses some unanswered questions regarding the existence of the corporate form of organization and examines the role of limited liability. Section 5 provides a synthesis of the basic concepts derived in sections 2–4 into a theory of the corporate ownership structure which takes account of the tradeoffs available to the entrepreneur–manager between inside and outside equity and debt. Some qualifications and extensions of the analysis are discussed in section 6, and section 7 contains a brief summary and conclusions.

2. The agency costs of outside equity

2.1. Overview

In this section we analyze the effect of outside equity on agency costs by comparing the behavior of a manger when he owns 100 percent of the residual claims on a firm to his behavior when he sells off a portion of those claims to outsiders. If a wholly owned firm is managed by the owner, he will make operating decisions which maximize his utility. These decisions will involve not only the benefits he derives from pecuniary returns but also the utility generated by various non-pecuniary aspects of his entrepreneurial activities

[14] This view of the firm points up the important role which the legal system and the law play in social organizations, especially, the organization of economic activity. Statutory law sets bounds on the kinds of contracts into which individuals and organizations may enter without risking criminal prosecution. The police powers of the state are available and used to enforce performance of contracts or to enforce the collection of damages for non-performance. The courts adjudicate conflicts between contracting parties and establish precedents which form the body of common law. All of these government activities affect both the kinds of contracts executed and the extent to which contracting is relied upon. This in turn determines the usefulness, productivity, profitability and viability of various forms of organization. Moreover, new laws as well as court decisions often can and do change the rights of contracting parties ex post, and they can and do serve as a vehicle for redistribution of wealth. An analysis of some of the implications of these facts is contained in Jensen and Meckling (1976b) and we shall not pursue them here.

such as the physical appointments of the office, the attractiveness of the sec-
retarial staff, the level of employee discipline, the kind and amount of chari-
table contributions, personal relations ("love", "respect", etc.) with employees, a larger than optimal computer to play with, purchase of production
inputs from friends, etc. The optimum mix (in the absence of taxes) of the
various pecuniary and non-pecuniary benefits is achieved when the marginal
utility derived from an additional dollar of expenditure (measured net of any
productive effects) is equal for each non-pecuniary item and equal to the marginal utility derived from an additional dollar of after tax purchasing power
(wealth).

If the owner–manager sells equity claims on the corporation which are
identical to his (i.e., share proportionately in the profits of the firm and have
limited liability) agency costs will be generated by the divergence between
his interest and those of the outside shareholders, since he will then bear only
a fraction of the costs of any non-pecuniary benefits he takes out in maximizing his own utility. If the manager owns only 95 percent of the stock, he will
expend resources to the point where the marginal utility derived from a dollar's expenditure of the firm's resources on such items equals the marginal
utility of an additional 95 cents in general purchasing power (i.e., *his* share
of the wealth reduction) and not one dollar. Such activities, on his part, can
be limited (but probably not eliminated) by the expenditure of resources on
monitoring activities by the outside stockholders. But as we show below, the
owner will bear the entire wealth effects of these expected costs so long as
the equity market anticipates these effects. Prospective minority shareholders
will realize that the owner–manager's interests will diverge somewhat from
theirs, hence the price which they will pay for shares will reflect the monitoring costs and the effect of the divergence between the manager's interest and
theirs. Nevertheless, ignoring for the moment the possibility of borrowing
against his wealth, the owner will find it desirable to bear these costs as long
as the welfare increment he experiences from converting his claims on the
firm into general purchasing power[15] is large enough to offset them.

As the owner–manager's fraction of the equity falls, his fractional claim
on the outcomes falls and this will tend to encourage him to appropriate larger
amounts of the corporate resources in the form of perquisites. This also makes
it desirable for the minority shareholders to expend more resources in monitoring his behavior. Thus, the wealth costs to the owner of obtaining additional cash in the equity markets rise as his fractional ownership falls.

We shall continue to characterize the agency conflict between the owner–

---

[15]For use in consumption, for the diversification of his wealth, or more importantly, for the
financing of "profitable" projects which he could not otherwise finance out of his personal
wealth. We deal with these issues below after having developed some of the elementary analytical
tools necessary to their solution.

manager and outside shareholders as deriving from the manager's tendency to appropriate perquisites out of the firm's resources for his own consumption. However, we do not mean to leave the impression that this is the only or even the most important source of conflict. Indeed, it is likely that the most important conflict arises from the fact that as the manager's ownership claim falls, his incentive to devote significant effort to creative activities such as searching out new profitable ventures falls. He may in fact avoid such ventures simply because it requires too much trouble or effort on his part to manage or to learn about new technologies. Avoidance of these personal costs and the anxieties that go with them also represent a source of on the job utility to him and it can result in the value of the firm being substantially lower than it otherwise could be.

2.2. A simple formal analysis of the sources of agency costs of equity and who bears them

In order to develop some structure for the analysis to follow we make two sets of assumptions. The first set (permanent assumptions) are those which shall carry through almost all of the analysis in section 2–5. The effects of relaxing some of these are discussed in section 6. The second set (temporary assumptions) are made only for expositional purposes and are relaxed as soon as the basic points have been clarified.

Permanent assumptions.

- (P.1) All taxes are zero.
- (P.2) No trade credit is available.
- (P.3) All outside equity shares are non-voting.
- (P.4) No complex financial claims such as convertible bonds or preferred stock or warrants can be issued.
- (P.5) No outside owner gains utility from ownership in a firm in any way other than through its effect on his wealth or cash flows.
- (P.6) All dynamic aspects of the multiperiod nature of the problem are ignored by assuming there is only one production–financing decision to be made by the entrepreneur.
- (P.7) The entrepreneur–manager's money wages are held constant throughout the analysis.
- (P.8) There exists a single manager (the peak coordinator) with ownership interest in the firm.

Temporary assumptions

- (T.1) The size of the firm is fixed.
- (T.2) No monitoring or bonding activities are possible.

(T.3) No debt financing through bonds, preferred stock, or personal borrowing (secured or unsecured) is possible.

(T.4) All elements of the owner–manager's decision problem involving portfolio considerations induced by the presence of uncertainty and the existence of diversifiable risk are ignored.

Define:

X $= \{x_1, x_2, \ldots, x_n\}$ = vector of quantities of all factors and activities within the firm from which the manager derives non-pecuniary benefits;[16] the x_i are defined such that this marginal utility is positive for each of them;

$C(X)$ = total dollar cost of providing any given amount of these items;

$P(X)$ = total dollar value to the firm of the productive benefits of X;

$B(X)$ = $P(X) - C(X)$ = net dollar benefit to the firm of X ignoring any effects of X on the equilibrium wage of the manger.

Ignoring the effects of X on the manager's utility and therefore on his equilibrium wage rate, the optimum levels of the factors and activities X are defined by X^* such that

$$\frac{\partial B(X^*)}{\partial X^*} = \frac{\partial P(X^*)}{\partial X^*} - \frac{\partial C(X^*)}{\partial X^*} = 0.$$

Thus for any vector $X \geqq X^*$ (i.e., where at least one element of X is greater than its corresponding element of X^*), $F \equiv B(X^*) - B(X) > 0$ measures the dollar cost to the firm (net of any productive effects) of providing the increment $X - X^*$ of the factors and activities which generate utility to the manager. We assume henceforth that for any given level of cost to the firm, F, the vector of factors and activities on which F is spent are those, $\hat{X}$, which yield the manager maximum utility. Thus $F \equiv B(X^*) - B(\hat{X})$.

We have thus far ignored in our discussion the fact that these expenditures on X occur through time and therefore there are tradeoffs to be made across time as well as between alternative elements of X. Furthermore, we have ignored the fact that the future expenditures are likely to involve uncertainty (i.e., they are subject to probability distributions) and therefore some allowance must be made for their riskiness. We resolve both of these issues by defining C, P, B, and F to be the *current market values* of the sequence of probability distributions on the period by period cash flows involved.[17]

---

[16] Such as office space, air conditioning, thickness of the carpets, friendliness of employee relations, etc.

[17] And again we assume that for any given market value of these costs, F, to the firm the allocation across time and across alternative probability distributions is such that the manager's current expected utility is at a maximum.

Given the definition of F as the current market value of the stream of manager's expenditures on non-pecuniary benefits we represent the constraint which a single owner–manager faces in deciding how much non-pecuniary income he will extract from the firm by the line $\bar{V}F$ in fig. 1. This is analogous to a budget constraint. The market value of the firm is measured along the vertical axis and the market value of the manager's stream of expenditures on non-pecuniary benefits, F, are measured along the horizontal axis. $0\bar{V}$ is the value of the firm when the amount of non-pecuniary income consumed is zero. By definition $\bar{V}$ is the maximum market value of the cash flows generated by the firm for a given money wage for the manager when the manager's consumption of non-pecuniary benefits are zero. At this point all the factors and activities within the firm which generate utility for the manager are at level X^* defined above. There is a different budget constraint $\bar{V}F$ for each possible scale of the firm (i.e., level of investment, I) and for alternative levels of money wage, W, for the manager. For the moment we pick an arbitrary level of investment (which we assume has already been made) and hold the scale of the firm constant at this level. We also assume that the manager's money wage is fixed at the level W^* which represents the current market value of his wage contract[18] in the optimal compensation package which consists of both wages, W^*, and non-pecuniary benefits, F^*. Since one dollar of current value of non-pecuniary benefits withdrawn from the firm by the manager reduces the market value of the firm by \$1, by definition, the slope of $\bar{V}F$ is -1.

The owner–manager's tastes for wealth and non-pecuniary benefits is represented in fig. 1 by a system of indifference curves, U_1, U_2, etc.[19] The indifference curves will be convex as drawn as long as the owner–manager's marginal rate of substitution between non-pecuniary benefits and wealth diminishes with increasing levels of the benefits. For the 100 percent owner–manager, this presumes that there are not perfect substitutes for these benefits available on the outside, i.e., to some extent they are job specific. For the fractional

---

[18] At this stage when we are considering a 100% owner-managed firm the notion of a "wage contract" with himself has no content. However, the 100% owner-managed case is only an expositional device used in passing to illustrate a number of points in the analysis, and we ask the reader to bear with us briefly while we lay out the structure for the more interesting partial ownership case where such a contract does have substance.

[19] The manager's utility function is actually defined over wealth and the future time sequence of vectors of quantities of non-pecuniary benefits, X_t. Although the setting of his problem is somewhat different, Fama (1970a, 1972) analyzes the conditions under which these preferences can be represented as a derived utility function defined as a function of the money value of the expenditures (in our notation F) on these goods conditional on the prices of goods. Such a utility function incorporates the optimization going on in the background which define $\hat{X}$ discussed above for a given F. In the more general case where we allow a time series of consumption, $\hat{X}_t$, the optimization is being carried out across both time and the components of X_t for fixed F.

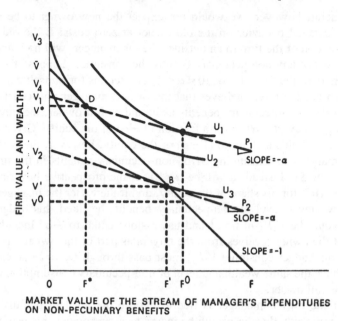

Figure 1. The value of the firm (V) and the level of non-pecuniary benefits consumed (F) when the fraction of outside equity is $(1-\alpha)V$, and U_j ($j = 1, 2, 3$) represents owner's indifference curves between wealth and non-pecuniary benefits.

owner–manager this presumes the benefits cannot be turned into general purchasing power at a constant price.[20]

When the owner has 100 percent of the equity, the value of the firm will be V^* where indifference curve U_2 is tangent to VF, and the level of non-pecuniary benefits consumed is F^*. If the owner sells the entire equity but remains as manager, and if the equity buyer can, at zero cost, force the old owner (as manager) to take the same level of non-pecuniary benefits as he did as owner, then V^* is the price the new owner will be willing to pay for the entire equity.[21]

---

[20] This excludes, for instance, (a) the case where the manager is allowed to expend corporate resources on anything he pleases in which case F would be a perfect substitute for wealth, or (b) the case where he can "steal" cash (or other marketable assets) with constant returns to scale – if he could the indifference curves would be straight lines with slope determined by the fence commission.

[21] Point D defines the fringe benefits in the optimal pay package since the value to the manager of the fringe benefits F^* is greater than the cost of providing them as is evidenced by the fact that U_2 is steeper to the left of D than the budget constraint with slope equal to -1.

That D is indeed the optimal pay package can easily be seen in this situation since if the conditions of the sale to a new owner specified that the manager would receive no fringe benefits

221

In general, however, we would not expect the new owner to be able to enforce identical behavior on the old owner at zero costs. If the old owner sells a fraction of the firm to an outsider, he, as manager, will no longer bear the full cost of any non-pecuniary benefits he consumes. Suppose the owner sells a share of the firm, $1 - \alpha$, $(0 < \alpha < 1)$ and retains for himself a share, α. If the prospective buyer believes that the owner–manager will consume the same level of non-pecuniary benefits as he did as full owner, the buyer will be willing to pay $(1 - \alpha)V^*$ for a fraction $(1 - \alpha)$ of the equity. Given that an outsider now holds a claim to $(1 - \alpha)$ of the equity, however, the *cost* to the owner–manager of consuming \$1 of non-pecuniary benefits in the firm will no longer be \$1. Instead, it will be $\alpha \times \$1$. If the prospective buyer actually paid $(1 - \alpha)V^*$ for his share of the equity, and if thereafter the manager could choose whatever level of non-pecuniary benefits he liked, his budget constraint would be V_1P_1 in fig. 1 and has a slope equal to $-\alpha$. Including the payment the owner receives from the buyers as part of the owner's post-sale wealth, his budget constraint V_1P_1, must pass through D, since he can if he wishes have the same wealth and level of non-pecuniary consumption he consumed as full owner.

But if the owner–manager is free to choose the level of perquisites, F, subject only to the loss in wealth he incurs as a part owner, his welfare will be maximized by increasing his consumption of non-pecuniary benefits. He will move to point A where V_1P_1 is tangent to U_1 representing a higher level of utility. The value of the firm falls from V^*, to V^0, i.e., by the amount of the cost to the firm of the increased non-pecuniary expenditures, and the owner–manager's consumption of non-pecuniary benefits rises from F^* to F^0.

If the equity market is characterized by rational expectations the buyers will be aware that the owner will increase his non-pecuniary consumption when his ownership share is reduced. If the owner's response function is known or if the equity market makes unbiased estimates of the owner's response to the changed incentives, the buyer will not pay $(1 - \alpha)V^*$ for $(1 - \alpha)$ of the equity.

---

after the sale he would require a payment equal to V_3 to compensate him for the sacrifice of his claims to V^* and fringe benefits amounting to F^* (the latter with total value to him of $V_3 - V^*$). But if $F = 0$, the value of the firm is only $\bar{V}$. Therefore, if monitoring costs were zero the sale would take place at V^* with provision for a pay package which included fringe benefits of F^* for the manager.

This discussion seems to indicate there are two values for the 'firm', V_3 and V^*. This is not the case if we realize that V^* is the value of the right to be the residual claimant on the cash flows of the firm and $V_3 - V^*$ is the value of the managerial rights, i.e., the right to make the operating decisions which include access to F^*. There is at least one other right which has value which plays no formal role in the analysis as yet – the value of the control right. By control right we mean the right to hire and fire the manager and we leave this issue to a future paper.

222

Theorem. For a claim of the firm of $(1-\alpha)$ the outsider will pay only $(1-\alpha)$ times the value he expects the firm to have given the induced change in the behavior of the owner–manager.

Proof. For simplicity we ignore any element of uncertainty introduced by the lack of perfect knowledge of the owner–manager's response function. Such uncertainty will not affect the final solution if the equity market is large as long as the estimates are rational (i.e., unbiased) and the errors are independent across firms. The latter condition assures that this risk is diversifiable and therefore equilibrium prices will equal the expected values.

Let W represent the owner's total wealth after he has sold a claim equal to $1-\alpha$ of the equity to an outsider. W has two components. One is the payment, S_0, made by the outsider for $1-\alpha$ of the equity; the rest, S_i, is the value of the owner's (i.e., insider's) share of the firm, so that W, the owner's wealth, is given by

$$W = S_0 + S_i = S_0 + \alpha V(F,\alpha),$$

where $V(F,\alpha)$ represents the value of the firm given that the manager's fractional ownership share is α and that he consumes perquisites with current market value of F. Let V_2P_2, with a slope of $-\alpha$, represent the tradeoff the owner–manager faces between non-pecuniary benefits and his wealth after the sale. Given that the owner has decided to sell a claim $1-\alpha$ of the firm, his welfare will be maximized when V_2P_2 is tangent to some indifference curve such as U_3 in fig. 1. A price for a claim of $(1-\alpha)$ on the firm that is satisfactory to both the buyer and the seller will require that this tangency occur along $\bar{V}F$, i.e., that the value of the firm must be V'. To show this, assume that such is not the case – that the tangency occurs to the left of the point B on the line $\bar{V}F$. Then, since the slope of V_2P_2 is negative, the value of the firm will be larger than V'. The owner–manager's choice of this lower level of consumption of non-pecuniary benefits will imply a higher value both to the firm as a whole and to the fraction of the firm $(1-\alpha)$ which the outsider has acquired; that is, $(1-\alpha)V' > S_0$. From the owner's viewpoint, he has sold $1-\alpha$ of the firm for less than he could have, given the (assumed) lower level of non-pecuniary benefits he enjoys. On the other hand, if the tangency point B is to the right of the line $\bar{V}F$, the owner–manager's higher consumption of non-pecuniary benefits means the value of the firm is less than V', and hence $(1-\alpha)V(F,\alpha) < S_0 = (1-\alpha)V'$. The outside owner then has paid more for his share of the equity than it is worth. S_0 will be a mutually satisfactory price if and only if $(1-\alpha)V' = S_0$. But this means that the owner's post-sale wealth is equal to the (reduced) value of the firm V', since

$$W = S_0 + \alpha V' = (1-\alpha)V' + \alpha V' = V'. \qquad \text{Q.E.D.}$$

The requirement that V' and F' fall on $\bar{V}F$ is thus equivalent to requiring that the value of the claim acquired by the outside buyer be equal to the amount he pays for it and conversely for the owner. *This means that the decline in the total value of the firm ($V^* - V'$) is entirely imposed on the owner–manager.* His total wealth after the sale of $(1 - \alpha)$ of the equity is V' and the decline in his wealth is $V^* - V'$.

The distance $V^* - V'$ is the reduction in the market value of the firm engendered by the agency relationship and is a measure of the "residual loss" defined earlier. In this simple example the residual loss represents the total agency costs engendered by the sale of outside equity because monitoring and bonding activities have not been allowed. The welfare loss the owner incurs is less than the residual loss by the value to him of the increase in non-pecuniary benefits $(F' - F^*)$. In fig. 1 the difference between the intercepts on the Y axis of the two indifference curves U_2 and U_3 is a measure of the owner–manager's welfare loss due to the incurrence of agency costs,[22] and he would sell such a claim only if the increment in welfare he achieves by using the cash amounting to $(1 - \alpha)V'$ for other things was worth more to him than this amount of wealth.

. . . .

2.4. The role of monitoring and bonding activities in reducing agency costs

In the above analysis we have ignored the potential for controlling the behavior of the owner–manager through monitoring and other control activities. In practice it is usually possible by expending resources to alter the opportunity the owner–manager has for capturing non-pecuniary benefits. These methods include auditing, formal control systems, budget restrictions, and the establishment of incentive compensation systems which serve to more closely identify the manager's interests with those of the outside equity holders, etc. Fig. 2 portrays the effects of monitoring and other control activities in the simple situation portrayed in fig. 1. Figs. 1 and 2 are identical except for the curve BCE in fig. 2 which depicts a "budget constraint" derived when monitoring possibilities are taken into account. Without monitoring, and with outside equity of $(1 - \alpha)$, the value of the firm will be V' and non-pecuniary expenditures F'. By incurring monitoring costs, M, the equity holders can restrict the manager's consumption of perquisites to amounts less than F'. Let $F(M, \alpha)$ denote the maximum perquisites the manager can consume for alternative

---

[22]The distance $V^* - V'$ is a measure of what we will define as the gross agency costs. The distance $V_3 - V_4$ is a measure of what we call net agency costs, and it is this measure of agency costs which will be minimized by the manager in the general case where we allow investment to change.

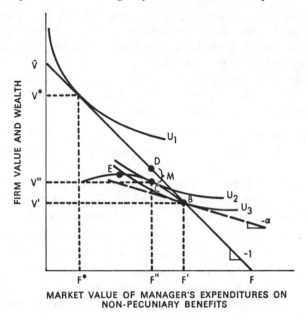

Figure 2. The value of the firm (V) and level of non-pecuniary benefits (F) when outside equity is $(1-\alpha)$, U_1, U_2, U_3 represent owner's indifference curves between wealth and non-pecuniary benefits, and monitoring (or bonding) activities impose opportunity set BCE as the tradeoff constraint facing the owner.

levels of monitoring expenditures, M, given his ownership share α. We assume that increases in monitoring reduce F, and reduce it at a decreasing rate, i.e., $\partial F/\partial M < 0$ and $\partial^2 F/\partial M^2 > 0$.

Since the current value of expected future monitoring expenditures by the outside equity holders reduce the value of any given claim on the firm to them dollar for dollar, the outside equity holders will take this into account in determining the maximum price they will pay for any given fraction of the firm's equity. Therefore, given positive monitoring activity the value of the firm is given by $V = \bar{V} - F(M,\alpha) - M$ and the locus of these points for various levels of M and for a given level of α lie on the line BCE in fig. 2. The vertical difference between the $\bar{V}F$ and BCE curves is M, the current market value of the future monitoring expenditures.

If it is possible for the outside equity holders to make these monitoring expenditures and thereby to impose the reductions in the owner–manager's consumption of F, he will voluntarily enter into a contract with the outside equity holders which gives them the rights to restrict his consumption of non-pecuniary items to F''. He finds this desirable because it will cause the value of the firm to rise to V''. Given the contract, the optimal monitoring expendi-

225

ture on the part of the outsiders, M, is the amount $D - C$. The entire increase in the value of the firm that accrues will be reflected in the owner's wealth, but his welfare will be increased by less than this because he forgoes some non-pecuniary benefits he previously enjoyed.

If the equity market is competitive and makes unbiased estimates of the effects of the monitoring expenditures on F and V, potential buyers will be indifferent between the following two contracts:

  (i) Purchase of a share $(1 - \alpha)$ of the firm at a total price of $(1 - \alpha)V'$ and no rights to monitor or control the manager's consumption of perquisites.
 (ii) Purchase of a share $(1 - \alpha)$ of the firm at a total price of $(1 - \alpha)V''$ and the right to expend resources up to an amount equal to $D - C$ which will limit the owner–manager's consumption of perquisites to F.

Given contract (ii) the outside shareholders would find it desirable to monitor to the full rights of their contract because it will pay them to do so. However, if the equity market is competitive the total benefits (net of the monitoring costs) will be capitalized into the price of the claims. Thus, not surprisingly, the owner–manager reaps all the benefits of the opportunity to write and sell the monitoring contract.

An analysis of bonding expenditures. We can also see from the analysis of fig. 2 that it makes no difference who actually makes the monitoring expenditures – the owner bears the full amount of these costs as a wealth reduction in all cases. Suppose that the owner – manager could expend resources to guarantee to the outside equity holders that he would limit his activities which cost the firm F. We call these expenditures "bonding costs", and they would take such forms as contractual guarantees to have the financial accounts audited by a public accountant, explicit bonding against malfeasance on the part of the manager, and contractual limitations on the manager's decision making power (which impose costs on the firm because they limit his ability to take full advantage of some profitable opportunities as well as limiting his ability to harm the stockholders while making himself better off).

If the incurrence of the bonding costs were entirely under the control of the manager and if they yielded the same opportunity set BCE for him in fig. 2, he would incur them in amount $D - C$. This would limit his consumption of perquisites to F'' from F', and the solution is exactly the same as if the outside equity holders had performed the monitoring. The manager finds it in his interest to incur these costs as long as the net increments in his wealth which they generate (by reducing the agency costs and therefore increasing the value of the firm) are more valuable than the perquisites given up. This optimum occurs at point C in both cases under our assumption that the bonding expenditures yield the same opportunity set as the monitoring expenditures. In general, of course, it will pay the owner–manager to engage in bonding activities and to write contracts which allow monitoring as long as the marginal benefits of each are greater than their marginal cost.

. . .

2.5. Pareto optimality and agency costs in manager-operated firms

In general we expect to observe both bonding and external monitoring activities, and the incentives are such that the levels of these activities will satisfy the conditions of efficiency. They will not, however, result in the firm being run in a manner so as to maximize its value. The difference between V^*, the efficient solution under zero monitoring and bonding costs (and therefore zero agency costs), and V'', the value of the firm given positive monitoring costs, are the total gross agency costs defined earlier in the introduction. These are the costs of the "separation of ownership and control" which Adam Smith focused on in the passage quoted at the beginning of this paper and which Berle and Means (1932) popularized 157 years later. The solutions outlined above to our highly simplified problem imply that agency costs will be positive as long as monitoring costs are positive – which they certainly are.

The reduced value of the firm caused by the manager's consumption of perquisites outlined above is "non-optimal" or inefficient only in comparison to a world in which we could obtain compliance of the agent to the principal's wishes at zero cost or in comparison to a *hypothetical* world in which the agency costs were lower. But these costs (monitoring and bonding costs and 'residual loss') are an unavoidable result of the agency relationship. Furthermore, since they are borne entirely by the decision maker (in this case the original owner) responsible for creating the relationship he has the incentives to see that they are minimized (because he captures the benefits from their reduction). Furthermore, these agency costs will be incurred only if the benefits to the owner–manager from their creation are great enough to outweigh them. In our current example these benefits arise from the availability of profitable investments requiring capital investment in excess of the original owner's personal wealth.

In conclusion, finding that agency costs are non-zero (i.e., that there are costs associated with the separation of ownership and control in the corporation) and concluding therefrom that the agency relationship is non-optimal, wasteful or inefficient is equivalent in every sense to comparing a world in which iron ore is a scarce commodity (and therefore costly) to a world in which it is freely available at zero resource cost, and concluding that the first world is "non-optimal" – a perfect example of the fallacy criticized by Coase

227

(1964) and what Demsetz (1969) characterizes as the "Nirvana" form of analysis.[23]

2.6. Factors affecting the size of the divergence from ideal maximization

The magnitude of the agency costs discussed above will vary from firm to firm. It will depend on the tastes of managers, the ease with which they can exercise their own preferences as opposed to value maximization in decision making, and the costs of monitoring and bonding activities.[24] The agency costs will also depend upon the cost of measuring the manager's (agent's) performance and evaluating it, the cost of devising and applying an index for compensating the manager which correlates with the owner's (principal's) welfare, and the cost of devising and enforcing specific behavioral rules or policies. Where the manager has less than a controlling interest in the firm, it will also depend upon the market for managers. Competition from other potential managers limits the costs of obtaining managerial services (including the extent to which a given manager can diverge from the idealized solution which would obtain if all monitoring and bonding costs were zero). The size of the divergence (the agency costs) will be directly related to the cost of replacing the manager. If his responsibilities require very little knowledge specialized to the firm, if it is easy to evaluate his performance, and if replacement search costs are modest, the divergence from the ideal will be relatively small and vice versa.

The divergence will also be constrained by the market for the firm itself, i.e., by capital markets. Owners always have the option of selling their firm, either as a unit or piecemeal. Owners of manager-operated firms can and do sample the capital market from time to time. If they discover that the value of the future earnings stream to others is higher than the value of the firm to them given that it is to be manager-operated, they can exercise their right to sell. It is conceivable that other owners could be more efficient at monitoring or even that a single individual with appropriate managerial talents and with sufficiently large personal wealth would elect to buy the firm. In this latter case the purchase by such a single individual would completely eliminate the agency costs. If there were a number of such potential owner-manager pur-

---

[23] If we could establish the existence of a feasible set of alternative institutional arrangements which would yield net benefits from the reduction of these costs we could legitimately conclude the agency relationship engendered by the corporation was not Pareto optimal. However, we would then be left with the problem of explaining why these alternative institutional arrangements have not replaced the corporate form of organization.

[24] The monitoring and bonding costs will differ from firm to firm depending on such things as the inherent complexity and geographical dispersion of operations, the attractiveness of perquisites available in the firm (consider the mint), etc.

chasers (all with talents and tastes identical to the current manager) the owners would receive in the sale price of the firm the full value of the residual claimant rights including the capital value of the eliminated agency costs plus the value of the managerial rights.

Monopoly, competition, and managerial behavior. It is frequently argued that the existence of competition in product (and factor) markets will constrain the behavior of managers to idealized value maximization, i.e., that monopoly in product (or monopsony in factor) markets will permit larger divergences from value maximization.[25] Our analysis does not support this hypothesis. The owners of a firm with monopoly power have the same incentives to limit divergences of the manager from value maximization (i.e., the ability to increase their wealth) as do the owners of competitive firms. Furthermore, competition in the market for managers will generally make it unnecessary for the owners to share rents with the manager. The owners of a monopoly firm need only pay the supply price for a manager.

Since the owner of a monopoly has the same wealth incentives to minimize managerial costs as would the owner of a competitive firm, both will undertake that level of monitoring which equates the marginal cost of monitoring to the marginal wealth increment from reduced consumption of perquisites by the manager. Thus, the existence of monopoly will not increase agency costs.

Furthermore the existence of competition in product and factor markets will not eliminate the agency costs due to managerial control problems as has often been asserted [cf. Friedman (1970)]. If my competitors all incur agency costs equal to or greater than mine I will not be eliminated from the market by their competition.

The existence and size of the agency costs depends on the nature of the monitoring costs, the tastes of managers for non-pecuniary benefits and the supply of potential managers who are capable of financing the entire venture out of their personal wealth. If monitoring costs are zero, agency costs will be zero or if there are enough 100 percent owner–managers available to own and run all the firms in an industry (competitive or not) then agency costs in that industry will also be zero.

[25] "Where competitors are numerous and entry is easy, persistent departures from profit maximizing behavior inexorably leads to extinction. Economic natural selection holds the stage. In these circumstances, the behavior of the individual units that constitute the supply side of the product market is essentially routine and uninteresting and economists can confidently predict industry behavior without being explicitly concerned with the behavior of these individual units.

When the conditions of competition are relaxed, however, the opportunity set of the firm is expanded. In this case, the behavior of the firm as a distinct operating unit is of separate interest. Both for purposes of interpreting particular behavior within the firm as well as for predicting responses of the industry aggregate, it may be necessary to identify the factors that influence the firm's choices within this expanded opportunity set and embed these in a formal model." (Williamson, 1964, p. 2)

CHAPTER 18

Vertical integration, appropriable rents, and the competitive contracting process

BENJAMIN KLEIN, ROBERT CRAWFORD, and
ARMEN ALCHIAN

Benjamin Klein was born in 1943 in New York City. He received the
Ph.D. in economics at the University of Chicago in 1970. Since 1978,
he has been Professor of Economics at the University of California, Los
Angeles.

Robert Crawford was born in 1943 in Medicine Hat, Alberta, Canada.
He received the Ph.D. in economics from Carnegie-Mellon University
in 1976. Since 1978, he has been Associate Professor of Economics at
Brigham Young University.

Armen Alchian is Emeritus Professor of Economics at the University of
California, Los Angeles. See also his paper coauthored with Harold
Demsetz in this volume.

More than forty years have passed since Coase's fundamental insight that
transaction, coordination, and contracting costs must be considered explicitly
in explaining the extent of vertical integration.[1] Starting from the truism that
profit-maximizing firms will undertake those activities that they find cheaper
to administer internally than to purchase in the market, Coase forced economists to begin looking for previously neglected constraints on the trading
process that might efficiently lead to an intrafirm rather than an interfirm
transaction. This paper attempts to add to this literature by exploring one
particular cost of using the market system – the possibility of post-contractual
opportunistic behavior.

Opportunistic behavior has been identified and discussed in the modern
analysis of the organization of economic activity. Williamson, for example,
has referred to effects on the contracting process of "*ex post* small numbers
opportunism,"[2] and Teece has elaborated:

Reprinted with abridgements from Benjamin Klein, Robert Crawford, and Armen Alchian,
"Vertical Integration, Appropriable Rents, and the Competitive Contracting Process," *Journal
of Law and Economics,* 21 (1978): 297–326. Copyright 1978. Reprinted with the permission of
the University of Chicago Press.

[1] R. H. Coase (1937).   [2] Oliver E. Williamson (1975).

Even when all of the relevant contingencies can be specified in a contract, contracts are still open to serious risks since they are not always honored. The 1970's are replete with examples of the risks associated with relying on contracts . . . [O]pen displays of opportunism are not infrequent and very often litigation turns out to be costly and ineffectual.[3]

The particular circumstance we emphasize as likely to produce a serious threat of this type of reneging on contracts is the presence of appropriable specialized quasi rents. After a specific investment is made and such quasi rents are created, the possibility of opportunistic behavior is very real. Following Coase's framework, this problem can be solved in two possible ways: vertical integration or contracts. The crucial assumption underlying the analysis of this paper is that, as assets become more specific and more appropriable quasi rents are created (and therefore the possible gains from opportunistic behavior increase), the costs of contracting will generally increase more than the costs of vertical integration. Hence, *ceteris paribus*, we are more likely to observe vertical integration.

I. Appropriable quasi rents of specialized assets

Assume an asset is owned by one individual and rented to another individual. The quasi-rent value of the asset is the excess of its value over its salvage value, that is, its value in its next best *use* to another renter. The potentially appropriable specialized portion of the quasi rent is that portion, if any, in excess of its value to the second highest-valuing *user*. If this seems like a distinction without a difference, consider the following example,

Imagine a printing press owned and operated by party A. Publisher B buys printing services from party A by leasing his press at a contracted rate of $5,500 per day. The amortized fixed cost of the printing press is $4,000 per day and it has a current salvageable value if moved elsewhere of $1,000 (daily rental equivalent). Operating costs are $1,500 and are paid by the printing-press owner, who prints final printed pages for the publisher. Assume also that a second publisher C is willing to offer at most $3,500 for daily service. The current quasi rent on the installed machine is $3,000 ($=\$5,500-\$1,500-\$1,000$), the revenue minus operating costs minus salvageable value. However, the daily quasi rent from publisher B relative to use of the machine for publisher C is only $2,000 ($=\$5,500-\$3,500$). At $5,500 revenue daily from publisher B the press owner would break even on his investment. If the publisher were then able to cut his offer for the press from $5,500 down to almost $3,500, he would still have the press service available to him. He would be appropriating $2,000 of the quasi rent from the

---

[3] David J. Teece (1976).

press owner. The $2,000 difference between his prior agreed-to daily rental of $5,500 and the next best revenue available to the press once the machine is purchased and installed is less than the quasi rent and therefore is potentially appropriable. If no second party were available at the present site, the entire quasi rent would be subject to threat of appropriation by an unscrupulous or opportunistic publisher.

Our primary interest concerns the means whereby this risk can be reduced or avoided. In particular, vertical integration is examined as a means of economizing on the costs of avoiding risks of appropriation of quasi rents in specialized assets by opportunistic individuals. This advantage of joint ownership of such specialized assets, namely, economizing on contracting costs necessary to insure nonopportunistic behavior, must of course be weighed against the costs of administering a broader range of assets within the firm.[4]

An appropriable quasi rent is not a monopoly rent in the usual sense, that is, the increased value of an asset protected from market entry over the value it would have had in an open market. An appropriable quasi rent can occur with no market closure or restrictions placed on rival assets. Once installed, an asset may be so expensive to remove or so specialized to a particular user that if the price paid to the owner were somehow reduced the asset's services to that user would not be reduced. Thus, even if there were free and open competition for entry to the market, the specialization of the installed asset to a particular user (or more accurately the high costs of making it available to others) creates a quasi rent, but no "monopoly" rent. At the other extreme, an asset may be costlessly transferable to some other user at no reduction in value, while at the same time, entry of similar assets is restricted. In this case, monopoly rent would exist, but no quasi rent.

We can use monopoly terminology to refer to the phenomenon we are discussing as long as we recognize that we are not referring to the usual monopoly created by government restrictions on entry or referring to a single supplier or even highly concentrated supply. One of the fundamental premises of this paper is that monopoly power, better labeled "market power," is pervasive. Because of transaction and mobility costs, "market power" will exist in many situations not commonly called monopolies. There may be many potential suppliers of a particular asset to a particular user but once the investment in the asset is made, the asset may be so specialized to a particular user that monopoly or monopsony market power, or both, is created.

---

[4] Vertical integration does not completely avoid contracting problems. The firm could usefully be thought of as a complex nonmarket contractual network where very similar forces are present. Frank Knight stressed the importance of this more than 50 years ago when he stated: "[T]he internal problems of the corporation, the protection of its various types of members and adherents against each other's predatory propensities, are quite as vital as the external problem of safeguarding the public interest against exploitation by the corporation as a unit." Frank H. Knight (1964).

Vertical integration, appropriable rents, competitive contracting process

A related motive for vertical integration that should not be confused with our main interest is the optimal output and pricing between two successive monopolists or bilateral monopolists (in the sense of marginal revenue less than price). A distortion arises because each sees a distorted marginal revenue or marginal cost.[5] While it is true that this successive monopoly distortion can be avoided by vertical integration, the results of the integration could, for that purpose alone, be achieved by a long-term or a more detailed contract based on the true marginal revenue and marginal costs. Integrated ownership will sometimes be utilized to economize on such precontractual bargaining costs. However, we investigate a different reason for joint ownership of vertically related assets – the avoidance of postcontractual opportunistic behavior when specialized assets and appropriable quasi rents are present. One must clearly distinguish the transaction and information costs of reaching an agreement (discovering and heeding true costs and revenues and agreeing upon the division of profits) and the enforcement costs involved in assuring compliance with an agreement, especially one in which specialized assets are involved. It is this latter situation which we here explore as a motivation for intrafirm rather than interfirm transactions.

We maintain that if an asset has a substantial portion of quasi rent which is strongly dependent upon some other particular asset, both assets will tend to be owned by one party. For example, reconsider our printing press example. Knowing that the press would exist and be operated even if its owner got as little as $1,500, publisher B could seek excuses to renege on his initial contract to get the weekly rental down from $5,500 to close to $3,500 (the potential offer from publisher C, the next highest-valuing user at its present site). If publisher B could effectively announce he was not going to pay more than, say, $4,000 per week, the press owner would seem to be stuck. This unanticipated action would be opportunistic behavior (which by definition refers to unanticipated non-fulfillment of the contract) if the press owner had installed the press at a competitive rental price of $5,500 anticipating (possibly naively) good faith by the publisher. The publisher, for example, might plead that his newspaper business is depressed and he will be unable to continue unless rental terms are revised.

Alternatively, and maybe more realistically, because the press owner may have bargaining power due to the large losses that he can easily impose on the publisher (if he has no other source of press services quickly available), the press owner might suddenly seek to get a higher rental price than $5,500 to capture some newly perceived increase in the publisher's profits. He could

---

[5] This matter of successive and bilateral monopoly has long been known and exposited in many places. See, for example, Robert Bork (1954); Fritz Machlup & Martha Taber (1960), where the problem is dated back to Cournot's statement in 1838.

do this by alleging breakdowns or unusually high maintenance costs. This type of opportunistic behavior is difficult to prove and therefore litigate.

As we shall see, the costs of contractually specifying all important elements of quality varies considerably by type of asset. For some assets it may be essentially impossible to effectively specify all elements of quality and therefore vertical integration is more likely. But even for those assets used in situations where all relevant quality dimensions can be unambiguously specified in a contract, the threat of production delay during litigation may be an effective bargaining device. A contract therefore may be clearly enforceable but still subject to postcontractual opportunistic behavior. For example, the threat by the press owner to break its contract by pulling out its press is credible even though illegal and possibly subject to injunctive action. This is because such an action, even in the very short run, can impose substantial costs on the newspaper publisher.[6]

This more subtle form of opportunistic behavior is likely to result in a loss of efficiency and not just a wealth-distribution effect. For example, the publisher may decide, given this possibility, to hold or seek standby facilities otherwise not worthwhile. Even if transactors are risk neutral, the presence of possible opportunistic behavior will entail costs as real resources are devoted to the attempt to improve posttransaction bargaining positions in the event such opportunism occurs. In particular, less specific investments will be made to avoid being "locked in."[7] In addition, the increased uncertainty of quality and quantity leads to larger optimum inventories and other increased real costs of production.

This attention to appropriable specialized quasi rents is not novel. In addi-

[6] While newspaper publishers generally own their own presses, book publishers generally do not. One possible reason book publishers are less integrated may be because a book is planned further ahead in time and can economically be released with less haste. Presses located in any area of the United States can be used. No press is specialized to one publisher, in part because speed in publication and distribution to readers are generally far less important for books than newspapers, and therefore appropriable quasi rents are not created. Magazines and other periodicals can be considered somewhere between books and newspapers in terms of the importance of the time factor in distribution. In addition, because magazines are distributed nationally from at most a few plants, printing presses located in many different alternative areas are possible competitors for an existing press used at a particular location. Hence, a press owner has significantly less market power over the publisher of a magazine compared to a newspaper and we find magazines generally printed in nonpublisher-owned plants. (See W. Eric Gustafson, 1959.) But while a magazine printing press may be a relatively less specific asset compared to a newspaper printing press, appropriable quasi rents may not be trivial (as possibly they are in the case of book printing). The magazine printing contract is therefore unlikely to be of a short-term one-transaction form but will be a long-term arrangement.

[7] The relevance for private investments in underdeveloped, politically unstable, that is, "opportunistic," countries is painfully obvious. The importance for economic growth of predictable government behavior regarding the definition and enforcement of property rights has frequently been noted.

tion to Williamson's[8] pathbreaking work in the area, Goldberg's[9] perceptive analysis of what he calls the "hold up" problem in the context of government regulation is what we are discussing in a somewhat different context. Goldberg indicates how some government regulation can usefully be considered a means of avoiding or reducing the threat of loss of quasi rent. (Goldberg treats this as the problem of providing protection for the "right to be served.") He also recognizes that this force underlies a host of other contractual and institutional arrangements such as stockpiling, insurance contracts, and vertical integration. Our analysis will similarly suggest a rationale for the existence of particular institutions and the form of governmental intervention or contractual provisions as alternatives to vertical integration in a wide variety of cases.

II. Contractual solutions

The primary alternative to vertical integration as a solution to the general problem of opportunistic behavior is some form of economically enforceable long-term contract. Clearly a short-term (for example, one transaction, non-repeat sale) contract will not solve the problem. The relevant question then becomes when will vertical integration be observed as a solution and when will the use of the market-contracting process occur. Some economists and lawyers have defined this extremely difficult question away by calling a long-term contract a form of vertical integration.[10] Although there is clearly a continuum here, we will attempt not to blur the distinction between a long-term rental agreement and ownership. We assume the opportunistic behavior we are concentrating on can occur only with the former.[11]

For example, if opportunism occurs by the owner–lessor of an asset failing to maintain it properly for the user–lessee and hence unexpectedly increasing the effective rental price, legal remedies (proving contract violation) may be very costly. On the other hand, if the user owned the asset, then the employee who failed to maintain the asset properly could merely be fired.[12] If the em-

---

[8] Oliver E. Williamson (1971) and Williamson (1975).   [9] Victor P. Goldberg (1976).

[10] See, for example, Friedrich Kessler & Richard H. Stern (1959).

[11] It is commonly held that users of assets that can be damaged by careless use and for which the damage is not easy to detect immediately are more likely to own rather than rent the assets. However, these efficient maintenance considerations apply to short-term contracts and are irrelevant if the length of the long-term rental contract coincides with the economic life of the asset. Abstracting from tax considerations, the long-term contract remains less than completely equivalent to vertical integration only because of the possibility of postcontractual opportunistic reneging. These opportunistic possibilities, however, may also exist within the firm; see note 4 *supra*.

[12] We are abstracting from any considerations of a firm's detection costs of determining proper maintenance. Ease of termination also analytically distinguishes between a franchisor-franchisee arrangement and a vertically integrated arrangement with a profit-sharing manager. If cheating occurs, it is generally cheaper to terminate an employee rather than a franchisee. (The law has

ployee could still effectively cheat the owner–user of the asset because of his specific ability to maintain the asset, then the problem is that vertical integration of a relevant asset, the employee's human capital, has not occurred. For the moment, however, we will concentrate solely on the question of long-term rental versus ownership of durable physical assets.[13]

Long-term contracts used as alternatives to vertical integration can be assumed to take two forms: (1) an explicitly stated contractual guarantee legally enforced by the government or some other outside institution, or (2) an implicit contractual guarantee enforced by the market mechanism of withdrawing future business if opportunistic behavior occurs. Explicit long-term contracts can, in principle, solve opportunistic problems, but, as suggested already, they are often very costly solutions. They entail costs of specifying possible contingencies and the policing and litigation costs of detecting violations and enforcing the contract in the courts.[14] Contractual provisions specifying compulsory arbitration or more directly imposing costs on the opportunistic party (for example, via bonding) are alternatives often employed to economize on litigation costs and to create flexibility without specifying every possible contingency and quality dimension of the transaction.

Since every contingency cannot be cheaply specified in a contract or even known and because legal redress is expensive, transactors will generally also rely on an implicit type of long-term contract that employs a market rather than legal enforcement mechanism, namely, the imposition of a capital loss by the withdrawal of expected future business. This goodwill market-enforcement mechanism undoubtedly is a major element of the contractual alternative to vertical integration. Macaulay provides evidence that relatively informal, legally unenforceable contractual practices predominate in business relations and that reliance on explicit legal sanctions is extremely rare.[15] Instead, business firms are said to generally rely on effective extralegal market

been changing recently to make it more difficult to terminate either type of laborer.) But the more limited job-tenure rights of an employee compared to a franchisee reduce his incentive to invest in building up future business, and the firm must trade off the benefits and costs of the alternative arrangements. A profit-sharing manager with an explicit long-term employment contract would essentially be identical to a franchisee.

[13] The problems involved with renting specific human capital are discussed below.

[14] The recent Westinghouse case dealing with failure to fulfill uranium-supply contracts on grounds of "commercial impossibility" vividly illustrates these enforcement costs. Nearly three years after outright cancellation by Westinghouse of their contractual commitment, the lawsuits have not been adjudicated and those firms that have settled with Westinghouse have accepted substantially less than the original contracts would have entitled them to. A recent article by Paul L. Joskow (1977) analyzes the Westinghouse decision to renege on the contract as anticipated risk sharing and therefore, using our definition, would not be opportunistic behavior. However, the publicity surrounding this case and the judicial progress to date are likely to make explicit long-term contracts a less feasible alternative to vertical integration in the situations we are analyzing.

[15] Stewart Macaulay (1963).

236

sanctions, such as the depreciation of an opportunistic firm's general goodwill because of the anticipated loss of future business, as a means of preventing nonfulfillment of contracts.

One way in which this market mechanism of contract enforcement may operate is by offering to the potential cheater a future "premium," more precisely, a price sufficiently greater than average variable (that is, avoidable) cost to assure a quasi-rent stream that will exceed the potential gain from cheating.[16] The present-discounted value of this future premium stream must be greater than any increase in wealth that could be obtained by the potential cheater if he, in fact, cheated and were terminated. The offer of such a long-term relationship with the potential cheater will eliminate systematic opportunistic behavior.[17]

The larger the potential one-time "theft" by cheating (the longer and more costly to detect a violation, enforce the contract, switch suppliers, and so forth) and the shorter the expected continuing business relationship, the higher this premium will be in a nondeceiving equilibrium. This may therefore partially explain both the reliance by firms on long-term implicit contracts with particular suppliers and the existence of reciprocity agreements among firms. The premium can be paid in seemingly unrelated profitable reciprocal business. The threat of termination of this relationship mutually suppresses opportunistic behavior.[18]

[16] The following discussion of the market enforcement mechanism is based upon the analysis of competitive equilibrium under costly quality information developed in Benjamin Klein & Keith Leffler (1979), which formally extends and more completely applies the analysis in Benjamin Klein (1974). It is similar to the analysis presented in Gary S. Becker & George J. Stigler (1974), of insuring against malfeasance by an employer. This market-enforcement mechanism is used in Benjamin Klein & Andrew McLaughlin, (1978) (unpublished manuscript), to explain franchising arrangements and particular contractual provisions such as resale price maintenance, exclusive territories, initial specific investments, and termination clauses.

[17] Formally, this arrangement to guarantee nonopportunistic behavior unravels if there is a last period in the relationship. No matter how high the premium, cheating would occur at the start of the last period. If transactors are aware of this, no transaction relying on trust (that is, the expectation of another subsequent trial) will be made in the penultimate period, because it becomes the last period, and so on. If some large lump-sum, final-period payment such as a pension as part of the market-enforcement scheme, as outlined by Gary S. Becker & George J. Stigler (1974), this last-period problem is obvious. One solution to this unrecognized last-period problem is the acceptance of some continuing third party (for example, escrow agents or government enforcers) to prevent reneging on the implicit contracts against reneging we are outlining. Alternatively, the potential loss of value of indefinitely long-lived salable brand-name assets can serve as deterrents to cheating even where the contract between two parties has a last period. If one party's reputation for nonopportunistic dealings can be sold and used in later transactions in an infinite-time-horizon economy, the firm that cheats in the "last" period to any one buyer from the firm experiences a capital loss. This may partially explain the existence of conglomerates and their use of identifying (not product-descriptive) brand names.

[18] Although it may not always be in one's narrow self-interest to punish the other party in such a reciprocal relationship since termination may impose a cost on both, it may be rational for one to adopt convincingly such a reaction function to optimally prevent cheating. R. L. Trivers (1971), discusses similar mechanisms such as "moralistic aggression" which he claims have

The premium stream can be usefully thought of as insurance payments made by the firm to prevent cheating.[19] As long as both parties to the transaction make the same estimate of the potential short-run gain from cheating, the quantity of this assurance that will be demanded and supplied will be such that no opportunistic behavior will be expected to occur.[20] If postcontractual reneging is anticipated to occur, either the correct premium will be paid to optimally prevent it or, if the premium necessary to eliminate reneging is too costly, the particular transaction will not be made.

We are not implicitly assuming here that contracts are enforced costlessly and cannot be broken, but rather that given our information-cost assumptions, parties to a contract know exactly when and how much a contract will be broken. An unanticipated broken contract, that is, opportunistic behavior, is therefore not possible in this particular equilibrium. In the context of this model, expected wealth maximization will yield some opportunistic behavior only if we introduce a stochastic element. This will alter the informational equilibrium state such that the potential cheater's estimate of the short-run gain from opportunistic behavior may be at times greater than the other firm's estimate. Hence, less than an optimal premium will be paid and opportunistic behavior will occur.

The firms collecting the premium payments necessary to assure fulfillment of contractual agreements in a costly information world may appear to be earning equilibrium "profits" although they are in a competitive market. That is, there may be many, possibly identical, firms available to supply the services of nonopportunistic performance of contractual obligations yet the premium will not be competed away if transactors cannot costlessly guarantee contractual performance. The assurance services, by definition, will not be supplied unless the premium is paid and the mere payment of this premium produces the required services.

Any profits are competed away in equilibrium by competitive expenditures on fixed (sunk) assets, such as initial specific investments (for example, a

been genetically selected to protect reciprocating altruists against cheaters. Similarly, throughout the discussion we implicitly assume that cheating individuals can only cheat once and thereafter earn the "competitive" rate of return. They may, however, be forced to earn less than the competitive wage if they are caught cheating, that is, take an extra capital loss (collusively, but rationally) imposed by other members of the group. This may explain why individuals may prefer to deal in business relations with their own group (for example, members of the same church or the same country club) where effective social sanctions can be imposed against opportunistic behavior. Reliance on such reciprocal business relationships and group enforcement mechanisms is more likely where governmental enforcement of contracts is weaker. Nathaniel H. Leff (1978), for example, documents the importance of such groups in less-developed countries. Industries supplying illegal products and services would likely be another example.

[19] It is, of course, an insurance scheme that not only pools risks but also alters them.

[20] As opposed to the analysis of Michael R. Darby & Edi Karni (1973), the equilibrium quantity of opportunistic behavior or "fraud" will be zero under our assumptions of symmetrical information.

sign) with low or zero salvage value if the firm cheats, necessary to enter and obtain this preferred position of collecting the premium stream.[21] These fixed (sunk) costs of supplying credibility of future performance are repaid or covered by future sales on which a premium is earned. In equilibrium, the premium stream is then merely a normal rate of return on the "reputation," or "brand-name" capital created by the firm by these initial expenditures. This brand-name capital, the value of which is highly specific to contract fulfillment by the firm, is analytically equivalent to a forfeitable collateral bond put up by the firm which is anticipated to face an opportunity to take advantage of appropriable quasi rents in specialized assets.

While these initial specific investments or collateral bonds are sometimes made as part of the normal (minimum-cost) production process and therefore at small additional cost, transaction costs and risk considerations do make them costly. We can generally say that the larger the appropriable specialized quasi rents (and therefore the larger the potential short-run gain from opportunistic behavior) and the larger the premium payments necessary to prevent contractual reneging, the more costly this implicit contractual solution will be. We can also expect the explicit contract costs to be positively related to the level of appropriable quasi rents since it will pay to use more resources (including legal services) to specify precisely more contingencies when potential opportunities for lucrative contractual reneging exist.

Although implicit and explicit contracting and policing costs are positively related to the extent of appropriable specialized quasi rents, it is reasonable to assume, on the other hand, that any internal coordination or other ownership costs are not systematically related to the extent of the appropriable specialized quasi rent of the physical asset owned. Hence we can reasonably expect the following general empirical regularity to be true: the lower the appropriable specialized quasi rents, the more likely that transactors will rely on a contractual relationship rather than common ownership. And conversely, integration by common or joint ownership is more likely, the higher the appropriable specialized quasi rents of the assets involved.

III. Example of appropriable specialized quasi rent

This section presents examples of specialized quasi rents where the potential for their appropriation serves as an important determinant of economic organization. A series of varied illustrations, some quite obvious and others rather subtle, will make the analysis more transparent and provide suggestive evidence for the relevance of the protection of appropriable quasi rents as an

---

[21] A more complete analysis of market equilibrium by the use of specific capital in guaranteeing contract enforcement is developed in Benjamin Klein & Keith Leffler (1979).

incentive to vertically integrate. It also suggests the direction of more systematic empirical work that obviously is required to assess the significance of this factor relative to other factors in particular cases. Where this force towards integration (that is, the economizing on contracting costs necessary to assure nonopportunistic behavior in the presence of appropriable quasi rents) does not appear to dominate, important insights regarding the determinants of particular contracting costs and contract provisions are thereby provided.[22]

. . .

B. Petroleum industry

Appropriable quasi rents exist in specialized assets of oil refineries, pipelines, and oil fields. This leads to common ownership to remove the incentive for individuals to attempt to capture the rents of assets owned by someone else.

Suppose several oil wells are located along a separately owned pipeline that leads to a cluster of independently owned refineries with no alternative crude supply at comparable cost. Once all the assets are in place (the wells drilled and the pipeline and refineries constructed) the oil-producing properties and the refineries are specialized to the pipeline. The portion of their value above the value to the best alternative user is an appropriable specialized quasi rent. The extent of the appropriable quasi rent is limited, in part, by the costs of entry to a potential parallel pipeline developer. Since pipelines between particular oil-producing properties and particular refineries are essentially natural monopolies, the existing pipeline owner may have a significant degree of market power.

These specialized producing and refining assets are therefore "hostage" to the pipeline owner. At the "gathering end" of the pipeline, the monopsonist pipeline could and would purchase all its oil at the same well-head price regardless of the distance of the well from the refinery. This price could be as low as the marginal cost of getting oil out of the ground (or its reservation value for future use, if higher) and might not generate a return to the oil-well owner sufficient to recoup the initial investment of exploration and drilling. At the delivery-to-refinery end of the pipeline, the pipeline owner would be able to appropriate the "specialized-to-the-pipeline quasi rents" of the refineries. The pipeline owner could simply raise the price of crude oil at least to the price of alternative sources of supply to each refinery that are specialized

---

[22] It is important to recognize that not only will contracting and enforcement costs of constraining opportunistic behavior determine the form of the final economic arrangement adopted by the transacting parties, but they will also influence the firm's production function. That is, the level of specific investment and therefore the size of the potentially appropriable quasi rent is not an independent "technological" datum in each of these following cases, but is economically determined in part by transaction costs.

to the pipeline. Given the prospects of such action, if the pipeline owner were an independent monopsonist facing the oil explorers and a monopolist to the refinery owners, everyone (explorers and refiners) would know in advance their vulnerability to rent extraction. Therefore oil-field owners and refinery owners would, through shared ownership in the pipeline, remove the possibility of subsequent rent extraction.

The problem would not be completely solved if just the oil field or the refineries (but not both) were commonly owned with the pipeline, since the local monopoly (or monopsony) would persist vis-à-vis the other. Prospectively, one would expect the common ownership to extend to all three stages. If several refineries (or oil fields) were to be served by one pipeline, all the refinery (or oil field) owners would want to jointly own the pipeline. A common practice is a jointly owned company which "owns" the pipeline with the shares by producers and refiners in the pipeline company corresponding roughly to the respective shares of oil to be transported.[23]

Consider other inputs in the production process. The oil tanker, for example, is specialized to crude oil transportation. But since it is essentially equi-valued by many alternative users, the appropriable quasi rent is near zero. So we would expect oil tankers not to be extensively owned by refiners or producers. Similarly, the assets used for refinery construction are not specialized to any single refiner or refinery and they should also not be commonly owned with the refinery.

· · ·

C. Specific human capital

The previous analysis has dealt with examples of physical capital. When specific human capital is involved, the opportunism problem is often more complex and, because of laws prohibiting slavery, the solution is generally some form of explicit or implicit contract rather than vertical integration.

For example, consider the following concrete illustration from the agricul-

[23] Jane Atwood & Paul Kobrin (1977) find an extremely high positive correlation between a firm's crude production and its share of ownership in the pipeline. On the other hand, natural gas pipelines, although apparently economically similar in terms of potentially appropriable quasi rents, do not appear to be vertically integrated. Rather than joint-ownership arrangements with the gas producers, these pipelines are often independently owned. The difference may be due to more effective FPC (and now the Federal Energy Regulatory Commission) regulation (of the wellhead and citygate gas prices and the implied pipeline tariff) compared to the direct Interstate Commerce Commission regulation of oil pipelines as common carriers. Regulation of oil pipeline tariffs could, for example, be easily evaded by opportunistic decreases in the wellhead prices paid for oil. More complete government regulation of gas prices may effectively prevent opportunistic behavior by the natural gas pipeline owners, and thereby serve as an alternative to vertical integration (see Victor P. Goldberg, 1976). Edmund Kitch informs us that the evidence does indicate a much greater degree of vertical integration of natural gas pipelines in the period before FPC regulation.

tural industry. Suppose someone owns a peach orchard. The ripened peaches, ready for harvest, have a market value of about $400,000. So far costs of $300,000 have been paid and the remaining harvesting and shipping costs will be $50,000 ($5,000 transport and $45,000 labor), leaving $50,000 as the competitive return on the owner's capital. Assume the laborers become a union (one party to whom the crop is now specialized) and refuse to pick unless paid $390,000. That would leave $5,000 for transport and only $5,000 for the owner of the peach orchard, instead of the $350,000 necessary to cover incurred costs and the cost of capital. If the union had power to exclude other pickers, it could extract all the appropriable quasi rent of that year's crop specialized to that particular labor union's service. The union would be extracting not just the usual monopoly rents involved in raising wages, but also the short-run appropriable quasi rents of the farmer's specific assets represented by the ripened peaches. This gain to the union is a one-period return because obviously the farmer will not make any additional specific investments in the future if he knows it will be appropriated by the union.

To reduce this risk of appropriation, the farmer may have a large clan family (or neighbors of similar farms) do his picking. Because of diseconomies of scale, however, this "cooperative" solution is not generally the lowest-cost arrangement and some reliance on market contracting will be necessary. The individual farmer, for example, may want the labor union to put up a forfeitable bond to compensate him in the event the union under threat of strike asks for more wages at harvest time. Alternatively, but equivalently, the collateral put up by the union could be the value of the brand-name capital of the union, a value which will depreciate if its leaders engage in opportunistic behavior. The farmer would then make a continuing brand-name payment to the union (similar to the premium payment noted above) for this collateral.[24]

The market value of the union's reputation for reliability of contract observance is the present-discounted value of these brand-name payments which will be greater than any short-run opportunistic gain to the union leaders that could be obtained by threats at harvest time. These payments which increase the cost to the union of opportunistic behavior would be substantial for a perishable product with a large appropriable quasi rent. It is therefore obvious why producers of highly perishable crops are so antagonistic to unionization of field labor. They would be especially hostile to unions without established

[24] If the premium is a payment of the union per unit time, then the arrangement is identical to a collateral-bond arrangement where the union collects the interest on the bond as long as no opportunistic behavior occurs. Because of possible legal difficulties of enforcing such an arrangement, however, the premium may be reflected in the price (that is, a higher wage).

reputations regarding fulfillment of contract and with politically motivated (and possibly myopic) leaders.[25]

In addition to implicit (brand-name) contracts, opportunistic union behavior may be prevented by use of explicit contracts, often with some outside arbitration as an element of the contract-enforcement mechanism. Although it is difficult for an outsider to distinguish between opportunistic behavior and good-faith modifications of contract, impartial arbitration procedures may reduce the necessity of explicitly specifying possible contingencies and thereby reduce the rigidity of the explicit long-term contract.[26]

When the problem is reversed and quasi rents of firm-specific human capital of employees may be opportunistically appropriated by the firm, implicit and explicit long-term contracts are also used to prevent such behavior. Because of economies of scale in monitoring and enforcing such contracts, unions may arise as a contract cost-reducing institution for employees with investments in specific human capital.[27]

In addition to narrow contract-monitoring economics of scale, a union creates a continuing long-term employment relationship that eliminates the last-period (or transient employee) contract-enforcement problem and also creates bargaining power (a credible strike threat) to more cheaply punish a firm that violates the contract. Even when the specific human-capital investment is made

[25] It is interesting to note in this context that California grape farmers preferred the established Teamsters Union to the new, untried, and apparently more politically motivated field-workers union organized by Cesar Chavez.

Since unions are not "owned," union leaders will not have the proper incentive to maximize the union's value; they will tend more to maximize returns during their tenure. If, however, union leadership (ownership) were salable, the leaders would have the optimal incentive to invest in and conserve the union's brand-name capital. They therefore would not engage in opportunistic actions that may increase current revenue while decreasing the market value of the union. "Idealistic" union leaders that do not behave as if they own the union may, in fact, produce less wealth-maximizing action than would "corrupt" leaders, who act if they personally own the union. Alternatively, the current members of the union may have control, not in the sense of having directly salable shares, but in the sense that the valuable union asset can be transferred to their children or relatives. If government regulations force union members to give away these rights to future rents (for example, by forcing them to admit minorities and eliminate nepotism), we can expect them to intentionally depreciate or not create the reputation capital of the union by opportunistic strikes. See Benjamin Klein (1974) where similar problems with regard to the supply of money by nonprivately owned, nonwealth-maximizing firms are discussed.

[26] An interesting legal case in this area is Publishers' Ass'n v. Newspaper & Mail Del. Union, 114 N.Y.S. 2d, 401 (1952). The union authorized and sanctioned a strike against the New York Daily News although the collective bargaining agreement had "no-strike" and arbitration clauses. The Daily News took the union to arbitration, and the arbitrator found actual damages of $2,000 and punitive damages of $5,000 if the union again violated the contract. (The court, however, overturned the punitive damages for technical reasons.) See David E. Feller (1973) for a discussion of the flexibility obtained with arbitration provisions in labor contracts.

[27] We should explicitly note that we are not considering unions as cartelizing devices, the usually analyzed motivation for their existence. This force is obviously present in many cases (for example, interstate trucking) but is distinct from our analysis.

by the firm, a union of employees may similarly reduce the contract-enforcement costs of preventing individual-worker opportunism. There are likely to be economies of scale in supply credibility of contract fulfillment, including the long-term continuing relationship aspect of a union. The existence of a union not only makes it more costly for a firm to cheat an individual worker in his last period but also makes it more costly for an individual worker in his last period to cheat the firm, because the union has the incentive (for example, withholding pension rights) to prevent such an externality on the continuing workers. Therefore unions are more likely to exist when the opportunistic cheating problem is greater, namely, when there is more specific human capital present.[28]

. . .

D. Leasing inputs and ownership of the firm

Examination of leasing companies should reveal that leases are less common (or too expensive) for assets with specialized quasi rents that could be appropriated by the lessee or lessor. Leasing does not occur in the obvious cases of elevators or the glass of windows in an office building where postinvestment bilaterally appropriable quasi rents are enormous, while the furniture in the building is often rented. In banks, the safe is owned by the bank, but computers (though not the memory discs) are sometimes rented.[29] Though this may seem like resorting to trivialities, the fact that such leasing arrangements are taken for granted merely corroborates the prior analysis.

The standard example of leasing arrangements occurs with transportation capital, such as the planes, trucks, or cars used by a firm. This capital is generally easily movable and not very specific. But leasing arrangements are far from universal because some of this capital can be quite specific and quasi rents appropriated. For example, early American steam locomotives were specialized to operating conditions such as high speed, hill climbing, short hauls, heavy loads, sharp corners, as well as types of coal for fuel. Slight differences in engines created significant differences in operating costs. High specialization made it desirable for the rail companies to own locomotives (as well as the land on which water was available for steam). The advent of the

[28] When allowing for this "reverse" effect of employee-specific capital, and therefore higher wages, on the formation of unions, the usual positive effect of unions on wages appears to vanish. See, for example, O. Ashenfelter & G. Johnson (1972) and Peter Schmidt & Robert P. Strauss (1976).

[29] In addition to computers being less specific and hence possessing smaller appropriable quasi rents than elevators, firms (for example, IBM) that supply computers generally posses extremely valuable brand names per unit of current sales due to a large anticipated growth in demand. Since there are some quasi rents associated with the use of a computer by a bank that could possibly be appropriated by threat of immediate removal, we would expect that if rental contracts existed they would be more likely be with highly credible firms with high anticipated demand growth.

more versatile, less specialized, diesel locomotive enabled more leasing and equipment trust financing. Similarly, Swift, the meat packer and innovator of the refrigerator car for transporting slaughtered beef, owned the specialized refrigerator cars it used.[30]

On the other hand, some capital may be quite specific to other assets in a firm's productive process and yet leased rather than owned. These cases provide useful insights into the nature of the contracting costs underlying our analysis. For example, consider the fact that agricultural land, a highly specific asset, is not always owned but often is rented. Land rented for farming purposes is typically for annual crops, like vegetables, sugar beets, cotton, or wheat, while land used for tree crops, like nuts, dates, oranges, peaches, apricots, or grape vines – assets that are highly specialized to the land – is usually owned by the party who plants the trees or vines.[31] However, long-term rental arrangements even for these "specialized asset" crops are not entirely unknown.

It is instructive to recognize why land-rental contracts, rather than vertical integration, can often be used without leading to opportunistic behavior. The primary reason is because it is rather cheap to specify and monitor the relevant contract terms (the quality of the good being purchased) and to enforce this particular rental contract. In addition, the landowner generally cannot impose a cost on the farmer by pulling the asset out or reducing the quality of the asset during the litigation process. Note the contrast with labor rental where it is essentially impossible to effectively specify and enforce quality elements (for example, all working conditions and the effort expended by workers) and where the possibility of withdrawal by strike or lockout is real and costly. Therefore, we do observe firms making highly specific investments in, for example, trees or buildings on land they do not own but only rent long term.[32] This is because credible postcontractual opportunistic threats by the landowner are not possible. However, if the landowner can vary the quality of the land, for example, by controlling the irrigation system to the crops or the electricity supply to a building, then a significant possibility of postinvestment

---

[30] The great bulk of all refrigerator cars are not owned by the railroads, but rather by shipper-users such as packers and dairy companies. See Robert S. Henry (1942).

[31] While 25% of vegetable and melon farms in California in 1974 were fully owned by the farm operator, 82% of fruit and nut tree farms were fully owned, a significantly different ownership proportion at the 99% confidence interval. Similarly, the ownership proportions of cash grain and cotton farms were 40% and 39%, respectively, both also significantly different at the 99% confidence interval from the proportions of fruit and nut tree farm ownership. See 1 U.S. Dep't of Commerce, Bureau of the Census, 1974 Census of Agriculture, State and County Data, pt. 5, at tab. 28. Summary by Tenure of Farm Operator and Type of Organization, *id.*, 1974, California, pp. 1–29 to 1–30.

[32] Rental terms may be related to sales of the firm using the land in order to share the risk of real-value changes and to reduce the risk of nominal land-value changes involved with a long-term contract.

opportunistic behavior exists and we would therefore expect vertical integration.[33]

One specific asset that is almost always owned by the firm is its trade-name or brand-name capital and, in particular, the logo it uses to communicate to consumers. If this asset were rented from a leasing company, the problems would be obvious. The firm would be extremely hesitant to make any investments to build up its goodwill, for example, by advertising or by successful performance, because such investments are highly specific to that "name." The quasi rents could be appropriated by the leasing company through increases in the rental fee for the trade name. Not only would the firm not invest in this specific asset, but there would be an incentive for the firm to depreciate a valuable rented brand name. Although these problems seem insurmountable, rental of the capital input of a firm's brand name is not entirely unknown. In fact, franchisors can be thought of as brand-name leasing companies. A franchisee is fundamentally a renter of the brand-name capital (and logo) owned by the franchisor. Because of the specific capital problems noted above, direct controls are placed on franchisee behavior. The rental payment is usually some form of profit-sharing arrangement and, although the franchisee is legally considered to be an independent firm, the situation is in reality much closer to vertical integration than to the standard contractual relationship of the independent market.

Finally, the analysis throws light on the important question of why the owners of a firm (the residual claimants) are generally also the major capitalists of the firm.[34] As we have seen, owners may rent the more generalized capital, but will own the firm's specific capital. This observation has implications for recent discussions of "industrial democracy," which fail to recognize that although employees may own and manage a firm (say, through their union), they will also have to be capitalists and own the specific capital. It will generally be too costly, for example, for the worker-owners to rent a plant because such a specific investment could be rather easily appropriated from its owners after it is constructed. Therefore it is unlikely to be built. A highly detailed contractual arrangement together with very large brand-name premium payments by the laborers would be necessary to assure nonoppor-

[33] Coase's example of a monopolist selling more of a durable good, say land, after initially selling a monopoly quantity at the monopoly price is analytically identical to the problem of postcontractual opportunistic behavior. Existing contractual relationships indicate, however, that the land case may be relatively easy to solve because it may not be expensive to make a credible contract regarding the remaining land. But, one of Coase's indicated solutions, the short-term rental rather than sale of the land is unlikely because it would discourage specific (to land) investments by the renter (such as building a house, developing a farm, and so forth) for fear of appropriation. See R. H. Coase (1972).

[34] We are grateful to Earl Thompson for discerning this implication.

tunistic behavior. This is generally too expensive an alternative and explains why capitalists are usually the owners of a firm.[35]

E. Social institutions

Much of the previous analysis has dealt with tangible capital. Contractual arrangements involving such assets are often cheaper than complete vertical integration, even when the assets are highly specific (for example, the land-rental case). As the discussion on human capital suggests, however, when the specific assets involved are intangible personal assets, the problems of contract enforcement become severe. In addition, when the number of individuals involved (or the extent of the specific capital) becomes very large, ownership arrangements often become extremely complex.

For example, consider country clubs. Golf country clubs are social, in addition to being golfing, organizations. Sociability of a country club involves substantial activities away from the golf course: dinners, dances, parties, cards, games, and general social activities with friends who are members of the club. However, some golf courses are operated with very few social activities for the set of members and their families. The social clubs (usually called "country clubs") are mutually owned by the members, whereas golf courses with virtually no off-course social activity often are privately owned with members paying daily golf fees without owning the golf course.

Mutual ownership is characteristic of the social country club because the specialized quasi rent of friendship is collected by each member whose friendship is specialized to the other members. The members' behavior toward one another constitutes an investment in forming valuable friendships, a congenial milieu, and rapport among the members. Each member has invested in creating that congenial milieu and atmosphere specialized to the other members. And its value could be stolen or destroyed by opportunistic behavior of a party authorized to admit new members.

---

[35] Armen A. Alchian & Harold Demsetz, Production, Information Costs, and Economic Organization, 62 Am. Econ. Rev. 777 (1972), claim that if the owner of the firm also owns the firm's capital it supplies evidence that he can pay for rented inputs, including labor. This appears to be incorrect since the owner could supply credibility by using some of his assets completely unrelated to the production process, such as treasury bonds, for collateral. Michael C. Jensen & William H. Meckling, (unpublished manuscript, Feb. 1977), emphasize the costs of monitoring managerial performance and the maintenance of rented capital, and the problems of efficiently allocating risks in a pure-rental firm. They also note that is is "impossible" for a firm to rent all the productive capital assets because many of them are intangible and therefore "it is impossible to repossess the asset if the firm refused to pay the rental fee" (1977, p. 20). This argument is similar to our analysis of opportunistic behavior. However, rather than asserting that such rentals are impossible, we would merely recognize the extremely high contracting costs generally present in such situations. More importantly, we claim that such an argument also extends to the rental of tangible specific capital.

To see how, suppose the club were owned by someone other than the members. Once the membership value is created by the interpersonal activities of the members, the owner of the club could then start to raise the fees for continuing members. Assuming some costs of the members moving away en masse and forming a new club, the owner could expropriate by higher fees some of the specialized quasi-rent value of the sociability created by the members' specialization to each other in their own group. Alternatively, the owner could threaten to break the implicit contract and destroy some of the sociability capital by selling admission to "undesirable" people who want to consort with the existing members.

Similarly, if the social country club were owned by the members as a corporation with each member owning a share of stock salable without prior approval of existing members (as is the case for the business corporation), a single member could, by threatening to sell to an "undesirable" potential member, extract some value of congeniality from the current members, as a payment for not selling.[36]

An extreme case of this general problem is a marriage. If each mate had a transferable share salable to a third party, there would be far fewer marriages with highly specific investments in affection and children. If a relationship is not one of specialized interest (specialized to a particular other party) or if it required no investment by any member, then the marriage relationship would be more like a corporation. As it is one of highly specific investments, marriages have historically been mutually owned entities, with permission of both parties generally required for alteration of membership. Government arbitration of this relationship to prevent postinvestment opportunistic behavior by either party can contribute toward lower bargaining costs and investments of resources (recoverable dowries) by both parties to improve their respective postinvestment bargaining positions, and, most importantly, create confidence that opportunistic behavior will not be successful. The legislative movement to "no-fault" divorce suggests that modern marriages may have less specific assets than formerly.[37]

[36] The "free-rider" problems of bribing an opportunistic member to prevent sale to an "undesirable" member are obvious. This analysis could be applied to social clubs such as Elks, Masonic Order, and so forth.

[37] Similarly, people whose work is highly specialized to each other will be partners (common ownership). For example, attorneys that have become highly specialized to their coattorneys will become partners, whereas new associates will at first be employees. A small team of performers (Laurel and Hardy, Sonny and Cher) who were highly specialized to each other would be "partners" (co-owners) rather than employee and employer. While it is still difficult to enforce such contracts and prevent postcontractual opportunistic behavior by either party, joint ownership creates an incentive for performance and specific investment not present in an easily terminable employer-employee contract that must rely solely on the personal brand-name reputation of contracting parties. Trust, including the reputation of certifying institutions such as theatrical agents, law schools, and so on, and the presence of social sanctions against opportunistic partners remain important.

. . .

IV. Concluding comment

We should emphasize in conclusion that most business relationships are neither likely to be as simple as the standard textbook polar cases of vertical integration or market contract nor as easily explained as some of the above examples. When particular examples are examined in detail, business relationships are often structured in highly complex ways not represented by either a simple rental contract or by simple vertical integration. . . .

. . .

. . . Once we attempt to add empirical detail to Coase's fundamental insight that a systematic study of transaction costs is necessary to explain particular forms of economic organization, we find that his primary distinction between transactions made within a firm and transactions made in the marketplace may often be too simplistic. Many long-term contractual relationships (such as franchising) blur the line between the market and the firm. It may be more useful to merely examine the economic rationale for different types of particular contractual relationships in particular situations, and consider the firm as a particular kind or set of interrelated contracts.[38] Firms are therefore, by definition, formed and revised in markets and the conventional sharp distinction between markets and firms may have little general analytical importance. The pertinent economic question we are faced with is "what kinds of contracts are used for what kinds of activities, and why?"

[38] If we think of firms as collections of interrelated contracts rather than the collection of goods operative in the contracts, the question of who "owns" the firm (the set of contacts) appears somewhat nonsensical. It may be useful to think solely of a set of claimants to various portions of the value consequences of the contractual coalition, with no "owner" of the firm.

CHAPTER 19

Towards an economic theory of the multiproduct firm

DAVID TEECE

David Teece was born in 1948. He received a Ph.D. in economics from the University of Pennsylvania in 1975. When this paper was published, he was Professor of Business Administration in the School of Business at the University of California, Berkeley, where he has also been Director of the Center for Research in Management since 1983.

1. Introduction

"Of all outstanding characteristics of business firms, perhaps the most inadequately treated in economic analysis is the diversification of their activities" (Penrose, 1959, p. 104). Little progress has been made since Penrose registered her dismay. Accordingly, the theory of the firm has yet to accommodate one of the principal features of the modern business enterprise – its multiproduct character. The mission of this paper is to outline how this deficiency might be rectified. To accomplish this objective it turns out to be necessary to modify the neoclassical theory of the firm to emphasize the distinctive properties of organizational knowledge and the transactions cost properties of market exchange. It is also necessary to make an analytical separation between a theory of diversification and a theory of growth since growth and diversification are not inextricably linked. A central issue for a theory of multiproduct organization is to explain why firms diversify into related and unrelated product lines rather than reinvesting in traditional lines of business or transferring assets directly to stockholders.

An earlier paper (Teece, 1980) argued that the multiproduct firm could not be explained by reference to neoclassical cost functions. Panzar and Willig (1975, p. 3) have argued that economies of scope explain multiproduct organization.[1] While economies of scope explain joint production, they do not explain why joint production must be organized within a single multiproduct

Reprinted in abridged form from David Teece, "Towards an Economic Theory of the Multiproduct Firm," *Journal of Economic Behavior and Organization,* 3 (1982): 39–63, by permission of the publisher.

[1] Economies of scope exist when for all outputs y_1 and y_2, the cost of joint production is less than the cost of producing each output separately (Panzar and Willig, 1975). That is, it is the condition, for all y_1 and y_2: $C(y_1,y_2) < C(y_1,0) + C(0,y_2)$.

enterprise. Joint production can proceed in the absence of multiproduct organization if contractual mechanisms can be devised to share the inputs which are yielding the scope economies. Whereas the earlier paper had the limited objective of exploring the relationship between economies of scope and the scope of the enterprise, the objective here is more ambitious – to outline a theory of multiproduct enterprise.

.   .   .

3. Nature of the firm

In microtheory textbooks, and in much contemporary research, it is accepted practice "to represent the business enterprise abstractly by the productive transformations of which it is capable, and to characterize these productive transformations by a production function or production set regarded as a datum" (Winter, 1982, p. 58).[2] Furthermore, production functions and hence firms can be eliminated or replicated with amazing alacrity, as when prices a whisker above competitive levels attract new entrants. New entry in turn drives profits back down to equilibrium levels. Embedded in this conceptualization is the notion that a firm's knowhow is stored in symbolic form in a "book of blueprints". Implicit in this commonly used metaphor is the view that knowledge can be and is articulated. Following Winter (1982), and Nelson and Winter (1980, 1982), the appropriateness of this abstraction is examined below, and the implications for multiproduct organization explored.

3.1. Individual and organizational knowledge

Polanyi has stressed, in obvious contradiction to the book of blueprints metaphor, that individual knowledge has an important tacit dimension, in that very often knowhow and skills cannot be articulated. It is a "well known fact that the aim of a skillful performance is achieved by the observance of a set of rules which are not known as such to the person following them"[3] (Polanyi, 1958, p. 49). In the exercise of individual skill, many actions are taken that are not the result of considered choices but rather are automatic responses that constitute aspects of the skill.[4]

---

[2] In modern general equilibrium theory (Arrow, 1951; Arrow and Debreu, 1954; Debreu, 1959) "commodity outputs in amounts represented by $q = (q_1, . . ., q_m)$ may or may not be producible from input commodities in amounts represented by $X = (\chi_1, . . . \chi_n)$. If q is producible from χ, then the input/output pair (χ, q) is 'in the production set'. Whatever is known or considered plausible as a property of the structure of technical knowledge is treated as a postulate about the properties of the production set" (Winter, 1982, p. 63).

[3] "The premises of a skill cannot be discovered focally prior to its performance, not even understood if explicitly stated by others, before we ourselves have experienced its performance, whether by watching it or engaging in it ourselves" (Polanyi, 1958, p. 1962).

[4] Polanyi illustrates this point by discussing how a bicyclist keeps his balance: "I have come to the conclusion that the principle by which the cyclist keeps his balance is not generally known.

251

Similarly, in the routine operation of an organization such as a business firm, much that could in principle be deliberated is instead done automatically in response to signals arising from the organization or its environment. Articulation of the knowledge underlying organizational capabilities is limited in the same respects and for the same reasons as in the case of individual capabilities though for other reasons as well, and to a greater extent. This routinization of activity in an organization itself constitutes the most important form of storage of the organization's specific operational knowledge. In a sense, organizations "remember by doing". Routine operation is the organizational counterpart of the exercise of skills by an individual. (Nelson and Winter, 1982 quoted in part from an earlier draft.)

Thus, routines function as the basis of organizational memory. To utilize organizational knowledge, it is necessary not only that all members know their routines, but also that all members know when it is appropriate to perform certain routines. This implies that the individual must have the ability to interpret a stream of incoming messages from other organizational members and from the environment. Once received and interpreted, the member utilizes the information contained in a message in the selection and performance of an appropriate routine from his own repertoire.[5] Thus to view organizational memory as reducible to individual member memories is to overlook, or undervalue, the linking of those individual memories by shared experiences in the past, experiences that have established the extremely detailed and specific communication system that underlies routine performance (Nelson and Winter, 1982, p. 105).

While there is abundant reason to believe that remembering-by-doing may in a wide range of circumstances surpass symbolic storage in cost effectiveness, one circumstance where complications arise is where the knowledge is to enter market exchange for subsequent transfer to a different organizational context. The transfer of key individuals may suffice when the knowledge to be transferred relates to the particulars of a separable routine. The individual in such cases becomes a consultant or a teacher with respect to that routine.

The rule observed by the cyclist is this. When he starts falling to the right he turns the handlebars to the right, so that the course of the bicycle is deflected along a curve towards the right. This results in a centrifugal force pushing the cyclist to the left and offsets the gravitational force dragging him down to the right. This maneuver presently throws the cyclist out of balance to the left which he counteracts by turning the handlebars to the left; and so he continues to keep himself in balance by winding along a series of appropriate curvatures. A simple analysis shows that for a given angle of unbalance the curvature of each winding is inversely proportional to the square of the speed at which the cyclist is proceeding. But does this tell us exactly how to ride a bicycle? No. You obviously cannot adjust the curvature of your bicycle's path in proportion to the ratio of your unbalance over the square of your speed; and if you could you would fall off the machine, for there are a number of these factors to be taken into account in practice which are left out in the formulation of this rule" (Polanyi, 1958, pp. 49–50).

[5] An organizational member's repetoire is the set of routines that could be performed in some appropriate environment (Nelson and Winter, 1982).

However, only a limited range of capabilities can be transferred if a transfer activity is focused in this fashion. More often than not, the transfer of productive expertise requires the transfer of organizational as well as individual knowledge.[6] In such cases, external transfer beyond an organization's boundary may be difficult if not impossible, since taken out of context, an individual's knowledge of a routine may be quite useless.

3.2. Fungible knowledge

Another characteristic of organizational knowledge is that it is often fungible to an important degree. That is, the human capital inputs employed by the firm are not always entirely specialized to the particular products and services which the enterprise is currently producing. This is particularly true of managerial talent, but it is also true for various items of physical equipment and for other kinds of human skills as well. Of course, various items of capital may have to be scrapped or converted if an organization's product mix is changed but these costs may in fact be quite low if the opportunity cost of withdrawing the equipment from its current use is minimal.

Accordingly, the final products produced by a firm at any given time merely represent one of several ways in which the organization could be using its internal resources. (Penrose, 1959). As wartime experience demonstrated, automobile manufacturers suddenly began making tanks, chemical companies began making explosives, and radio manufacturers began making radar. In short, a firm's capability lies upstream from the end product – it lies in a generalizable capability which might well find a variety of final product applications. Economies of specialization assume a different significance when viewed from this conceptual vantage point, as specialization is referenced not to a single product but to a generalized capability. (It might be "information processing" rather than computers, "dairy products" rather than butter and cheese, "farm machinery" rather than tractors and harvestors, and "time measurement" rather than clocks and watches.) The firm can therefore be considered to have a variety of end products which it can produce with its organizational technology. Some of these possibilities may be known to it and some may not. What needs to be explained is the particular end product or configuration of end products which the firm chooses to produce.

This view of the nature of the firm turns the neoclassical conceptualization on its head. Whereas the neoclassical firm selects, according to factor prices, technologies off the shelf to manufacture a given end product, the organization theoretic firm depicted here selects an end product configuration, consis-

---

[6] "Over the years an individual may learn a piece of the company puzzle exceptionally well and he may even understand how the piece fits into the entire puzzle. But he may not know enough about the other pieces to reproduce the entire puzzle" (Lieberstein, 1979).

tent with its organizational technology, which is defined yet fungible over certain arrays of final products. In short, the firm has end product as well as technological choices to confront.

4. Dynamic considerations

4.1. General

Whether the firms' knowhow is embedded in a book of blueprints or in individual and organizational routines will not explain its multiproduct scope unless other dimensions of the neoclassical model of firms and markets are modified. Thus following Schumpeter (1950) and others, the competitive process is viewed as dynamic, involving uncertainty, struggle, and disequilibrium. In particular, two fundamental characteristics of a dynamic competitive system are recognized: (a) firms accumulate knowledge through R & D and learning, some of it incidental to the production process, (b) the market conditions facing the firm are constantly changing, creating profit opportunities in different markets at different times. Furthermore, the demand curve facing a specialized firm is rarely infinitely elastic, as is assumed in the perfectly competitive model.

4.2. Learning, teaching, and "Penrose-effects"

Edith Penrose (1959) has described the growth processes of the firm in a way that is both unconventional and convincing. According to Penrose, at any time a firm has certain productive resources, the services of which are used to exploit the production opportunities facing the firm. Opportunities for growth exist because there are always unused productive services which can be placed into employment – presumably in new as well as existing lines of business. Unused resources exist not only because of indivisibilities, but also because of the learning which occurs in the normal process of operating a business. Thus, even with a constant managerial workforce, managerial services are released for expansion without any reduction in the efficiency with which existing operations are run. Not only is there continuous learning, but also as each project becomes established so its running becomes more routine and less demanding on managerial resources. The managerial workforce can also be expanded, at least within limits. Existing managers can teach new managers. However, the increment to total managerial services provided by each additional manager is assumed to decrease the faster the rate at which they are reoriented. (The "Penrose-effect".)

A specialized firm's generation of excess resources, both managerial and technical, and their fungible character is critical to the theory of diversification advanced here. What has to be explained, however, is (1) why diversification is likely to lead to the productive utilization of 'excess' resources, and (2) the sequence in which this assignment is likely to occur.

4.3. Demand conditions

A specialized firm's excess resources can of course be reinvested in the firm's traditional business. Indeed, if the firm confronts a perfectly elastic demand curve, has a distinctive capability (lower costs) in its traditional business, and markets elsewhere are competitive, it has incentives to reinvest in its traditional line of business, both at home and abroad. Assume, however, that at some point competitive returns can no longer be obtained through reinvestment at home or abroad, either because of a secular decline of demand due to life cycle considerations (Grabowski and Mueller, 1975; Mueller, 1972), or because the firm is facing a finite degree of elasticity to its demand curve, in which case reinvestment and expansion will serve to lower prices and profits. Confronted with this predicament, a profit seeking firm confronts three fundamental choices:

(1) It can seek to sell the services of its unused assets to other firms in other markets.
(2) It can diversify into other markets, either through acquisition or de novo entry.
(3) If the unused resource is cash, it can be returned to stockholders through higher dividends or stock repurchase.

A theory of diversification for a profit seeking enterprise emerges when conditions are established under which the second option appears the more profitable. The first option involves the use of markets for capturing the employment value of the unused assets. Multiproduct diversification (option 2) will be selected by profit seeking firms over the market alternative (option 1) when transactions cost problem are likely to confound efficient transfer. Accordingly, an assessment of the efficiency properties of factor and financial markets is warranted.

4.4. Market failure considerations: physical and human capital

If excess resources are possessed by a single product firm, there is the possibility of disposal in factor markets, i.e., sale and transfer to other specialized firms. This strategy permits standard specialization economies to be obtained, and if transaction costs are zero, ought to usurp incentives for diversification. Consider, therefore, whether efficient employment of these resources is likely to involve multiproduct organization. Assume, furthermore, that the excess resources are either indivisible or fungible, so that scope economies exist.[7] Four classes of scope economies are identified and analyzed.

Class I. Indivisible but *non-specialized* physical capital as a common input into two or more products:

Scope economies may arise because some fixed item of capital equipment is indivisible. It may be a machine – such as heavy gauge sheet metal shears – which is needed occasionally in the production process for product A but is otherwise idle. Assume that the machine could be used to manufacture both products A and B. Even if this is the case it need not indicate that an efficient solution is for the manufacturer of A to diversify into the manufacture of B. There are at least two other options. The manufacturer of A could rent the services of another firm's machine, or it could acquire its own machine and lease access to it when it would otherwise remain idle.

To the extent that there is not a thin market for the services of the machinery in question – which will often be the case – there does not appear to be a compelling reason for diversification on account of the hazards of exposure to opportunism (Williamson, 1975; Klein, Crawford and Alchian, 1978). Market solutions would appear to be superior.[8]

Class II. Indivisible *specialized* physical capital as a common input to two or more products:

Assume that the piece of equipment is specialized but not entirely so. Assume specifically that it can only be used for making products A and B, that there is some idle capacity if it is only used to manufacture A, and that the market for A and B will only support a small number of producers. In these circumstances there may be incentives for the manufacturer of A to also manufacture B because of the transactional difficulties which might otherwise be encountered in the small numbers markets assumed. Since the fixed asset is

---

[7] As a general matter, "economies of scope arise from inputs that are shared, or utilized jointly without complete congestion. The shared factor may be imperfectly divisible, so that the manufacture of a subset of the goods leaves excess capability in some stage of production, or some human or physical capital may be a public input which, when purchased for use in one production process, is then freely available to another" (Willig, 1979, p. 346).

[8] A related example would be the provision of air services between points A and B. An airport will be needed at both A and B and in the absence of complete congestion, service can also be provided from both points to C (which has an airport) once airport terminals A and B are constructed. Hence $C(AB, BC, AC) < C(AB,0,0) + C(0,BC,0) + C(0,0,AC)$. While economies of scope exist, it need not imply that one airline ought provide services AB, BC, and CA. Individual airlines could specialize on each route and access to terminals (the source of the assumed indivisibility) could be shared via contracts. Only in the extent to which transactional difficulties can be expected in writing, executing, and enforcing contracts will common ownership be necessary to capture the scope of economies.

256

highly specialized, and the number of potential lessees is assumed to be quite small, markets for the services of the fixed assets will be thin. Bilateral monopoly situations can then arise in which lessees may attempt to extract the quasi-rents associated with the utilization of the leasor's fixed and specialized asset[9] (Williamson, 1975, 1979; Klein, Crawford and Alchian, 1978; Monteverde and Teece, 1982a, 1982b). In order to avoid these hazards, intrafirm trading – that is, multiproduct diversification – can be substituted for market exchange. Internal trading changes the incentives of the parties and enables the firm to bring managerial control devices to bear on the transaction, thereby attenuating costly haggling and other manifestations of non-cooperative behavior. Exchange can then proceed more efficiently because of lower transactions costs.

Class III. Human capital as a common input to two or more products:

To the extent that knowhow has fungible attributes, it can represent a common input into a variety of products. Knowhow may also display some of the characteristics of a public good in that it may be used in many different non-competing applications without its value in any one application being substantially impaired. Furthermore, the marginal cost of employing knowhow in a different endeavor is likely to be much less than the average cost of production and dissemination (transfer). Accordingly, the transfer and application of proprietary information to alternative production activities is likely to generate important economies.

However, internal organization (multiproduct enterprise) is generally needed for these economies to be realized. Markets do not work well as the institutional mode for trading knowhow. One reason is that an important component of organizational knowledge is tacit. As discussed above, the transfer of tacit knowledge from one enterprise to another is likely to be difficult and costly. A temporary if not permanent transfer of employees may be needed, especially if the technology involved is state of the art and has not as yet been stabilized and formalized. If this is the case, multiproduct organization is likely to have appeal because it provides a more efficient technology transfer mode.

Besides the logistical problems surrounding the transfer of tacit knowledge, technology transfer must confront an important class of transactions cost problems. These can be summarized in terms of (1) recognition, (2) disclosure, and (3) team organization (Teece, 1980; Williamson and Teece, 1982). Thus consider a firm which has accumulated knowhow which can potentially find application in the fields of industrial activity beyond its existing product

---

[9] The quasi-rents will be the difference between the asset value if the equipment is used to produce multiple products and its value when it is used to produce the single product.

line(s). If there are other firms in the economy which can apply this knowhow with profit, then according to received microtheory, trading will ensue until Pareto Optimality conditions are satisfied. Or, as Calabresi has put it, "if one assumes rationality, no transactions costs, and no legal impediments to bargaining, all misallocations of resources would be fully cured in the market by bargains" (Calabresi, 1968). However, one cannot in general expect this result in the market for proprietary knowhow. Not only are there high costs associated with obtaining the requisite information but there are also organizational and strategic impediments associated with using the market to effectuate transfer.

Consider, to begin with, the information requirements associated with using markets. In order to carry out a market transaction it is necessary to discover who it is that one wishes to deal with, to inform people that one wishes to deal and on what terms, to conduct negotiations leading up to the bargain, to draw up the contract, to undertake the inspection needed to make sure that the terms of the contract are being observed, and so on (Coase, 1960, p. 15). Furthermore, the opportunity for trading must be identified. As Kirzner (1973, pp. 215–216) has explained:

. . . for an exchange transaction to be completed it is not sufficient merely that the conditions for exchange which prospectively will be mutually beneficial be present; it is necessary also that each participant be aware of his opportunity to gain through exchange . . . It is usually assumed . . . that where scope for (mutually beneficial) exchange is present, exchange will in fact occur . . . In fact of course exchange may fail to occur because knowledge is imperfect, in spite of conditions for mutually profitable exchange.

The transactional difficulties identified by Kirzner are especially compelling when the commodity in question is proprietary information, be it of a technological or managerial kind. This is because the protection of the ownership of technological knowhow often requires suppressing information on exchange possibilities. For instance, by its very nature industrial R & D requires disguising and concealing the activities and outcomes of R & D establishment. As Marquis and Allen (1966, p. 1055) point out, industrial laboratories, with their strong mission orientation, must

. . . cut themselves off from interaction beyond the organizational perimeter. This is to a large degree intentional. The competitive environment in which they operate necessitates control over the outflow of messages. The industrial technologist or scientist is thereby essentially cut off from free interaction with his colleagues outside of the organization.

Except as production or marketing specialists within the firm perceive the transfer opportunity, transfer may fail by reason of non-recognition.

Even where the processor of the technology recognizes the opportunity, market exchange may break down because of the problems of disclosing value to buyers in a way that is both convincing and does not destroy the basis for exchange. A very severe information inpactedness problem exists, on which account the less informed party (in this instance the buyer) must be wary of opportunistic representations by the seller. If, moreover, there is insufficient disclosure, including veracity checks thereon, to assure the buyer that the information possesses great value, the "fundamental paradox" of information arises: "its value for the purchaser is not known until he has the information, but then he has in effect acquired it without cost" (Arrow, 1971, p. 152).

Suppose that recognition is no problem, that buyers concede value, and are prepared to pay for information in the seller's possession. Occasionally that may suffice. The formula for a chemical compound or the blueprints for a special device may be all that is needed to effect the transfer. However, more is frequently needed. As discussed above, knowhow has a strong tacit and learning-by-doing character, and it may be essential that human capital in an effective team configuration accompany the transfer. Sometimes this can be effected through a one-time contract (a knowhow agreement) to provide a "consulting team" to assist start-up. Although such contracts will be highly incomplete, and the failure to reach a comprehensive agreement may give rise to dissatisfaction during execution, this may be an unavoidable, which is to say irremediable, result. Plainly, multiproduct organization is an extreme response to the needs of a one-time exchange. In the absence of a superior organizational alternative, reliance on market mechanisms is thus likely to prevail.

Where a succession of proprietary exchanges seems desirable, reliance on repeated contracting is less clearly warranted. Unfettered two way communication is needed not only to promote the recognition and disclosure of opportunities for information transfer but also to facilitate the execution of the actual transfer itself. The parties in these circumstances are joined in a small numbers trading relation and as discussed by Williamson, such contracting may be shot through with hazards for both parties (Williamson, 1975, 1979). The seller is exposed to hazards such as the possibility that the buyer will employ the knowhow in subtle ways not covered by the contract, or the buyer might 'leap frog' the licensor's technology and become an unexpected competitive threat. The buyer is exposed to hazards such as the seller asserting that the technology has better performance or cost reducing characteristics than is actually the case; or the seller might render promised transfer assistance in a prefunctory fashion. While bonding or the execution of performance guarantees can minimize these hazards, they need not be eliminated since costly haggling might ensue when measurement of the performance characteristics of the technology is open to some ambiguity. Furthermore, when a lateral transfer is contemplated and the technology has not therefore been previously commercialized by either party in the new application, the

259

execution of performance guarantees is likely to be especially hazardous to the seller because of the uncertainties involved (Teece, 1977). In addition, if a new application of a generic technology is contemplated, recurrent exchange and continuous contact between buyer and seller will be needed. These requirements will be extremely difficult to specify ex ante. Hence, when the continuous exchange of proprietary knowhow between the transferor and transferee is needed, and where the end use application of the knowhow is idiosyncratic in the sense that it has not been accomplished previously by the transferor, it appears that something more than a classical market contracting structure is required. As Williamson notes ''The nonstandardized nature of (these) transactions makes primary reliance on market governance hazardous, while their recurrent nature permits the cost of the specialized governance structure to be recovered'' (Williamson, 1979, p. 250). What Williamson refers to as ''relational contracting'' is the solution; this can take the form of bilateral governance, where the autonomy of the parties is maintained; or unified structures, where the transaction is removed from the market and organized within the firm subject to an authority relation (Williamson, 1979, p. 250). Bilateral governance involves the use of ''obligational contracting'' (Wachter and Williamson, 1978; Williamson, 1979). Exchange is conducted between independent firms under obligational arrangements, where both parties realize the paramount importance of maintaining an amicable relationship as overriding any possible short-run gains either might be able to achieve. But as transactions become progressively more idiosyncratic, obligational contracting may also fail, and internal organization (intrafirm transfer) is the more efficient organizational mode. The intrafirm transfer of knowhow avoids the need for repeated negotiations and ameliorates the hazards of opportunism. Better disclosure, easier agreement, better governance, and therefore more effective execution of knowhow transfer are likely to result. Here lies an incentive for multiproduct organization.

The above arguments are quite general and extend to the transfer of many different kinds of proprietary knowhow. Besides technological knowhow, the transfer of managerial (including organizational) knowhow, and goodwill (including brand loyalty) represent types of assets for which market transfer mechanisms may falter, and for which the relative efficiency of intrafirm as against interfirm trading is indicated.

Class IV. External economies:

George Stigler has cast the Coase theorem (Coase, 1960) in the following form: ''Under perfect competition and any assignment of property rights, market transactions between a firm producing a nuisance and one consuming it will bring about the same composition of output as would have been determined by a single firm engaged in both activities. That is, market transactions will have the same consequences as internal management no matter what the property structure, *provided transactions costs are negligible.''* (Stigler, 1966, p. 113, emphasis added). The converse of this is that external economies – which can generate economies of scope – will dictate multiproduct organization when there are significant transaction costs.

External economies in the production of various goods are quite common. For instance, there are locational externalities if a new airport opens up a previously remote area and stimulates tourism.[10] There are also externalities if a cost saving innovation in one industry lowers costs in another. If these externalities can be captured at low cost by common ownership, then multiproduct organization is suggested.

Of course there are limits to the economies which can be captured through diversification. If diversification is based on scope economies, then there will eventually be a problem of congestion associated with accessing the common input. For instance, if the common input is knowhow, then while the value of the knowhow may not be impaired by repeated transfer, the costs of assessing it may increase if the simultaneous transfer of the information to a number of different applications is attempted. This is because knowhow is generally not embodied in blueprints alone; the human factor is critically important in technology transfer. Accordingly, as the demands for sharing knowhow increase, bottlenecks in the form of over-extended scientists, engineers, and managers can be anticipated.[11] Congestion associated with assessing common inputs will thus clearly limit the amount of diversification which can be profitably engaged. However, if the transfers are arranged so that they occur in a sequential fashion, then the limits imposed by congestion are relieved, at least in part (Teece, 1977).

Control loss considerations may also come into play. However, the establishment of a decentralized divisionalized "M-Form" (Williamson, 1975) structure is likely to minimize control loss problems. In fact Chandler argues that the M-Form innovation made diversification a viable strategy (Chandler, 1969). It is also important to note that diversification need not represent abandonment of specialization. It is simply that a firm's particular advantage is defined not in terms of products but in terms of capabilities. The firm is seen as possessing a specialized knowhow or asset base from which it extends its operations in response to competitive conditions. This element of common-

---

[10] Common ownership may also be needed if the external economies are in the form of skills. Suppose firm X_1 is a monopolist in industry A. A new industry Y emerges which requires labor skills developed in industry X. Because of the transactional difficulties which confront X_1 in appropriating the skills with which it has imbued its employees, X_1 may generate an externality in industry Y. Diversification of X_1 into Y enable the externality to be internalized.

[11] The "Penrose-effect" discussed earlier focuses on the problem with respect to managerial resources.

ality simplifies the control problem, at least compared to other forms of diversification.

4.5. Market failure considerations and financial capital

Suppose that cash is the only excess capacity possessed by a specialized firm. Assuming, for the moment, that taxation of dividends and capital gains is unimportant, I wish to investigate whether allocative efficiency and/or a firm's market value can possibly be improved by diversification if financial markets are "efficient". Oliver Williamson, among others, has postulated that multidivisional firms can establish internal capital markets with resource allocation properties superior to those obtained by the (external) capital market. In particular, he postulates "a tradeoff between breadth of information, in which respect the banking system may be presumed to have the advantage, and depth of information, which is the advantage of the specialized firm" (Williamson, 1975, p. 162). Inferior access to inside information and the weak control instruments exercised by financial intermediaries and the stock market provides the foundation for Williamson's assertion that the "miniature capital market" within the firm has distinctive efficiency properties.

Financial theorists, however, are often quick to reply that since the financial markets have been shown to be "efficient", no improvement in allocative efficiency or market value can possibly derive from managers usurping the role of financial markets. Myers (1968), Schall (1972), and Mossin (1973) have all argued that value is conserved (value additivity obtains) under the addition of income streams, as would occur with diversification by merger. However, the notions of "efficiency" as used by financial theorists is highly specialized and do not accord with the concept of allocative efficiency used in welfare economics. Nor does it deny that stockholder wealth can be improved through the operations of the firm's internal capital markets. These issues are critical to the analysis to follow and so are examined below.

In the finance literature, the term "efficient markets" has taken on a specialized and misleading meaning. One widely employed definition refers to informational efficiency. For example, according to Fama (1970b, p. 383) "A market in which prices fully reflect available information is called 'efficient' ",[12] and according to Jensen (1978), "A market is efficient with re-

---

[12] Fama (1970b, 1976) actually defines three types of efficiency, each of which is based on a different notion or the type of information understood to be relevant in the phrase "prices fully reflect available information". Specifically, he recognizes:

(1) *Weak-form efficiency.* No investor can earn excess returns if he develops trading rules based on historical price of return information. In other words, the information in past prices or returns is not useful or relevant in achieving excess returns.

(2) *Semistrong-form efficiency.* No investor can earn excess returns from trading rules based on any publicly available information. Examples of publicly available information are: annual

spect to information set Θ_t if it is impossible to make economic profits by trading on the basis of information set Θ_t''. The other widely employed definition is what can be called mean-variance efficiency. The market is mean-variance efficient if capital market prices correspond to an equilibrium in which all individuals evaluate portfolios in terms of their means and variances, about which they all have identical beliefs. Unfortunately, these concepts have nothing to do with allocative efficiency. As Stiglitz (1981) has shown, neither informational efficiency or mean variance efficiency are necessary or sufficient conditions for the Pareto optimality of the economy. In short, 'there is no theoretical presumption simply because the financial markets appear to be competitive, or ''pass'' the standard finance literature tests concerning efficiency, that they are efficient' (Stiglitz, 1981, p. 237).

One reason for this result is that it is costly to obtain and transmit information about investment opportunities. Since managers are obviously more informed about investment opportunities available to the firm, they must somehow convey this information to potential investors if efficient outcomes are to be obtained solely through utilization of the (external) capital market. However, capital markets in which it is costly to obtain and transmit information look substantially different from those in which information is assumed to be perfect, and they fail to possess the standard optimality properties' (Stiglitz, 1981, p. 244).

The capital market clearly does not fully reflect all information – which is what is necessary for Pareto optimality to obtain.[13] If markets were perfectly efficient in transmitting information from the informed to the uninformed, informed individuals wouldn't obtain a return on their investment in information; thus, the only information which can, in equilibrium, be efficiently transmitted is costless information. With costly information, markets cannot be fully arbitraged (Grossman and Stiglitz, 1976, 1980).

The above considerations indicate why a useful economic function can be performed by the internal allocation of capital within the firm. If managers have access to an information set which is different from investors, and if it is difficult and costly to transmit the content of this information set to investors, then managers may be able to increase stockholder wealth by making

reports of companies, investment advisory data such as ''Heard on the Street'' in *The Wall Street Journal,* or ticker tape information.

(3) *Strong-form efficiency.* No investor can earn excess returns using any information, whether publicly available or not.

Obviously, the last type of market efficiency is very strong indeed. If markets were efficient in their strong form, prices would fully reflect all information even though it might be held exclusively by a corporate insider. Suppose, for example, he knows that his company has just discovered how to control nuclear fusion. Even before he has a chance to trade based on the news, the strong form of market efficiency predicts that prices will have adjusted so that he cannot profit.

[13] Strong form efficiency, defined in the previous footnote, would be necessary for Pareto optimality to hold.

263

investment decisions on behalf of the stockholders. In the process, resource allocation is likely to be improved over a situation in which all earnings are returned to stockholders who then make all reinvestment decisions. The transactions cost properties of such an arrangement render it absurd in most circumstances. Accordingly, the existence of internal capital markets and the (partial) internalization of the capital allocation process within the firm appear to possess a compelling rationale – both in terms of stockholder wealth enhancement and allocative efficiency.

In this context it is possible to recognize that if a specialized firm possesses financial resources beyond reinvestment opportunities in its traditional business, there are circumstances under which both stockholder wealth and allocative efficiency can be served if managers allocate funds to new products. However, the domain within which an efficiency gain is likely swings on empirical factors, and is likely to be quite narrow, given the relative efficiencies within which managers and stockholders can scan investment opportunities. It is generally only with respect to related businesses – businesses related functionally, technologically and geographically – that a relative advantage seems likely. It is for those investment opportunities in which the firm has a decided information advantage that managers are likely to possess such an advantage. Broader investment opportunities are better assessed by mutual funds which specialize in that function and can make portfolio investments at low transactions costs.

. . .

5.4. Some historical observations

The economic theory of the multiproduct firm outlined above has firms adopting multiproduct features due to the coupling of market failures and the emergence of excess capacity. Implicit in the analysis is a conviction that this model explains a substantial portion of the diversification activity which has occurred in the American economy. To demonstrate this convincingly would involve a major empirical effort. I settle here for a more limited objective – to establish that the historical trends appear broadly consistent with the theory.

Diversification has unquestionably made for great changes in the profile of American industry during the last half century (Chandler, 1969, p. 247). Furthermore, the Depression apparently triggered the trend towards diversification. Historians point out that the purpose of diversification was not to reduce portfolio risk or to pursue managerial motives, but rather to put slack resources to work. Furthermore, it was the technologically sophisticated firms which led the way. As Chandler (1969, p. 275) observed:

264

Precisely because these firms had accumulated vast resources in skilled manpower, facilities, and equipment, their executives were under even greater pressure than those of smaller firms to find new markets as the old ones ceased to grow. In the 1920's, the chemical companies, each starting from a somewhat different technological base, began to widen their product lines into new industries. In the same decade, the great electrical manufacturers – General Electric and Westinghouse – which had concentrated primarily on the manufacture of light and power equipment, diversified into production of a wide variety of household appliances. They also entered electronics with radios and X-ray equipment. During the Depression General Motors (and to a lesser extent other firms in the auto industry) moved into diesels, appliances, tractors, and airplanes. Some makers of primary metals, particularly aluminum and copper, turned to consumer products like kitchenware and household fittings, while rubber firms developed the possibilities of rubber chemistry to compensate for declining tire sales. In the same period food companies employed their existing distribution organizations to market an increasing variety of products.

Whereas the Depression triggered diversification by generating excess capacity, the Second World War stimulated the demand for new products because the world market for many raw materials was severely disrupted while the war effort generated demand for a wide range of military products. The synthetic rubber program caused both rubber and petroleum firms to make far greater use of chemical technologies than they had ever done before. Similarly, the demand for radar and other electronic equipment carried the electrical, radio, and machinery firms farther into this new field, and the production of tanks, high-speed aircraft, and new drugs all created skills and resources (Chandler, 1969, p. 275). Once these capabilities were created, they were applied, where possible, in the production of civilian goods for the peace time economy. Thus, "the modern diversified enterprise represents a calculated rational response of technically trained professional managers to the needs and opportunities of changing technologies and markets" (Chandler, 1969, p. 279).[14]

. . .

[14] While Chandler's original focus was on managerial and technological considerations, his more recent writings indicate that he has been able to identify additional sources of underutilized resources – such as marketing and purchasing knowhow – which could also provide the foundation for an efficient diversification strategy. In the years after the first world war, "many American companies . . . added lines that permitted them to make more effective use of their marketing and purchasing organizations and to exploit the by-products of their manufacturing and processing operations" (Chandler, 1977, p. 473).

PART IV

Efficiency or control? Radical perspectives and commentaries

CHAPTER 20

What do bosses do? The origins and functions of hierarchy in capitalist production

STEPHEN MARGLIN

Stephen Marglin was born in Los Angeles, California, in 1938. He received the Ph.D. in economics at Harvard University in 1965. When this article was published, he was Associate Professor of Economics at Harvard University. He is currently Walter S. Barker Professor of Economics at Harvard.

1. Introduction: does technology shape social and economic organization or does social and economic organization shape technology?

Is it possible for work to contribute positively to individual development in a complex industrial society, or is alienating work the price that must be paid for material prosperity? Discussions of the possibilities for meaningful revolution generally come down, sooner or later, to this question. If hierarchical authority is essential to high productivity, then self-expression in work must at best be a luxury reserved for the very few regardless of social and economic organization. And even the satisfactions of society's elite must be perverted by their dependence, with rare exception, on the denial of self-expression to others. But is work organization determined by technology or by society? Is hierarchical authority really necessary to high levels of production, or is material prosperity compatible with nonhierarchical organization of production?

Defenders of the capitalist faith are quite sure that hierarchy is inescapable. Indeed their ultimate line of defense is that the plurality of capitalist hierarchies is preferable to a single socialist hierarchy. To seal the argument the apologist may call on as unlikely a source of support as Friedrich Engels. Perhaps it was a momentary aberration, but at one point in his career at least Engels saw authority as technologically rather than socially determined:

If man, by dint of his knowledge and inventive genius, has subdued the forces of nature, the latter avenge themselves upon him by subjecting him, in so far as he employs them, to a veritable despotism, *independent of all social organization*. Wanting to abolish authority in large-scale industry is tantamount to wanting to abolish industry itself, to destroy the power loom in order to return to the spinning wheel.[1]

Reprinted in abridged form from Stephen Marglin, "What Do Bosses Do? The Origins and Functions of Hierarchy in Capitalist Production," *The Review of Radical Political Economy*, 6(1974): 33–60, by permission of the author.
[1] F. Engels (1894) p. 483. Emphasis added.

269

Going back to the spinning wheel is obviously absurd, and if the producer must typically take orders, it is difficult to see how work could in the main be anything but alienating.

Were the social sciences experimental, the methodology for deciding whether or not hierarchical work organization is inseparable from high material productivity would be obvious. One would design technologies appropriate to an egalitarian work organization, and test the designs in actual operation. Experience would tell whether or not egalitarian work organization is utopian. But social science is not experimental. None of us has the requisite knowledge of steel-making or cloth-making to design a new technology, much less to design one so radically different from the present norm as a serious attempt to change work organization would dictate. Besides in a society whose basic institutions – from schools to factories – are geared to hierarchy, the attempt to change one small component is probably doomed to failure. For all its shortcomings, neoclassical economics is undoubtedly right in emphasizing *general* equilibrium over *partial* equilibrium.

Instead of seeking alternative designs, we must take a more round-about tack. In this paper it is asked why, in the course of capitalist development, the actual producer lost control of production. What circumstances gave rise to the boss-worker pyramid that characterizes capitalist production? And what social function does the capitalist hierarchy serve? If it turns out that the origin and function of capitalist hierarchy has relatively little to do with efficiency, then it becomes at least an open question whether or not hierarchical production is essential to a high material standard of living. And workers – manual, technical, and intellectual – may take the possibility of egalitarian work organization sufficiently seriously to examine their environment with a view to changing the economic, social, and political institutions that relegate all but a fortunate few to an existence in which work is the means to life, not part of life itself.

It is the contention of this paper that neither of the two decisive steps in depriving the workers of control of product and process – (1) the development of the minute division of labor that characterized the putting-out system and (2) the development of the centralized organization that characterizes the factory system – took place primarily for reasons of technical superiority. Rather than providing more output for the same inputs, these innovations in work organization were introduced so that the capitalist got himself a larger share of the pie at the expense of the worker, and it is only the *subsequent* growth in the size of the pie that has obscured the class interest which was at the root of these innovations. The social function of hierarchical work organization is not technical efficiency, but accumulation. By mediating between producer and consumer, the capitalist organization sets aside much more for expanding and improving plant and equipment than individuals would if they could control the pace of capital accumulation. These ideas, which are developed in the body of this paper, can be conveniently divided into four specific propositions.

I.   The capitalist division of labor, typified by Adam Smith's famous example of pin manufacture, was the result of a search not for a technologically superior organization of work, but for an organization which guaranteed to the entrepreneur an essential role in the production process, as integrator of the separate efforts of his workers into a marketable product.

II. Likewise, the origin and success of the factory lay not in technological superiority, but in the substitution of the capitalist's for the worker's control of the work process and the quantity of output, in the change in the workman's choice from one of how much to work and produce, based on his relative preferences for leisure and goods, to one of whether or not to work at all, which of course is hardly much of a choice.

III. The social function of hierarchical control of production is to provide for the accumulation of capital. The individual, by and large and on the average, does not save by a conscious and deliberate choice. The pressures to spend are simply too great. Such individual (household) savings as do occur are the consequence of a lag in adjusting spending to a rise in income, for spending, like any other activity, must be learned, and learning takes time. Thus individual savings is the consequence of growth, and not an independent cause. Acquisitive societies – precapitalist, capitalist or socialist – develop institutions whereby collectivities determine the rate of accumulation. In modern capitalist society the pre-eminent collectivity for accumulation is the corporation. It is an essential social function of the corporation that its hierarchy mediate between the individual producer (and shareholder) and the market proceeds of the corporation's product, assigning a portion of these proceeds to enlarging the means of production. In the absence of hierarchical control of production, society would either have to fashion egalitarian institutions for accumulating capital or content itself with the level of capital already accumulated.

IV. The emphasis on accumulation accounts in large part for the failure of Soviet-style socialism to "overtake and surpass" the capitalist world in developing egalitarian forms of work organization. In according first priority to the accumulation of capital, the Soviet Union repeated the history of capitalism, at least as regards the relationship of men and women to their work. Theirs has not been the failure described by Santayana of those who, not knowing history, unwittingly repeat

271

it. The Soviets consciously and deliberately embraced the capitalist mode of production. And defenders of the Soviet path to economic development would offer no apology: after all, they would probably argue, egalitarian institutions and an egalitarian (and community oriented) man could not have been created over night, and the Soviet Union rightly felt itself too poor to contemplate an indefinite end to accumulation. Now, alas, the Soviets have the "catch-up-with-and-surpass-the-U.S.A." tiger by the tail, for it would probably take as much of a revolution to transform work organization in that society as in ours.

The following sections of this paper take these propositions one by one, in the hope of filling in sufficient detail to give them credibility.

II. Divide and conquer

Hierarchy was of course not invented by capitalists. More to the point, neither was hierarchical production. In precapitalist societies, industrial production was organized according to a rigid master-journeyman-apprentice hierarchy, which survives today in anything like its pure form only in the graduate departments of our universities. What distinguished precapitalist from capitalist hierarchy was first that the man at the top was, like the man at the bottom, a producer. The master worked along with his apprentice rather than simply telling him what to do. Second, the hierarchy was linear rather than pyramidal. The apprentice would one day become a journeyman and likely a master. Under capitalism it is a rare worker who becomes even a foreman, not to mention independent entrepreneur or corporate president. Third, and perhaps most important, the guild workman had no intermediary between himself and the market. He generally sold a product, not his labor, and therefore controlled both product and work process.

Just as hierarchy did not originate with capitalism, neither did the division of labor. The *social* division of labor, the specialization of occupation and function, *is* a characteristic of all complex societies, rather than a peculiar feature of industrialized or economically advanced ones. Nothing, after all, could be more elaborate than the caste division of labor and its accompanying hierarchy in traditional Hindu society. Nor is the *technical* division of labor peculiar to capitalism or modern industry. Cloth production, for example, even under the guild system was divided into separate tasks, each controlled by specialists. But, as we have said, the guild workman controlled product and process. What we have to account for is why the guild division of labor evolved into the capitalist division of labor, in which the workman's task typically became so specialized and minute that he had no product to sell, or at least none for which there was a wide market, and had therefore to make

272

use of the capitalist as intermediary to integrate his labor with the labor of others and transform the whole into a marketable product.

Adam Smith argues that the capitalist division of labor came about because of its technological superiority; in his view, the superiority of dividing work into ever more minutely specialized tasks was limited only by the size of the market.[2] To understand the limitations of this explanation requires clarity and precision on the meaning of "technological superiority," and the related ideas of technological efficiency and inefficiency; indeed, these ideas are central to the whole story told in this paper. We shall say, in accordance with accepted usage, that a method of production is technologically superior to another if it produces more output with the same inputs. It is not enough that a new method of production yield more output per day to be technologically superior. Even if labor is the only input, a new method of production might require more hours of labor, or more intensive effort, or more unpleasant working conditions, in which case it would be providing more output for more input, not for the same amount. It will be argued here that – contrary to neoclassical logic – a new method of production does not have to be technologically superior to be adopted; innovation depends as much on economic and social institutions – on who is in control of production and under what constraints control is exercised.

The terms "technological efficiency" and "technological inefficiency," as used by economists, have meanings that are slighty at variance with the ordinary, every-day ideas of better and worse that they evoke. A method of production is technologically efficient if no technologically superior alternative exists. It is inefficient if a superior alternative does exist. Thus more than one method of production may be – and generally is – technologically efficient if one looks only as a single product. Wheat, for example, can be efficiently produced with a lot of land and relatively little fertilizer, as in Kansas, or with a lot of fertilizer and relatively little land, as in Holland.

But if one views technological superiority and efficiency from the point of view of the whole economy, these concepts reduce, under certain circumstances, to *economic* superiority and efficiency. Under text-book assumptions of perfect and universal competition, the technologically efficient method of production is the one that costs least, and cost reduction is an index of technological superiority.[3] The relationship between minimum cost and technological efficiency is a purely logical one and does not depend at all on whether

---

[2] The attribution of the division of labor to efficiency antedates Adam Smith by a least two millenia. Plato, indeed, argued for the political institutions of the Republic on the basis of an analogy with the virtue of specialization in the economic sphere. Smith's specific arguments were anticipated by Henry Martyn three quarters of a century before the publication of the *Wealth of Nations*. See Martyn (1701).

[3] For a concise and elegant discussion of the relationship between technological efficiency and least-cost methods of production, see Tjalling Koopmans (1957) essay 1, especially pp. 66–126.

or not the world exhibits the assumptions of the model. On the other hand, the relevance of the identification of technological with economic efficiency depends absolutely on the applicability of the assumptions of the competitive model to the development of capitalism. In critical respects the development of capitalism necessarily required denial, not fulfillment, of the assumptions of perfect competition.

In a way it is surprising that the development of capitalist methods of work organization contradicts essential assumptions of perfect competition, since perfect competition has virtually nothing to say about the organization of production! Indeed, even the firm itself, a central economic institution under capitalism, plays no essential role in models of the competitive economy[4]; it is merely a convenient abstraction for the household in its role as producer and does nothing that households could not equally well do for themselves. Defenders of the faith from Wicksell to Samuelson have grandly proclaimed the perfect neutrality of perfect competition – as far as the model goes, workers could as well hire capital as capitalist workers![5] Alas, the failure of the competitive model to account for one of the most distinctive features of capitalism (and of socialism imitating capitalism) – the pyramidal work order – is for neoclassical economists a great virtue rather than a shortcoming; it is supposed to show the great generality of the theory. Generality indeed: neoclassical theory says only that hierarchy must be technologically efficient to persist, but denies the superiority of capitalist hierarchy (workers can just as well hire capital, remember!). This is to say very little, and that little, it will be argued, quite wrong.

To return to Adam Smith. *The Wealth of Nations* advances three arguments for the technological superiority of dividing labor as finely as the market will allow.

(This) great increase of the quantity of work, which, in consequence of the division of labor, the same number of people are capable of performing, is owing to three different circumstances; first, to the increase of dexterity in every particular workman; secondly, to the saving of the time which is commonly lost in passing from one species of work to another; and lastly, to the invention of a great number of machines which facilitate labor and abridge labor, and enable one man to do the work of many.[6]

Of the three arguments, one – the saving of time – is undoubtedly important. But this argument has little or nothing to do with the minute specializa-

---

[4] At least in the constant-returns-to-scale version of the competitive economy. Any other version implies the existence of a factor of production (like "entrepreneurial effort") that is not traded on the market, and with respect to which the model is therefore noncompetitive.

[5] "We may, therefore, assume either that the landowner will hire laborers for a wage . . . or that the laborers will hire the land for rent." Knut Wicksell (1934) Volume 1, p. 109.

"Remember that in a perfectly competitive market it really doesn't matter who hires whom; so have labor hire 'capital' ". . . , Paul Samuelson (1957).

[6] A. Smith (1937) p. 7.

tion that characterizes the capitalist division of labor. A peasant, for example, will generally plow a whole field before harrowing it rather than alternating plow and harrow, furrow by furrow – in order to economize on the set-up line. But peasant agriculture is the antithesis of capitalist specialization; the individual peasant normally undertakes all the activities necessary to bring a crop from seed to marketable product. In respect of set-up time, there is nothing to differentiate agriculture from industry. To save "the time that is commonly lost in passing from one species of work to another" it is necessary only to continue in a single activity long enough that the set-up time becomes an insignificant proportion of total work time. The saving of time would require at most only that each worker continue in a single activity for days at a time, not for a whole life time. Saving of time implies *separation* of tasks and *duration* of activity, not *specialization*.

Smith's third argument – the propensity to invention – is not terribly persuasive. Indeed, the most devastating criticism was noticed by Smith himself in a later chapter of *The Wealth of Nations:*

In the progress of the division of labor, the employment of the far greater part of those who have by labor, that is, of the great body of the people, come to be confined to a few very simple operations, frequently to one or two. But the understandings of the greater part of men are formed by their ordinary employments. The man whose life is spent in performing a few simple operations, of which the effects too are, perhaps, always the same, or very nearly the same, has no occasion to exert his understanding, or to exercise his invention in finding out expedients for difficulties which never occur. He naturally loses, therefore, the habit of such exertion and generally becomes as stupid and ignorant as it is possible for a human creature to become. . . .

It is otherwise in the barbarous societies, as they are commonly called, of hunters, of shepherds, and even of husbandman in that crude state of husbandry which precedes the improvement of manufactures. In such societies the varied occupations of every man oblige every man to exert his capacity, and to invent expedients for removing difficulties which are continually occurring. Invention is kept alive, and the mind is not suffered to fall into that drowsy stupidity, which, in a civilized society, seems to benumb the understanding of almost all the inferior ranks of people.[7]

The choice does not, however, seem really to lie between stupidity and barbarity, but between the workman whose span of control is wide enough that he sees how each operation fits into the whole and the workman confined to a small number of repetitive tasks. It would be surprising indeed if the workman's propensity to invent has not been diminished by the extreme specialization that characterizes the capitalist division of labor.

This leaves "the increase of dexterity in every particular workman" as the basis of carrying specialization to the limits permitted by the size of the market. Now if Adam Smith were talking about musicians or dancers or surgeons,

[7] Smith (1937) pp. 734–5.

or even if he were speaking of the division of labor between pin-making and cloth-making, his argument would be difficult to counter. But he is speaking not of esoteric specializations, nor of the social division of labor, but of the minute division of ordinary, run-of-the-mill, industrial activities into separate skills. Take his favorite example of pin manufacture:

. . . in the way of which this business is now carried on, not only the whole work is a peculiar trade, but it is divided into a number of branches, of which the greater part are likewise peculiar trades. One man draws out the wire, another straights it, a third cuts it, a fourth points it, a fifth grinds it at the top for receiving the head; to make the head requires two or three distinct operations; to put it on, is a peculiar business, to whiten the pins is another; it is even a trade by itself to put them into the paper; and the important business of making a pin is, in this manner, divided into about eighteen distinct operations, which in some manufactories, are all performed by distinct hands, though in others the same man will sometimes perform two or three of them. I have seen a small manufactory of this kind where ten men only were employed, and where some of them consequently performed two or three distinct operations. But though they were very poor, and therefore but indifferently accommodated with the necessary equipment, they could, when they exerted themselves, make among them about twelve pounds of pins in a day. There are in a pound upwards of four thousand pins of a middling size. Those ten persons, therefore could make among them upwards of forty-eight thousand pins in a day. Each person, therefore, making a tenth part of forty-eight thousand pins, might be considered as making four thousand eight hundred pins in a day. But if they had all wrought separately and independently, and without any of them having been educated to this peculiar business, they certainly could not each of them have made twenty, perhaps not one pin in a day. . . .[8]

To the extent that the skills at issue are difficult to acquire, specialization is essential to the division of production into separate operations. But, judging from the earnings of the various specialists engaged in pin-making, these were no special skills. At least there were none that commanded premium wages. In a pin manufactory for which fairly detailed records survive from the early part of the nineteenth century, T. S. Ashton reported wages for adult males of approximately 20 shillings per week, irrespective of the particular branch in which they were engaged.[9] Women and children, as was customary, earned less, but again there appear to be no great discrepancies among the various branches of pin production. It would appear to be the case that the mysteries of pin-making were relatively quickly learned, and that the potential increase in dexterity afforded by minute division of tasks was quickly exhausted. Certainly it is hard to make a case for specialization of workmen to particular tasks on the basis of the pin industry.[10]

[8] Smith (1937) pp. 4–5.
[9] T. S. Ashton (1925) pp. 281–92.
[10] For another example, cotton handloom weaving, though described by J. L. and Barbara Hammond (1919), was apparently a skill quickly learned (p. 70). A British manufacturer testified

The dichotomy between specialization and the separate crafting of each individual pin seems to be a false one. It appears to have been technologically possible to obtain the economics of reducing set-up time *without* specialization. A workman, with his wife and children, could have proceeded from task to task, first drawing out enough wire for hundreds or thousands of pins, then straightening it, then cutting it, and so on with each successive operation, thus realizing the advantages of dividing the overall production process into separate tasks.

Why, then, did the division of labor under the putting-out system entail specialization as well as separation of tasks? In my view the reason lies in the fact that without specialization, the capitalist had no essential role to play in the production process. If each producer could himself integrate the component tasks of pin manufacture into a marketable product, he would soon discover that he had no need to deal with the market for pins through the intermediation of the putter-outer. He could sell directly and appropriate to himself the profit that the capitalist derived from mediating between the producer and the market. Separating the tasks assigned to each workman was the sole means by which the capitalist could, in the days preceding costly machinery, ensure that he would remain essential to the production process as integrator of these separate operations into a product for which a wide market existed; and specialization of men to tasks at the sub-product level was the hall mark of the putting-out system.

The capitalist division of labor, as developed under the putting-out system, embodied the same principles that "successful" imperial powers have utilized to rule their colonies: divide and conquer. Exploiting differences between Hindu and Muslim in India – if not actually creating them – the British could claim to be essential to the stability of the sub-continent. And they could sometimes with ill-concealed satisfaction, point to the millions of deaths that followed Partition as proof of their necessity to stability. But this tragedy proved only that the British had *made* themselves essential as mediators, not

before a parliamentary committee that "a lad of fourteen may acquire a sufficient knowledge of it in six weeks." Duncan Bythell (1969), which is my immediate source for the manufacturer's testimony, is quite explicit: "Cotton handloom weaving, from its earliest days, was an unskilled, casual occupation which provided a domestic by-trade for thousands of women and children. . . ." (p. 270)

The apparent ease with which, according to the Hammonds, women replaced male woolen weavers gone off to fight Napoleon suggests that woolen weaving too was not such a difficult skill to acquire (1969, pp. 60–162). Indeed the competition of women in some branches of the woolen trade was such that in at least one place the men felt obliged to bind themselves collectively "not to allow any women to learn the trade" (1969, p. 162), an action that would hardly have been necessary if the requisite strength or skill had been beyond the power of women to acquire. The role of war-induced labor shortages in breaking down artificial sex barriers, and the subsequent difficulties in re-establishing these barriers is reminiscent of American experience in World War II.

that there was any inherent need for British mediation of communal differences.

Similarly, the development of an industrial system dependent on capitalist integration does not prove that the capitalist division of labor was technologically superior to integration by the producer himself. The putter-outer's peculiar contribution to production was handsomely rewarded not because of any genuine scarcity of the ability to integrate separate functions; rather the scarcity was artifically created to preserve the capitalist's role.

How could the capitalist withstand competition if his role was an artificial one? What prevented each producer from integrating his own work, and thereby coming directly into contact with a wide market? The capitalist putter-outer, who, by hypothesis, was technologically superfluous, would have been eliminated by such competition; for integrated producers would have produced pins and cloth and pottery more cheaply. Why didn't some enterprising and talented fellow organize producers to eliminate the capitalist putter-outer? The answer is that there was no profit in such a line of endeavor. If the organizer became a producer himself, he would have had to settle for a producer's wage. His co-workers might have subscribed a dinner or gold watch in his honor, but it is doubtful that their gratitude would have led them to do much more. To glean rewards from organizing, one had to become a capitalist putter-outer! The point is that no collusion was necessary between the men of talent, enterprise, and means that formed the capitalist class of putting-out days. It was the interest of each as well as in the interest of all to maintain the system of allocating separate tasks to separate workmen. Not much wit was required to see that their prosperity, as well as their survival as mediators, depended on this system.[11]

. . .

[11]This is not to say that the putter-outer, or "master manufacturer" never contributed anything of technological importance to the production process. But where the capitalist did contribute a useful technological innovation, he could effectively appropriate to himself the gains (of what in economic terms is a "public good") by preventing others, particularly his workers, from learning and imitating his trade secrets. What better way to achieve secrecy than to insist that each worker know only a part of the whole? The patent system was notoriously ineffective, and the benefactions of a grateful nation all too haphazard to rely upon, especially for the marginal improvements that are the most all but a handful of innovators could possible achieve.

CHAPTER 21

From *Contested Terrain*

RICHARD EDWARDS

Richard Edwards was born in 1944 in Minot, North Dakota. He received the Ph.D. in economics at Harvard University in 1972. When the work excerpted here was published, he was a member of the Department of Economics at the University of Massachusetts, Amherst, where he currently is Professor and Chairman.

Three faces from the hidden abode

Conflict and control in the workplace

Capitalism itself came into being when labor power (as opposed to merely labor's products) became a commodity, that is, a thing bought and sold in the market. Employers, in business to make profits, begin by investing their funds (money capital) in the raw materials, labor power, machinery, and other commodities needed for production; they then organize the labor process itself, whereby the constituents of production are set in motion to produce useful products or services; and finally, by selling the products of labor, capitalists reconvert their property back to money. If the money capital obtained at the end of this cycle exceeds that invested initially, the capitalists have earned a profit.

Focusing on the central role of the labor process in this sequence, Karl Marx noted that:

> The money-owner buys everything necessary for [production], such as raw material [and labor power], in the market, and pays for it at its full value . . . The consumption of labor power is completed, as in the case of every other commodity, outside the limits of the market. . . . Accompanied by Mr. Moneybags and by the possessor of labor power, we therefore take leave for a time of this noisy sphere, where everything takes place on the surface and in view of all men, and follow them both into the hidden abode of production, on whose threshold there stares us in the face, "No admittance except on business." Here we shall see, not only how capital produces, but how capital is produced. We shall at last force the secret of profit making.
>
> On leaving this sphere of [the market], . . . we think we can perceive a change in

the physiognomy of our dramatis personae. He, who before was the money-owner, now strides in front as capitalist; the possessor of labor power follows as his laborer. The one with an air of importance, smirking, intent on business; the other, timid and holding back, like one who is bringing his own hide to market and has nothing to expect but – a hiding.[1]

The market equality between buyer and seller of the commodity labor power disappears in this "hidden abode," and the capitalist takes charge. No wonder the capitalist strides ahead, "intent on business," for it turns out that the commodity he had purchased is not what is useful to him. What the capitalist buys in the labor market is the right to a certain quantity of what Marx has called *labor power,* that is, the worker's capacity to do work.[2] Labor power can be thought of as being measured in time units (hours, days) and it may be improved or expanded by any skills, education, or other attributes that make it more productive than "simple" labor power. Thus, the capitalist, in hiring a carpenter for a day, buys one day's quantity of carpenter labor power.

But the capacity to do work is useful to the capitalist only if the work actually gets done. Work, or what Marx called *labor,* is the actual human effort in the process of production. If labor power remains merely a potentiality or capacity, no goods get produced and the capitalist has no products to sell for profit. Once the wages-for-time exchange has been made, the capitalist cannot rest content. He has purchased a given quantity of labor power, but he must now "stride ahead" and strive to extract actual labor from the labor power he now legally owns.

Workers must provide labor power in order to receive their wages, that is, they must show up for work; but they need not necessarily provide *labor,* much less the amount of labor that the capitalist desires to extract from the labor power they have sold. In a situation where workers do not control their own labor process and cannot make their work a creative experience, any exertion beyond the minimum needed to avert boredom will not be in the workers' interest. On the other side, for the capitalist it is true (without limit) that the more work he can wring out of the labor power he has purchased, the more goods will be produced; and they will be produced without any increased wage costs. It is this discrepancy between what the capitalist can buy in the market and what he needs for production that makes it imperative for him to control the labor process and the workers' activities. The capitalist need not be motivated to control things by an obsession for power; a simple desire for profit will do.

[1] Karl Marx (1967 [1867]) pp. 175–6.
[2] "By labor-power or capacity for labor is to be understood the aggregate of those mental and physical capabilities existing in a human being, which he exercises whenever he produces a use-value of any description." Marx (1967 [1867]) p. 167.

These basic relationships in production reveal both the basis for conflict and the problem of control at the workplace.[3] Conflict exists because the interests of workers and those of employers collide, and what is good for one is frequently costly for the other. Control is rendered problematic because, unlike the other commodities involved in production, labor power is always embodied in people, who have their own interests and needs and who retain their power to resist being treated like a commodity. Indeed, today's most important employers, the large corporations, have so many employees that to keep them working diligently is itself a major task, employing a vast workforce of its own. From the capitalist's perspective, this is seen as the problem of management, and it is often analyzed simply in terms of the techniques of administration and business "leadership." But employment creates a two-sided relationship, with workers contributing as much to its final form as managers or capitalists.

In some cases, the management task may be trivial. Employers may, for example, contract for particular labor services when workers are hired; if the exact nature of the duties can be spelled out beforehand, competition among job applicants – i.e., the labor market – effectively enforces the contract. Similarly, employers may pay only for work actually done; if each worker's output is independent, piece-rate pay compels adequate production. Other workplace schemes may be directed toward the same end.

In general, however, capitalists have found it neither practical nor profitable to rely on such devices. Complete market contracting (by exhaustively specifying the worker's duties before hire) is usually impossible and almost always too expensive. Piece-rate pay has limited application and frequently engenders conflict over the rates themselves. In both cases, evaluation of the contracted work raises further problems. Other schemes – profit sharing, the distributing of company stock to workers, and more elaborate incentive schemes – also fail. Most importantly, all these devices founder because their targets, the workers, retain their ability to resist. Typically, then, the task of extracting labor from workers who have no direct stake in profits remains to be carried out in the workplace itself. Conflict arises over how work shall be organized, what work pace shall be established, what conditions producers must labor under, what rights workers shall enjoy, and how the various em-

---

[3] Of course, this conflict is only superficially confronted with regard to an individual worker. Any worker who, once on the job, refuses to work or who even works less than the most eager job-seeking unemployed person will simply be fired. Individual resistance by a worker, if it is detected, is easily dealt with, so long as a replacement is standing by the unemployment line. Meaningful conflict arises, then, with regard to groups of workers or an employer's or an entire industry's workforce. The amount of labor that can be extracted from the purchased labor power depends on the workforce's willingness to perform useful work and the enterprise's ability to compel or evoke such work.

ployees of the enterprise shall relate to each other. The workplace becomes a battleground, as employers attempt to extract the maximum effort from workers and workers necessarily resist their bosses' impositions.

An academic observer at the beginning of the 1930s gives us a glimpse of this workplace conflict in his account of one worker's experience:

"Red," a beginner in industry, was working on an assembly line in a phonograph factory, producing small motors, on hourly rate. The line was turning out an average of only 30 motors a day. "Red" found it so easy to keep up his part of the work that he would pile up parts ahead of the next worker in the line. He would then move over and help perform the next operation until the other worker caught up. This went on until "Red" was shifted by the foreman to the final operation in the assembly line. Here he was in a position to work as fast as he liked so far as passing on his completed work was concerned, but he was constantly waiting for the man behind. In order not to appear slow this man had to put through a few more parts, which had its effect all along the assembly line. The process of speeding up developed slowly until the gang, which formerly put through about 30 motors a day, was turning out an average of 120 a day. To "Red's" surprise, the men objected strenuously to this increase, argued with him and even threatened to "meet him in the alley" unless he slowed down his production. "Red" said that when production got up above 100 motors a day the threats became so insistent he began to fear "they might really mean something."[4]

When he placed "Red" at the end of the line, the foreman initiated the conflict by forcing a speed-up on all workers, and in self-defense they responded. In this case, our observer tells us, the workers won and " 'Red's' problem was 'solved' by his transfer to another department."

A similar situation, more recent, concerns a General Motors plant in 1971:

At Lordstown, efficiency became the watchword. At 60 cars an hour, the pace of work had not been exactly leisurely, but after [new managers] came in the number of cars produced almost doubled. Making one car a minute had been no picnic, especially on a constantly moving line. Assembly work fits the worker to the pace of the machine. Each work station is no more than 6 to 8 feet long. For example, within a minute on the line, a worker in the trim department had to walk about 20 feet to a conveyor belt transporting parts to the line, pick up a front seat weighing 30 pounds, carry it back to his work station, place the seat on the chassis, and put in four bolts to fasten it down by first hand-starting the bolts and then using an air gun to tighten them according to standard. It was steady work when the line moved at 60 cars an hour. When it increased to more than 100 cars an hour, the number of operations on this job were not reduced and the pace became almost maddening. In 36 seconds the worker had to perform at least eight different operations, including walking, lifting, hauling, lifting the carpet, bending to fasten the bolts by hand, fastening them by air gun, replacing the carpet, and putting a sticker on the hood. Sometimes the bolts fail to fit

[4] S. B. Mathewson (1931) pp. 16–17.

into the holes; the gun refuses to function at the required torque; the seats are defective or the threads are bare on the bolt. But the line does not stop.[5]

These illustrations involve assembly-line production, but the basic relations exist in all workplaces; indeed, the shopfloor, the office, the drafting room, the warehouse, the hospital ward, the construction site, and the hotel kitchen all become places of continuing conflict. Workers resist the discipline and the pace that employers try to impose. At most times the workers' efforts are solitary and hidden; individual workers find relief from oppressive work schedules by doing what their bosses perceive as slacking off or intentionally sabotaging work. At other times resistance is more conspiratorial; informal work groups agree on how fast they will work and combine to discipline ratebusters; or technicians work to rules, sticking to the letter of the production manual and thereby slowing work to a fraction of normal efficiency. More openly, workers or even union locals (often against the commands of their leaders) walk off the job to protest firings, arbitrary discipline, unsafe working conditions, or other grievances. More public still, established unions or groups seeking to achieve bargaining rights strike in order to shut down production entirely.

The struggle in the workplace has a closely intertwined parallel in the bargaining that goes on in the marketplace. Here conflict concerns wages, as labor and capital contend over the reward for the laborer's time. Sometimes this bargaining occurs collectively; sometimes it takes an individual form. At times wage bargaining creates a crisis; at other times it assumes an entirely pacific form. But here, too, the clash of interests persists.

Thus, in the slogan, "A fair day's work for a fair day's pay," *both* elements become matters of conflict. "A fair day's work" is as much an issue for bargaining, resistance, and struggle as is the "fair day's pay." The old Wobbly[6] demand – "Good Pay or Bum Work!" – expressed one connection. But especially in times (such as the 1910s and 1930s) when self-consciously anticapitalist groups have appeared, these two conflicts merge to challenge the very basis of capitalist production itself.

Conflict in the labor process occurs under definite historical circumstances, or, what is the same, within a specific economic and social context. Most importantly, production is part of the larger process of capital accumulation, that is, the cycle of investment of prior profits, organization of production, sale of produced commodities, realization of profits (or loss), and reinvestment of new profits. This process constitutes the fundamental dynamic of a capitalist economy. But capital accumulation, while it remains the basic theme,

[5] Stanley Aronowitz (1973) pp. 22–3.
[6] A member of the radical Industrial Workers of the World (IWW), a labor organization that was a strong force between 1905–1920.

is played out with substantial variations, and a whole set of factors – the degree of competition among capitalists, the size of corporations, the extent of trade union organizations, the level of class consciousness among workers, the impact of governmental policies, the speed of technological change, and so on – influence the nature and shape and pace of accumulation. Taken together, these various forces provide both possibilities for and constraints on what can occur within the workplace. What was possible or successful in one era may be impossible or disastrous in another. Conflict at work, then, must be understood as a product of both the strategies or wills of the combatants and definite conditions not wholly within the grasp of either workers or capitalists. As Marx put it,

> People make their own history, but they do not make it just as they please; they do not make it under circumstances chosen by themselves, but under circumstances directly found, given, and transmitted from the past.[7]

Conflict occurs within limits imposed by a social and historical context, yet this context rarely determines everything about work organization. After technological constraints, the discipline of the market, and other forces have been taken into account, there remains a certain indeterminacy to the labor process. This space for the working out of workplace conflict is particularly evident within the large corporation, where external constraints have been reduced to a minimum. Here especially, the essential question remains: how shall work be organized?

The labor process becomes an arena of class conflict, and the workplace becomes a contested terrain. Faced with chronic resistance to their effort to compel production, employers over the years have attempted to resolve the matter by reorganizing, indeed revolutionizing, the labor process itself. Their goal remains profits; their strategies aim at establishing structures of control at work. That is, capitalists have attempted to organize production in such a way as to minimize workers' opportunities for resistance and even alter workers' perceptions of the desirability of opposition. Work has been organized, then, to contain conflict. In this endeavor employers have sometimes been successful.

The dimensions of control

How much work gets done every hour or every day emerges as a result of the struggle between workers and capitalists. As later chapters will describe, each side seeks to tip the balance and influence or determine the outcome with the weapons at its disposal. On one side, the workers use hidden or open resis-

---

[7] Karl Marx (1972 [1852]) p. 457.

tance to protect themselves against the constant pressure for speed-up; on the other side, capitalists employ a variety of sophisticated or brutal devices for tipping the balance their way. But this is not exactly an equal fight, for employers retain their power to hire and fire, and on this foundation they have developed various methods of control by which to organize, shape, and affect the workers' exertions.

Control in this sense differs from coordination, a term that appears more frequently in popular literature describing what managers do, and it may be useful at the outset to distinguish the two. Coordination is required, of course, in all social production, since the product of such production is by definition the result of labor by many persons. Hence, whether a pair of shoes is produced in a Moroccan cobbler's shop, a Chinese commune, or an American factory, it is an inherent technical characteristic of the production process that the persons cutting and tanning the leather must mesh their efforts with those who sew the leather, those who attach the heels, and others. Without such coordination, production would be haphazard, wasteful, and – where products more complex than shoes are involved – probably impossible as well. Hence, coordination of social production is essential.[8]

Coordination may be achieved in a variety of ways, however, and the differences are crucial. Coordination may be achieved by tradition – through long-established ways of doing the work and the passing on of these trade secrets from master to apprentices. Or it may be achieved directly by the producers themselves, as occurs when the members of a cooperative or commune discuss their parts in the production process to ensure that their tasks are harmonized. As the scale of production increases, workers may designate one member (or even choose someone from the outside) to act as a full-time coordinator of their interests, thus establishing a manager. As long as the managerial staff, no matter how large, remains accountable to the producers themselves, we may properly speak of their efforts as "coordination" or "administration."

A different type of coordination characterizes capitalist workplaces, however; in capitalist production, labor power is purchased, and with that purchase – as with the purchase of every commodity in a capitalist economy – goes the right to designate the use (consumption) of the object bought. Hence there is a presumption, indeed a contractual right backed by legal force, for the capitalist, as owner of the purchased labor power, to direct its use. A

---

[8] As Marx (1967 [1867] pp. 330–1) put it: "All combined labor on a large scale requires, more or less, a directing authority, in order to secure the harmonious working of the individual activities, and to perform the general functions that have their origin in the action of its separate organs. A single violin player is his own conductor; an orchestra requires a separate one." See also S. A. Marglin (1974), F. Roosevelt (1975), and Theodore Anderson and Seymour Warkov (1961).

corollary presumption (again backed by legal force) follows: that the workers whose labor power has been purchased have no right to participate in the conception and planning of production. Coordination occurs in capitalist production as it must inevitably occur in all social production, but it necessarily takes the specific form of top-down coordination, for the exercise of which the top (capitalists) must be able to control the bottom (workers). In analyzing capitalist production, then, it is more appropriate to speak of control than of coordination, although of course, control is a means of coordination.[9]

"Control" is here defined as the ability of capitalists and/or managers to obtain desired work behavior from workers. Such ability exists in greater or lesser degrees, depending upon the relative strength of workers and their bosses. As long as capitalist production continues, control exists to some degree, and the crucial questions are: to what degree? how is control obtained? and how does control lead to or inhibit resistance on a wider scale? At one extreme, capitalists try to avoid strikes, sit-downs, and other militant actions that stop production; but equally important to their success, they attempt to extract, day by day, greater amounts of labor for a given amount of labor power.

In what follows, the *system of control* (in other words, the social relations of production within the firm) are thought of as a way in which three elements are coordinated:

1. Direction, or a mechanism or method by which the employer directs work tasks, specifying what needs to be done, in what order, with what degree of precision or accuracy, and in what period of time.
2. Evaluation, or a procedure whereby the employer supervises and evaluates to correct mistakes or other failures in production, to assess each worker's performance, and to identify workers or groups of workers who are not performing work tasks adequately.
3. Discipline, or an apparatus that the employer uses to discipline and reward workers, in order to elicit cooperation and enforce compliance with the capitalist's direction of the labor process.

---

[9] As this implies, control is thus not a form of coordination unique to capitalism, since it obtains, for example, in slave societies and in socialist societies like the U.S.S.R., where democratic coordination over the labor process has not been established. Coercive coordination is required in all class-based social systems.

Even where workers and capitalists enjoyed precisely the same objective interests in the efficiency or productivity of production – as would be true, for example, where each worker's wage was simply a fixed percentage of the firm's "profits" – coordination would take the form of control. Imagine that the capitalist and workers of a firm disagreed on how best to pursue maximum profits; as long as the capitalist has the final say, rather than being accountable to the workers, management must be able to force the workers to follow the capitalist's program rather than the workers'. As this example illustrates, coordination need not involve coercion, but control does.

The types of control

Systems of control in the firm have undergone dramatic changes in response to changes in the firm's size, operations, and environment and in the workers' success in imposing their own goals at the workplace. The new forms did not emerge as sharp, discrete discontinuities in historical evolution, but neither were they simply points in a smooth and inevitable evolution. Rather, each transformation occurred as a resolution of intensifying conflict and contradiction in the firm's operations. Pressures built up, making the old forms of control untenable. The period of increasing tension was followed by a relatively rapid process of discovery, experimentation, and implementation, in which new systems of control were substituted for the older, more primitive ones. Once instituted, these new relations tend to persist until they no longer effectively contain worker resistance or until further changes occur in the firm's operations.

In the nineteenth century, most businesses were small and were subject to the relatively tight discipline of substantial competition in product markets. The typical firm had few resources and little energy to invest in creating more sophisticated management structures. A single entrepreneur, usually flanked by a small coterie of foremen and managers, ruled the firm. These bosses exercised power personally, intervening in the labor process often to exhort workers, bully and threaten them, reward good performance, hire and fire on the spot, favor loyal workers, and generally act as despots, benevolent or otherwise. They had a direct stake in translating labor power into labor, and they combined both incentives and sanctions in an idiosyncratic and unsystematic mix. There was little structure to the way power was exercised, and workers were often treated arbitrarily. Since workforces were small and the boss was both close and powerful, workers had limited success when they tried to oppose his rule. This system of "simple" control survives today in the small-business sector of the American economy, where it has necessarily been amended by the passage of time and by the borrowings of management practices from the more advanced corporate sector, but it retains its essential principles and mode of operation. It is the system of simple control that governs Maureen Agnati's job at Digitex.

Near the end of the nineteenth century, the tendencies toward concentration of economic resources undermined simple control; while firms' needs for control increased, the efficacy of simple control declined. The need for coordination appeared to increase not only with the complexity of the product but also with the scale of production. By bringing under one corporate roof what were formerly small independent groups linked through the market, the corporation more than proportionately raised the degree of coordination needed. Production assumed an increasingly social character, requiring greater "social"

287

planning and implying an increased need for control. But as firms began to employ thousands of workers, the distance between capitalists and workers expanded, and the intervening space was filled by growing numbers of foremen, general foremen, supervisors, superintendents, and other minor officials. Whereas petty tyranny had been more or less successful when conducted by entrepreneurs (or foremen close to them), the system did not work well when staffed by hired bosses. The foremen came into increasingly severe conflict with both their bosses and their workers.

The workers themselves resisted speed-up and arbitrary rule more successfully, since they were now concentrated by the very growth of the enterprise.[10] From the Homestead and Pullman strikes to the great 1919–1920 steel strike, workers fought with their bosses over control of the actual process of production. The maturing labor movement and an emergent Socialist Party organized the first serious challenge to capitalist rule. Intensifying conflict in society at large and the specific contradictions of simple control in the workplace combined to produce an acute crisis of control on the shop floor.

The large corporations fashioned the most far-reaching response to this crisis. During the conflict, big employers joined small ones in supporting direct repression of their adversaries. But the large corporations also began to move in systematic ways to reorganize work. They confronted the most serious problems of control, but they also commanded the greatest resources with which to attack the problems. Their size and their substantial market power released them from the tight grip of short-run market discipline and made possible for the first time planning in the service of long-term profits. The initial steps taken by large companies – welfare capitalism, scientific management, and company unions – constituted experiments, trials with serious inherent errors, but useful learning experiences nonetheless. In retrospect, these efforts appear as beginnings in the corporations' larger project of establishing more secure control over the labor process.

Large firms developed methods of organization that are more formalized and more consciously contrived than simple control; they are ''structural'' forms of control. Two possibilities existed: more formal, consciously contrived controls could be embedded in either the physical structure of the labor process (producing ''technical'' control) or in its social structure (producing ''bureaucratic'' control). In time, employers used both, for they found that the new systems made control more institutional and hence less visible to

[10] Again we may quote Marx (1967 [1867] p. 331): "As the number of the cooperating laborers increases, so too does their resistance to the domination of capital, and with it, the necessity for capital to overcome this resistance by counter-pressure. The control exercised by the capitalist is not only a special function, due to the nature of the social labor-process, and peculiar to that process, but it is, at the same time, a function of the exploitation of a social labor-process, and is consequently rooted in the unavoidable antagonism between the exploiter and the living and laboring raw material he exploits.

workers, and they also provided a means for capitalists to control the "intermediate layers," those extended lines of supervision and power.

Technical control emerged from employers' experiences in attempting to control the production (or blue-collar) operations of the firm. The assembly line came to be the classic image, but the actual application of technical control was much broader. Machinery itself directed the labor process and set the pace. For a time, employers had the best of two worlds. Inside the firm, technical control turned the tide of conflict in their favor, reducing workers to attendants of prepaced machinery; externally, the system strengthened the employer's hand by expanding the number of potential substitute workers. But as factory workers in the late 1930s struck back with sit-downs, their action exposed the deep dangers to employers in thus linking all workers' labor together in one technical apparatus. The conflict at the workplace propelled labor into its "giant step," the CIO.

These forces have produced today a second type of work organization. Whereas simple control persists in the small firms of the industrial periphery, in large firms, especially those in the mass-production industries, work is subject to technical control. The system is mutually administered by management and (as a junior partner) unions. Jobs in the GE plant where Fred Doyal works fit this pattern.

There exists a third method for organizing work, and it too appeared in the large firms. This system, bureaucratic control, rests on the principle of embedding control in the social structure or the social relations of the workplace. The defining feature of bureaucratic control is the institutionalization of hierarchical power. "Rule of law" – the firm's law – replaces "rule by supervisor command" in the direction of work, the procedures for evaluating workers' performance, and the exercise of the firm's sanctions and rewards; supervisors and workers alike become subject to the dictates of "company policy." Work becomes highly stratified; each job is given its distinct title and description; and impersonal rules govern promotion. "Stick with the corporation," the worker is told, "and you can ascend up the ladder." The company promises the workers a *career*.

Bureaucratic control originated in employers' attempts to subject nonproduction workers to more strict control, but its success impelled firms to apply the system more broadly than just to the white-collar staff. Especially in the last three decades, bureaucratic control has appeared as the organizing principle in both production and nonproduction jobs in many large firms, and not the least of its attractions is that the system has proven especially effective in forestalling unionism. Stanley Miller's job at Polaroid is subject to bureaucratic control.

Continuing conflict in the workplace and employers' attempts to contain it have thus brought the modern American working class under the sway of three quite different systems for organizing and controlling their work: simple control, technical control (with union participation), and bureaucratic control. Of course, the specific labor processes vary greatly: Maureen Agnati's coil wrapper might have been a typewriter or a cash register, Fred Doyal's job might have been in a tire plant or a tractor factory, and Stanley Miller's work might have involved being a supervisor or skilled craftsman. Yet within this variety of concrete labors, the three patterns for organizing work prevail.

The typology of control embodies both the pattern of historical evolution and the array of contemporary methods of organizing work. On the one hand, each form of control corresponds to a definite stage in the development of the representative or most important firms; in this sense structural control succeeded simple control and bureaucratic control succeeded technical control, and the systems of control correspond to or characterize stages of capitalism. On the other hand, capitalist production has developed unevenly, with some sectors pushing far in advance of other sectors, and so each type of control represents an alternate method of organizing work; so long as uneven development produces disparate circumstances, alternate methods will coexist.

The following chapters explore the dynamic of class conflict within the labor process; but the impact of this dynamic extends far beyond the workplace. The redivision of labor splintered the working class; rather than creating new "classes," it has established enduring *fractions* of the same class, and, as the last chapter will·suggest, by changing the constellation of class forces in society it has reconstituted the basis of American politics.

Class-fraction politics may well have created a situation in which American society is stuck between capitalism and its future. On the one hand, the fractionalizing of the working class in the economic sphere has probably made class confrontation unlikely; in the foreseeable future, it has certainly left the working class too weak and too seriously divided to challenge capitalist hegemony. On the other hand, the continuing class-rooted conflict (in the form of class-fraction politics) has steadily expanded the role of government and pushed it to impose increasingly costly (for capitalists) limitations on business. Within the context of the long post–World War II boom, and while the United States' international position went unchallenged, the contradictions in this process could be patched up by sharing the spoils of rapid growth. In the harsher times of the 1970s, no such easy solution seemed possible.

This impasse in the class struggle has momentous consequences for the future of democracy. As will be argued later, capitalists have sought over the past few decades to restrict the tendency toward deadlock by restricting democratic government itself. They have continued to defend the form of democratic rule, but they have lent their weight to the long-term erosion of its content. The rise of rule by the great state bureaucracies, the "imperial presidency,'' and government by executive or administrative order provides the undemocratic substance of modern democratic government.

On the other hand, it appears that working-class fractions will increasingly be pressed to defend and extend political democracy as a way of pushing for their more immediate economic and social needs. In this, concerns at the workplace intersect directly with larger-scale issues, for the great contradiction in bureaucratic control is its implicit tyranny. Workers are treated fairly within the rules, but they have no say in establishing the rules. The (perhaps inevitable) response, already apparent within the past few years, is the call for democracy at work. But if it is to be genuine and not merely the latest wrinkle in employer control, democracy at work requires socialism. Industrial democracy alongside political democracy – long a dream of socialists – thus appears as a unifying demand in the working class's disunity.

The present situation represents an historic conjuncture. Society once again faces the basic questions of capitalism, socialism, and democracy. How these questions will be answered is by no means certain.

291

CHAPTER 22

The organization of work: a comparative institutional assessment

OLIVER WILLIAMSON

Oliver Williamson is Gordon Tweedy Professor of Economics of Law and Organization at Yale University. See also his paper co-authored with Michael Wachter and Jeffrey Harris in this volume.

1. Introduction

The organization of work is of long-standing interest to and elicits frequent commentary by academics, social reformers, and men of affairs (politicians, businessmen, labor leaders, bureaucrats). Although all of the social sciences have something to contribute, none would appear to have a greater stake in the issues than economics. In fact, however, the interests of economists have been of a selective kind. Partly this is because questions regarding alternative modes of internal organization do not arise naturally within, and in some respects are even alien to, the neoclassical tradition.[1] Among contemporary economists, it has mainly been those who are associated with the New Left that have pressed the issues. What appears to be a consensus position within the New Left has been summarized by Bowles and Gintis (1976, ch. 3).

The leading features of this consensus are reviewed in section 2. The argument of special interest is whether, as alleged, hierarchical modes of organization lack redeeming efficiency attributes. Assessing this is facilitated by (1) focussing on a specific production process, (2) expressly describing alternative organizational modes, across which the degree of hierarchy varies, for accomplishing the task, and (3) evaluating each mode with respect to a common set of performance attributes. Transaction costs, which have been relatively neglected in the recent literature, turn out to be central to this exercise. These efficiency issues are addressed in sections 3 and 4.

Some of the historical evidence bearing on the evolution of work modes

Reprinted in abridged form from Oliver Williamson, "The Organization of Work: A Comparative Institutional Assessment," *Journal of Economic Behavior and Organization*, 1 (1980):5–38, by permission of the publisher.

[1]Aaron Gordon's (1976, p. 3) remarks in his 1975 Presidential Address to the American Economic Association suggest as much: ". . . we should not ignore the extent to which rigorous formulations of the theory of the firm have had to be relaxed in order to obtain useful results in empirical work. Nor . . . should we forget the extent to which conventional theory ignores how and why work is organized within the firm and establishment in the way that it is. . . .".

and issues of alienation are briefly examined in section 5. Concluding remarks appear in section 6.

Very briefly, I argue that the New Left has a legitimate complaint that neoclassical economics makes little useful contact with organization of work issues. The principal reason for this is that the neoclassical firm is characterized as a production function. Economizing thus takes the form of efficient choice of factor proportions, while issues relating to the organization of work mainly involve economizing on transaction costs. The latter rarely surface, much less are prominently featured, under the production function approach.

Economizing on transaction costs involves choice among alternative modes of organization. A comparative institutional assessment of the properties of alternative modes thus supplants the conventional calculus of cost minimization. While the New Left is to be commended for recognizing the limits of the neoclassical calculus, radical economists unfortunately make very little use of systematic comparative institutional analysis. Instead, having established that neoclassical analysis is unsuited, the New Left simply asserts that non-hierarchical work modes have excellent transaction cost properties and are superior to hierarchical modes in work satisfaction respects. An examination of these assertions does not stand up to scrutiny. What is needed, and what I attempt to do, is (1) expressly identify the relevant transaction cost dimensions, (2) expressly describe the organizational and operating properties of alternative modes, and (3) perform a comparative institutional assessment. This microanalytic strategy for investigating work mode attributes would appear to have general applicability beyond the specific (and time honored) pin-making example studied here.

. . .

3. The microanalytic approach

3.1. Efficiency

Consistent with the production function orientation of received microtheory, the prevailing tendency in economics is to attribute efficiency differences to differences in technology. Technologies for which a large number of workers are required to work coordinately at a single station are implicitly assumed to be very common. Joining these workers under an employment relation is thought to be the ''natural'' way to organize production. What is referred to as the firm is then the outcome of these underlying technological conditions.

In reality, however, most large firms are not large, single station facilities. Instead, large size is the result of joining a series of stations, across which intermediate product is successively passed, within a single administrative entity.

In principle, the interfaces between successive stations could be mediated by market exchanges. That such market mediated exchanges are supplanted by an administrative process is a *prima facie* indication that internal organization serves to economize on transaction costs that would otherwise be incurred in the market. Vertical integration is thus to be understood principally in transaction cost rather than technological terms (Williamson, 1975, chs. 4–5).

Transferring a transaction (or related set of transactions) out of the market into the firm still leaves open, however, the matter of how these transactions are going to be organized internally. Two propositions are relevant in this connection: (1) just as market structure matters in assessing the performance properties of market organization, so does internal structure matter in assessing the efficacy of alternative internal modes, and (2) transaction costs are central to performance assessments of both kinds. Accordingly, holding the degree of vertical integration constant, the choice between alternative internal modes for organizing successive stages of production turns mainly on transaction cost rather than technological considerations.

I do not by this, however, mean to imply that choices of technology and internal organization are independent. To the contrary, technological changes may render some organizing modes inoperable. But as between *feasible* organizing modes (of which there are normally several), differential performance is to be understood as a transaction cost issue.

Basically, the question of efficient versus inefficient modes of internal organization comes down to an examination of their properties in bounded rationality and opportunism respects. Organizing modes that economize on scarce information processing and decision-making capability have superior properties in transaction cost terms, *ceteris paribus*. Similarly, modes that serve to attenuate subgoal pursuit and discourage information hoarding and distortion are favored, *ceteris paribus*. Economizing on bounded rationality and attenuating opportunism are thus the core issues on which a comparative assessment of transaction costs turns.

3.2. A description of alternative modes

Marglin contends that the non-experimental nature of the social sciences contributes to the continuing neglect of internal organization. Were this not the case, alternative modes of organization, including egalitarian work modes, would be designed and tested experimentally (Marglin, 1974, pp. 33–34). While I agree that experimental testing of this kind has great merit, I submit that a great deal can be discovered about the efficacy of alternative work modes by an abstract assessment of their transactional properties. At the very least, a priori analysis of the transactional attributes of alternative modes should permit the empirical issues to be greatly delimited.

So that alternative modes will be on a parity in technological and locational respects, it will be useful first to specify the common manufacturing characteristics associated with each. One of the more serious problems with the work mode literature is that such assumptions are rarely made explicit.

The following assumptions will be maintained in this and the next two sections and, except where noted to the contrary, will apply across all modes:

(1) Specialized equipment, provided that it can be utilized at design capacity, facilitates low cost pin manufacture.

(2) Workers acquire dexterity by repeated operations of the same kind, though this is subject to diminishing returns.

(3) It is economical, so as to economize on transportation expense, that all pinmaking operations be completed at a common location, whence, the putting-out system excepted, all work is performed under one roof.

(4) The common building is leased and, whatever the station ownership and utilization arrangements, no problems arise with respect to building lease payments.

(5) Successive stages of manufacture are separable in the sense that placing a buffer inventory between them permits work at each stage to proceed independently of the other.

(6) The production line is balanced in the following very special sense: work stations are designed such that, absent untoward events, a steady flow of intermediate product between stations is assured by placing a single, fully occupied worker at each station.

(7) Market transactions for intermediate product are very costly.

(8) The workers employed under each mode are a random sample of the technically qualified population of which they are a part.

(9) Replacement investment occurs routinely and investment for expansion purposes is ignored.

The first four assumptions are relatively uncontroversial. The fifth assumption (separability) means that differences among work modes turn on transactional rather than technological considerations. Coupling this with the one-man-each station condition [assumption (6)] effectively means that the technology associated with the putting-out system is not inferior; rather, the same technology is feasible for and is common to all modes.

As noted, this one-man-each station assumption is very special. It serves to concentrate attention on transaction cost issues, which have hitherto been neglected, and suppress technological considerations, the importance of which has previously been exaggerated. Redressing this imbalance by way of the one-man-each station device scarcely yields a ''representative'' outcome. It is nevertheless noteworthy that the very same transaction cost attributes of work organization which this device serves to isolate also appear in the multiperson station context. The assumption will accordingly be retained throughout the paper.

The assumption that intermediate product markets work badly permits us to focus entirely on the transactional properties of *internal* organization. Were it that market alternatives to internal exchange could be exercised at slight cost, choice among alternative internal modes becomes less important since market relief can always be obtained when internal modes threaten to break down. Assumption (7) forecloses this possibility.

The assumption that the workers employed under each mode are a random sample of the population precludes the possibility that workers will match preferences toward work modes in a discriminating way. Thus although certain work modes may be competitively viable if they are staffed with workers with *special* attributes, this is foreclosed by the random assignment stipulation wherein all modes are assessed with respect to a common workforce.

Assumption (9) permits new investment issues to be set aside; attention is focused on the operating and adaptive attributes of alternatives modes instead. This has two advantages. First, the investment properties of alternative ownership arrangements can be and have been investigated within the neoclassical framework. The studies of Vanek (1970), Meade (1972), and Furubotn (1976), all confirm that collective ownership models are beset with investment problems. Secondly, the operating and adaptive attributes of alternative work modes have been relatively neglected in the prior literature. Omitting investment from the performance attributes under scrutiny serves to compensate for this imbalance.

So much for the assumptions; I turn now to a description of alternative modes. Six different modes are described, first in ownership and then in contracting terms. Both for transaction cost purposes and for the purposes of studying hierarchy, the latter is more basic. Ownership, however, is the more familiar way of describing work modes and will be employed first.

3.2.1. Alternative modes/ownership

Three types of station ownership relations – entrepreneurial, collective ownership, and capitalist – with two variants within each will be considered.

(a) Entrepreneurial modes. Entrepreneurial modes are ones in which each station is owned and operated by a specialist.

(i) Putting-Out system. A merchant-coordinator here supplies the raw materials, owns the work-in-process inventories, and makes contracts with the individual entrepreneurs, each of whom performs one of the basic operations at his home using his own equipment. Material is moved from station to

296

station (home to home) in batches under the direction of the merchant-coordinator.

The Putting-Out system has been described by Landes (1966, p. 12) as follows:

. . . merchant-manufacturers "put out" raw materials – raw wool, yarn, metal rods, as the case might be – to dispersed cottage labor, to be worked up into finished or semifinished products. Sometimes the household was responsible for more than one step in the production process: spinning and weaving were a typical combination. But the system was also compatible with the most refined division of labor, and in the cutlery manufacture of Solingen or Thires or in the needle trade of Iserlohn, the manufacturing process was broken down into as many as a dozen stages, with each cottage shop specializing in one. Putting-Out was a major step on the path to industrial capitalism. For one thing, it brought industrial organization closer to the modern division between employers who own the capital and workers who sell their labor. To be sure, most domestic weavers owned their loom and nailers their forge. They were not, however, independent entrepreneurs selling their products in the open market; rather they were hirelings, generally tied to a particular employer, to whom they agreed to furnish a given amount of work at a price stipulated in advance.

(ii) Federated. Stations are here located side by side in a common facility. Intermediate product is transferred across stages according to contract. So as to avoid the need for supervision or continuous coordination, buffer inventories are introduced at each station. Subject to the condition that buffer inventories do not fall below prescribed levels, in which event penalties are assessed, each worker proceeds at his own pace.

Whether this mode was ever widely used in uncertain and perhaps doubtful. Thus although Landes (1966, p. 14) observes that the practice of "leasing space and power in a mill to individual artisans, each conducting his own enterprise" was common in nineteenth century England, it is unclear whether intermediate product was traded among stations or if each station was self-contained.

It is nevertheless useful to consider the Federated mode as an evolutionary development, even if only of a hypothetical kind. For one thing, it illustrates the use of comparative analysis of a microanalytic kind to investigate the properties of new forms of organization. Once an abstract mode has been described, its incentive and contracting properties, in relation to other modes, are relatively easy to establish. Additionally, the Federated mode has the attractive property that it preserves considerable worker autonomy.[2] Egalitarian work relations are presumably favored in the process.

[2]An alternative mode, of a less autonomous kind, would be to transfer the Putting-Out mode into the factory. Thus instead of each work station striking contracts with predecessor and successor stations, all contracts would be mediated instead by a central agent – the merchant-coordinator. Since, except in transportation expense respects, the simple efficiency properties of this

297

(b) Collective ownership. Work stations are here owned in common by the entire group of workers.

(i) Communal-emh. Although stations are owned in common, every man has a claim to the output associated with his own labors. So as to facilitate the acquisition of dexterity and economize on set-up costs, each worker engages in batch process manufacture. The orderly movement of product is accomplished by having workers move between successive stations at prescribed intervals (hourly, daily, weekly, or whatever appears most appropriate), each bringing his own work-in-process inventory with him and selling his final product in the market.

The suffix "emh" is used to emphasize that this is an every-man-for-himself system.[3] Thus although workers pool their resources with respect to the ownership of plant and equipment and orderly station moves are accomplished by calendar, there is no specialization among workers. Such a joining of common ownership with an every-man-for-himself rule is what Demsetz (1967, p. 54) has described elsewhere as the communal mode. Unsurprisingly, the combination of community ownership with emh appropriability leads to mixed performance results. To conclude, however, that collective ownership is inferior to private ownership because of defects in the Communal-emh mode is unwarranted. If collective modes, such as the Peer Group, can be devised that have better properties than does Communal-emh, these presumably should be considered.[4]

(ii) Peer groups. The same ownership arrangement obtains here as in the Communal-emh mode, but workers are compensated not on the basis of their own product but are paid the average product of the group instead.[5] Workers may rotate among stations or specialize at one or a few stations. Moreover, so as to avoid the need for full group discussion whenever an adaptation needs to be made and/or to better assure coordination among the members with respect to work breaks, variable rates of production, and the like, Peer Groups may elect temporary "leaders", who make operating – but not strategic – decisions on behalf of the group. It is important, however, that leadership

mode are substantially identical to those of the Putting-Out system, the Federated mode, with bilateral contracting between stations, has more interesting properties. [Freudenberger and Redlich (1964, p. 394) conjecture that "Very probably the first consolidated, centrally managed workshops were little more than concentrated Putting-Out arrangements".]

[3]Alternatively, the suffix "eph/h" could be used, where this refers to every-person-for his/herself. For purposes of economy, I use emh.

[4]Demsetz was concerned with land use rather than batch manufacturing in his discussion of communal ownership. I conjecture that the Peer Group typically has superior properties to the Communal-emh mode for land use as well.

[5]Specifying average group product is unnecessary. Any of a variety of non-marginal product reward schemes will do.

rotate among group members if rigid hierarchical relations are to be avoided. Mandel's (1968, p. 677) proposal for self-management "in which everybody will take a turn to carry out administrative work in which the differences between 'director' and 'directed' will be abolished" is in this spirit. The joining of a non-marginal productivity sharing rule with democratic decision-making is what characterizes Peer Group organization.[6]

(c) Capitalist modes. Inventories of all kinds (raw materials, intermediate product, finished goods) as well as plant and equipment are owned by a single party under capitalist modes.

(i) Inside contracting. The Inside Contracting mode of organization has been succinctly described by Buttrick (1952, pp. 201–202) in the following way:

Under the system of inside contracting, the management of a firm provided floor space and machinery, supplied raw materials and working capital, and arranged for the sale of the final product. The gap between raw material and finished product, however, was filled not by paid employees arranged in [a] descending hierarchy . . . but by [inside] contractors, to whom the production job was delegated. They hired their own employees, supervised the work process, and received a [negotiated] piece rate from the company.

The Inside Contracting system permits a capitalist who has relatively little technical knowledge to employ his capital productively while limiting his involvement to negotiating contracts with inside contractors, inspecting and coordinating the flow of intermediate product, and taking responsibility for final sales.[7]

(ii) Authority relation. The Authority Relation mode involves capitalist ownership of equipment and inventories coupled with an employment relationship between capitalist and worker. The employment relation is, by design, an incomplete form of contracting. Flexibility is featured as the employee stands ready to accept authority regarding work assignments provided only that the behavior called for falls within the "zone of acceptance" of the contract. Joining an organization under the Authority Relation mode thus entails an agreement "that within some limits (defined both explicitly and implicitly by the terms of the employment contract) [the employee] will accept as premises of his behavior orders and instructions supplied to him by the organization" (March and Simon, 1958, p. 90). Rather than enjoy the contractual autonomy of an inside contractor, who is subject to only very loose performance constraints (e.g., that minimum quality standards be met and that buffer inven-

---

[6]For an elaboration, see Williamson (1975, ch. 3).
[7]For an evaluation of the limits of Inside Contracting, see Williamson, (1975, pp. 96–9).

tories not fall below prescribed levels more than a certain percentage of the time), the worker now is subject to much more detailed supervision.

3.2.2. Alternative modes/contracting

Contractual differences of two kinds should be distinguished. The first and more important compares alternative modes in terms of their degree of reliance on contractual detail to coordinate production. This is the distinction emphasized here and in section 4. The second has reference to the bargaining relation between the contracting agents. This aspect is examined in section 3.3 below.

The six alternative modes under examination in this paper differ significantly in the degree to which they rely on comprehensive contracting. For three of the modes, contracting (and recontracting) is the exclusive basis by which product is exchanged and interfaces are brought into adjustment. For the other three modes, contract is used to provide framework, which framework is subject to renegotiation at the contract renewal interval. Within the context of this framework, however, day-to-day operations are governed by an administrative process. These two different styles of organization will be referred to as continuous contracting and periodic contracting, respectively.

(a) Continuous contracting. Both types of entrepreneurial modes (Putting-Out and Federated) as well as the Inside Contracting mode rely extensively on contracting. The putter-outer and the capitalist serve as the common contracting agent in the first and third instances while the workers in the Federated mode engage in bilateral contracts with the owners of predecessor and successor stations. A common characteristic of contracting modes is that each worker maintains considerable autonomy and, once the terms of the contract are struck, lays claims to a distinct profit stream. Since the gains of one agent are frequently made at the expense of another, relations among the parties are of a highly calculative kind.

The problem with such contracting modes are of two kinds. First, can the requisite complex contract be described, negotiated, and enforced in a low cost manner? Bounded rationality considerations preclude comprehensive contracting from being realized. Confronted with the infeasibility of such complete contracting, the hazards of incomplete contracting then need to be addressed.

Since bargaining relations between successive stations are necessarily of a small numbers kind, bilateral monopoly problems abound. To be sure, a long-term recurring relationship between the parties is contemplated. Unrestrained, myopic subgoal pursuit is accordingly discouraged. But it is unrealistic to expect autonomous parties to adapt to unforeseen, hence unplanned, circumstances in a joint profit maximizing way without first settling their respective claims on profit streams through intensive, self-interested bargaining. The prospect and actuality of such recurrent bargaining is a major impediment to autonomous contracting work modes.

(b) Periodic contracting. There is no exchange of intermediate product among members of Communal-emh firms, whence there is little occasion for contracting under this mode. *Ad hoc* contracts might, however, be negotiated if workers were to become disabled, since work-in-process inventories would otherwise stand idle. Also, original investment, re-investment, and maintenance agreements will need to be worked out. Although these are not trivial matters, the problems of recurring contracting which arise in connection with day-to-day operations in each of the above described contracting modes do not appear.

Members of Peer Groups have even less need for contracting. Work left undone by a disabled worker would be completed by his associates. To be sure, membership affiliation and disaffiliation terms would have to be reached. But no bilateral contracting between successive stations on operating matters would occur. Democratic decision-making, effected by the rotating leader or by full group discussion, is used to bring station interfaces into adjustment.

Contracting under the Authority Relation is apt to be somewhat more complete, in that explicit and implicit understandings regarding the zone of acceptance of the employment relation (Barnard, 1962; Simon, 1957) need to be reached. Once agreement has been reached, however, this is an essentially non-contractual mode. Adaptations of an operating kind are made within the framework of this rather general contract, whereby boss and worker essentially agree to "tell and be told". And strategic decisions affecting the overall configuration of the enterprise are mainly left to the boss's discretion.

3.3. The degree of hierarchy

The degree of hierarchy is usually assessed in decision-making respects. Where the responsibility for effecting adaptations is concentrated on one or a few agents, hierarchy is relatively great. Where instead adaptations are taken by individual agents or are subject to collective approval, hierarchy is slight. A less common but nonetheless useful way to characterize hierarchy is in contractual terms. If one or a few agents are responsible for negotiating all contracts, the contractual hierarchy is great. If instead each agent negotiates each interface separately, the contractual hierarchy is weak.[8] Although there is a

---

[8]Note in this connection that the term contractual hierarchy has reference to the relation between the contracting agents, not to the reliance on contracting to effect adaptations. Modes that are described above as periodic may (and some do) have strong hierarchical properties at contract renewal intervals.

strong, positive rank correlation between these two ways of characterizing hierarchy for the work modes investigated here, the correlation is not perfect. What is perhaps more interesting is that ownership is imperfectly correlated with hierarchies of both kinds. Using E, Co, and Cap to denote Entrepreneurial, Collective and Capitalist modes respectively and using brackets to denote ties (or near ties), the rank ordering of modes from least to most hierarchical in contractual and decision-making respects is as follows:

Degree of hierarchy (least to most)

Contractual	Decision-making
(1) Federated (E) Communal-emh (Co) Peer Group (Co) (2) Putting-Out (E) (3) Inside Contracting (Cap) Authority Relation (Cap)	(1) Federated (E) Communal-emh (Co) (2) Putting-Out (E) Inside Contracting (Cap) (3) Peer Group (Co) (4) Authority Relation (Cap)

There is no central contracting agent in the Federated, Communal-emh, or Peer Group modes of organization, whence a contractual hierarchical relationship is altogether absent for these. By contrast, there is a central agent for the other three modes. Although characterizing the hierarchical relation between central agent and workers is not simple, a plausible case for the relations shown between Putting-Out, Inside Contracting, and the Authority Relation can be made in terms of bargaining strength of the workers vis-à-vis the central agent at the contract renewal interval. This varies with (1) the extent to which workers have acquired firm-specific skills and knowledge, (2) collective organization among workers, and (3) physical asset ownership.

Skill acquisition is the same under all three periodic contracting modes, since each involves specialization in identical degree. Collective organization may be slightly stronger under the Authority Relation, since workers here are less autonomous than under Putting-Out (where they are dispersed) and Inside Contracting (where they appropriate separate profit streams). Physical assets are owned by each worker under Putting-Out, but the central agent owns the stations in both instances under the Authority Relation and Inside Contracting. The upshot is that the contractual hierarchy is weak for Putting-Out, while the Authority Relation and Inside Contracting are somewhat stronger in contractual hierarchy respects.

Consider now the decision-making hierarchy. There is no command relation whatsoever between the members of the Federated and Communal-emh

302

modes. The former is governed by rules and bilateral contractual relations; the latter is governed by rules and democratic decision-making. A relatively weak command relation exists for Inside Contracting and the Putting-Out modes. The central agent to the contracts can appeal to the workers to adapt in coordinated ways to changed circumstances, but the contracts govern as responsibility for operating matters has been extensively delegated. Thus bargaining and bribes may be needed if interim changes favored by the central agent are to be effected. The Peer Group acknowledges the benefits of a command structure by designating a leader to coordinate day-to-day affairs. The leadership position turns over regularly, however, and strategic decisions are reached only after a full group discussion. Democratic decision-making effectively prevails. The Authority Relation posits at the outset that a superior-subordinate relation will govern in both operating and strategic respects. To be sure, the zone of acceptance of the employment relation, within which workers will accept orders without resistance, is limited by formal and informal agreement. But a command hierarchy is a prominent feature of the Authority Relation.

Although capitalist modes are more hierarchical than are collective ownership modes from a contractual point of view, the more critical hierarchy for performance purposes is the decision-making hierarchy. The observed relation between ownership and hierarchy is very weak in decision-making respects. The least hierarchical modes, Federated and Communal-emh, are of different ownership kinds (entrepreneurial and collective ownership, respectively). The Peer Group, Putting-Out, and Inside Contracting modes have intermediate degrees of hierarchy and each is from a different ownership class. Although the most hierarchical decision-making mode is a capitalist mode, the next strongest command hierarchy features collective ownership.

4. Efficiency properties of alternative modes

The issue to be addressed here is, socioeconomic attributes of the enterprise aside, do alternative work modes differ systematically in efficiency respects? A set of simple efficiency criteria are proposed first. Crude rankings of work modes with respect to these criteria are then attempted.

4.1. Simple efficiency criteria

None of the eleven efficiency measures described below is unfamiliar. Not only will each be recognized as a relevant efficiency dimension, but, at one time or another, the ramifications of each for the organization of work have been discussed previously by others. What has been missing is an overview of the issues. No single mode has been systematically assessed with respect

303

to all of the eleven criteria. Neither has there been an effort to make comparisons across modes in terms of these criteria.

The eleven efficiency indicators are usefully grouped into three types: attributes associated with the flow of product, the efficiency with which workers are assigned to tasks, and the incentive properties of alternative modes. Note that each of the eleven performance statements that follow is of a *ceteris paribus* kind.

(a) Product flow[9]. Transportation expense, buffer inventory requirements, and the "leakage" of product at successive processing stages are the matters to be evaluated here.

(i) Transportation expense. The physical transport of work-in-process inventories from one station to the next is costly. *Ceteris paribus,* modes which economize on transportation expense are favored.

(ii) Buffer inventories. Temporal separability between successive work stations is effected by creating a buffer inventory. Modes which economize on the level of these inventories are favored.

(iii) Interface leakage. Interface leakage has reference to actual or effective losses of product during manufacture. Modes which at low cost discourage embezzlement and/or the disguise of the true quality attributes of intermediate product as product is transferred across stages are favored.

(b) Assignment attributes. Assignment issues of three kinds arise. First, there is the matter of assignment workers to work stations. Second is the issue of leadership. Third is the matter of contracting with nonoperating specialists.

(i) Station assignments. Talents will be effectively utilized to the extent that workers are assigned to tasks for which they are relatively well suited. This is a specialization of labor issue. In the normal case where workers are not equally skilled in every task, modes that make discriminating job assignments on the basis of comparative advantage are favored.

(ii) Leadership. Modes vary in the degree to which coordination is required and the efficacy with which leadership assignments are made. Modes which economize on coordination needs and make discriminating leadership assignments are favored.

[9]These product flow economies are often advanced as the reason for supplanting the Putting-Out system by the factory. See Babbage (1835, pp. 135, 213, 219) and Freudenberger and Redlich (1964, p. 395). As described below, however, there is much more to it than this.

(iii) Contracting. The capacity to aggregate demands and contract with specialists which service the needs of many stations (e.g., maintenance specialists)[10] is the issue here. Modes in which such contracting is easily accomplished are favored.

(c) Incentive attributes. Differential steady state and intertemporal incentives give rise to performance differences. Of special interest are:

(i) Work intensity. Work intensity refers to the amount of productive energy expended on the job. Modes which discourage workers from malingering are favored.

(ii) Equipment utilization. The issue here is whether equipment is utilized with appropriate care. Modes which disfavor equipment abuse and neglect are favored.

(iii) Local shock responsiveness. Local shocks are those which affect an individual work station. Work stoppages due to machine breakdown or worker illness are examples. Modes which facilitate quick recovery are favored.

(iv) Local innovation. Local innovations involve process improvements at individual stations. Modes that promote local cost economizing process changes are preferred.

(v) System responsiveness. The capacity to respond to system shocks and to recognize and implement system innovations (of process, product, or organizational kinds) are the matters of interest here.[11] Modes that adapt easily to changing market circumstances and which permit systems improvements to be made without requiring extensive contract renegotiation are favored.

4.2. Efficiency ratings

Although there are some dimensions for which best or worst efficiency ratings are easily made (e.g., the Putting-Out mode has the worst transportation expense features; the Communal-emh mode, where workers move successively across stations and appropriate the fruits of their own labors, has the best work

---

[10]Among the advantages of the factory identified by Baines (1835, p. 460) and Babbage (1835, pp. 214–15) was the fact that it allowed specialists to perform maintenance functions on a number of machines in a single location.

[11]These could be treated as separate performance categories. As it turns out, the rankings of modes across system shock and system innovation dimensions are substantially identical, whence the composite system responsiveness category.

intensity and interface leakage properties but is worst in equipment utilization respects; the Authority Relation has the best system responsiveness properties; etc.), there is little to be gained by using a four-fold ranking system (best, good, poor, worst) rather than a simpler bivariate ranking in which best or good modes are assigned the value 1 and poor or worst modes are rated 0.[12]

Bivariate assignments for each of the simple efficiency dimensions are reported in table 1, where modes are grouped according to ownership type. Although a detailed rationale for the assignments is not attempted here, one is reported elsewhere (Williamson, 1976, pp. 30–50). I submit, however, that most of the assignments are transparent or are evident from the discussions of ownership comparisons and contracting comparisons that appear below.

(a) Ownership comparisons. Putting-Out and Federated modes, which are the entrepreneurial ownership modes, have rather poor product flow attributes, mixed assignment attributes, and are indistinguishable in incentive respects. Inasmuch as the Federated mode involves concentrating work stations at a common location, transportation expense economies are realized over the Putting-Out mode. Buffer inventories for each mode are high, however – though the reasons differ. For the Putting-Out mode, inventories are high because each station works on its own schedule (subject to daily or weekly output agreements) and product is moved in discrete shipments. Buffer inventories are high for the Federated mode so as to reduce the temporal dependence on predecessor stages, which are linked by bilateral contracts. Small buffer inventories would predictably result in numerous disputes if, as is commonly the case, it is costly to assess responsibility for delivery failures.

Interface leakage for both entrepreneurial modes is high. Chronic theft and quality problems are reported in connection with the Putting-Out mode (Babbage, 1835, pp. 135, 219; Freudenberger and Redlich, 1964, p. 395; and Marglin, 1974, p. 51). Theft is not a problem with the Federated mode, but quality control is. Not only is there an incentive for each stage to shade quality, but there are complex attribution problems when complaints are registered.[13]

The Putting-Out mode has leadership advantages over the Federated mode

---

[12]For an earlier rating scheme in which the four-fold assignments were used, see Williamson (1976). For earlier efforts to assess the efficiency of alternative organizing modes by rank ordering their efficiency properties, see Udy, Jr. (1970) and Sen (1975, ch. 3). Both are concerned with broader economic development issues (Udy from an anthropoligical point of view) than are of concern to me here; and both are of limited immediate relevance to an assessment of batch process manufacturing – though Sen might be extended in this direction.

[13]Thus if putting a head on a pin depends on the manner in which wire is drawn and straightened but not on pointing, if pointing precedes head attachment in order of progression, and if carelessness in the pointing operation can result in bent shafts, determining the responsibility for the condition of the shafts at the head attachment stage may not be easy: Was the straightening defective or are the bent shafts due to careless handling by the pointer?

Table 1

Simple efficiency properties of alternative modes, ownership grouping.

Mode	Product flow attributes			Assignment attributes			Incentive attributes				
	Transportation expense	Buffer inventories	Interface leakage	Station	Leadership	Contracting	Work intensity	Equipment utilization	Local responsiveness	Local innovation	System responsiveness
Entrepeneurial Putting-Out	0	0	0	1	1	0	1	1	0	1	0
Federated	1	0	0	1	0	0	1	1	0	1	0
Collective Communal-emh	1	0	1	0	1	0	1	0	0	0	0
Peer Group	1	1	1	0	0	1	0	1	1	1	1
Capitalist Inside Contracting	1	0	0	1	1	1	1	0	0	1	0
Authority Relation	1	1	1	1	1	1	0	1	1	0	1

since there is a central contracting agent. The dispersed location of the stages, however, makes it difficult for leadership to be exercised in contracting, local responsiveness, or system responsiveness respects – whence Putting-Out is rated no better than Federated on these dimensions.

The two collective ownership modes have generally good product flow attributes, rather poor assignment properties, and very different incentive properties. The Communal-emh mode has higher buffer inventory requirements, since each worker moves successively across all stages, taking his own work-in-progress inventory with him. Assuming that setup costs are not negligible, each worker will remain at each stage for a considerable period. Inventory requirements, thus, are correspondingly great.

The Communal-emh mode has excellent work intensity incentives, since every worker appropriates the fruits of his own labors. The Peer Group, by contrast, is subject to free rider abuses. (Although careful screening of candidates for Peer Group membership could serve to check such abuses, this would violate the random assignment assumption.) In other respects, however, the Peer Group has superior incentive properties to the Communal-emh mode. This is because the Peer Group is a cooperative mode whereas the Communal-emh mode is given to aggressive suboptimization.

Such suboptimization is especially evident in the case of equipment utilization. The benefits attributable to careful utilization of equipment are realized mainly by others while the costs of intensive or careless utilization are shifted mainly to others; adverse incentives proliferate. A complex bargain would have to be struck and policed to alter this adverse outcome. Peer Group members, by contrast, experience no such myopic equipment use incentives. The suboptimization versus cooperative aspects of these two modes explain other incentive differences as well.

The Authority Relation has superior product flow attributes to the other capitalist mode, Inside Contracting. Absent penalties on excess work-in-process inventories, contractors have the incentive to accumulate such inventories so as to realize greater operating autonomy. By contrast, the Authority Relation does not need to rely on pecuniary penalties to move inventories: fiat will do. And it can carry low inventories because of its superior responsiveness attributes. Interface leakage is also a problem with Inside Contracting because contractors have an incentive to suboptimize (shade quality) that is not operative among hourly employees.[14]

Inside Contracting and the Authority Relation have uniformly good assignment attributes. They have very different incentive properties, however. This

---

[14]Piece rates for employees under the Authority Relation create worker incentives closer to that of Inside Contracting. More generally, piece rate workers have less incentive to act cooperatively than do hourly workers when adaptations are proposed. This type of limitation of piece rates has not received the attention it deserves.

Table 2

Simple efficiency properties at alternative modes, contracting grouping.

Mode	Product flow attributes			Assignment attributes			Incentive attributes				
	Transportation expense	Buffer inventories	Interface leakage	Station	Leadership	Contracting	Work intensity	Equipment utilization	Local responsiveness	Local innovation	System responsiveness
Continuous contracting modes											
Putting-Out	0	0	0	1	1	0	1	1	0	1	0
Federated	1	0	0	1	0	0	1	1	0	1	0
Inside Contracting	1	0	0	1	1	1	1	0	0	1	0
Periodic contracting modes											
Communal-emh	1	0	1	0	1	0	1	0	0	0	0
Peer Group	1	1	1	0	0	1	0	1	1	1	1
Authority Relation	1	1	1	1	1	1	0	1	1	0	1

is mainly because inside contractors have greater autonomy, appropriate the fruits of their own labors more fully, and need to be bribed to adapt cooperatively while employees working in an Authority Relation mode are less given to aggressive subgoal pursuit and do not resist adaptations because they do not possess the requisite property rights. Thus inside contractors work intensively and introduce local innovations, but respond to local or system adaptation requirements much less readily. Also since inside contractors do not own the equipment, malutilization may occur.

Specifically, the relevant time horizon to which inside contractors refer is the contract termination date. Repairs that generate benefits which more than recover costs within the contract interval will be made, but those for which the benefits can be recovered only if the contractor wins the bid for successive contracts will not.[15] Equipment repairs of a major kind will thus be deferred and left to the capitalist at the contract renewal interval. Even minor repairs may be postponed as contract termination dates approach.

(b) Contracting comparisons. Consider now table 2, where the same rankings are displayed – only here the modes are grouped by contracting attributes. The striking features of this table are: (1) continuous contracting modes have generally poor product flow attributes and uniformly poor local and system responsiveness attributes, (2) continuous contracting modes are uniformly good in station assignment, work intensity, and local innovation respects, (3) periodic contracting modes have generally good product flow attributes, and (4) although some periodic contracting modes are good in assignment and incentive respects, no general statements can be made for periodic contracting modes as a group in either of these general categories.

(c) Aggregation. Aggregation to obtain an overall efficiency rating for each mode requires that the relative importance of the eleven efficiency indicators be addressed. This will obviously vary across industries. Suppose, however, that each is weighted equally and a composite rating is obtained by taking the row sum for each mode. The following rankings then emerge:

Mode	Row sum
Communal-emh	4
Putting-Out	5
Federated	5
Inside Contracting	6
Peer Group	8
Authority Relation	9

[15]This assumes that inside contractors are compensated neither for repairs which yield benefits that extend beyond the contract termination date nor are they reimbursed for idle time if the

Even allowing for the fact that the rankings are very rough, several interesting relations warrant comment:

(1) The Communal-emh mode, which accords workers the greatest degree of job variety and appears to be greatly favored by Marglin, is the least efficient mode. Although it is possible to ascribe the nonexistence of the Communal-emh mode to pernicious efforts by vested interests to annihilate it, a more plausible explanation is that the Communal-emh mode is dragged down by its own efficiency disabilities.

(2) The least hierarchical modes, in both contracting and decision-making respects (see 2.3, above), have the worst efficiency properties. By contrast both the Peer Group and the Authority Relation rely extensively on a decision-making hierarchy – which indeed goes far to explain the superior performance of each. Hostility to hierarchy, thus, is evidently misguided. There may be more and less preferred types of hierarchy; but hierarchy itself is unavoidable unless efficiency sacrifices are made.

(3) The Communal-emh mode aside, periodic contracting modes have superior efficiency properties to continuous contracting modes.

(4) Modes are listed roughly in the same order as they appeared historically. Although it is possible to argue that later modes displaced earlier modes because the 'interests' were determined to stamp out autonomy, an alternative hypothesis is that successor modes have superior efficiency properties to predecessor modes. The progression from Putting-Out to Inside Contracting to the Authority Relation is especially noteworthy in this respect.

(5) Ranking the six modes in terms of power differentials between boss and workers is difficult for lack of a power metric. One nevertheless has the impression that there is a positive rank correlation between row sum efficiency and power. At the same time, this correlation seems to be less than perfect. (Thus Putting-Out, which accords the boss greater power than does the Peer Group or Federated modes, has worse efficiency properties than both.) The best evidence that power is driving organizational outcomes would be a demonstration that less efficient modes that serve to concentrate power displace more efficient modes in which power is more evenly distributed.

. . .

capitalist were to make repairs during the contract interval. The former poses serious benefit estimation problems while compensating for idle time would set up incentives to utilize equipment carelessly.

CHAPTER 23

On some recent explanations of why capital hires labor

LOUIS PUTTERMAN

Louis Putterman was born in 1952 in New York City. He received the Ph.D. in economics at Yale University in 1980. Since 1982, he has been Associate Professor of Economics at Brown University.

I. Introduction

In recent years, interest in forms of enterprise wherein workers exercise substantial control over basic decision-making has been growing in many academic and non-academic corridors. Within Western economics, the presumed superiority of the conventional firm has been attacked on at least two fronts: by "radicals" who contend that the usual structure of firms is dictated by power rather than efficiency considerations; and by "neoclassical" analysts of self-management, who argue the efficiency of worker-managed enterprises on the basis of relatively orthodox microeconomic theory.

Both of these currents have helped to stimulate attempts to explain why the conventional structure, wherein *capital hires labor,* prevails in most market economies. Several of the "mainstream" contributors to these recent efforts accept the premise that orthodox economic theory lacks a general explanation of the structure of firms; from there, they proceed to face the challenge of providing such an explanation within the framework of efficiency analysis. This paper consists of a critical discussion of three such attempts to explain the "capitalistic" nature of production.

One crucial warning is in order before proceeding. In evaluating the success of our authors in explaining why capital, and not labor, runs the firm, some general understanding about what "labor running the firm" means must be established. The procedure is to call a firm *worker-managed* when the workforce of the firm, in a politically egalitarian and democratic manner, has ultimate authority over the decisions of the enterprise, *including the right to delegate some or all decisions to managerial organs.*

This approach will be controversial, for both traditional proponents of "workplace democracy," and their detractors, have tended to assume that workers'

Reprinted with abridgements from Louis Putterman, "On Some Recent Explanations of Why Capital Hires Labor," *Economic Inquiry,* 22 (1984): 171–87, by permission of the Western Economic Association.

control might mean *additional* things, such as egalitarianism in income distribution, direct democracy in decision-making, and anti-specialization within the workforce. Nevertheless, for present purposes, the author argues that the more general definition given above should be adopted because, while some or all of the mentioned characteristics might be chosen by certain worker-run enterprises, arguments to the effect that *capital-hiring-labor* is *intrinsically* more efficient than *labor-hiring-capital* cannot be considered as adequate *in a general sense* if they *presuppose* characteristics that, if the term ''workers-management'' is to be taken seriously, must themselves be viewed as elements in the set of *workers' organizational options*.

II. Alchian and Demsetz' metering story

A set of individuals with certain endowments of labor and, perhaps, of non-labor factors of production, may benefit from *team* production if economies of scale can be captured through joint effort and division of labor. But in moving from production as individuals to production as a team, an incentive problem arises whenever the attribution of fractions of the joint output to the effort of specific individuals is difficult and/or costly.[1] If a team member can reduce his effort without a proportionate reduction in his income, an individual motive exists for shirking. Equally, if the benefits of *increased* effort cannot be fully captured by a worker, but are in effect shared by the group, then an inadequate incentive exists to *increase* effort.

In such a situation, joint production becomes attractive only if a tolerable relationship between effort and income shares can be achieved. From the standpoint of the individual engaging in team production, the closer his realizable set of leisure-income possibilities comes to the true physical possibilities, the higher the level of welfare he can reach. Hence, the worker can benefit from such *monitoring* of his labor as will improve this correspondence.

But as with labor in general, so with monitoring in particular. The individual contribution to the monitoring of team labor is difficult to ascertain, so the benefits of monitoring activity tend to be spread among the team members, and the individual incentive to monitor might be small. According to Alchian and Demsetz, the ''classical capitalist firm'' is established in order to circumvent this problem by assigning the task of monitoring to a specialist whose incentive to monitor is his claim to the team's ''residual'' income.

If owners of cooperating inputs agree with the monitor that he is to receive any residual product above prescribed amounts (hopefully, the marginal products of the other inputs), the monitor will have added incentive not to shirk as monitor.[2]

---

[1] Alchian and Demsetz (1972).　　[2] Alchian and Demsetz (1972) p. 782.

Even a self-managing team would, therefore, have an interest in appointing one member as measurer of real inputs, determiner of input rewards, and residual claimant. However, in order to fulfill his functions efficiently, say Alchian and Demsetz, the team monitor must also have the right to hire and fire owners of cooperating inputs, which rules out team democracy. Finally, because the cost of monitoring the use of certain capital goods makes owner-ship more efficient than rental, it is desirable that the monitor be owner of the team's fixed inputs. The "classical capitalist firm" is born.

Is centralized monitoring and residual claimancy necessary?

As the narration above has implied, it may be noted that if it *were* true that effective team production mandated a centralized monitoring structure, this in itself would not rule out workers' control of production. In the most egalitarian of producers' cooperatives, the *kibbutz*,[3] each work branch has its head, who supervises and tries to assure the effective work performance of its members. A relatively conventional supervisory structure marks many collective enterprises, such as those of the Mondragon network of cooperatives in Northeastern Spain, in which incomes are directly tied to labor input.

The conjunction of centralized monitoring with profit-claiming status by the monitor is, however, more problematic. It could be argued, to be sure, that a fully democratic enterprise could elect to operate under such an arrangement, without forfeiting workers' control as such. (It is, then, only the further conjunction of these features with the contract-making and other powers of the monitor, which unambiguously controverts the idea of enterprise democracy.) But we know of no real-world examples of worker-run firms which make the monitor the residual claimant. Do Alchian and Demsetz show it to be a general necessity?

The intuitive logic of the argument is that incentives to work depend upon the correspondence between effort and reward, and that the incentive to establish that correspondence by monitoring, can only arise from a claim to the team's residual income, because the rewards to monitoring, including *monitoring the monitor,* would otherwise be too diffusely shared to constitute an adequate inducement. The logic does seem to be coherent; but the argument falls short of a demonstration of logical necessity.

Suppose that the general claim that workers' effort, incomes, and welfare would increase with better monitoring is accepted, and that rights to the residual would induce *an individual* to provide such monitoring. Without addi-

---

[3] Some references are: on the *kibbutz,* Barkai (1977); on Mondragon, Johnson and Whyte (1977).

tional restrictions, the alternative contention that a *shared claim* to profit would be too diluted to generate comparable monitoring (*i.e.*, at the aggregate level), could still not be rigorously proven.[4] Moreover, while Alchian and Demsetz consider only the *incentive to monitor,* other factors which must be weighed in determining the most efficient assignment of monitoring responsibilities include the *technology of monitoring,* the process of translating observations into pay-out schedules, the effects of monitoring arrangements upon worker motivation, well-being, and behavior, and the *direct costs* of monitoring.

At a *technological* level, whether centralized monitoring or, rather, mutual or self-supervision, will be more efficient, depends upon the nature of tasks and the spatial characteristics of the workplace. Some activities allow individuals to work and to observe one another's performance simultaneously, for example, so that output and monitoring are joint products. While Alchian and Demsetz point out that monitoring is made difficult by technologically non-separable activities, the implication that a third party can better assess the effort levels of team members cannot be asserted to hold universally – for example, in the authors' own example of a team loading heavy objects onto a truck.[5] In the terminology of Oliver Williamson, information may be *"impacted" within the team.* In other cases, where individuals work in spatially separated environments, or on tasks requiring so much initiative and judgment that detailed work evaluation is extremely costly, provision of self-supervisory incentives may be mandated.[6]

Once information on job performance is obtained, it must be translated into changes in workers' remuneration, if a direct material stimulus is desired. This stage requires collation and communication of information, processes that may favor vertical or hierarchical structures in all but the smallest of enterprises. But much information may be lost, whether because of the "coarseness" imposed by aggregation, or the poor motivation and even adverse incentives of subordinates, in a hierarchy in which monitoring is per-

---

[4] For example, in one of the more formidable attempts to model the monitoring problem rigorously, Mirrlees (1976) remarks that he has not established

under what circumstances it would pay a group of workers to have one of their number undertake all the performance observation, and when it would pay instead to have a symmetric solution in which each worker devotes some of his time to "monitoring." (p. 128.)

And, significantly, he concludes that "[i]t is not obvious that the asymmetric solution . . . assumed optimal by Alchian and Demsetz (1972) is in fact optimal . . ."

[5] That a supervisor can efficiently monitor work levels is the implication of their discussion on p. 780 ff. But a supervisor would appear to be poorly placed to detect effective labor, compared to the team members themselves, especially if cost considerations prevent him from watching his team more than a small fraction of the time. One reason is that his performance sample will probably be a nonrandom one, unless he can observe without himself being seen.

[6] The latter factor is mentioned by Alchian and Demsetz, but seen as significant only in professional and artistic work. At issue, then, is whether judgment and initiative are important aspects of more than a handful of jobs.

formed by agents of varying ranks. At this remove from the one-monitor "classical" firm, the incentive function of *enterprise profits* inevitably is diminished.

Alchian and Demsetz downplay the fact that for many workers, *being monitored* itself has psychic costs. The effects on employee performance and morale, as Williamson (1975) notes, may argue against excessive monitoring and frequent revisions of reward schedules. The possibility of employee efforts to affect the monitor's observations, efforts which are both directly unproductive and detrimental to the productivity of monitoring, must also be considered.[7]

It may not be surprising, in light of these factors, that American corporations currently experimenting with programs encouraging employee initiative and self-supervision are observing not only positive productivity effects from the relaxing of conventional supervision, but list among the more problematic implications of these programs the question of what to do with expensive and redundant supervisory personnel. This suggests that the *direct costs* of monitoring may have received inadequate attention not only in arguments such as that of Alchian and Demsetz, but also in the actual design of conventional supervision systems.

Profits, motivation, and hierarchy

Another set of doubts about the Alchian–Demsetz thesis arises because its implication that the primary function of the profit claim is to serve as an incentive to monitoring, must contend with other, at least equally cogent, views of the role of profit. As Stiglitz (1974) has shown, rights to a variable stream of income should optimally serve both *incentive* and *risk-distributing* functions. Where monitoring is difficult, Stiglitz finds, profit-sharing, rather than fixed-wage contracts, is a more efficient arrangement from the standpoint of both principal and agent. Notably, the profit share here serves as a direct incentive to work effort itself, rather than monitoring. On the other hand, to the extent that revenue fluctuation reflects stochastic or exogenous factors which are not controlled by the behavior of team members, residual claimancy has no efficiency relation to either monitoring or labor effort, and Pareto-optimality calls instead for a distribution related to individual risk aversion. The relevance of the risk-bearing question to democratic enterprises will resurface in section IV, below.

We have still not considered the issue of the broader bundle of rights which, Alchian and Demsetz say, is associated with monitoring and profit claimancy. Discussion of the necessity of hierarchical decision-making and private own-

---

[7] Compare Mirrlees (1976) p. 121.

ership is most efficiently left to subsequent sections; the principal question to be addressed presently is whether Alchian and Demsetz actually show that monitoring, management, and ownership must be linked in a single individual (or organization apex).

The simple answer is that they do not even attempt to do this. While they suggest that intra-firm resource allocation and monitoring are joint outcomes of the same activity, a proposition that might contribute to such a demonstration, their linking of the bundle of rights which constitutes "classical" capitalist entrepreneurship is essentially justified by observation, rather than logical necessity. This procedure is entirely appropriate for descriptive purposes, but it would, then, be erroneous to conclude that they present any case at all for the necessity, from an efficiency standpoint, of such a bundle of rights.

It should also be mentioned, at this point, that one of the gravest weaknesses of Alchian and Demsetz' argument lies precisely in its assertion that authority is an irrelevant category for the analysis of the conventional firm. Although their monitor is granted the powers of hiring, firing, and wage-setting, in order to "discipline team members and reduce shirking," they insist that these powers do not constitute authority, since "[t]he employee can terminate the contract as readily as can the employer." This approach not only glides over the asymmetrical nature of a relationship wherein one party can dismiss any or all of the other team members, while being immune to such actions on the part of any coalition of the latter; it also denies the long-term nature of actual employment contracts, and the dimension of *authority* in the employment relation. The latter criticisms, especially, have been spelled out quite effectively by Williamson (1975, pp. 67–70), and require no further treatment here.

III. Williamson on the necessity of hierarchy

Recent work by Oliver Williamson (1975, 1980) responds explicitly to radical critiques of the hierarchical organization of production. Williamson agrees with the radicals that standard microeconomic theory fails to confront the issues of organization, but argues that the dominance of hierarchical modes of organization may be explained in terms of comparative efficiency, provided that the question of *transaction costs* is addressed.

Idiosyncratic exchange

The central problem to be solved by the employment relation in Williamson's (1975) analysis is one of bilateral monopoly between workers who come to possess firm-specific skills, and employers who can offer or refuse renewal of contract for the corresponding jobs. At the initiation of employment, the employer recruits from a large pool of undifferentiated applicants, who can be hired at competitive wages. After a period, job incumbents become distinguished from outside bidders for their jobs by the possession of idiosyncratic knowledge of their work environment that makes them potentially more productive than these competitors. They are thus in a monopoly position with respect to the firm and can hold out for wages higher, by the prospective costs of training, than the going rate for non-incumbents. To prevent workers from exploiting such monopoly power in the short-run, firms structure employment opportunities so as to encourage a long-term association with the firm and to discourage individual bargaining by tying pay to well-defined jobs, rather than to individuals, and by filling higher slots through internal promotion and making promotion itself contingent upon performance.

Williamson's emphasis on the *firm's* attenuation of workers' bargaining advantages does not seem promising from the standpoint of establishing an association between firm structure and *worker's welfare*. He suggests that the *worker's* monopolistic exploitation of idiosyncratic skills threatens to make investment in training unprofitable. But this view neglects the *bilateral* aspect of the monopoly. Workers have gained skills on the job, but those skills may be worth little elsewhere. The employer can threaten to make workers ordinary members of the labor pool, once again, by terminating employment.

If training is viewed as an investment that will be undertaken only when its stream of expected returns outweighs its costs (discounted at the appropriate rate), then firms will need to anticipate earning back at least the future value of their present outlay before engaging in any training. The relevant range of bilateral monopolistic conflict between firms and workers with foresight, then, concerns the returns from training investments which *exceed* their costs. The distribution of these returns on "inframarginal" training projects, between the firm and the worker, must be determined by their respective bargaining strengths. In the limit, if firms capture the entire profit, workers gain nothing from training. Thus, if structured employment relations give firms the upper hand in such bargaining, it is unclear how the arrangement serves the workers' interests.

Calculation and "atmosphere"

Williamson's analysis includes a refreshing treatment of "metering" or rating questions. In contrast to Alchian and Demsetz, Williamson emphasizes that monitoring of labour inputs and revision of rewards creates the externality of a calculative atmosphere with negative effects upon the employment relation. While the firm incurs the *direct* costs of monitoring, the employee incurs less tangible psychic penalties from *being monitored*. Disputes over monitoring observations and reward adjustments are costly in time and good will, and the atmosphere engendered by constant "metering" is one in which employees perform their jobs in a minimal or "perfunctory" rather than a maximal or "consummate" fashion.

Since monitoring will be imperfect in any event, many firms strategically refrain from short-run assessments of productivity and adjustments of rewards, writes Williamson, in favor of long-term assessments and discrete reward changes through promotion. If employees feel that the employer is "fair" and offers an attractive chance of long-term advancement in exchange for good performance on the job, they may undertake to fulfill their assignments well, and may even develop a sense of identification with the company and its goals. With incentives partly internalized by the workers, both direct and external costs of monitoring are reduced.[8]

Williamson's concern with atmosphere and with the nonpecuniary attributes of working relations leads him to a relatively sympathetic view of cooperative modes of work organization. In very small enterprises, in which selectiveness may be exercised over membership and mutual monitoring and discipline can be effective, a democratically-run collective enterprise may be as efficient, or more efficient, than a hierarchical one. When efficient enterprise size is large, however, the advantages of hierarchy become decisive. The primary reason is that democratic decision-making becomes inefficient and ultimately impossible as the volume of information required by decision-makers expands. Specialization between managerial and other roles becomes imperative, as do vertical channels of information flow. The analysis essentially echoes Simon's view that "[h]ierarchy is the adaptive form for finite intelligence to assume in the face of complexity" (1971, p. 204). However the argument receives a sociological twist: democratic teams may improvise in response to these needs by electing temporary and rotating managements, but

to the extent that the requisite information-processing and decision-making talents are not widely distributed, efficiency will be served by reserving the central information collection and decision-making position to the one or few individuals who have superior information processing capacities and exceptional oratorical and decision-making skills. Something of an elite thereby results, as the select subset bears an asymmetrical relation to everyone else. Not only does the peak coordinator enjoy the power which authority and expertise accord him . . . , but having more complete information gives him a strategic advantage over everyone else. The peak coordinatior has inordinate influence over both the value and factual premises of other members of the group. It is really a fiction, when such an elite develops, to maintain that a peer group any longer exists – even if, in principle, the group can always challenge and even reverse individual decisions. Simple hierarchy effectively obtains (Williamson, 1975, pp. 52–53).

---

[8] However, it also seems necessary to point out that such an analysis may be relevant only to limited sectors of the job market, at best; see Edwards (1979).

"Peer group" and hierarchy

This view is elaborated and extended when Williamson (1980) explicitly takes on radical critics of mainstream theory, such as Bowles, Gintis, Marglin, and Stone, attempting to show that *efficiency* rather than *power* considerations determine questions of organizational form in a free market setting.[9] In "The Organization of Work," he contends that while the democratic "peer group" possesses superior sociological attributes,[10] it is inferior to hierarchical alternatives because it fails to assign workers to their most productive uses. An additional liability is that of limited differentiation of rewards, which reduces work incentives. But to grasp these points, we must first understand the "peer group" as Williamson defines it.

Williamson's "peer group" is not just a worker-run enterprise in the sense that ultimate authority resides in the democratic vote of the working membership. It is, rather, a utopian form of cooperative in which social, political, and economic equality are sought through rotation of members between all jobs, and in which incomes must be divided in a way *not* requiring direct monitoring of individual productivities. This choice of features for the alternative to the conventional firm may be a natural one, given the stream of radical literature to which Williamson is responding. However, it is all too easy for the reader to draw unwarranted conclusions from the discussion, by overlooking the fact that the strictures of definition, just elaborated, immediately account for the liabilities of task assignment and labor incentives mentioned above.[11] The conclusion that the necessary hierarchical decision-making structure rules out true "peer groups" for large organizations has already been referred to, and now can be seen to be related similarly to the strictures of Williamson's definition. Finally, Williamson's "peer group" entails collective capital ownership, which produces other undesirable attributes.[12]

Thus, while Williamson's arguments may serve to clarify intuitive thinking

[9] For space economy, the reader is referred to the work cited, by Williamson, for references to Bowles, *et al.*

[10] The earlier version of the paper (Williamson, 1976) includes a discussion and ratings of five "socio-economic" characteristics: security, affiliation, social esteem, latitude, and self-realization. Williamson gives the "peer group" positive scores for the four out of five dimensions which he evaluates, whereas the "authority relation" scores well in one and badly in two out of three dimensions. In terms of a four point rating system (p. 51), "peer group" dominance over the "authority relation" is complete in these "socio-economic" categories.

[11] Consider the inferior ratings of the "peer group" for "station and leadership assignment attributes" in Williamson (1980) p. 38. Inferiority in "work intensity incentives" is lost through aggregation into the bimodal ratings of the latter, but appears in Williamson (1976) p. 51, where the "peer group" and "authority relation" receive "worst" and "poor" ratings, respectively, for work intensity.

[12] These problems receive some emphasis in the critiques of Jensen and Meckling, Furubotn and Pejovich, and others, and are commented upon in section IV, below, and in Putterman (1981).

about the relative "inefficiency" of an organizational structure as horizontal as the pure "peer group" in complex and large-scale production processes,[13] they actually say very little about worker-controlled enterprise as such. Just as Alchian and Demsetz' concerns suggested that worker-controlled enterprises might hire or assign specialized monitors to "meter" labor productivity under particular technological situations, so Williamson's discussion points to the probability that workers' groups which attach sufficient importance to productivity as such would institute some degree of hierarchy and job specialization in their enterprises, *as do, in fact, almost all known producers' cooperatives.* But in what sense does navigation among the trade-offs between informational economies and direct decision-making participation, and between income and non-material benefits, *imply* the conventional capitalist firm, so long as the steering is in the hands of the working body of the enterprise?

Contributions to a theory of cooperation?

A major flaw in Williamson's analysis is his tendency to consider *any* degree of hierarchy within the organization to be not only the end for the pure "peer group," but also the beginning of the capitalist structure of production *in toto.* There is no room for partially democratic organizational forms which might fit somewhere in the spectrum between the "peer group" and the managerial corporation. The fact of formal powers of recall is of no account.

Williamson's discussion here, even more so than on "idiosyncratic exchange," also inadvertently gives strong ammunition to the proponents of worker control. By pointing out the considerable consequences of "asymmetries" of power, he suggests just how important checks on that power might be. The workers' ability to achieve optimal trade-offs in the workplace, which is dependent upon job mobility when firms are not directly controlled by workers, is impaired by the type of long-term, internal promotional structure that Williamson describes. If workers are, to an important extent, tied to firms, and if managers, "having more complete information," have "a strategic advantage over everyone else," and "inordinate influence over both the value and factual premises of other members of the group," why should workers relinquish all controls over management? It would seem altogether irrational on their parts to follow Williamson's implied conclusion that since "hierarchy effectively obtains," there is no more reason for discussing workers' control over it.

That hierarchy is a necessity in complex organizations and that leadership

---

[13] Strictly speaking, even lower productivity is not automatically *inefficient* in welfare terms, because individuals may prefer to trade material benefits for social ones, as Williamson notes.

imparts advantages and power is hardly to be disputed. Do we therefore conclude that in the political arena there is no purpose in maintaining the structures of representative government? Do we argue that since citizens can move from state to state, and since any hierarchy subverts democratic control, then governments might just as well be autocratic, for people can satisfy their wants by finding states offering them desired trade-offs of environmental protection, taxes, etc.? This analogy, although obviously imperfect, nonetheless suggestively highlights the issues in an argument which commends "exit" to the exclusion of "voice."[14]

While Williamson's attempt to argue that the capitalist organization of production is advantageous from the workers' own vantage point seems deficient, his positive contribution to the understanding of the firm is significant. Among its greatest virtues is its detection of the utility of cooperative strategies in a world in which the material and psychological costs of individualism are high. More generally, in its rich and realistic emphasis upon human-relations elements and their considerable economic importance in a world of bounded rationality and imperfect information, Williamson's work is an important corrective to more mechanistic models of behavior. It might be argued, indeed, that the normative extension of this analysis into "system justification" is so far at odds with many of the leads in the core of the analysis that Williamson might rightly be claimed by proponents of self-management as one of their own.[15]

IV. The manager as agent: Jensen and Meckling

Where Williamson's references to cooperatives are responses to the "radical" critiques, a recent paper by Jensen and Meckling (1979) on labor-management and co-determination is directed toward answering the "neoclassical theory of self-management."[16] Although their principal concerns are with property rights, rather than transaction costs, Jensen and Meckling share Williamson's perception that orthodox theory is flawed by its treatment of the firm (in their

[14] Hirschman (1970). The discussion above may suggest a quite different conclusion, however. It is that, instead of trying to maintain formal control of the firm in the face of the necessity of hierarchy, workers may find the organization of an independent opposition – i.e., a labor union – to be a superior strategy. This possibility will be pursued no further here, except to point out one way in which the analogy between a union and a political opposition is inapt: a union, presumably, is not a contender for direct management of the firm.

[15] See Sandler and Cauley (1980) pp. 18–19. This paper is explicitly written "to formalize Williamson's analysis." While the passage referred to contains no mention of workers' participation, it would seem difficult to find a more appropriate language for analyzing the structure, not of a modern corporation, but of a decentralized labor-controlled enterprise.

[16] That is, the literature by Ward, Vanek, Meade, and others, analyzing the behavior of labor-run enterprises using standard neoclassical microeconomic methodology. For references not given below, the reader is referred to Jensen and Meckling's paper.

words) as a "black box." The resulting insensitivity to the variation of individual motivation and behavior with organizational form is, they imply, largely responsible for the unrealistically positive conclusions of many formal studies of self-management.

The brunt of Jenson and Meckling's critique centers on questions of finance and risk-bearing. They begin by arguing that labor-management's theoretical optimality[17] hinges on the assumption that all capital is rented at competitive rates. This assumption is then attacked on the grounds that: (a) investment in such intangibles as research and development cannot take the form of renting physical assets only, and (b) given the monitoring costs associated with asset use, ownership rather than rental is frequently the most efficient decision even with respect to physical capital. With "pure rental" thus ruled out, the authors proceed to catalogue the arguments on the inefficiency of internal finance or collective ownership of capital, including the familiar Furubotn–Pejovich horizon problem and the "self-extinction" problem of Vanek.[18] These arguments are already well-known and accepted by advocates of self-management, however.

The interesting portions of the critique for present purposes are those that are less concerned with the internal finance option. Three arguments, in particular, will be addressed here. The first is that, without a stock market and marketable claims to firms, little incentive exists for professional and public evaluation of firms, and therefore there will be insufficient monitoring of managerial behavior. To this point are added two others already found in the literature on self-management. One is that if shares of the firm's equity are in fact marketed, optimality requires decision-making participation by the shareowners. The second is that members of a labor-managed enterprise are forced to bear risk that would be insurable in a capitalist system, and are unable to reach individually preferred positions with respect to risk-bearing.

Markets as monitors

The first argument, on the need for financial markets as monitors of management, deserves special attention. Its background is developed at length in the authors' (1976) treatment of the theory of agency and property rights, and it may be viewed as the "managerial" analogue of Alchian and Demsetz (1972). According to the latter argument, discussed in section II of this paper,

[17] That is, the allocative equivalence of self-managed firms and industries to their capitalist counterparts, under conditions of perfect competition, perfect factor mobility, and free entry, and in the long run, as shown by Ward, *et al.*, in a partial equilibrium framework, and by Dréze in that of Walrasian general equilibrium. See Jensen and Meckling (1979) p. 477.

[18] Jensen and Meckling (1979) pp. 481–4 and 495–6; Furubotn and Pejovich (1974); Vanek (1977). See also McCain (1977) pp. 356–7, for a brief review of the problems of internal finance under labor-management.

workers' inadequate incentives to control their own shirking in the course of team production, give rise to the demand for specialized monitors and, hence, to the "classical capitalist firm." Jensen and Meckling pointing out, though, that the modern corporation is not a classical firm, because the manager is not sole, or even majority, owner of the firm's assets.

As sole owner, a manager might engage in non-profit-seeking activities which reduce his pecuniary income but increase his utility in nonpecuniary respects. Such activity remains efficient, because the capitalist foregoing the profits incurs all relevant costs himself. As the manager's share in the firm and its profits falls, however, his incentives to deviate from profit-maximization increase to the extent that such behavior is undetected, since he enjoys all of the benefits but bears only a fraction of the costs. If such behavior is expected but controlled, and if investors are rational, the manager ultimately will bear the full costs by paying a higher price to raise capital, or accepting a lower valuation on marketed equity. Thus, like the *workers* in Alchian and Demsetz' argument, the *managers* of corporations, as well as the capital owners, have an interest in reducing non-profit-seeking behavior to the extent that the costs of such reduction do not exceed the benefits. Monitoring, including independent audits ordered by management, and contractual restrictions on managerial discretion, are among the means adopted for controlling managerial behavior. In addition, the work of financial analysts, and the evaluation processes which give rise to publicly available assessments of managerial efficiency in the form of stock market prices, help to reduce the efficiency losses from the separation of ownership and management.

When they turn to the labor-managed firm, Jensen and Meckling argue that

[e]mployees of the pure-rental firm will also have an interest in monitoring the performance of management, but no one in the pure-rental economy will have the same incentive to specialize in performance evaluation (monitoring) as exists in a corporate economy, because there is no way for any individual employee to capture more than a small fraction of the potential gains from such activities. It is therefore naive to believe that pure-rental managers will take the same pains as would corporate executives to seek out high-payroll new projects, to weed out projects which have negative payoffs, to control waste and shirking, etc. (1979, p. 485).

The problem of managerial control is thus effectively insoluble under labor-management.

Finance and management under workers' control

In order to address this issue and the other investment-related questions raised, it is necessary to posit a particular structure of ownership for the labor-managed firm. Having argued the impossibility of "pure rental," Jensen and Meckling carry out their discussion primarily in terms of the specific institutional structure of one known system, that of Yugoslavia. Here, the principal source of investment funds is government. With government the primary lender, and no real capital market, bureaucratic management of the capital stock becomes an easy target for the authors' critique.

While this approach may satisfy some readers, students of both *self-management* and *Yugoslavia* can reject the equation of the two. As has been pointed out, for example, by Vanek (1978), the Yugoslav economy is inefficient in the realm of investment because, suspicious of scarcity rents on capital and anxious to maintain a high ratio of investment to output, authorities set interest rates far below capital's marginal productivity. Ideological and political constraints on economic policy also steer the State away from principles of economic efficiency in the allocation of capital. Thus, Yugoslavia hardly provides ideal conditions for testing the performance of a bureaucratic method of managing a country's capital stock.

It is not necessary, however, to grapple with the difficult political-economic question of whether an 'ideal' *bureaucratic* system could *ever* be established, because at least one alternative system, that of the "external" finance of worker-run enterprises, is entirely feasible, consistent with self-management principles, and resistant to the Jensen and Meckling attack on "pure rental." In other words, while *collective asset ownership* by a firm's workers may produce economic inefficiencies, and while a *bureaucratic system of investment allocation* may be subject to its own flaws, it is possible for a worker run enterprise, without inefficiency, to enjoy the use of fully owned assets, provided that investments are financed at scarcity reflecting interest rates, so that firms are of zero *net* worth.

A starting point is for private savings to be channeled through financial intermediaries which in turn loan funds to worker-run enterprises at competitive interest rates. If the intermediary institutions (*e.g.*, banks) are themselves labor-managed, loans can be expected to be evaluated on sound economic criteria so as to provide a maximum return to the financiers. Competition among firms for loanable funds would produce an efficient allocation of capital. The *Caja Laboral Popular* in the Mondragon network of cooperatives is an example of this on a modest scale.[19]

Bond finance could provide either an alternative or a complement to the system just described. Self-managed enterprises could raise capital by selling fixed claims to individuals, and/or other enterprises, including those in the finance and insurance sectors. Now, both banks and bond financing of self-management investment, if the environment is sufficiently competitive, should lead to *efficient* allocation of an economy's savings, since all projects with

---

[19] See Johnson and Whyte (1977).

expected returns above the demand-and-supply equilibrating interest rate, and only those projects, can be expected to be undertaken. Unlike "internal" finance systems, wherein worker-managers must forego current consumption for the sake of an anticipated future income stream, there is no "horizon problem" of differential desires to invest within an enterprise's workforce.[20]

It has been noted, however, that observed large capitalist firms rely not only on debt financing, but also on equity, because raising adequate capital for risky ventures requires an instrument that allows the investor to share not only in the risk of default, but also in the full range of potential *high* returns. On these grounds, McCain (1977) has proposed an equity-like "risk-participation bond" for the labor-managed firm. Its principal difference from ordinary equity is simply that its owner can have no voting control over enterprise decisions, or over the election of enterprise management. After a lengthy technical analysis, McCain finds that the labor-managed firm whose objective is to maximize profit-per-worker, having both ordinary and "risk participation" bonds at its disposal, would "attain the same allocation of resources as would a capitalist corporation, under comparable circumstances and informationally efficient markets" (1977, p. 382).

Having described a plausible range of external financing instruments, we are now prepared to address the *monitoring* issue raised by Jensen and Meckling. We will do so within the context of a completely labor-managed economy, for simplicity. The main thing to be noticed is that all of the forms of the monitoring of managerial behavior on the part of investors and financial institutions which are discussed in Jensen and Meckling (1976a) potentially are present here. Self-managed enterprises depend, for their capital requirements, on the willingness of a variety of investors and institutions to lend to them. On the opposite side of the market, lenders have an incentive to study the performance records of their potential creditors. Since the price of finance capital to the firm will, as in the capitalist case, reflect the firm's "reputation" and, hence, its performance, the checks upon mismanagement, squandering of resources, and personal indulgences at social expense, are the same as in the case described by Jensen and Meckling. Not only will enterprises be impelled toward responsible management of their assets, on an ongoing basis,

[20] On the "horizon problem," see the sources cited in note 18. It may also be added here that the inefficiencies introduced by the Yugoslav asset maintenance rule, which are often presented as part of the "horizon problem," are intrinsic to neither *internal* nor *external* finance, but are rather an outgrowth of historical fears that workers would "eat" the value of State assets turned over to them under the self-management reforms. In principle, the danger of managerial consumption of assets is present in the capitalist corporation as much as in the self-managed enterprise, and there is no reason to suppose that the operative checks, in the form of legal accountability to creditors plus the constraints imposed by the need for future finance, could not function similarly in the latter case. This is one area in which the virtues of an active and ongoing relationship between enterprises and financial institutions, ramifying in the kind of *monitoring* described by Jensen and Meckling, may merit particular attention.

but they might even invite outside audits and enter into self-constraining "covenants" with investors, if this would lead to a desired exchange of managerial discretion for easier credit terms, from the standpoint of the working body.[21]

Aside from challenging the consistency of such a picture with the principles of self-management, the major counter-argument to be anticipated here is that, although the interests of the enterprises and institutions on both sides of the financial markets just described might *appear* to be isomorphic to those in similar capitalist markets, the behavior of these units would be qualitatively different, due to their self-managed character. For example, a member of a worker-run banking institution would not be as careful in investing that institution's funds as would a capitalist banker, because the consequences would be diluted among the larger working group; but unless we are viewing the alternative as a one-man capitalist bank, obviously a parody of reality, the issue is not really one of the private profit motive and its dilution in the collective. It is, instead, a matter of comparing the potential achievement of accountability in the multi-person cooperative with that in the multi-person capitalistic firm. Thus, the argument is only as good as are all others which suppose that top-down enterprises must, *a priori,* be superior to democratic ones in bringing about behavioral-consonance between the individual and the organization. As suggested in the previous sections, such arguments rely mostly on the rigid characterization of cooperatives, or the idealization of capitalist firms.

Shareholders' control

Being aware of the suggestions regarding "external finance," in the labor-management literature, Jensen and Meckling raise the further problem [this time echoing Dréze (1976, pp. 1136–7), as well as Meade (1972), and others] that if shares of equity in the firm are marketed, efficiency requires the participation of the share-owners in enterprise decision-making. The best counter to this point, however, would seem to be in the authors' own work, in which

---

[21] To interpret this as indicating that self-managed enterprises will be forced into mimicking capitalist counterparts with respect to the organization of production, characteristics of the workplace, and so on, would be quite incorrect, however. The point is that the trade-offs between desirable features of the enterprise, and ease of finance, will be "negotiated" by the working body along a socially-efficient frontier. Their final choices in the dimensions of working hours, effort levels, technology, degree of decision-making participation, etc. etc., would reflect the "tangency" of their own particular values, as aggregated through a democratic decision process, with the objective possibilities confronting them, including those determined by the attitudes of potential lenders. While the managerial "rationality" induced through the monitoring of financial institutions thus flows from the same set of relationships, between debtor and creditor, as described by Jensen and Meckling, the self-managed firm maintains its peculiar character because of the democratic nature of its internal governance. Compare Dréze (1976) pp. 1128–30.

it is difficult to detect any real enthusiasm for the notion of decision-making participation in an active sense. Jensen and Meckling (1976a), in fact, develop their entire theory of agency and property ownership under an assumption that equity share are *nonvoting*. Given their general mistrust of political decision-making, seen especially in the 1979 paper, it is clear that they consider these powers to be at most a hopefully-unutilized threat. *Real* control over managerial behavior is exercised not through direct participation in decision-making, but through market assessment of performance, which determines the firm's ability to raise capital, and through monitoring, convenants, and the like. All of the latter forms of "control" could exist in the labor-managed economy just considered.

One interesting point ought to be made here, however. If voting rights remain a valued source of control to shareholders, then presumably the labor-managed firm which wanted to keep full decision-making power in its workers' hands would have to pay for this privilege by accepting a lower valuation of its equity (or paying higher dividends). This fact would then help to explain why conventional firms resist efforts to share decision-making powers with their workers, and why workers in individual firms would be unlikely to take steps toward co-determination unless all firms were to do so simultaneously, under the influence of legislation. Such legislation would not then, necessarily, represent coercion of the majority by a minority, as Jensen and Meckling assume. Rather, it might better be seen under the rubric of enforcement of a socially preferred cooperative "game" solution.[22]

. . .

Conclusion

None of what has been said above may be seen as constituting a case *for* self-management, as that has not been the purpose of this paper. Moreover, the case for the economic *superiority* of enterprise democracy, whether based on theory or on the "success stories," is still open to discussion and debate. Nevertheless, a critical survey of the economics literature which proclaims the *conventional forms* to be superior has failed to reveal a theoretical reason why "labor" cannot manage production at least as efficiently as "capital."

---

[22] While from one point of view such legislation would appear to *restrict* workers' *rights* to enter into certain types of employment relationship, the same change in the "social constitution" may also be seen as an affirmation of a different right: the right of the worker to govern enterprise decision-making along with fellow workers. For society to outlaw the alienation of this right to an enterprise's capital owners, even if by mutually voluntary contracts, may not be entirely dissimilar to the outlawing of voluntarily entered relations of slavery, prostitution, or sale of the vote in public elections On conflicts between freedom of exchange and rights, see Okun (1975) chapter 1.

328

The production process in a competitive economy: Walrasian, neo-Hobbesian, and Marxian models

SAMUEL BOWLES

Samuel Bowles was born in 1939 in New Haven, Connecticut. He received the Ph.D. in economics at Harvard University in 1965. He is currently Professor of Economics at the University of Massachusetts, Amherst.

Recent years have witnessed a growing interest in the internal organization of the firm. Many, taking the work of Ronald Coase (1937) as their starting point, have developed insights based on the concept of transactions costs. Others, building on the work of J. R. Commons (1918, 1935), have developed an historical and institutional analysis of the structure of collective bargaining and internal labor markets. Others, starting from Marx's distinction between work ("labor") and labor time ("labor power") have developed an analysis of class conflict within the firm.

A careful reading of this diverse body of literature suggests that there are many common points of reference. All, for example, have stressed the social and nonmarket aspects of the production process.[1] But there are important differences as well.

In this essay I develop an underlying microeconomic logic of the Marxian model, and contrast it with two alternative views. The first is the simple Walrasian model in which the production process is represented as a set of input–output relations selected from an array of feasible technologies by a process of cost minimization with respect to market-determined prices. The Walrasian model presents no analysis of the internal social organization of the firm.

The second group of models stems from Coase's seminal work, and is exemplified by the important recent contributions of Armen Alchian and Harold Demsetz (1972), Oliver Williamson (1980), Guillermo Calvo (1979), Edward Lazear (1981), and others. Like the Marxian approach, and unlike the

Reprinted from Samuel Bowles, "The Production Process in a Competitive Economy: Walrasian, Neo-Hobbesian, and Marxian Models," *The American Economic Review*, 75 (1985):16–36, by permission of the editors.

[1] The list of approaches is quite partial as it excludes, for example, the interesting and related work on social norms and economic processes. See George Akerlof (1980) and Robert Solow (1980).

Walrasian, these models present a well-developed model of the firm as a social organization. I refer to these models as neo-Hobbesian because according to them the key to understanding the internal structure of the firm is the concept of malfeasance. Also known as shirking or free riding, malfeasance gives rise to the archetypal Hobbesian problem of reconciling self-interested behavior on the part of individuals with collective or group interests. Moreover, the neo-Hobbesian explanation of the functional nature of the hierarchical organization of the modern workplace bears a close resemblance to the original Hobbesian rationale for the state as a socially necessary form of coercion.[2]

By contrast, the basic commitment of the Marxian models is to the fundamental importance of class as an economic concept. While the Marxian model does not deny the importance of the Hobbesian conflict between individual and collective rationality as an underlying social problem central to an understanding of the production process in any social system, it focuses on those problems which may be traced to the structure of ownership and control of the means of production.[3]

What is at issue between Marxian and non-Marxian economists is not the general relevance of class concepts to the analysis of social groupings, institutions, or political action, but the status of class as an *economic* concept. Even within the realm of economics, terminological differences aside, there is general agreement on the relevance to a wide range of issues of what Marxian economists would term the class structure. Few economists of any persuasion would question the importance of the distribution of the ownership of assets as a determinant of the distribution of income, patterns of consumption, or levels of saving.

The Marxian model is distinct, however, in that it asserts that consideration of the ownership of the means of production, and the command over the production process which this ownership permits, is essential to a coherent analysis of the production process itself, and to the analysis of market equilibration and competition. It is thus not only in its macroeconomic theory and its theory of collective action that the Marxian model makes substantive use of the idea of class, but in its microeconomics as well.[4]

The distinctiveness of the Marxian microeconomics with respect to the neo-

[2] Thus, for example, it is argued that a team of workers would rationally hire a supervisor to monitor their work activities, an economic analogue to the Hobbesian position which asserts that uncoerced citizens in a state of nature would in their own interests commit themselves to obey the dictates of a state.

[3] I will specify what I take to be the principal differences between the neo-Hobbesian and the Marxian models in the penultimate section. The relationship between the Marxian model and what Marx wrote is suggested in various notes.

[4] I would thus take strong exception to Oskar Lange's (1935) view that the specificity and strength of Marxian economics resides in its institutional and sociological content and not in its microeconomic theory per se.

Hobbesian and Walrasian approaches, as we shall see, has little to do with the labor theory of value, however. Its primary focus is on the interactions between the voluntary relations of the marketplace and the command relationships of the workplace. Thus Marxian economists take strenuous exception to Paul Samuelson's assertion that "in the competitive model it makes no difference whether capital hires labor or the other way around" (1957, p. 894).

The structure of the Marxian model may be illustrated by reference to three propositions central to its analysis of capitalist production.

First, capitalists (owners of firms or their representatives) will generally select methods of production which forego improvements in productive efficiency in favor of maintaining their power over workers. For this reason, the technologies in use in a capitalist economy, as well as the direction of technical change, cannot be said to be an efficient solution to the problem of scarcity, but rather, at least in part, an expression of class interest. This proposition is fundamental to the Marxian assertion that the productive potential of a society (the "forces of production") is inhibited (or "fettered") by the specifically capitalist institutional structure of the economy (the "social relations of production").

Second, it will generally be in the interest of capitalists to structure pay scales and the organization of the production process to foster divisions among workers, even to the extent of treating differently workers who are identical from the standpoint of their productive capacities. This proposition is central to the Marxian divide and rule interpretation of internal labor markets, segmented labor markets, and discrimination.

Third, involuntary unemployment is a permanent feature of capitalism central to the perpetuation of its institutional structure and growth process. In a capitalist economy, product and labor markets will not function so as to eradicate Marx's familiar "reserve army of the unemployed." Moreover, even public policy towards this objective will be unable to maintain full employment.

To economists trained in the Walrasian or more generally neoclassical tradition, these assertions are often thought to be either non-sensical, or based on a radically different model of production and competition. Specifically, it is often thought that these propositions require one or more of the following assumptions: that capitalists collude in pursuit of their collective interests, that capitalists do not maximize profits, that product and factor markets are not competitive, or that the economy is characterized by important institutional rigidities such as sticky wages. Under these assumptions, it is not difficult to demonstrate the above propositions and thus affirm the importance of the Marxian concept of class.

But, while sufficient, these assumptions are not necessary to the demon-

331

stration of the above basic propositions of Marxian economics. (Nor, one might add in passing, are they particularly central to Marx's own theoretical writings, which generally presumed a highly competitive economy based on profit maximization.) The basic difference between the Marxian and Walrasian models is thus not in the structure of markets or in concepts of collective vs. atomistic action, or in institutional rigidities, but in the analysis of the process of production itself, or in what Marxists term the labor process.[5]

In this essay I develop a simple model of the production process in a competitive capitalist economy. To the familiar two-equation Walrasian model of production (production function and cost function), I add a third equation representing class conflict within the production process. I then derive the above three propositions from the expanded model. I close with some observations on the closely related but quite distinct neo-Hobbesian model of the production process.

My intent is not so much to advance the discussion of technical change, discrimination, or involuntary unemployment per se, as to provide a single coherent microeconomic framework capable of integrating important modern Marxian contributions in these fields. To cite only a few: those of Stephen Marglin (1974), William Lazonick (1982), and Harry Braverman (1974), on technology; of Richard Edwards, David Gordon, and Michael Reich (1982), Herbert Gintis (1976), and John Roemer (1979), on divide and rule strategies; and of Michel Kalecki (1943), Andrew Glyn and Robert Sutcliffe (1972), Raford Boddy and James Crotty (1975), and Richard Goodwin (1967), on unemployment.

I. The extraction of labor from labor power

The Marxian model comprises an analysis of three quite distinct aspects of the production process, broadly construed: market exchanges (modeled as voluntary contractual or contract-like interactions), physical input-output relations (which in principal might be represented by an engineering production function), and social relationships among workers and between workers and their employer (which are modeled in an entirely different manner).

Central to the Marxian approach is the distinction between those social relationships that take the form of market exchanges between firms and other ownership units, on the one hand, and relationships of command that take place within firms. The market arena in which contractual exchanges take place, Marx termed "a very Eden of the innate rights of man." By contrast

---

[5] Partly as a result of the differing treatment of the labor process and partly for other reasons, the Marxian and Walrasian views of the competitive process differ somewhat. Both stress the importance of unlimited entry and a multiplicity of buyers and sellers. Marxists, however, generally assume price-making rather than price-taking behavior by firms.

the internal structure of the firm – which Marx termed the "hidden abode of production" – is represented (as Coase was later to do) as a mini-command economy.[6]

The distinction between the two types of social relationships would be of little theoretical importance, of course, if the command relations of the firm were simply effects entirely derived from the technological structure of production and the market relationships into which the firm enters. Indeed, this is precisely the logic of Samuelson's remark quoted above.

But, according to the Marxian model, the structure and effects of the social relations within the firm – of command, cooperation, competition, and the like – while influenced by technology and market relations, are not entirely reducible to them, but rather depend on the class structure of the productive process, and hence require a distinct form of modeling. By contrast, Walrasian theory denies the need for a distinct modeling of the social relationships within the firm, while the neo-Hobbesian approach insists that a distinct modeling of the firm as a command economy is necessary, but has nothing to do with the class structure, for hierarchical relationships between managers and workers reflect nothing more than an efficient solution to the universal problem of malfeasance.

The importance of the social structure of the firm, the necessity of a distinct modeling of these social interactions, and the centrality of the class structure to their analysis may be traced within the Marxian model to three characteristics of the production process. First, labor is embodied in people, and hence labor services are inseparable from the person supplying the service. Second, whether for reasons of technology or of economies of supervision, production is generally less costly when it is done by a considerable number of workers together in one location. And third, the production process is always a process of joint production, as the workers' attitudes, capacities, and beliefs are transformed in the production process as surely as the raw materials and other goods in process are transformed into final outputs. I will refer to these three characteristics respectively as the human embodiment of labor, the social nature of production, and the endogeneity (or joint production) of workers.

---

[6] The distinction is perhaps the most fundamental in Marxian economics. Marx wrote:

If we consider the exchange between capital and labor, then, we find that it splits into two processes which are not only formally but also qualitatively different. . . : (1) the worker sells his commodity . . . (labor power) . . . which has . . . as a commodity . . . a price. . . . (2) The capitalist obtains labor itself . . . he obtains the productive force which maintains and multiplies capital. . . . The separation of these two processes is so obvious that they can take place at different times and need by no means coincide. The first can be and usually, to a certain extent, is completed before the second even begins. . . . *In the exchange between capital and labor the first act is an exchange and falls entirely within ordinary circulation; the second is a process qualitatively different from exchange, and only by misuse could it have been called any kind of exchange at all.* (1973, pp. 274–5)

333

Two types of social interaction within the firm are central to understanding the production process: relations among workers (of competition, solidarity, or whatever) and relations between workers and their employer. I focus on the second at the outset, representing the capital-labor relationship as a simple bilateral relationship between two individuals. Relations among workers will be introduced later.

The relationship between workers and their capitalist employer is formally structured by the ownership and control of the means of production. It is thus (by definition) a class relationship. In what follows, two characteristics of this relationship will be central. Both may be considered axioms with respect to the proposition to be demonstrated below. First, quite apart from the level of wages, employers and workers have a conflict of interest in the production process in the specific sense that the employer's interests (as measured by profits) are enhanced by being able to compel the worker to act in a manner that he or she otherwise would not choose. This conception of a conflict of interest does not imply that the employer and the worker have no common interests, or that, if left to their own devices, labor would choose not to produce anything at all. It simply states that within a given legal and economic context, the employer can do better than to simply hire workers and let them work as they please. The level of profits therefore depends – at least to some extent – on the power of capital over labor.

While this conflict of interest may extend to such issues as the safety or comfort of the workplace and the amount, type, and location of new investment, I focus in what follows on the conflict over the amount of work done per hour, or what may be termed the intensity of labor. This is often termed the conflict over extraction of labor from labor power. It might better be called the extraction of work from the worker.

The second axiomatic characteristic of the capital–labor relationship is that the strategies that capital may adopt in order to enhance or exercise its power over labor are costly. The basis of the power of capital over labor is the ability of the owner to impose costs on workers who refuse to (or otherwise fail to) carry out the wishes of the employer. In liberal capitalist societies, the only means by which this cost may be imposed is via the employer's control over the terms of employment (wage and other conditions) and the possibility of job termination. For reasons of simplicity, I focus initially on the threat of job loss.

The expected cost to the worker of resisting (or otherwise not carrying out) the command (explicit or implicit) of the employer will depend on the likelihood that the worker's resistance will be detected, and on the cost to the worker of losing his or her job. (Assume for the present that any worker who is observed performing below the employer's expectation will be fired; I will

334

later modify this assumption.) Because the cost (to the worker) of job loss will depend on the wage, enhancing the threat of job loss (by raising the wage) will be costly to the employer. Similarly, the employer cannot cost-lessly know what each worker is doing at any given moment even if the employer knows all of the workers' production capacities and personality characteristics. However, the employer can increase the probability of detect-ing below-standard work intensity through employing surveillance personnel and equipment, and by using production methods that produce (as a joint product) information on individual worker performance. Both methods of en-hancing the worker's expected cost of working below expectation are thus costly to the employer.

These two characteristics of the production process – the conflict of interest between capital and labor, and the costliness of employer strategies – form the basis of the propositions that follow. The underlying reasoning may be made more precise with the aid of a simple model.

Let us assume that labor is homogeneous, that the employed and unem-ployed are otherwise indistinguishable, that there are no employer costs of selection or on-the-job training, that workers are risk neutral, and that all markets are competitive in the sense of a multiplicity of noncolluding buyers and sellers.[7]

Let the output of a firm be a function of the level of inputs.

$$Q = f(X,L), \tag{1}$$

where Q is the number of units of output over some period of time, X is the vector of material inputs and services, and L is the input of labor over this same time period. All inputs and output are measured in physical terms. La-bor is thus counted in effective work done, or effort units. For simplicity, the price of the output is taken by the firm as given and is set equal to one.

As is quite evident, the treatment of total sales and the physical input-output aspect of production in the model is similar to its neoclassical – or Walrasian – analogue. The difference emerges when we consider the cost function. The labor argument in the production function – work effort – bears no market price, for it is labor time, not work itself, that is purchased. Hence the cost of labor – work – cannot be expressed in the firm's cost function as a market-determined hourly wage rate multiplied by the number of labor hours

---

[7] Unlike search models or Arthur Okun's (1981) toll model, I assume that workers have com-plete information about job and wage conditions throughout the economy, that employees know all (actual and potential) employee characteristics, and that what Okun called "the attachment between employer and employees (mutual), . . . the key component of the toll model that was absent in the simple search model" (p. 75) is absent here as well. Unlike contract theory, I assume away problems of risk aversion and issues of reputation (workers and capitalists alike have no memories).

hired.[8] To express the cost function and the production and total sales function in the same terms, a third equation is required – the labor extraction function – representing the amount of labor done per hour of labor hired as a function of the costly inputs used to elicit work from workers.[9]

We may write L, the total labor input, as the product of the hours of labor power hired, Lp, and the amount of work done per hour l^*, or $L = Lpl^*$. The amount of work done per hour is determined by the worker in response to the constraints devised by the employer, given the availability of other jobs, unemployment insurance, and the like. At this point, attention need only be given to those determinants of the worker's effort that appear as instruments from the standpoint of the employer.

The amount of work done per hour will depend upon the worker's perception of the cost of pursuing a nonwork activity, that is, of acting on the basis of any of his or her nonwork (and work-reducing) objectives. Assuming that a worker's job will be terminated if the worker's nonwork activities are detected, the expected cost of pursuing nonwork activities, $E(n)$, is the product of two terms: the probability that a worker's nonwork strategy will be observed by the employer, p^o, and the cost of being fired, if observed, w^*. It is assumed that p^o is positively affected by the amount of surveillance inputs (material or human) purchased per hour of production labor hired, s, or

---

[8] Marx (1976) dramatized the fact that labor itself cannot be bought and hence has no price as follows. "On the surface of bourgeois society the worker's wage appears as the price of labor, as a certain quantity of money that is paid for a certain quantity of labor" (p. 675). But "it is not labor which daily confronts the possessor of money (the capitalist, SB) on the commodity market, but rather the worker. What the worker is selling is his labor power" (p. 677). As a result, "according to the amount of actual labor supplied every day, the same . . . wage may represent very different prices of labor, i.e., very different sums of money paid for the same quantity of labor" (p. 683). Marx then makes it clear that the cost of a given amount of labor may vary through the extension of the length of the working day, or through an increase in the intensity of work in any given hour. "The rise in . . . wages may therefore be unaccompanied by any change in the price of labor, or may even be accompanied by a fall in the latter" (p. 684). Henry Ford may have understood this when he paid his workers in Detroit the unheard of sum of $5 a day. That labor itself cannot be purchased has long been recognized outside the Marxian tradition as well. Gary Becker observed that "any enforceable contract could at best specify the hours required on a job, not the quality of the performance" (1962, p. 6). But this fact has not been given the importance it has received among Marxian economists.

[9] Note that if labor costs did *not* depend on hours of labor hired but only on the amount of labor done, or if the relationship between hours hired and work effort performed were exogenously determined, or if the extraction of work from workers were costless, the third equation would be unnecessary. However, even the use of straight piece-rate payments will not render costs independent of the hours of labor hired unless the piece-rate workers use no inputs owned by the firm, and the determination of the number of pieces produced requires no surveillance inputs and hence is costless. But in this extreme case, there is no reason – by conventional definitions – to consider the piece-rate workers part of the firm that purchases their output, for their sole relationship to the firm is an exchange. The necessity for the third equation is thus based on assumptions no different from those used in the Coasian tradition to explain the existence of firms. The manner in which this function is developed is quite different, as we shall see, from its Coasian analogue.

$p^o = p^o(s)$, and $p^o(0) = 0$, and $p_{os} > 0$ for $s > 0$. (Here and below subscripted functions indicate the partial derivative of the function with respect to the variable indicated by the subscript.)

Surveillance labor does not enter into the transformation of inputs into outputs, and is thus distinct from what may be termed coordination labor, which is a production input represented in the production function as a component of L. (Here I abstract from the far from trivial problem of extracting work from surveillance employees. Thus, I represent surveillance services, s, as purchasable at price p_s.) The cost of an hour of labor power, c_{Lp}, is thus $(w + p_s s)$, and the cost of an effort unit of labor, c_l, or what Marx called the price of labor, is $(w + p_s s)/l^*$.

The money cost of being fired is measured by w^*, the difference between the wage offered and the worker's expected income if fired. (I assume for simplicity that the worker has no nonwage income if employed.) This latter term is simply a weighted average of w^c, the worker's nonwage income if fired and not reemployed (unemployment insurance, means-tested income support payments, and the like), and $\hat{w}$ the expected wage in some other job, should the fired worker find employment elsewhere. It is assumed that both wages $(w, \hat{w})$ exceed w^c. Thus assuming a time horizon of a single period and letting j represent the probability of finding another job (or equivalently, the fraction of the period during which the worker expects to remain unemployed), the expected income loss, $\hat{w}^d$, is

$$\hat{w}^d = w - [j\hat{w} + (1-j)w^c].$$

All of these wage terms, including w^c, are expressed in real units.[10]

A particularly simple model of the worker's response to the employer's choice of various combinations of surveillance and wage-loss threat results if we assume that at any moment the worker's decision is to work at a level of intensity satisfactory to the employer or not to work. The intensity of labor, l^*, then is just the percentage of time on the job during which the worker is actually working. It is assumed that the worker chooses a desired level of l^*, and then selects the moments of work and nonwork randomly. The probability that the worker will be detected not working, and hence dismissed, (p^d), is equal to the probability of being observed at any moment (p^o), multiplied by the probability that at that moment the worker will not be working $(1 - l^*)$, or $p^d = p^o(1 - l^*)$. The probability of job retention is simply $(1 - p^d)$, setting aside reasons for jobs termination other than observed nonwork. Thus, for $l^* = 1$, $p^d = 0$.

---

[10] Note that because the employer clearly may directly set only nominal variables, but seeks to implement a real strategy, the general price level will enter into the employer's wage setting even in the absence of cost-of-living provisions in contracts. But I will not develop this point here.

Let us assume for simplicity a two-period framework in which hiring occurs only at the beginning of a period and firing occurs only at the end of a period. The worker's time preference is assumed to be zero. The worker's expected income over two periods is thus the first-period's (assured) wage plus the expected wage or nonwage income for the second period:

$$\hat{y} = w + (1 - p^d)w + p^d(j\hat{w} + (1 - j)w^c).$$

Assuming identical workers and employers makes it reasonable to represent the worker as perceiving the alternative wage as identical to the present wage, or $w = \hat{w}$, and thus the expected income in the second period, if dismissed at the end of the first period would be $w - \hat{w}^d$, and rewriting the above expression for $\hat{y}$:

$$\hat{y} = 2w - p^d\hat{w}^d. \tag{2}$$

The worker's expected effort over two periods is both the effort expended in the current job, and the effort expended in the next job, should the worker be terminated and then reemployed. (Given the assumption that the worker has full information and hence nothing to learn, it is reasonable to suppose that the worker's choice concerning work effort when reemployed will be identical to the prejob loss choice.) Thus, the expected level of effort is

$$l^* = l^* + (1 - p^d)l^* + p_d j l^*. \tag{3}$$

The worker values income and, on the margin at least, finds increased work intensity displeasing.[11] The risk-neutral worker's response to the employer's strategy will be that which maximizes

$$\hat{u} = \hat{u}(\hat{y}, l^*) \tag{4}$$

by equating the expected marginal disutility of effort (from equations (3) and (4)) with the expected marginal utility of income associated with an increment of effort (from equations (2) and (4)).[12]

Because the expected marginal income return to an increment in work will depend positively on $\hat{w}^d$, under quite general assumptions it can be shown that the worker's choice of l^* will be a positive function of $\hat{w}^d$.[13] By similar reasoning it can be shown that work intensity will be a positive function of s.

---

[11] This does not require a marginal disutility of labor (or effort). Even on the margin, the worker may enjoy the process of work, or despise it; what is essential to my argument is the assumption that the workers' objective function includes some positively valued on-the-job activities (or inactivity) that are associated with a positive opportunity cost in terms of working.

[12] That is, by equating $(\partial u/\partial \hat{y})(\partial \hat{y}/\partial l^*)$ with $-(\partial \hat{u}/\partial l^*)(\partial l^*/\partial l^*)$.

[13] Assuming the second-order conditions for the worker's utility maximization to be met, it can be shown that effort will be an increasing function of $\hat{w}^d$ for $\hat{w}^d \geq 0$, $l^* < 1$, and $s > 0$. This is because an increase in $\hat{w}^d$ will increase $(\partial \hat{u}/\partial \hat{y})(\partial \hat{y}/\partial l^*)$. This follows readily from the independence of $\partial \hat{u}/\partial \hat{y}$ from $\hat{w}^d$ and the fact that $\partial \hat{y}/\partial l^* = p^d\hat{w}^d$. Thus, $(\partial^2 \hat{y}/\partial l^* \partial \hat{w}^d)$ must also be positive (for $s, \hat{w}^d > 0$). The upward shift of $(\partial \hat{u}/\partial \hat{y})(\partial \hat{y}/\partial l^*)$ associated with an increment in effort will

We may now represent the amount of work done per hour of labor power purchased, l^*, as

$$l^* = h(s, \hat{w}^d). \tag{5}$$

The function h – the labor extraction function – summarizes the effects of all of the relevant preferences of the worker, as well as the worker's sense of commitment, injustice, resentment, deference, patriotism, or whatever may affect the difficulty or ease of extracting labor from labor power, or influence the efficacy of surveillance or the threat of income loss as instruments towards this objective.[14]

necessarily result in an increase in effort as long as the disutility associated with a marginal increment in effort is not infinite. Thus the derivative of work effort with respect to the cost of job loss will be positive for positive $\hat{w}^d$ and s. Assuming the expected marginal utility of effort is independent of s, the analogous result for s follows.

[14] Before bringing together the three functions – production, cost, and extraction – to consider formally the capitalist's profit-maximizing problem, it may be useful to scrutinize more carefully the nature of the extraction problem. Is this not just another case of the economics of lemons, in which the employer must pay some costs to find out which workers will work hard (or well) and which will not? While some of the results are similar, not all are, and the mechanisms are quite different. The problem for the employer is not to find out what the worker *is*, but to find out what the worker *does*. To see that this is the case, the extreme assumption is made that the employer may know at zero cost the workers' skills and personality characteristics relevant to work motivation and capacities including exact knowledge of the determinants of the typical (and therefore every) worker's work effort. One of the determinants of work effort is the threat of job loss and hence the level of surveillance. The employer, by these assumptions, knows exactly how much work each worker will do on the average once the employer has selected the level of surveillance and the wage (given external wages, unemployment probabilities and unemployment insurance). At a given moment, however, the employer does not know what the worker is doing, unless the worker is being observed at that moment. And unless the worker is observed not working up to standard, it would not be rational for the employer to fire him or her, for this would convince the remaining workers that the probability of job loss did not depend on work effort, and would thus lower the efficacy of the surveillance inputs. Note that by firing the worker the employer does not eliminate a "bad worker" in favor of a chance at getting a "better worker" from the unemployment pool, for all workers are identical. The purpose of firing the nonworking worker is to convince workers that the surveillance system is effective, and that firing is related to low work effort. In other words, without firings or with firings not based on observed low work effort, the h function would shift adversely from the standpoint of the employer. Strictly speaking, then, the cost of surveillance is not an information cost at all (or at least a very peculiar one) as surveillance will affect increases in effort (over some range) even if the "surveillors" do not pass the information along to the employer, as long as the workers believe that the probability that a nonwork strategy will be detected is a positive function of the level of surveillance. But if employers know exactly how much work each worker will do once the wage and level of surveillance is selected, would it not be optimal to pay workers according to the amount of work done? It might. But this in no way would affect the results below, for the firm's costs will still depend on the number of hours hired (because surveillance s is proportional to hours of labor engaged, not the amount of work done and because workers use inputs owned by the firm). And as long as costs are not independent of the number of hours hired, employers will not be indifferent to how hard each particular worker works. (We will see below that the limiting case of no surveillance inputs cannot be optimal. It is, of course, possible to devise combinations of incentive pay and surveillance such that costs would be independent of hours hired. But it would be quite accidental if that scheme coincided with the optimal incentive structure, given workers' preference and other relevant information.)

It is assumed that the employer knows the h functions of each worker and that each is identical, thus allowing one to argue in terms of a representative worker. Further, on the basis of the reasoning above, for both s and $\hat{w}^d$ positive and $l^* < 1$, h_s, and $h_{\hat{w}d}$ are positive, and $h_{s\hat{w}d}$ is also positive.[15]

Letting p_x represent a vector of prices of nonlabor inputs, the problem for the employer is now to maximize

$$R = f(X,L) - p_x X - (w + p_s s)Lp, \tag{6}$$

subject to

$$L = l^* Lp = h(s, \hat{w}^d)Lp, \tag{7}$$

or to maximize

$$R = f[X, h(s, \hat{w}^d)Lp] - p_x X - (w + p_s s)Lp. \tag{8}$$

Because it has been assumed for the moment that the nonlabor inputs X do not affect the labor extraction process, the production function and the extraction function (equations (1) and (5)) are separable, and the employer's maximizing problem may be solved sequentially. The first problem for the employer, and the one that interests us here, is to minimize the cost of a unit of work done, or

$$\min c_l = (w + p_s s)/h(s, \hat{w}^d). \tag{9}$$

Having solved this problem, its solution, c_l^o, can then be considered the minimum cost of a unit of labor and entered into the employer's new maximand

$$R = f(X,L) - c_l^o L - p_x X. \tag{8'}$$

Assuming, for the moment, an interior solution, and noticing that the marginal cost of a unit increase in $\hat{w}^d$ is one by definition, minimizing (9) requires that

$$h_{\hat{w}d} = h(s, \hat{w}^d)/(w + p_s s) = h_s/p_s, \tag{10}$$

or that the average effort per dollar of wage and surveillance cost equal the marginal effort per dollar increase in either wage cost or surveillance cost. Analogously the profit-maximizing employer's strategy must satisfy the condition

$$p_s = h_s/h_{\hat{w}d}, \tag{10'}$$

---

[15] More formally, because the derivative of expected income with respect to work intensity is simply $\hat{w}^d p^d$, the effect of an increase in $\hat{w}^d$ on the workers' optimal effort level will depend positively on the level of s, and conversely.

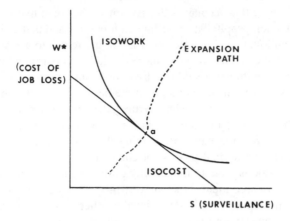

Figure 1

or the price of surveillance must be equal to the "marginal rate of substitution" between income loss if fired and probability of detection in the labor-extraction function (5).

We may represent this graphically as in Figure 1. The isocost function is a locus of equally costly employer strategies. Because the cost to the employer of a unit increment in $\hat{w}^d$ is one by definition, the slope of the isocost function can be seen to be $-p_s$. The isowork function, derived from the labor extraction function (5), is one of a family of loci of equally effective employer strategies: points describing an equal extraction of labor from a given number of hours of labor power hired. Its slope is $-h_s/h_{\hat{w}d}$. The expansion path is the locus of all possibly profit-maximizing strategies, namely, those satisfying (10'). Some point on the expansion path, say point a, minimizes the cost of a unit of labor and is therefore the solution to (9) and is the profit-maximizing strategy. (It cannot be read directly off the figure.)

I now use this model to demonstrate the three substantive propositions with which I began.

II. The reserve army of the unemployed

The more or less permanent existence of involuntary unemployment is central not only to the Marxian critique of capitalist society, but to the analytical underpinnings of its theory of profit (or of surplus value) as well. Because profits in the Marxian model are not a return to a scarce input but are simply a deduction from total output made possible by capital's power over labor, a complete Marxian model must provide a compelling account of how this power is perpetuated in an economically competitive and politically liberal environ-

341

ment. The basis of this account is the asymmetry between two forms of competition: that among capitalists in selling their outputs and that among workers in seeking employment. Because profit is not the return to a scarce input, in the absence of such an asymmetry, there would be no reason why price competition among capitalists would not drive the profit rate to zero.

The necessary asymmetry is based on the permanent existence of involuntary unemployment, or what Marx termed the reserve army of the unemployed.[16] The effect of involuntary unemployment is to render labor power nonscarce and hence incapable of claiming the whole product (net of depreciation) through the normal process of competitive price and wage determination. The puzzle is then no longer why profits are not competed away, but why does a nonscarce input, labor power, receive any competitive remuneration at all. The capital-labor distributional conflict thus appears as one taking place between and among two sets of actors, none of which exercise their claims on the product on the basis of a competitively determined return to scarcity in the usual general equilibrium sense.

The Marxian solution to this puzzle is to not reject the competitive assumptions underlying the general equilibrium model, but to pose a distinct theory of the long-term determination of wages and effort in which the former varies negatively and the latter positively with the level of unemployment.[17] Only *involuntary* unemployment will affect the bargaining power of capital and labor; hence the centrality of involuntary unemployment to the Marxian theory of the capitalist economy.

On what basis can involuntary unemployment be represented as a general – rather than ephemeral – characteristic of the capitalist economy? The endogenous perpetuation of the reserve army of the unemployed could be assured by a variety of mechanisms: for example, an infinitely elastic supply of labor from other countries or from declining domestic noncapitalist economic systems, such as household production, or rapid structural and technical change accompanied by downwardly sticky wages.[18] The above model of the extraction of labor from labor power points to another possibility, and one more consistent with competitive assumptions, namely, that the labor market does

---

[16] Marx (1976): "... relative surplus population (i.e., unemployment, SB) is therefore the background against which the demand and supply of labor does its work" (p. 792). And, "The pressure of unemployment compels those who are employed to furnish more labor and therefore makes the supply of labor to a certain extent independent of the supply of workers. The movement of the law of supply and demand on this basis completes the domination of capital" (p. 793).

[17] The macroeconomic and general equilibrium characteristics of this solution are the subject of two of my other papers (1983a,b).

[18] If the supply of labor hours is infinitely elastic at a given wage, those who are not employed cannot be said to be involuntarily unemployed strictly speaking, as they are unwilling to offer any labor time at a lower wage.

not clear in equilibrium. Put somewhat differently, excess supply in labor markets does not imply a competitive response of wage reductions.

By equilibrium in the labor market, I mean a level of wages, employment, and labor intensity that none of the agents would have both the motivation and the ability to alter. A non-clearing-labor-market equilibrium requires that profit-maximizing employers offer workers a wage and surveillance package such that, given the levels of work effort that workers will choose to expend under the package offered, workers are not indifferent between working and being unemployed. This is, of course, tantamount to saying that a profit-maximizing employer would refuse the offer by a currently unemployed worker to work as hard as the current work force for a wage less than the current wage. We shall see why this counterintuitive result may quite generally occur.

It is clear then that a market-clearing wage would imply that in our model the cost of job loss is zero, for if the cost is not zero the worker cannot be indifferent between employment and unemployment. Under what conditions could a wage-surveillance package that rendered the worker indifferent between employment and nonemployment be a profit-maximizing strategy for the individual employer, and hence a possible equilibrium? Or, in terms of Figure 1, could an optimal strategy lie on our horizontal axis, indicating a zero income loss associated with being fired? Because $h_s \to 0$ as $\hat{w}^d \to 0$, and analogously $h_{\hat{w}^d} \to 0$ as $s \to 0$, the expansion path for any $p_s > 0$ will lie entirely within the range of positive values of s and $\hat{w}^d$. As long as the employer has hired some surveillance inputs, a market-clearing wage ($\hat{w}^d = 0$) cannot be optimal (because $h_s = 0$ for $\hat{w}^d = 0$). The critical role of the cost of surveillance is here clearly indicated, for with $p_s = 0$ the isocost functions in Figure 1 would be horizontal: (free) surveillance would be substituted for (costly) job loss threat and the cost minimum would occur at $\hat{w}^d = 0$, a result consistent with the traditional market-clearing equilibrium.

But what of the "no income loss, no surveillance strategy" represented by the origin in Figure 1? In order for this strategy to be optimal, it would have to be the case that

$$h(0,0)/w > h(s,\hat{w}^d)/(w + p_s s) \tag{11}$$

for all possible levels of s and w. In this case, surveillance and job loss threats are sufficiently ineffective or costly to prohibit their use at any level. But this implies that, even when it is possible for the employer to exercise power over the worker, it is not profitable to do so. But this could only be true if there were no conflict of interest between the worker and the employer. In this case, employer and workers have a "conflict of interest" only in the socially irrelevant sense that sunbathers and drought-stricken farmers have a conflict of interest (barring the possibility of rainmaking).

This result does not depend on the manner in which the probability of

343

reemployment (j) is determined. Assume for the moment that the government committed itself to achieving full employment, either through fiscal and monetary policy, or simply by guaranteeing any unemployed worker a job at the going wage. With $j = 1$ the employer might either set $\hat{w}^d > 0$ by offering a wage higher than other employers, or set $\hat{w}^d = 0$. The former is consistent with equilibrium. This can be readily seen by rewriting the cost of being fired as an equilibrium condition (with $w = \hat{w}$) or $\hat{w}^d = (1 - j)(w - w^c)$. By the logic of the previous paragraph, the latter is inconsistent with the assumed conflict of interest between worker and capitalist.

Let us summarize these results. Given a positive cost of surveillance and a conflict of interest between employer and worker over work effort, the wage rate offered by the competitive profit-maximizing employer will exceed the worker's next best alternative. This is possible in general only if the probability of reemployment is less than one. Therefore, labor market competition cannot clear the labor market. Correspondingly, market clearing – the absence of involuntary unemployment – implies labor market disequilibrium.[19]

Other than ruling out market clearing as a possible labor market equilibrium, this model bears no direct implications concerning the determination of the general level of unemployment or the probability of reemployment. But it does provide a microeconomic foundation consistent with Kalecki's suggestion that sustained full employment and the long-run survival of capitalist enterprise may be inconsistent. Indeed, given a conflict of interest between employer and worker, labor market clearing implies either escalating wage increases, or a reduction in work effort to those levels chosen by workers. Particularly in an open economy, neither result would likely be conducive to investment levels capable of sustaining full employment (but to pursue this argument we would have to go considerably beyond the microeconomic confines of this paper).[20]

These results would be modified, of course, if employers were assumed to have not prohibitively expensive ways of imposing effective sanctions on workers even in the absence of involuntary unemployment. The extent to

[19] This result is similar to that produced – with somewhat different models – by Calvo, B. Curtis Eaton and William White (1982), James Malcomson (1981), Hajime Miyazaki (1981), Tekashi Negishi (1979), Solow (1980), Carl Shapiro and Joseph Stiglitz (1984) and others. In all of the above, actual amount of work done is directly or indirectly a positive function of the wage rate. Miyazaki focuses on the problem of worker free riding against other workers in a work group. Eaton and White focus on "trust jobs." Malcomson assumes "at least two types of individuals with different productivities who cannot be discriminated perfectly by observation at work" (p. 865). Negishi and Solow both base their models on problems of worker morale and "affront" (Negishi, p. 114). Closest in spirit to my model (though lacking the surveillance element) is Calvo, who, however, while demonstrating the possibility of nonclearing equilibria, assumes an interior solution to a problem analogous to the minimization of (6), thus eliminating the market-clearing equilibrium by assumption.

[20] I develop this argument in my 1981, 1983a,b papers. See also Gintis and Tsuneo Ishikawa (1983).

which such alternative sanctions are feasible and effective is in part an empirical issue that cannot be resolved here. For whatever reason, the practical import of most of the alternatives to the threat of involuntary unemployment appears to be quite limited in the U.S. economy.[21]

III. Capitalist technology

Central to the Marxian critique of capitalist society is the idea that the competitive pursuit of profits requires employers to organize the production process so as to maintain their power over workers, and that at least some of the boredom, fragmentation, and other undesirable aspects of the work experience may be attributed to this fact and not to the requirements of technical rationality. According to this view, the prevailing organization of production – including the technologies in use – cannot be derived solely from an interaction of exogenously given technical possibilities and worker and consumer preference for goods, leisure, and various kinds of work environment, but rather reflect the class interest of capital as well. Hence the expression "capitalist technology."

To suggest that technology may be an instrument of class conflict does not mean, of course, that employers may select technologies without regard to the competitive requirements of cost minimization. Nor does it require that capitalists collude in their choice of production methods or in the development

---

[21] If workers could instantaneously find alternative employment, but nonetheless bore significant costs of job changing – either through moving costs, training costs not borne by their new employer, employment bonds, or job entry fees that are forfeited upon job loss, a tax levied by the government on job changers, or through any other means, or if on-the-job nonwork activities were treated as a criminal offense subject to fines or imprisonment, the attainment of full employment could not be ruled out on theoretical grounds. While possible substitutes (or complements) to the threat of unemployment are thus readily imaginable, their actual or potential relevance to the problem of getting workers to work may be questioned. First, to replace the threat of unemployment, the costs imposed must be quite substantial, considerably more than reasonable moving or training costs, and in excess of what most workers can readily borrow for payment of an employment bond. Juliet Schor and I (1983) estimate that in 1983, for example, the mean cost of job loss (roughly an after-tax estimate of $\hat{w}^d$) was about one-half the mean after-tax annual income of a fully employed production worker. (This is a low estimate, as it abstracts from the costs associated with the loss of job seniority.) Moreover, the variance among individuals of the expected cost of job loss is probably quite large, due to the high variance of unemployment duration, suggesting that if we were to drop the unrealistic assumption that workers are risk neutral, the certainty equivalent of the cost of job loss might be considerably greater than Schor's and my estimates. Consideration of the social or psychological costs of unemployment – even with a generous accounting of the joys of free time – would further augment the estimate of the costs of job loss. Second, the imposition of these alternative sanctions by either employers or through the government may involve private or social enforcement costs, or other welfare losses sufficiently large to inhibit their use. Third, some otherwise promising methods of eliciting work effort other than the threat of unemployment may be considered to be socially unacceptable or politically infeasible. Even assuming that effective alternative sanctions were feasible would only modify rather than nullify my results unless these alternatives were so cost effective as to totally eclipse the expedient of paying workers more than their supply price.

of future technologies. Rather, the concept of capitalist technology is based on the proposition that cost minimization by competitive employers implies the selection of profitable but inefficient technologies even in the absence of market failures arising from collusion, externalities, extended time horizons, and the like.

I will say that the capitalist has chosen an inefficient technology when there exists some other method of production that, per unit of output, uses less of at least some input and not more of any. The logic of the concept of capitalist technology is that a technology that is inefficient in the above sense may nonetheless be cost minimizing if it allows the capitalist to lower the cost of some input. This is possible in the Marxian model because the firm is not a price taker with respect to the price of labor, but rather may alter this cost through the selection of various labor extraction strategies. The most obvious case of this is the adoption of machine-paced production as a means of increasing the intensity of labor.[22] In this case, costs may be lowered not only by producing more with the same inputs – labor – for the same price, and thus lowering the unit cost of labor. Machine-paced production may of course also be efficient. But it is simple to show that it *need not* be efficient in order to be adopted.

Capital goods may be considered to be capable of joint production, simultaneously contributing to the marketed output of the firm and producing or contributing to the acquisition of information on the work performance of the workforce. The assembly line, and even factory production itself (in contradistinction to more decentralized production methods), as well as modern information-processing systems are important cases of surveillance information-producing technologies.

The implications for efficient technical choice may be readily seen by modifying the labor extraction function to take account of this form of joint production. We now have

$$l^* = h[p^o(s,x), \hat{w}^d], \tag{5'}$$

where x is the vector of inputs (per labor hour) of production equipment and intermediate goods, and $p^o(s,x)$ is the worker's expected probability that a nonwork strategy will be detected. For some x we have $p_{ox} > 0$ and hence $h_x > 0$: given the cost of job loss ($\hat{w}^d$) and the level of (pure) surveillance inputs (s), the use of larger amounts of some input in the production process will increase the amount of work done per hour by increasing the probability that a nonwork strategy will be detected, thus increasing the worker's expected cost of pursuing a nonwork strategy.

---

[22] Edwards (1979) refers to this as "technical control" in contradistinction to "bureaucratic control" or "simple control" of the production process.

The production process in a competitive economy

It can be seen in this case that even if all relative goods prices were optimal (in the sense that they accurately reflected relative scarcities), the familiar conditions for efficient technical choice (i.e., $f_x = p_x$) would be violated. For it will now be the case that the profit-maximizing employer will maximize profits by observing the following condition:

$$f_x + f_{l^*} h_x = p_x. \tag{12}$$

The second term on the left-hand side reflects the contribution of a marginal increment in x to production via its contribution to the extraction of labor from labor power. (It is redundant to observe that under these conditions the relative general equilibrium prices would also not be optimal.)

The implication of this point is that a competitive profit-maximizing capitalist could choose a technology using more of both x and l^* per unit of output. This may be readily seen by noting that the isocost function slope is

$$dl^*/dx = -(p_x + l^* c_{lx})/c_l, \tag{13}$$

where c_{lx}, the derivative of the cost of a unit of effort with respect to x, is negative and hence the numerator is not necessarily negative. Thus the isocost function may be positively sloped, leading to the possibility that cost minimization may result in the choice of an inefficient technology, namely in the rejection of a technology using less of both l^* and x per unit of output.

It might be thought that this demonstration implies that the need for surveillance inputs is somehow illegitimate and should be abstracted from in consideration of efficiency. Indeed, as we shall see in the penultimate section, the assertion that the class structure of capitalism induces a particularly high level of work resistance and hence promotes the extensive use of surveillance inputs differentiates the Marxian from the neo-Hobbesian view. But the above argument involves neither abstracting from surveillance inputs, nor considering surveillance to be a kind of false need induced through an endogenously generated disutility of labor.

Quite the contrary, pure surveillance inputs s, with an *exogenously* determined labor extraction function, provide a particularly clear case of the above argument. Consider the indicated isowork function in Figure 1 as representing an amount of work effort capable of producing one unit of output. Starting at point a, were the firm to move along this isowork locus by raising wages and cutting surveillance inputs, the cost of labor would rise and hence the profit rate would fall, but output per unit of input would rise (l^* remaining constant and s falling). This result arises because there is a tradeoff between surveillance and the wage rate in the labor extraction function, and while surveillance inputs are resource-using, the wage rate is not; hence raising wages and lowering surveillance may be efficient but not profitable. Thus cost minimi-

347

zation and efficiency do not coincide: the tradeoff in this case is not efficiency vs. equity, but efficiency vs. profitability.

IV. Divide and rule

Central to recent Marxian research on racial and sexual discrimination, segmented labor markets, and internal labor markets is the proposition that divisions among workers may be in the interest of employers, and further that it may be in the interest of competitive noncolluding employers to discriminate among workers on the basis of ascriptive characteristics unrelated to the individual worker's ability or willingness to contribute to the production process.[23]

Reich, Roemer, Gintis, and others have recently proposed coherent models of discriminating competitive capitalists. The present model of the extraction of labor from labor power may be extended in a very simple way to capture the logic of these contributions.[24]

We say that an employer discriminates when he or she makes different wage-surveillance offers to workers of differing ascriptive characters (race, sex, age) who are otherwise identical with respect to their productive capacities and proclivities, that is, given that we have assumed that labor services are homogeneous, identical with respect to their labor extraction functions, h. I now introduce the possibility that workers may cooperate either to render surveillance more difficult or otherwise more expensive (for example by refusing to offer information on the work or nonwork activities of fellow workers), or to reduce or withdraw labor services should the employer treat a fellow worker in a manner thought to be unjust or simply contrary to the interests of other workers. Labor services may be withdrawn either through a reduction in work effort (an outward shift in the h function), or in an extreme case through a strike.

The extent of worker cooperation, including the possibility of forming institutions such as unions, varies positively with the extent of worker unity, u. Worker unity will depend on general social conditions external to the firm, but it will also be influenced by the firm's hiring and pay policies. Where a

[23] This view may be distinguished from that which maintains that the cost-minimizing process renders discrimination unprofitable to the individual employer, however beneficial it might be to the employer's class as a whole, and hence that discrimination is primarily an ideological or political phenomenon whose perpetuation is explained by inertia, ignorance, or by the collective action (in the media, schools, state, or elsewhere) of those who benefit from it.

[24] See Reich and the previously cited references to Roemer and Gintis. This model differs somewhat from those cited in stressing the costly nature of surveillance and the cost of job loss rather than bargaining strength based on worker unity. All of the Marxian models differ from the search theory approach to the stability of discrimination in a competitive environment in that the employer is assumed to know all of the relevant worker characteristics.

uniform wage surveillance package is offered to all workers, for example, opportunities for joint negotiations concerning wage and working conditions will be enhanced, and divisive sentiments such as envy and invidious distinction attenuated. With distinct pay and surveillance packages offered to different workers – particularly to groups of workers predominantly composed of individuals of different race, sex, age, and other characteristics – employers are more likely to be able to bargain separately with each group to foster competition, envy, or even hostility among the distinct groups, and thus to discourage unity. For simplicity we say that unity, u, will be a negative function of a measure of wage inequality of the workforce of the firm, v.[25]

I make an additional assumption, not necessary to my result but one which will enrich the model somewhat: let us now assume that there are some costs to the employer of replacing the worker (firm-specific training, or other), and that, for this reason, when a worker is detected pursuing a nonwork strategy, the employer may choose not to terminate the worker's employment.

In my expanded model, then, the expected cost to the worker of pursuing a nonwork strategy is

$$E(n) = p^o p^t \hat{w}^d, \tag{14}$$

where, as before $\hat{w}^d$ is the cost of job loss, p^o is the probability of being detected should the worker pursue a nonwork activity, and p^t, previously assumed to be unity, is now the variable probability of being terminated, if detected. By the above argument,

$$p^o = p^o(s,x,u) \quad \text{with } P_{ou} < 0;$$
$$p^t = p^t(u) \quad \text{with } P_{tu} < 0.$$

The labor extraction function thus becomes

$$l^* = h[p^o(s,x,u), p^t(u), \hat{w}^d] \tag{5''}$$

in which the derivative of l^* with respect to u is negative, taking account of the effects of unity on both the probability of detection and the probability of termination.

Under what conditions will the employer described in this model choose to discriminate? Assume that there are two "types" of worker, type i and type j. Why would the employer pay them different wages? It is clear at once that if the wage rates prevailing in the rest of the economy are different, or if the probability of reemployment or access to unemployment insurance is different, the optimal wage offers w_i and w_j will differ. Thus given differing external conditions, the firm will choose to offer differing wages to each type of

---

[25] Because u cannot readily be measured, this behavioral assumption cannot easily be tested. But it is strongly supported by the relevant works in labor economics and labor history. See Reich, and Edwards, Gordon, and Reich and the works cited therein.

worker. But it will be clear that the cost of a unit labor from one type of worker is less than the other, or $c_{lj} < c_{li}$ (assuming that type i workers are favored by higher wages and/or reemployment probabilities or access to unemployment insurance in the remainder of the economy). So the question arises, why would the employer chose to employ any of type i?

Assume that the employer hired no type i workers. In this case, there would be no wage inequality among the workforce ($v = o$). Hiring some type i workers will yield a positive v, thus increasing l^* and possibly lowering the average cost of labor for the firm as a whole, c_l. By the same reasoning, it could be in the interest of the employer to offer type i and type j workers different wages, even if in the rest of the economy they were treated perfectly equally. Moreover, given the existence of involuntary unemployment, such a strategy would not be rendered infeasible by the labor supply choices of the group which was offered the lower wage.

A related but distinct argument for paying identical workers different wages may also be offered, if the model is extended to more than one time period. Assume initially that all workers are paid the same wage. An employer could then offer a prospective worker a two-period wage package with a low first-period and high second-period wage. The difference in the first-period wages under the equal wage and the stepped-wage package may be considered an employment bond paid by the worker to the employer which will be returned to the worker in the form of higher second-period wages, unless, of course, the worker is fired in the interim. Let the wage cost to the firm of the two packages be the same, assuming the firm intends to make good its second-period offer, and expects the worker to neither quit, nor be fired. The "less now, more later" offer will elicit more work from the worker, however, because once it is accepted and work under its terms has commenced, the cost of job loss under the terms of that package is greater, because the worker has already performed some low wage labor and has an increasingly advantageous balance of high wage labor to look forward to should he or she retain the job. In a regime of generalized stepped-wage offers such as the primary labor market in the United States, the costs of failing to cash in on later-period high wages can be considerable.

The worker may not accept the stepped-wage offer, of course, if he or she believes that the probability of getting arbitrarily fired at the end of the first period is high. But should the worker accept the stepped-wage offer, the firm will have affected a reduction in its cost of labor c_l. As in the case of discrimination above, the fact that jobs are rationed will allow the firm to recruit labor using the less attractive stepped-wage offer.

Thus long-term contracts and internal labor markets – promotion ladders according to job tenure and unrelated to skill – may be a method of increasing the cost of job loss to the worker without increasing the wage bill, and hence an effective means of reducing the cost of labor (in effort units).[26]

The above explains why identical workers may be paid differently. It does not explain why discrimination exists, or why type i workers tend to be white, male, and neither very young nor very old. But it does present one possible argument for the reproducibility of discrimination and internal labor markets in a competitive capitalist economy.

V. Neo-Hobbesian and Marxian models

It may well be objected that while the labor extraction model provides an internally consistent analysis of involuntary unemployment, inefficient technical choice, and discrimination in a competitive equilibrium, any negative normative connotations would be misplaced, for these undesirable outcomes might be intrinsic to *any* system of production, irrespective of the social structure in which it is embedded. Indeed this is precisely the implication of what I have termed the neo-Hobbesian models of the production process.

Malfeasance is to the neo-Hobbesian models what class conflict is to Marxian models. The key difference between the two is this: malfeasance is a universal human proclivity – in this case based on the inherent nature of work as a disutility. By contrast, class conflict in the labor process of a capitalist economy is the result of a specific and mutable set of social institutions; the conflict over work intensity being *at least in part* the consequence of the particular organization of work and the resulting alienated nature of labor.

Samuelson's statement cited at the outset – while based on a Walrasian model – reflects the spirit of the neo-Hobbesian models as well, for it is consistent with the view that the form of the class relationship imparts nothing of importance to the production process.

Can the neo-Hobbesian position be sustained? Can the Marxian problem – class conflict over the extraction of labor from labor power – be reduced to the general problem of malfeasance? Differing ideological connotations aside,

[26] From quite different perspectives, a similar argument has been suggested by Edwards and by Lazear. The argument is quite distinct, however, from models based on search theory and screening costs, in which the employer has an interest in retaining the worker (because of hiring costs). See, for example, Okun. The post-World War II emergence of long-term contracts and internal labor markets as characteristic of a major segment of the U.S. economy may be attributable in part to their labor extraction cost-saving aspect, to the historically low rates of unemployment in the postwar period, and to the apparent decline in the cost of job loss associated with a spell of unemployment. Further, as Lazear has pointed out, the labor extraction advantages of long-term stepped-wage offers may help explain the otherwise anomalous phenomenon of returns to job tenure significantly in excess of any empirically compelling estimates of productivity enhancement through generalized on-the-job leaning. See James Medoff and Katherine Abraham (1980).

is the extraction of labor from labor power simply another way of addressing the universal problem of "shirking"?

Concern with the general problem of reconciling individual self-interest and collective rationality is hardly new, dating back at least to Hobbes. That the regulation of self-interest through the market provided a solution to the Hobbesian problem was suggested metaphorically by Mandeville during the eighteenth century and developed fully by Walras and by twentieth-century welfare economists. If all economic interactions are contractual exchanges, the conflict of self-interest and collective rationality is capable of resolution, or at least substantial attenuation.

But, as economists of all persuasions now recognize, not all economic interactions are exchanges. Coase's conception of the firm, as a command economy of nonexchange relations, is a necessary but possibly troublesome addition to any analysis of a specifically capitalist economy characterized by an employment relation. Strikingly, the Coasian view of the capitalist economy as a multiplicity of mini-command economies operating in a sea of market exchanges is radically different from the Walrasian foundations of welfare economics, and superficially indistinguishable from the Marxian view.

The question obviously arises, then, as to the compatibility of the Coasian insight (command) and the Mandevillian solution to the Hobbesian problem (markets). Are the command relations of the firm a rational solution to the problem of the coordination of individual and group rationality? Or are they, in some sense, a market failure attributable to the successful pursuit of the interests of those who command the firm? This is the central issue dividing the neo-Hobbesian from the Marxian analysis.

Coase, basing his concept of the firm on the notion that command relations supercede market relations when the transactions costs of markets exceed the analogous costs of command and nonmarket coordination, initiated a literature which affirmed the efficiency of the hierarchical structure of the firm.[27] Because malfeasance is no more than an expression of the natural self-interestedness of human beings, the cost of policing malfeasance cannot be considered evidence of a failure of markets. The logic of this position can be illustrated within the terms of the Marxian model.

Let us make the (neo-Hobbesian) assumption that the labor extraction function is given by human nature. People's attitude towards work – broadly, the disutility of labor – is unrelated to the social institutions that govern the process of work. In this case, the extraction function must be considered to be exogenous, not only to the firm but to the society as a whole. Hence the various employer strategies and their results must be considered to be little more than a consequence of the (possibly lamentable but ineradicable) human

---

[27] The recent literature was initiated by Alchian and Demsetz.

tendency to avoid work. A society might nonetheless choose to discourage discrimination, to minimize involuntary unemployment, or to discourage the use of surveillance equipment or personnel, but they would do so only at the cost of choosing to permit a higher level of what the neo-Hobbesian literature terms free riding or shirking, and consequently a lower average level of output per hour of labor.

But the assumptions required to sustain the neo-Hobbesian view are exceptionally restrictive and implausible. We have seen in the analysis of capitalist technology that even with an exogenously given labor extraction function, the choice of technology – including the level of surveillance – which is profit maximizing will not in general be efficient: it generally will be dominated by some other less profitable and less surveillance-intensive combination of inputs.[28]

Perhaps more fundamentally, the assumption of an exogenous extraction function appears to be quite arbitrary. If the organization of the work process and the principles determining the distribution of the net revenues arising therefrom influence workers' attitudes towards work and hence are among the determinants of the extraction function, the neo-Hobbesian conclusions are considerably altered. In this case, there may exist some alternative set of arrangements in which a bargain could be struck in which at least one of the participants was better off and none worse off. A possible argument may be illustrated. Rewrite the labor extraction function as

$$l^* = h(i,s,\hat{w}^d,u,x), \tag{5''}$$

where i is a vector reflecting the general institutional environment. If it could be shown that in an environment which workers perceived to be more fair, or more consistent with their self-respect, for example, they would choose to expend more effort for any given employer strategy, then it is a simple matter to demonstrate that the initial outputs could be produced with unchanged levels of labor effort in production and using less surveillance labor.[29] In Figure 1, the transformed institutional environment (the change in i) would be re-

---

[28] Because the efficient (less surveillance-intensive) technology is less profitable it might be objected that while the neo-Hobbesian position is faulty on static efficiency grounds, a dynamic efficiency perspective, taking account of optimal levels of investment and the relationship of profits to investment, would salvage their view. But this is not the case unless it is also assumed that the current levels of investment are at or below the optimal level and further (and dubiously) that a reduction in the profit rate is necessarily associated with a decline in investment. To the extent that capitalists consume rather than invest their profits (or invest them in other economies), a decline in the profit rate does not *require* a reduction in the level of investment, even if the economy is operating at the level of potential output. Of course, given the institutions that define the capitalist economy, such an effect is likely to result, but it is hardly reasonable to take as given the institutions which are themselves under evaluation.

[29] There seems to be considerable evidence that this is the case. See, for example, Raymond Katzell et al. (1975).

flected in an inward shift in the isowork loci such that the initial amount of work could be extracted with a reduced s.[30] The newly released surveillance labor could then be employed producing goods representing a new addition to the total product, achieved without increasing total labor hours worked and/or workers' efforts per hour.

The above argument draws directly on the third basic characteristic of the production process in the Marxian model, the joint production of commodities and workers or the endogenous nature of workers' preferences. The attitude towards work is not, according to this principle, simply a manifestation of human nature, but in part the result of the social institutions in which the production process takes place.

In the production of workers, of course, other institutions – schools, the family, political organizations, and the like – assume a critical importance. The structure of these institutions is, however, strongly albeit indirectly influenced by the structure of the production process.[31] Moreover, the structure of the production process itself undoubtedly has direct effects on attitudes towards work. A more democratic structure of decision making and a more egalitarian distribution of the firm's net revenues, for example, might both reduce the incentive to pursue nonwork activities and heighten the cost of so doing by enlisting fellow workers as more ardent enforcers of the pace of work, or more willing cooperators with the surveillance system.[32]

The neo-Hobbesian's normative position thus seems dubious on two grounds: the discrepancy between profitability and efficiency, and the endogeneity of

[30] A simple reduction of s would not be optimal, of course, but this is immaterial to my argument.

[31] The influence is mutual, of course, schools and families influencing the structure of production as well as conversely. See, from very different perspectives, my book with Gintis (1976), Melvin Kohn (1969), and William Lazonick (1978, 1981). Lazonick concluded, "Hence it can be argued that not only the institutional transformation of the capitalist enterprise but also, and perhaps more fundamentally, the institutional transformation of the larger society was required to stabilize the capital labor relation in the mass production industries" (1981, p. 36).

[32] Why are the potential gains to such an alternative form of work organization not sufficient to bring such worker-based enterprises into being and to assure their success in the competitive struggle with more hierarchically structured capitalist firms? If workers' attitudes toward work were determined solely and instantaneously by the work environment in which they worked, and if credit were readily available on terms no worse than those available to capitalist firms, any group of workers could form a co-op and reap the benefits of lessened surveillance. Both assumptions are highly questionable. To the extent that attitudes toward work are determined by an entire nexus of social institutions which change slowly, the opportunities for the atomistic movement towards a less socially irrational form of production are quite limited. Perhaps more important, because workers' own assets are not extensive, their access to credit is limited or costly by comparison to that enjoyed by the owners of firms. (It matters little for the issues treated here whether the different terms of credit available to capitalists and workers reflect rational profit-maximizing behavior by lenders or an imperfection in the credit market.) And it might be added that, perhaps for some of the reasons outlined in this paper, and despite the obstacles outlined in this note, the last decade has witnessed a substantial growth of workers' co-ops and worker-managed firms in the United States.

the labor extraction function. If the social nature of the labor extraction function is conceded and, further, if the feasibility of forms of social structure and work organization conducive of lower levels of work resistance or higher levels of work motivation is accepted, or, if the possible nonoptimality of the competitively determined profit rate is admitted, the command relationships within the firm and the associated patterns of involuntary unemployment, technical choice, and discrimination must be viewed as market failures rather than simply as unavoidable transactions costs. Moreover, because of the importance of the labor input in the production process, the quantitative importance of this source of market failure may overshadow the more commonly recognized environmental and other externalities.

VI. Conclusion

The model of the production process based on the extraction of labor from labor power thus provides an internally consistent microeconomic theory capable of supporting some of the most fundamental general propositions in Marxian economics concerning the reserve army of the unemployed, the determination of the profit rate, discrimination, and the irrationality of the organization of work and technology. The above arguments do not, of course, establish the superiority of the Marxian model. Nor do they provide any indication that the Marxian model is capable of generating plausible empirical accounts of such phenomena as movements in the unemployment rate, the profit rate, the structure of discrimination, or technical choice.

However, a significant amount of empirical work along the lines outlined above has been done, some of it with quite successful results. For example, econometric models of postwar U.S. productivity growth, the profit rate, Tobin's Q, and strike activity using an empirical measure of the cost of job loss, $\hat{w}^d$, have generated highly significant and robust estimates consistent with the expectations of this model.[33] Historical studies of technical choice and work organization based on the extraction of labor from labor power have produced compelling accounts of otherwise anomalous patterns of technical change. (See Lazonick, 1982, and Marglin.) And econometric studies of the distributional impact of discrimination have produced results quite consistent with the divide and rule interpretation. (See Reich.) None of these is alone decisive, but taken together they do suggest that the Marxian model offers a promising direction for empirical investigation.

[33] See Thomas Weisskopf et al. (1983), my paper with Gordon and Weisskopf (1983), and Schor's and my papers (1983, 1984). Michele Naples (1982) has estimated significant relationships between labor productivity and the structure of control of the labor process consistent with the above model.

References

Akerlof, George, 1980, "A Theory of Social Custom, of Which Unemployment May Be One Consequence," *Quarterly Journal of Economics,* 94: 749–75.

Alchian, Armen, 1951, "Uncertainty, Evolution, and Economic Theory," *Journal of Political Economy,* 58:211–21.

Alchian, A. A., 1965, "The Basis of Some Recent Advances in the Theory of Management of the Firm," *Journal of Industrial Economics,* 14: 30–44.

Alchian, Armen A., 1969, "Corporate Management and Property Rights," in Henry G. Manne, ed., *Economic Policy and the Regulation of Corporate Securities.* Washington: American Enterprise Institute Public Policy Research.

Alchian, Armen, 1984, "Specificity, Specialization, and Coalitions," *Journal of Institutional and Theoretical Economics,* 140: 34–49.

Alchian, Armen A. and Demsetz, Harold, 1972, "Production, Information Costs, and Economic Organization," *American Economic Review,* 62: 777–95.

Alchian, A. A. and Kessel, R. A., 1962, "Competition, Monopoly and the Pursuit of Pecuniary Gain," in *Aspects of Labor Economics.* New Jersey: National Bureau of Economic Research.

Anderson, Theodore R. and Warkov, Seymour, 1961, "Organizational Size and Functional Complexity," *American Sociological Review,* 26: 23–8.

Aoki, Masahiko, 1984, *The Co-operative Game Theory of the Firm.* London: Clarendon Press.

Argyle, M., Gardner, G., and Cioffi, F., 1958, "Supervisory Methods Related to Productivity, Absenteeism, and Labor Turnover," *Human Relations,* 10: 23–9.

Arnowitz, Stanley, 1973, *False Promises: The Shaping of American Working Class Consciousness.* New York: McGraw-Hill Co.

Arrow, K. J., 1951, "An Extension of the Basic Theorems of Classical Welfare Economics," in J. Neyman, ed., *Proceedings of the Second Berkeley Symposium on Mathematical Statistics and Probability.* Berkeley: University of California Press.

Arrow, K. J., 1969, "The Organization of Economic Activity," in *The Analysis and Evaluation of Public Expenditure: The PPB System,* Vol. 1, JEC, 91st Congress, 1st Session, 47–64.

Arrow, K. J., 1971, *Essays in the Theory of Risk Bearing.* Chicago, Illinois.

Arrow, K. J., 1974, *The Limits of Organization.* New York: Norton.

Arrow, K. J. and Debreu, G., 1954, "Existence of Equilibrium for a Competitive Economy," *Econometrica,* 22: 265–90.

Ashenfelter, O. and Johnson, G., 1972, "Unionism, Relative Wages, and Labor Quality in U. S. Manufacturing Industries, *International Economic Review,* 13: 488–508.

References

Ashton, T. S., 1925, "The Records of a Pin Manufactory – 1814–21," *Economica,* 5: 281–92.

Atwood, Jane and Kobrin, Paul, 1977, "Integration and Joint Ventures in Pipelines," (Research Study No. 5, American Petroleum Institute).

Babbage, C., 1925, *On the Economy of Machinery and Manfucturers.* London: C. Knight.

Baines, E., 1835, *History of the Cotton Manufacture in Great Britain.* London.

Barkai, Haim, 1982, *Growth Patterns of the Kibbutz Economy.* New York: North-Holland Publishing Co.

Barnard, Chester I., 1938, *The Functions of the Executive.* Cambridge, Massachusetts: Harvard University Press.

Barnard, C. I., 1962, *The Functions of the Executive,* 2nd edition. Cambridge, Massachusetts: Harvard University Press.

Batt, Francis R., 1929, *The Law of Master and Servant.* New York: Pitman Publishing Co.

Baumol, William J., 1959, *Business Behavior, Value and Growth.* New York: Macmillan.

Becker, G., 1962, "Investment in Human Capital: A Theoretical Analysis," *Journal of Political Economy,* Supplement, 70: 9–44.

Becker, Gary S. and Stigler, George J., 1974, "Law Enforcement, Malfeasance, and Compensation of Enforcers," *Journal of Legal Studies,* 3: 1–18.

Ben-Porath, Yoram, 1980, "The F-Connection: Families, Friends, and Firms and the Organization of Exchange," *Population and Development Review,* 6: 1–30.

Berhold, M., 1971, "A Theory of Linear Profit Sharing Incentives," *Quarterly Journal of Economics,* 85: 460–82.

Berle, Adolf and Means, Gardiner, 1932, *The Modern Corporation and Private Property.* New York: Commerce Clearing House.

Blau, P. and Scott, W., 1962, *Formal Organizations.* San Francisco: Chandler.

Blinder, A., "Who Joins Unions," Working Paper No. 36, Industrial Relations Section, Princeton University.

Boddy, Raford and Crotty, James, 1975, "Class Conflict and Macro Policy: The Political Business Cycle," *Review of Radical Political Economics,* 7: 1–19.

Bork, Robert, 1954, "Vertical Integration and the Sherman Act: The Legal History of an Economic Misconception," *University of Chicago Labor Review,* 22: 157–201.

Bornstein, Morris, ed., 1973, *Plan and Market: Economic Reform in Eastern Europe.* New Haven: Yale University Press.

Bookman, Ann, 1977, *The Process of Political Socialization Among Women and Immigrant Workers: A Case Study of Unionization in the Electronics Industry.* Unpublished Ph.D. Thesis, Harvard University.

Bowles, Samuel, 1981, "Competitive Wage Determination and Involuntary Unemployment," mimeo.

Bowles, Samuel, 1983a, "Long-Term Growth and Equilibrium Unemployment in an Open Competitive Capitalist Economy," mimeo.

Bowles, Samuel, 1983b, "The Cyclical Movement of Real Wages, Labor Productivity, and 'Overhead Labor' in a Competitive Non-Monetary Economy," mimeo.

357

REFERENCES

Bowles, Samuel and Gintis, Herbert, 1976, *Schooling in Capitalist America*. New York: Basic Books.

Bowles, Samuel, Gordon, David M. and Weisskopf, Thomas, 1983, "The Profit Rate in the Post-War U. S. Economy: An Econometric Investigation," mimeo.

Branch, B., 1973, "Corporate Objectives and Market Performance, *Financial Management,* 24–9.

Braverman, Harry, 1974, *Labor and Monopoly Capital*. New York: Monthly Review Press.

Brown, C. and Medoff, J., 1975, "Trade Unions in the Production Process," unpublished paper.

Burton, J. and Parker, J., 1969, "Interindustry Variations in Voluntary Labor Mobility," *Industrial and Labor Relations Review,* 22: 199–216.

Buttrick, J., 1952, "The Inside Contracting System," *Journal of Economic History,* 12: 205–21.

Bythell, Duncan, 1969, *The Handloom Weavers*. Cambridge, England: Cambridge University Press.

Cairnes, J. E., 1862, *The Slave Power*. London.

Calabresi, G., 1968, "Transactions Costs, Resource Allocation and Liability Rules: A Comment," *Journal of Law and Economics,* 11:67–74.

Calvo, Guillermo, 1979, "Quasi-Walrasian Theories of Unemployment," *American Economic Review,* 69: 102–7.

Chamberlain, N., 1962, *The Firm: Micro Economic Planning and Action*. New York: McGraw-Hill.

Chandler, A., 1969, "The Structure of American Industry in the Twentieth Century: A Historical Review," *Business History Review,* 63: 255–98.

Cheung, S. N. S., 1969, "Transaction Costs, Risk Aversion, and the Choice of Contractual Arrangements," *Journal of Law and Economics,* 12: 23–42.

Cheung, Steven, 1983, "The Contractual Nature of the Firm," *Journal of Law and Economics,* 26: 1–21.

Clark, J. B., 1900, *Distribution of Wealth*. New York: Macmillan Co.

Coase, R. H., 1937, "The Nature of the Firm," *Economica,* IV: 386–405 reprinted, pp. 331–351 in *Readings in Price Theory*. Chicago, Illinois: Irwin.

Coase, R. H., 1952, "The Nature of the Firm," Ch. 16 in American Economic Association, *Readings in Price Theory,* 6: 331–51.

Coase, R. H., 1959, "The Federal Communications Commission," *Journal of Law and Economics,* 2: 1–40.

Coase, R. H., 1960, "The Problem of Social Cost," *Journal of Law and Economics,* 3: 1–44.

Coase, R. H., 1964, "Discussion," *American Economic Review,* 54: 194–7.

Coase, R. H., 1972, "Durability and Monopoly," *Journal of Law and Economics,* 15: 143–50.

Commons, J. R., 1918, *History of Labor in the United States*. New York: Macmillan, Vols. 1,2; Vols. 3,4, 1935.

Commons, J., 1970, *The Economics of Collective Action*. Madison, Wisconsin: University of Wisconsin Press.

358

References

Cox, A., 1958, "The Legal Nature of Collective Bargaining Agreements," *Michigan Law Review*, 57: 1–36.

Cyert, R. M. and C. L. Hedrick, 1972, "Theory of the Firm: Past, Present and Future: An Interpretation," *Journal of Economic Literature*, 10: 398–412.

Cyert, R. M. and J. G. March, 1963, *A Behavioral Theory of the Firm*. Englewood Cliffs, New Jersey: Prentice-Hall.

Darby, Michael R. and Karni, Eli, 1973, "Free Competition and the Optimal Amount of Fraud," *Journal of Law and Economics*, 16: 67–88.

Dawes, Harry, 1934, "Labour Mobility in the Steel Industry," *The Economic Journal*, 44: 84–94.

Davison, J. P., Florence, P. S., Gray, B. and Ross, N., 1958, *Productivity and Economic Incentives*. London: Allen & Unwin.

Debreu, G., 1959, *Theory of Value*. New York: Wiley.

Demsetz, H., 1967, "Toward a Theory of Property Rights," *American Economic Review*, 57: 347–359.

Demsetz, H., 1969, "Information and Efficiency: Another Viewpoint," *Journal of Law and Economics*, 12: 1–22.

Dobb, Maurice, 1925, *Capitalist Enterprise and Social Progress*. London: George Routledge and Sons, Ltd.

Dobb, Maurice, 1928, *Russian Economic Development*. New York: F. P. Dutton and Co.

Doeringer, P. and Piore, M., 1971, *Internal Labor Markets and Manpower Analysis*. Boston: D. C. Heath.

Dreze, Jacques H., 1976, "Some Theory of Labor Management and Participation," *Econometrica*, 44: 1125–1140.

Dunlop, J., 1958, *Industrial Relations Systems*. New York: Holt.

Dunlop, J., 1957, "The Task of Contemporary Wage Theory," in G. W. Taylor and F. C. Pierson, eds., *New Concepts in Wage Determination*, New York: McGraw-Hill.

Durbin, E. F. M., 1936, "Economic Calculus in a Planned Economy," *Economic Journal*, 46: 676–90.

Eaton, B. Curtis and White, William D., 1982, "Agent Compensation and the Limits of Bonding," *Economic Inquiry*, 20: 330–43.

Edwards, Richard, 1979, *Contested Terrain: The Transformation of the Workplace in the Twentieth Century*. New York: Basic Books.

Edwards, Richard C., Gordon, David M. and Reich, Michael, 1982, *Segmented Work, Divided Workers: The Historical Transformation of Labor in the United States*. Cambridge: Cambridge University Press.

Engels, F., 1894, "On Authority," first published in *Atmenacco Republicano*, reprinted in Robert C. Tucker, ed., *The Marx-Engels Reader*. New York: W. W. Norton and Co.

Fama, E. F., 1970a, "Multiperiod Consumption-Investment Decisions," *American Economic Review*, 60: 163–74.

Fama, E. F., 1970b, "Efficient Capital Markets: A Review of Theory and Empirical Work," *The Journal of Finance*, 25: 383–417.

REFERENCES

Fama, E. F., 1972, "Ordinal and Measurable Utility," in M. C. Jensen, ed., *Studies in the Theory of Capital Markets*. New York: Praeger.

Fama, E. F., 1976, *Foundations of Finance*. New York: Basic Books.

Fama, Eugene and Jensen, Michael, 1983a, "Separation of Ownership and Control," *Journal of Law and Economics*, 26: 301–26.

Fama, Eugene and Jensen, Michael, 1983b, "Agency Problems and Residual Claims," *Journal of Law and Economics*, 26: 327–49.

Fama, Eugene F. and Miller, Merton H., 1972, *The Theory of Finance*. New York: Holt, Rinehart & Winston.

Feldman, J. and Kanter, H., 1965, "Organizational Decision-Making," pp. 614–49 in J. March, ed., *Handbook of Organizations*. Chicago: Rand McNally.

Feller, David E., 1973, "A General Theory of the Collective Bargaining Agreement," *California Labor Review*, 3: 663–856.

Ferguson, Adam, 1767, *An Essay on the History of Civil Society*. Edinburgh.

Ferguson, C. E., 1969, *The Neoclassical Theory of Production and Distribution*. London: Cambridge University Press.

Freeman, Richard, 1980, "The Exit-Voice Tradeoff in the Labor Market: Unionism, Job Tenure, Quits, and Separations," *Quarterly Journal of Economics*, 94: 643–73.

Freeman, Richard, 1981, "The Effect of Trade Unions on Fringe Benefits," *Industrial and Labor Relations Review*, 34: 489–509.

Freudenberger, H. and Radlich, F., 1964, "The Industrial Development of Europe: Reality, Symbols, Images," *Kyklos*, 17: 372–403.

Friedman, M., 1970, "The Social Responsibility of Business Is to Increase Its Profits," *New York Times Magazine*, September 13, 32ff.

Furubotn, E., 1976, "Worker Alienation and the Structure of the Firm," in S. Pejovich, ed., *Governmental Controls and the Free Market* (Texas: College Station), 195–225.

Furubotn, E. G. and Pejovich, S., 1972, "Property Rights and Economic Theory: A Survey of Recent Literature," *Journal of Economic Literature*, 10: 1137–62.

Furubotn, E. and Pejovich, S., 1974, "Property Rights and the Behavior of the Firm in a Socialist State: The Example of Yugoslavia," 227–251 in E. Furubotn and S. Pejovich, eds., *The Economics of Property Rights*. Cambridge, Massachusetts: Ballinger Publishing Company.

Garnier, Germain, 1815, *Abrege elementaire des principes de l'Economie Politique*. Paris.

Ghiselli, E. E. and Brown, C. W., 1948, *Personnel and Industrial Psychology*. New York: McGraw-Hill.

Gintis, Herbert, 1976, "The Nature of the Labor Exchange," *Review of Radical Political Economics*, 8: 36–54.

Gintis, Herbert and Ishikawa, Tsuneo, 1983, "Wages, Work Discipline, and Macroeconomic Equilibrium," mimeo.

Glyn, Andrew and Sutcliffe, Robert, 1972, *British Capitalism, Workers, and the Profit Squeeze*. London: Penguin.

Goldberg, Victor P., 1976, "Regulation and Administered Contracts," *Bell Journal of Economics*, 7: 426–48.

References

Goldberg, V. P., 1977, "Competitive Bidding and the Production of Precontract Information," *Bell Journal of Economics*, 8: 250–61.

Goldberg, V. P., 1979, "Protecting the Right to Be Served by Regulated Utilities," *Research in Law and Economics*, 1: 145–56.

Goldberg, Victor, 1980a, "Bridges Over Contested Terrain: Exploring the Radical Account of the Employment Relationship," *Journal of Economic Behavior and Organization*, 1: 249–74.

Goldberg, V. P., 1980b, "The Law and Economics of Vertical Restrictions: A Relational Perspective," *Texas Law Review*, 58: 91–129.

Goldberg, Victor, 1982, "A Relational Exchange Perspective on the Employment Relationship," Working Paper No. 208, Department of Economics, University of California, Davis.

Goodwin, Richard, 1967, "A Growth Cycle," in C. H. Feinstein, ed., *Capitalism and Economic Growth*. Cambridge: Cambridge University Press.

Gordon, R. A., 1976, "Rigor and Relevance in a Changing Institutional Setting," *American Economic Review*, 66: 1–14.

Grabowski, H. and Mueller, D., 1975, "Life Cycle Effects of Corporate Returns of Retentions," *Review of Economics and Statistics*, 57: 400–9.

Green, J. and Sheshinski, E., 1975, "Competitive Inefficiencies in the Presence of Constrained Transactions," *Journal of Economic Theory*, 10: 343–57.

Grossman, S. J. and Stiglitz, J. E., 1976, "Information and Competitive Price Systems," *American Economic Review*, 66: 246–53.

Gustafson, W. Eric, 1959, *Periodicals and Books*, in Max Hall, ed., *Case Studies in Metropolitan Manufacturing*. Cambridge: Harvard University Press.

Hammond, J. L. and Barbara, 1919, *The Skilled Laborer*. London: Longmans Green.

Harbison, F., 1956, "Entrepreneurial Organization as a Factor in Economic Development," *Quarterly Journal of Economics*, 70: 364–79.

Harrison, B., 1972, *Education, Training and the Urban Ghetto*, Baltimore: Johns Hopkins University Press.

Hayek, F. A., 1933, "The Trend of Economic Thinking," *Economica*, 13: 121–37.

Hayek, F. A., 1945, "The Use of Knowledge in Society," *The American Economic Review*, 35: 519–30.

Heckerman, D. G., 1975, "Motivating Managers to Make Investment Decisions," *Journal of Financial Economics*, 2: 273–92.

Henderson, Hubert D., 1922, *Supply and Demand*. New York: Harcourt, Brace and Co.

Henderson, James and Quandt, Richard, 1971, *Microeconomic Theory: A Mathematical Approach*. New York: McGraw-Hill.

Henry, Robert S., 1942, *This Fascinating Railroad Business*. New York: Bobbs-Merrill.

Hess, James, 1983, *The Economics of Organization*. Amsterdam: North-Holland.

Hicks, J., 1973, *Theory of Wages*. New York: St. Martin's Press.

Hirschman, Albert O., 1970, *Exit, Voice and Loyalty: Responses to Decline in Firms, Organizations, and States*. Cambridge: Harvard University Press.

Hodgeskin, Thomas, 1827, *Popular Political Economy*. London.

International Labor Organization, 1951, "Payment by Results," *ILO Studies and Reports*, New Series No. 27. Geneva.

361

REFERENCES

International Labor Organization, 1957, "ILO Productivity Missions to Underdeveloped Countries, Part 1," *International Labor Review*, 76: 1–29.

International Labor Organization, 1958, "ILO Productivity Missions to Underdeveloped Countries, Part 2," *International Labor Review*, 76: 139–66.

Jensen, Michael C., 1972, "Capital Markets: Theory and Evidence," *Bell Journal of Economics*, 3: 357–98.

Jensen, M. C., 1978, "Some Anomalous Evidence Regarding Market Efficiency," *Journal of Financial Economics*, 6: 95–101.

Jensen, Michael, 1983, "Organization Theory and Methodology," *Accounting Review*, 58: 319–39.

Jensen, Michael C. and Meckling, William H., 1976a, "Theory of the Firm: Managerial Behavior, Agency Costs and Ownership Structure," *Journal of Financial Economics*, 3: 305–60.

Jensen, M. C. and W. H. Meckling, 1976b, "Can the Corporation Survive?" Center for Research in Government Policy and Business Working Paper No. PPS 76-4. Rochester, New York: University of Rochester.

Jensen, M. C. and W. H. Meckling, 1977, "On the Labor-Managed Firm and the Co-determination Movement," (unpublished manuscript).

Jensén, M. C. and W. H. Meckling, 1979, "Rights and Production Functions: An Application to Labor-Managed Firms and Co-determination," *Journal of Business*, 52: 469–506.

Johnson, Ana Gutierrez and Whyte, William Foote, 1977, "The Mondragon System of Worker Production Cooperatives," *Industrial and Labor Relations Review*, 31: 18–30.

Johnson, Harry G., 1963, "The 'Higher Criticism' of the Modern Corporation," *Columbia Law Review*, 63: 399–432.

Jones, Eliot, 1927, *The Trust Problem*. New York: Macmillan Co.

Joskow, P. L., 1973, "Pricing Decisions of Regulated Firms: A Behavioral Approach," *Bell Journal of Economics*, 4: 118–40.

Joskow, Paul L., 1977, "Commercial Impossibility, the Uranium Market, and the Westinghouse Case," *Journal of Legal Studies*, 6: 119–76.

Kaldor, N., 1934, "A Classificatory Note of the Determinateness of Equilibrium," *The Review of Economic Studies*, 1: 122–36.

Kaldor, N., 1934, "The Equilibrium of the Firm," *The Economic Journal*, 44: 60–76.

Kalecki, Michel, 1943, "Political Aspects of Full Employment," *Political Quarterly*, 14: 322–30.

Katzell, Raymond A., *et al.*, 1975, *Work, Productivity and Job Satisfaction: An Evaluation of Policy Related Research*. New York: Harcourt Brace Jovanovich.

Kerr, C., 1954, "The Balkanization of Labor Markets," pp. 92–110 in E. Wight Bakke, *et al.*, *Labor Mobility and Economic Opportunity*. Cambridge, Massachusetts: Technology Press of MIT.

Kessler, Friedrich, and Stern, Richard H., 1959, "Competition, Contract, and Vertical Integration," *Yale Law Journal*, 69: 1–129.

Kirzner, I., 1973, *Competition and Entrepreneurship*. Chicago: University of Chicago Press.

References

Klein, Benjamin, 1974, "The Competitive Supply of Money," *Journal of Money, Credit and Banking*, 6: 423–53.

Klein, Benjamin, 1983, "Contracting Costs and Residual Claims: The Separation of Ownership and Control," *Journal of Law and Economics*, 26: 367–74.

Klein, Benjamin and McLaughlin, Andrew, 1978, "Resale Price Maintenance, Exclusive Territories, and Franchise Termination: The Coors Case," unpublished manuscript.

Klein, Benjamin, Crawford, Robert G., and Alchian Armen, 1978, "Vertical Integration, Appropriable Rents and the Competitive Contracting Process," *Journal of Law and Economics*, 21: 297–326.

Klein, Benjamin and Leffler, Keith, 1979, "The Role of Market Forces in Assuring Contractual Performance," *Journal of Political Economy*, 89: 615–41.

Klein, W. A., 1976, "Legal and Economic Perspectives on the Firm," unpublished manuscript. Los Angeles, California: University of California.

Knight, Frank H., 1964, *Risk, Uncertainty, and Profit*. New York: A. M. Kelley.

Kohn, Melvin, 1969, *Class and Conformity, A Study in Values*. Homewood: Dorsey Press.

Koopmans, Tjalling, 1957, *Three Essays on the State of Economic Science*. New York: McGraw-Hill.

Laband, David and John Sophocleus, 1985, "Revealed Preference for Economics Journals: Citations as Dollar Votes," *Public Choice*, 46: 317–24.

Landes, D. S., ed., 1966, *The Rise of Capitalism*. New York: Macmillan.

Landsberger, H. A., 1958, *Hawthorne Revisited*. Ithaca, New York: Cornell University Press.

Lange, Oskar, 1935, "Marxian Economics and Modern Economic Theory," *Review of Economic Studies*, 2: 189–201.

Langlois, Richard, 1981, "Why Are There Firms?" C. N. Starr Discussion Paper #81-30, New York University.

Lazear, Edward, 1981, "Agency, Earnings Profiles, Productivity, and Hours Restrictions," *American Economic Review*, 71: 606–20.

Lazonick, William, 1978, "The Subjugation of Labor to Capital: The Rise of the Capitalist System," *Review of Radical Political Economics*, 10: 1–31.

Lazonick, William, 1981, "Technological Change and the Control of Work: A Perspective on the Development of Capital Labor Relations in U. S. Mass Production Industries," Discussion Paper No. 821, Harvard Institute of Economic Research.

Lazonick, William, 1982, "Production, Productivity and Development, Theoretical Implications of Some Historical Research," Discussion Paper No. 876, Harvard Institute of Economic Research.

Leff, Nathaniel H., 1978, "Industrial Organization and Entrepreneurship in the Developing Countries: The Economic Groups," *Economic Development and Cultural Change*, 26: 661–76.

Leibenstein, H., 1966, "Allocative Efficiency vs. X-Efficiency," *American Economic Review*, 56: 392–415.

Leibenstein, Harvey, 1979, "A Branch of Economics Is Missing: Micro-Micro Theory," *Journal of Economic Literature*, 17: 477–502.

Leibenstein, Harvey, 1980, "X-Efficiency, Intrafirm Behavior and Growth," in Shlomo

Maital and Noah M. Meltz, eds., *Lagging Productivity Growth*. Cambridge: Ballinger.

Lester, R., 1967, "Benefits as a Preferred Form of Compensation," *Southern Economic Journal*, 33: 488–95.

Lewis, D., 1981, *Convention: A Philosophical Study*. Cambridge: Cambridge University Press.

Lewis, H. G., 1959, "Competitive Monopoly Unionism," in Philip Bradley, ed., *The Public Stake in Union Power*. Charlottesville: University of Virginia Press.

Lieberstein, S. H., 1979, *Who Owns What Is in Your Head*. New York: Hawthorn Publishers.

Lindbeck, Assar, 1977, *The Political Economy of the New Left: An Outsider's View*. New York: New York University Press.

Livernash, E., 1957, "The Internal Wage Structure," pp. 140–73 in G. W. Taylor and F. C. Pierson, eds., *New Concepts in Wage Determination*. New York: McGraw-Hill.

Macaulay, Stewart, 1963, "Non-Contractual Relations in Business: A Preliminary Study," *American Sociological Review*, 6: 55–66.

Macgregor, David H., 1906, *Industrial Combination*. London: George Bell and Sons.

Machlup, F., 1967, "Theories of the Firm: Marginalist, Behavioral, Managerial," *American Economic Review*, 57: 1–33.

Machlup, Fritz and Taber, Martha, 1960, "Bilateral Monopoly, Successive Monopoly, and Vertical Integration," *Economica*, 27: 101–19.

MacNeil, I. R., 1974, "The Many Futures of Contracts," *Southern California Law Review*, 47: 691–816.

Malcomson, James, 1981, "Unemployment and the Efficiency Wage Hypothesis," *Economic Journal*, 91: 848–66.

Malcomson, James, 1984, "Work Incentives, Hierarchy, and Internal Labor Markets," *Journal of Political Economy*, 92: 486–507.

Malmgren, H., 1961, "Information, Expectations, and the Theory of the Firm," *Quarterly Journal of Economics*, 75: 399–421.

Mandel, E., 1968, *Marxist Economic Theory* (translated by B. Pearce), Vol. 2, Rev. ed. New York: Monthly Review Press.

Manne, Henry G., 1962, "The 'Higher Criticism' of the Modern Corporation," *Columbia Law Review*, 62: 399–432.

Manne, Henry G., 1965, "Mergers and the Market for Corporate Control," *Journal of Political Economy*, 73: 110–20.

Manne, Henry G., 1967, "Our Two Corporate Systems: Laws and Economics," *Virginia Law Review*, 53: 259–85.

March, J. G. and Simon, H. A., 1958, *Organizations*. New York: Wiley.

Marglin, S. A., 1974, "What Do Bosses Do? The Origins and Functions of Heirarchy in Capitalist Production," *Review of Radical Political Economics*, 6: 60–112.

Marquis, D. and Allen, T., 1966, "Communication Patterns in Applied Technology," *American Psychologist*, 21: 1052–60.

Marris, R., 1964, *The Economic Theory of Managerial Capitalism*. Glencoe, Illinois: Free Press.

Marschak, Jacob, 1949, "Role of Liquidity under Complete and Incomplete Infor-

References

mation," *Papers and Proceedings, American Economic Review*, 39: 182–95; with discussion by F. Modigliani and J. Tobin. (Abstracts in *Econometrica*, 1949, 17: 180–84.)

Martyn, Henry, 1701, *Considerations Upon the East India Trade*. London.

Marx, Karl, 1967, *Capital: A Critique of Political Economy, Volume I. The Process of Capitalist Production*. Edited by Frederick Engels. Translated from the Third German Edition by Samuel Moore and Edward Aveling. New York: International Publishers.

Marx, Karl, 1972, "The Eighteenth Brumaire of Louis Bonaparte," reprinted in Robert C. Tucker, ed., *The Marx-Engels Reader*. New York: W.W. Norton. Originally published in 1852.

Marx, Karl, 1973, *The Grundrisse: Introduction to Critique of Political Economy*, New York: Vintage.

Marx, Karl, 1976, *Capital, Vol I*. Harmondsworth, England: Penguin.

Marx, K. and Engels, F., 1959, L. Feuer, ed., *Basic Writings in Politics and Philosophy*, Garden City, New York: Doubleday and Co.

Mathewson, S. B., 1969, *Restriction of Output Among Unorganized Workers*. Carbondale, Illinois: Southern Illinois University. Originally published in 1931.

McCain, Roger A., 1977, "On the Optimum Financial Environment for Worker Cooperatives," *Zeitschrift fur Nationalokonomie*, 37: 355–84.

McManus, J. C., 1975, "The Costs of Alternative Economic Organizations," *Canadian Journal of Economics*, 8: 334–50.

McNulty, Paul, 1980, *The Origins and Development of Labor Economics*. Cambridge: MIT Press.

McNaulty, Paul, 1984, "On the Nature and Theory of Economic Organization: The Role of the Firm Reconsidered," *History of Political Economy*, 16: 233–53.

McPherson, Michael S. and Winston, Gordon C., 1983, "The Economics of Academic Tenure: A Relational Perspective," *Journal of Economic Behavior and Organization*, 4: 163–84.

Meade, J., 1971, *The Controlled Economy*. London: G. Allen & Unwin.

Meade, J. E., 1972, "The Theory of Labour-Managed Firms and of Profit Sharing," *Economic Journal*, 82: 402–28.

Meckling, W. H., 1976, "Values and the Choice of the Model of the Individual in the Social Sciences," *Zeitschrift fur Volkswirtschaft und Statistik*, 112: 545–60.

Medoff, James and Abraham, Katherine, 1980, "Experience, Performance, and Earnings," *Quarterly Journal of Economics*, 95: 703–36.

Meij, J., 1963, *Internal Wage Structure*, Amsterdam: North-Holland Publishing Co.

Meyers, C. and Pigors, P., 1973, *Personnel Administration*. New York: McGraw-Hill.

Mirrlees, James A., 1976, "The Optimal Structure of Incentives and Authority Within an Organization," *The Bell Journal of Economics*, 7: 105–31.

Miyazaki, Hajime, 1980, "Work Norm and Involuntary Unemployment," Discussion Paper No. 7, Stanford Workshop on Factor Markets.

Monsen, R. J. and Downs, A., 1965, "A Theory of Large Managerial Firms," *Journal of Political Economy*, 73: 221–36.

REFERENCES

Monteverde, K. M. and Teece, D. J., 1982a, "Supplier Switching Costs and Vertical Integration," *Bell Journal of Economics,* 13: 206–13.

Monteverde, K. M. and Teece, D. J., 1982b, "Appropriable Rents and Quasi Vertical Integration," *Journal of Law and Economics,* 25: 321–28.

Mossin, J., 1973, *Theory of Financial Markets.* Englewood Cliffs, New Jersey: Prentice-Hall.

Mueller, D. C., 1972, "A Life Cycle Theory of the Firm," *Journal of Industrial Economics,* 20: 199–219.

Muth, John F., 1960, "Optimal Properties of Exponentially Weighted Forecasts," *Journal of American Statistical Association,* 55: 299–306.

Myers, S. C., 1968, "Procedures for Capital Budgeting Under Uncertainty," *Industrial Management Review,* 9: 1–19.

Naples, Michele, 1982, "The Structure of Industrial Relations, Labor Militance and the Rate of Growth of Productivity: The Case of U. S. Mining and Manufacturing, 1953–77," unpublished doctoral dissertation, University of Massachusetts.

Negishi, Tekashi, 1979, *Microeconomic Foundations of Keynesian Macroeconomics.* Amsterdam: North-Holland.

Nelson, Charles R., 1973, *Applied Time Series Analysis for Managerial Forecasting.* San Francisco: Holden-Day.

Nelson, Richard R. and Winter, Sidney G., 1980, "Firm and Industry Response to Changed Market Conditions: An Evolutionary Approach," *Economic Inquiry,* 18: 179–202.

Nelson, Richard R. and Winter, Sidney G., *An Evolutionary Theory of Economic Change.* Cambridge: Harvard University Press.

Neumann, John von, and Morgenstern, Oskar, 1944, *Theory of Games and Economic Behavior,* Princeton: Princeton University Press.

Nove, Alec, 1983, *The Economics of Feasible Socialism,* London: Allen and Unwin.

Ohlin, G., review of E. Lundberg, 1962, *Productivity and Profitability: Studies of the Role of Capital in the Swedish Economy* in *American Economic Review,* 52: 827–9.

Okun, Arthur M., 1975, *Equality and Efficiency: The Big Tradeoff.* Washington: The Brookings Institution.

Okun, Arthur, 1981, *Prices and Quantities, A Macroeconomic Analysis.* Washington: The Brookings Institution.

Panzar, John and Willig, R., 1975, "Economics of Scale and Economics of Scope in Multi-Output Production," Unpublished Working Paper. Murray Hill, New Jersey: Bell Laboratories.

Pejovich, S., 1969, "The Firm, Monetary Policy and Property Rights in a Planned Economy," *Western Economic Journal,* 42: 277–81.

Pencavel, J., 1970, *An Analysis of the Quit Rate in American Manufacturing Industry.* Princeton, New Jersey: Princeton University Press.

Penrose, E., 1958, *The Theory of the Growth of the Firm.* New York: Wiley.

Penrose, Edith T., 1959, *Theory of the Growth of the Firm.* Oxford: Blackwell.

Piore, M., 1973, "Fragments of a 'Sociological' Theory of Wages," *The American Economic Review,* 63: 377–84.

References

Plant, Arnold, 1932, "Trends in Business Administration," *Economica*, 12: 45–62.

Polanyi, Michael, 1958, *Personal Knowledge: Towards a Post-Critical Philosophy.* Chicago, Illinois: University of Chicago Press.

Preston, L. E., 1975, "Corporation and Society: The Search for a Paradigm," *Journal of Economic Literture*, 13: 434–53.

Putterman, Louis, 1981, "The Organization of Work: Comment," *Journal of Economic Behavior and Organization*, 2: 273–9.

Radner, R., 1970, "Problems in the Theory of Markets under Uncertainty," *The American Economic Review*, 60: 454–60.

Raimon, R., 1953, "The Indeterminateness of Wages of Semiskilled Workers," *Industrial and Labor Relations Review*, 6: 180–94.

Reich, Michael, 1980, *Racial Inequality*. Princeton: Princeton University Press.

Reich, Michael and Divine, James, 1981, "The Microeconomics of Conflict and Hierarchy in Capitalist Production," *Review of Radical Political Economy*, 2: 27–45.

Richardson, G. B., 1972, "The Organization of Industry," *Economic Journal*, 82: 883–96.

Robertson, D. H., 1930, *Control of Industry*. London: Nisbet & Co.

Robbins, L., 1932, *An Essay on the Nature and Significance of Economic Science.* New York: Macmillan.

Robinson, E. A. G., 1931, *The Structure of Competitive Industry*. London: Cambridge University Press.

Robinson, E. A. G., 1934, "The Problem of Management and the Size of the Firm," *The Economic Journal*, 44: 242–57.

Roemer, John, 1979, "Divide and Conquer: Micro Foundations of the Marxian Theory of Discrimination," *Bell Journal of Economics*, 10: 695–705.

Roethlisberger, F. T. and Dickson, W. J., 1939, *Management and the Worker*. Cambridge: Harvard University Press.

Roosevelt, Frank, 1975, "Cambridge Economics as Commodity Fetishness," *Review of Radical Political Economics*, 7: 1–32.

Ross, A., 1958, "Do We Have a New Industrial Feudalism?" *The American Economic Review*, 48: 903–20.

Ross, S. A., 1973, "The Economic Theory of Agency: The Principals Problem," *American Economic Review*, 62: 134–9.

Ross, S. A., 1974, "The Economic Theory of Agency and the Principle of Similarity," in M. D. Balch, McFadden & Wu, eds., *Essays on Economic Behavior under Uncertainty*. Amsterdam: North-Holland.

Samuelson, Paul, 1957, "Wage and Interest: A Modern Dissection of Marxian Economic Models," *American Economic Review*, 47: 884–912.

Sandler, Todd, and Cauley, Jon, 1980, "A Hierarchical Theory of the Firm," *Scottish Journal of Political Economic*, 27: 17–29.

Schall, L. D., 1972, "Asset Valuation, Firm Investment, and Firm Diversification," *Journal of Business*, 45: 11–28.

Schelling, T., 1971, "On the Ecology of Micromotives," *The Public Interest*, 25: 61–98.

367

REFERENCES

Schmidt, Peter and Strauss, Robert P., 1976, "The Effect of Unions on Earnings and Earnings on Unions: A Mixed Logit Approach, *International Economic Review,* 17: 204–12.

Schor, Juliet and Bowles, Samuel, 1983, "Conflict in the Employment Relation and the Cost of Job Loss," mimeo.

Schor, Juliet and Bowles, Samuel, 1984, "Employment Rents and Class Conflict: An Empirical Investigation," mimeo.

Schotter, Andrew, 1981, *Economic Theory of Social Institutions.* Cambridge: Cambridge University Press.

Schumpeter, Joseph A., 1950, *Capitalism, Socialism, and Democracy.* New York: Harper and Brothers.

Sen, A., 1975, *Employment, Technology and Development.* Oxford: Clarendon Press.

Shapiro, Carl and Stiglitz, Joseph, 1984, "Equilibrium Unemployment as a Worker Discipline Device," *American Economic Review,* 74: 433–44.

Shove, G. F., 1933, "The Imperfection of the Market: A Further Note," *The Economic Journal,* 116.

Shubik, M., 1970, "A Curmudgeon's Guide to Microeconomics," *Journal of Economic Literature,* 8: 405–34.

Silver, M. and Auster, R., 1969, "Entrepreneurship, Profit and Limits on Firm Size," *Journal of Business,* 42: 277–81.

Simon, Herbert A., 1947, *Administrative Behavior.* New York: Macmillan.

Simon, H. A., 1951, "A Formal Theory of the Employment Relation," *Econometrica,* 19: 293–305. Reprinted in *Models of Man,* 1957. New York: Wiley.

Simon, H. A., 1955, "A Behavioral Model of Rational Choice," *Quarterly Journal of Economics,* 69: 99–118.

Simon, H. A., 1957, *Models of Man.* New York: Wiley.

Simon, H., 1959, "Theories of Decision Making in Economics and Behavioral Science," *American Economic Review,* 253–83.

Simon, Herbert, 1962, "The Architecture of Complexity," *Proceedings of the American Philosophical Society,* 106: 467–82, reprinted in Herbert Simon, 1981, *The Sciences of the Artificial,* Second Edition. Cambridge: MIT Press.

Simon, H., 1971, "Decision Making and Organizational Design," in D. S. Pugh, ed., *Organizational Theory.* New York: Penguin Books.

Simon, Herbert, 1979, "Rational Decision Making in Business Organizations," *American Economic Review,* 69: 493–513.

Smith, A., 1937, *The Wealth of Nations,* Cannan edition. New York: Modern Library. Originally published 1776.

Snitzler, James R. and Byrnes, Robert J., 1958, *Interstate Trucking of Fresh and Frozen Poultry Under Agricultural Exemption.* Washington: U. S. Department of Agriculture.

Solow, Robert, 1979, "Alternative Approaches to Macroeconomic Theory: A Partial View," *Canadian Journal of Economics,* 12: 339–54.

Solow, Robert, 1980, "On Theories of Unemployment," *American Economic Review,* 70: 1–10.

Spence, Michael and Zeckhauser, Richard, 1971, "Insurance, Information and Individual Action," *American Economic Review,* 61: 380–7.

References

Stigler, George, 1966, *The Theory of Price*. New York: Macmillan.

Stiglitz, Joseph E., 1974, "Incentives and Risk Sharing in Sharecropping," *Review of Economic Studies*, 33: 361–71.

Stiglitz, Joseph, 1975, "Incentives, Risk and Information: Notes Towards a Theory of Hierarchy," *Bell Journal of Economics*, 6: 552–79.

Stiglitz, Joseph E., 1981, "The Allocation Role of the Stock Market: Pareto-Optimality and Competition," *Journal of Finance*, 36: 235–51.

Stoikov, V. and Raimon, R. L., 1968, "Determinants of Differences in the Quit Rates Among Industries," *American Economic Review*, 68: 1283–98.

Summers, C., 1969, "Collective Agreements and the Law of Contracts," *Yale Law Journal*, 78: 527–75.

Sweezy, Paul, ed., 1966, *Karl Marx and the Close of His System and Bohm-Bawerk's Criticism of Marx*. New York: Augustus M. Kelley.

Teece, David J., 1976, *Vertical Integration and Vertical Divestiture in the U. S. Petroleum Industry*. Stanford, California: Stanford University.

Teece, David J., 1977, "Technology Transfer by Multinational Firms: The Resource Cost of Transferring Technological Knowhow," *Economic Journal*, 87: 242–61.

Teece, David J., 1980, "Economies of Scope and the Scope of the Enterprise," *Journal of Economic Behavior and Organization*, No. 3, 1: 223–47.

Thompson, F. A., 1970, "Nonpecuniary Rewards and the Aggregate Production Function," *Review of Economics and Statistics*, 52: 395–404.

Thurow, L., 1971, "Measuring the Economic Benefits of Education," Report prepared for the Carnegie Commission on Higher Education.

Tomerkovic, T., 1962, "Levels of Knowledge of Requirements as a Motivational Factor in the Work Situation," *Human Relations*, 15: 197–216.

Trivers, R. L., 1971, "The Evolution of Reciprocal Altruism," *Quarterly Review of Biology*, 46: 35–57.

Tucket, J. D., 1846, *A History of the Past and Present State of the Labouring Population*. London.

Udy, S. H., Jr., 1970, *Work in Traditional and Modern Society*. Englewood Cliffs, New Jersey: Prentice-Hall.

Ullman-Margalit, Edna, 1978, *The Emergence of Norms*. New York: Oxford University Press.

Ure, Andrew, 1835, *The Philosophy of Manufactures or an Exposition of the Scientific, Moral and Commercial Economy of the Factory System of Great Britain*. London: 2nd edition.

Urquhart, David, 1843, *Familiar Words as Affecting England and the English*. London.

U. S. Department of Labor, 1972, *Characteristics of Agreements Covering 20,000 Workers or More*, Bulletin 17.29. Washington.

Usher, Abbott P., 1921, *Introduction to the Industrial History of England*. London: G. C. Harrap and Co., Ltd.

Vanek, J., 1970, *The General Theory of Labor Managed Market Economies*. Ithaca, New York: Cornell University Press.

Vanek, Jaroslav, 1977, "The Basic Theory of Financing of Participatory Firms,"

REFERENCES

186–98, in Jaroslav Vanek, *The Labor-Managed Economy: Essays by Jaroslav Vanek*. Ithaca, New York: Cornell University Press.

Vanek, Jaroslav, 1978, "Self-Management, Workers' Management, and Labour Management in Theory and Practice: A Comparative Study," *Economic Analysis and Workers' Management*, 12: 5–24.

Viscusi, W. K., 1979, *Employment Hazards: An Investigation of Market Performance*. Cambridge: Harvard University Press.

Vroom, V. and Deci, E., 1974, *Management and Motivation*. New York: Penguin.

Wachtel, H. and Betsy, C., 1972, "Employment at Low Wages," *Review of Economics and Statistics*, 54: 121–29.

Wachter, M. L. and O. E. Williamson, 1978, "Obligational Markets and the Mechanics of Inflation," *Bell Journal of Economics*, 9: 549–71.

Watts, Ross L. and Zimmerman, Jerod, 1978, "Auditors and the Determination of Accounting Standards, an Analysis of the Lack of Independence," University of Rochester, Graduate School of Management.

Weisskopf, Thomas, Gordon, David M. and Bowles, Samuel, 1983, "Hearts and Minds: A Social Model of U. S. Productivity Growth," *Brookings Papers on Economic Activity*, 2: 381–450.

Wicksell, Knut, 1934, *Lectures on Political Economy* (translated by E. Classen). London: Routledge & Kegan Paul.

Williamson, O. E., 1964a, "The Economics of Antitrust: Transaction Cost Cosiderations," University of Pennsylvania Law Review, 122: 1439–96.

Williamson, O. E., 1964b, *The Economics of Discretionary Behavior: Managerial Objectives in a Theory of the Firm*. Englewood Cliffs, New Jersey: Prentice-Hall.

Williamson, O. E., 1970, *Corporate Control and Business Behavior*. Englewood Cliffs, New Jersey: Prentice-Hall.

Williamson, O. E., 1971, "The Vertical Integration of Production: Market Failure Considerations," *American Economic Review*, 61: 112–23.

Williamson, Oliver E., 1975, *Markets and Hierarchies: Analysis and Anti-Trust Implications*. New York: The Free Press.

Williamson, Oliver, 1979, "Transaction-Cost Economics: The Governance of Contractual Relations," *Journal of Law and Economics*, 22: 233–61.

Williamson, Oliver, 1980, "The Organization of Work: A Comparative Institutional Assessment," *Journal of Economic Behavior and Organization*, 1: 5–38.

Williamson, Oliver, 1981, "The Modern Corporation: Origins, Evolution, Attributes," *Journal of Economic Literature*, 19: 1537–68.

Williamson, Oliver, 1983a, "Credible Commitments: Using Hostages to Support Exchange," *American Economic Review*, 83: 519–40.

Williamson, Oliver, 1983b, "Organization Form, Residual Claimants, and Corporate Control," *Journal of Law and Economics*, 26: 351–66.

Williamson, Oliver, 1984a, "Corporate Governance," *Yale Law Journal*, 93: 1197–230.

Williamson, Oliver, 1984b, "The Economics of Governance: Framework and Implication," *Journal of Institutional and Theoretical Economics*, 140: 195–223.

Williamson, Oliver, 1985, *The Economic Institutions of Capitalism: Firms, Markets, Relational Contracting*. New York: The Free Press.

References

Williamson, Oliver E. and D. J. Teece, 1982, "European Economic and Political Integration: The Markets and Hierarchies Approach," in Pierre Salmon, ed., *New Approaches to European Integration,* forthcoming.

Williamson, O., Wachter, M. and Harris, S., 1975, "Understanding the Employment Relation," *Bell Journal of Economics,* 6: 250–78.

Willig, Robert, 1979, "Multiproduct Technology and Market Structure," *American Economic Review,* 69: 346–51.

Wilson, R., 1968, "On the Theory of Syndicates," *Econometrica,* 36: 119–32.

Wilson, R., 1969, *La Decision: Agregation et Dynamique des Orders de Preference, Extrait.* Paris: Editions du Centre National de la Recherche Scientifique.

Winter, Sidney G., 1982, "An Essay on the Theory of Production," in S. H. Hymans, ed., *Economics and the World Around It.* Ann Arbor, Michigan: The University of Michigan Press.